MEASURING PRODUCTIVITY IN WORD FORMATION

STUDIES IN SEMITIC
LANGUAGES AND LINGUISTICS

EDITED BY

T. MURAOKA AND C.H.M. VERSTEEGH

VOLUME XXVII

MEASURING PRODUCTIVITY IN WORD FORMATION

MEASURING PRODUCTIVITY IN WORD FORMATION

The Case of Israeli Hebrew

BY

SHMUEL BOLOZKY

BRILL

LEIDEN · BOSTON · KÖLN

1999

This book is printed on acid-free paper.

Library of Congress Cataloging-in-Publication Data

Bolozky, Shmuel.
    Measuring productivity in word formation : the case of Israeli
Hebrew / by Shmuel Bolozky.
        p. cm. — (Studies in Semitic languages and linguistics, ISSN
    0081-8461 ; 27)
    Includes bibliographical references and index.
    ISBN 9004112529 (cloth : alk. paper)
    1. Hebrew language—Word formation. 2. Hebrew language—New
words. I. Title. II. Series.
PJ4603.B65   1998
492.4'5'–dc21   98-36385
                                                                           CIP

Die Deutsche Bibliothek-CIP-Einheitsaufnahme

Bolozky, Shmuel:
Measuring productivity in word formation : the case of Israeli
Hebrew / by Shmuel Bolozky. - Leiden ; New York ; Köln :
Brill, 1999
    (Studies in Semitic languages and linguistics ; 27)
    ISBN 90-04-11252-9

ISSN   0081-8461
ISBN   90 04 11252 9

PRINTED IN THE NETHERLANDS

CONTENTS

PREFACE

Somewhere in the heart of every speaker of Israeli Hebrew, placed between love of oriental food and passion for politics, there is a constant urge to form new words. Existing words, be they native or borrowed, are used as bases for innovative new forms for the purpose of capturing meanings beyond those associated with the bases. In Israel, as in most other countries, language is an essential component of national identity, and individuals take pride in contributing to its development. But there are other factors. Hebrew was revived as a spoken language only about a hundred years ago, and pragmatic needs still generate a sense of urgency in the search for new words. The Hebrew Language Academy tries to fill in the gaps, but only part of that is actually absorbed in everyday speech, through language educators at school, and mostly through the media. The media also introduce their own neologisms, often based on European language models. Some creative neologisms are the creation of literati, and the more natural and more transparent of them are absorbed as well. But the bulk of innovation is the work of the native speaking community in general, and it is mostly those one-time innovations by individuals that take hold, once they capture the imagination of the public. In the small, closely knit community that is Israel, everybody knows each other, hears the same news on the radio, watches the same television programs, and spends a month or two per year on reserve army duty with reservists from all over the country. Innovations thus spread very fast, and the more transparent and more appealing neologisms survive.

Today's purists complain about what they consider to be the deterioration of the Hebrew language. There indeed appear to be some reasons for concern when one reads the various tabloids mushrooming in every city, as well as the national evening papers, with their wholesale borrowing of English structures and English calques even when perfectly good native counterparts exist in everyday Hebrew. But as recent word formation indicates, the linguistic mechanism that underlies the neologism process is rich and complex, and certainly does not suggest that the morphological system is becoming impoverished. On the contrary, it appears that Israeli Hebrew word formation has become more sophisticated than it has ever been. In fact, the average educated Israeli has better command of all components of the language than his parents did. Rosén (1992) shows how the language of today is far more 'grammatical' and often closer to the 'language of the sources' than it was seventy years ago. Speakers of the 1920's were more dependent on substratum languages as models, and also used foreign words for which we have Hebrew counterparts today (some new, but others derived from the sources). There existed no truly integrated system, lexical items had very broad semantic scope, and constraints on collocability were very loose. The use of *binyanim* (verb patterns) and *miškalim* (other non-linear patterns) was inconsistent. Speakers had limited knowledge of the grammar, and they often analogized, albeit subconsciously, on the basis of substratal models. In comparison, Israelis today possess a better total language system, which is based on tradition and sources. They are more tuned to register differences, and in general, they have better knowledge of the grammar. Insofar as word formation is concerned, Israelis now have at their disposal much more specialized meanings associated with lexical units, and command a variety of derivation patterns and their specialized functions. The amazing growth of the new lexicon is living evidence to the vitality of Israeli Hebrew morphology.

The richness of Hebrew word formation also stems from its being a Semitic language. As such, its morphology employs a wide variety of non-linear derivation patterns, which are available to speakers in addition to the linear word formation devices typically used in Indo-European languages. The combination of the two types of derivation strategies, linear and non-linear, gives speakers a very powerful innovating tool, as explained in Chapter 2. Chapters 3–5 deal with the selection of a derivation pattern, demonstrating that it is semantically based for the most part: Chapter 3 for verbs, Chapter 4 for adjectives, Chapter 5 for nouns. A productivity ranking is established for each semantic category investigated, based on three evaluation measures: productivity tests, dictionary comparison, and corpus data. Chapter 6 considers the possibility of productivity ranking across semantic boundaries in the verb system, and separately for nouns/adjectives. Chapter 7 describes partial *miškal* mergers and back-formation phenomena and their implications to productivity. The central argument made is that since no single evaluation measure constitutes a sure criterion of productivity on its own, several criteria should be applied simultaneously, and that a process can be characterized as productive when findings based on different methodologies all converge and point to it as such.

I wish to thank the Graduate School of the University of Massachusetts at Amherst and the Dean of Humanities and Fine Arts for partial support of the research conducted in preparation for this volume and of its publication, the editor of *Hebrew Studies*, for permitting me to summarize the content of my article on the formation of diminutives in Modern Hebrew (1994:35, 47–63), as well as the arguments in my article with Ora R. Schwarzwald on the derivation of Hebrew nouns with the suffix +*ut* (1992:33, 51–69), and the editors of the *Hadassah Kantor Jubilee Book* for allowing me to reproduce the arguments on the non-linear structure of the segolates (1995, 17–26). I am also grateful to Dr. Dorit Ravid of Tel Aviv University and to Dr. Emanuel Allon of Beit Berl College for their help in running some of the productivity tests, as well as to students at the Hebrew Language department of Ben Gurion University of the Negev for their contribution as subjects. Special thanks are due to Professor Ruth A. Berman of Tel Aviv University, for her highly beneficial advice and comments regarding both content and form, to Professor Ora R. Schwarzwald, for her constructive timely comments, to Morris Rosenthal, who helped with the editing, to Aryeh Olman, for his useful suggestion regarding productivity ratio computation, and to Noemi Schwarz, for her assistance with corpus transcription. All errors are, of course, mine.

CHAPTER ONE

INTRODUCTION

The purpose of this volume is to suggest three separate ways of evaluating productivity in word formation. The proposed methods can be used for any language, but the research reported on below focuses on Modern Hebrew, or more precisely, Israeli Hebrew.

A word formation pattern is characterized as productive when speakers readily form or understand neologisms based upon it. The degree of its productivity can be defined as the 'statistical readiness' with which it is used, either in production or in perception (cf. Baayen & Renouf 1996, following Bolinger 1948). In English, for instance, the suffix *-ness* may be attached to most adjectives to form new abstract nouns, even to ones that conventionally take other suffixes such as +*ity*. To the contrary, the +*th* suffix, which is 'frozen' in nouns like *warmth*, will never attach to an adjective to form a new noun (Spencer 1991). In Hebrew, as shown in Bolozky (1994a), the mark of a truly productive diminution device, such as the suffix +*on* or its colloquial (loan) counterpart +*čik*, is the readiness with which it can be appended to any diminutivizable word. This includes words already incorporating another diminutive suffix.

Some researchers (e.g. Bauer 1983, following Lyons 1977; Lieber 1992, following Schultnik 1961) distinguish between productivity and creativity. Productivity is rule-governed. Its realizations are generally unintentional, their 'newness' going unnoticed. It is best measured in unintentional coinages, performed automatically and almost subconsciously (see Aronoff 1983, Lieber 1992, Baayen & Renouf 1996). Neologisms resulting from creativity, such as clever literary innovations, or sophisticated commercial names, are often unpredictable and haphazard, and thus may not represent productive processes as defined above. Aronoff (1976) points out that productive processes generate transparent, semantically-coherent structures, that apply across the board, unfettered by arbitrary restrictions on particular lexical items. Clark (1993) in particular emphasizes transparency: speakers prefer to select construction types that are easily analyzable and hence transparent, using forms in which the meaning of new combinations of identifiable stems and affixes are largely predictable. Furthermore, Clark assigns particular importance to the 'usefulness' of selecting a specific word formation pattern for a particular semantic need, e.g. a specific affix that captures the target meaning better than any other related device would.

Measuring productivity is also complicated by numerous restrictions on its application. An obvious constraint pointed out in Clark (1993) is that speakers need to select from structurally possible options in their language, and try to coin words that do not violate any of them. Bauer (1983) shows that productivity can be constrained by (a) pragmatic considerations, such as requirement of existence, nameability; (b) blocking due to previously occupied slots (Clark & Clark's 1979 and Clark 1993's 'preemption'); (c) phonological, morphological, lexical, and semantic restrictions. Taking morphology, for example, there are constraints on the types of stem to which an affix can be appended. Thus, +*ion* (or +*ation*) and +*ity* are restricted to latinate stems, while +*ment* and +*ness* are not. Should the total lexicon count when measuring productivity, or only realizations within the lexical sub-division concerned? Aronoff (1976) suggests comparison based on the ratio between potential and actually occurring forms. To control the comparison, he proposes that the set of bases undergoing the word formation processes to be compared be kept constant, e.g. adjectives ending in +*ous*, to which +*ity* and +*ness* would be appended to form nouns. +*ity* represents 'Class I' affixes, which are more closely bound to the stem, cause stress shift, and undergo non-automatic processes. +*ness* represents 'Class II' affixes that are less bound, do not cause stress shift, and do not undergo non-automatic processes (see Chomsky & Halle 1968, Siegel 1979). The process of appending +*ness* can be shown to be more productive, which Aronoff attributes to its transparency (no changes resulting from stress shift, as in the -*ity* cases,[1] or other processes) and greater semantic coherence, as well as to the absence of arbitrary lexical restrictions. But the distinction between actual and potential words required by such analyses is not straightforward. As pointed out in Lieber (1992), the difficulty with 'actual' is that the mental lexicon of a particular individual need not coincide with that of another,

---

[1] As Clark (1993) points out, however, transparency is affected only when the stem is distorted; stress shift alone does not seem to render the base less transparent (see Cutler 1980).

while a dictionary tends to reflect that of the lexicographer's. 'Potential' is problematic as well, since one has to distinguish between truly productive, sort-of-automatic formation, and an occasional creative neologism that reflects marginally productive processes. There are also occasional analogical formations which are unlikely to be repeated for any other form. Besides, how does one count potential appending of a productive suffix to a base ending with another productive suffix (e.g. +*ity* to +*able*)? This is virtually impossible in practice.

Precise measurement of word formation productivity thus would not seem to be a realistic goal. One could examine tendencies, and compare the relative productivity of specific processes in particular domains or registers, without aiming for fully exhaustive or 'scientific' accuracy. My proposal is that since no single method constitutes a sure criterion of productivity on its own, several criteria should be applied simultaneously, and a process be characterized as productive when findings based on different methodologies all converge and point to it as such.

Morphological productivity may be examined in a number of ways. The most direct method is by productivity tests, in which speakers are forced to innovate in set contexts. Open-ended coinage tests invoke creation of one-time potential words that 'make sense', but which do not occur in any dictionary. In judgment tests such coinages are evaluated for 'potential acceptability' through selection from a number of options (see Bolozky 1978, Berman 1987, etc.). Tests may be conducted at different registers, as well as on special groups of speakers (e.g. children).

Open-ended coinage tests elicit intuitive innovation, the speaker's first reaction when the need for a neologism arises. Usually (cf. Bolozky 1993), they reflect the subject's knowledge of the new lexicon (Berman 1987, Clark & Berman 1984, etc.), particularly its everyday component (comprising of the frequent and the familiar, as distinct from the formal/literary), and the most prominent, transparent patterns that easily come to mind. Speakers tend to look for patterns that are associated with broad semantic clues, such as *pi'el* for all agentive verbs including causatives, *hitpa'el* for all 'focus-on-the-theme' verbs, +*an* or *meCaCeC* for 'performer of an action' (incorporating both agents and instruments). They first access the more general categories, even when more normative alternatives are available in the broader lexicon, such as *hif'il* for causative agentive verbs, or *meCaCeC* for human agents as distinct from instruments.

But open-ended tests may also reflect individual creativity, manifest in imaginative, ingenious neologisms that might apply to a particular subject's mental lexicon.

Judgment tasks offer a wider variety of options, of which the speaker may not have been aware, and thus represent a fuller, more complex lexicon. They expand the range of options, which creates the potential for two opposite tendencies. First, the broader choice may direct the subject to more specific and possibly more normative options that would not immediately occur to him/her by first intuition. Second, the proposed choice of alternants may also remind speakers of what their default selection would have been in the open-ended test anyway, had they been aware of that option. The second tendency is more common, as evidenced by the fact the scores for the preferred options in the open-ended tests are often even higher in the judgment tests.

Most researchers agree that dictionary data do not in themselves provide a reliable gauge of productivity. Aronoff (1976), Lieber (1992), Clark (1993), Baayen & Renouf (1996), for example, all note that the productivity of a word formation pattern cannot be measured simply by the number of its realizations in the conventional dictionary. Dictionaries often fail to list the most predictable formations, such as all words in English that can take + *ness*, because lexicographers regard them as too obvious/automatic, and thus redundant. Lexicographers also rarely note ephemeral neologisms which often characterize true productivity (e.g. unusual use of the English suffix + *ly*, see Baayen & Renouf 1996). Furthermore, quantitative dictionary comparison cannot differentiate between patterns that are currently productive, and those that used to be productive. Clark (1993), for instance, claims that only non-established neologisms (such as those elicited in coinage and judgment tests described above, data gathered at different stages of language acquisition, etc.) truly reflect lexical productivity, since established items often represent idiosyncrasies of form-meaning relationships.

In spite of these inherent difficulties, it is possible to make effective use of dictionary data, for example, by a method proposed in Bolozky (1993) of identifying the new/recent lexicon through dictionary comparison. Most dictionaries do not identify exactly when an entry was introduced into the language. For example, the most comprehensive Hebrew dictionary available to date, Even-Shoshan (1970), only specifies the general period at which the word was first documented, i.e. Biblical, Mishnaic, Medieval or Modern. 'Modern' covers the entire period from the second part of the 19th century to the present, whereas 'recent' on the Israeli Hebrew scene would cover the last 20 or 30 years at most. Bolozky (1993) proposes that comparisons be made between an earlier and a later dictionary, as well as between a dictionary and its later supplement. This method allows one to determine which words constitute recent innovations, and may thus point to recent tendencies in word formation.

The proposed dictionary (or dictionary and supplement) juxtaposition must be employed with care. The data derived from it include accidental omissions, as well as colloquialisms which lexicographers were aware of, but unwilling to include earlier. Also, as noted above, in their quest for efficient representation and elegance, compilers of dictionaries often make a point of excluding automatic derivations. But Bolozky (1993) shows that dictionary comparison is still a reasonable alternative for determining relative chronology of lexical entrance: most of the data added in later dictionaries are indeed innovations, and there is usually a correlation between dictionary comparison and data extracted from productivity tests. Occasionally, a truly productive pattern may be poorly represented in a particular recent dictionary, since its occurrences have been regarded as self-evident. But examination of another dictionary published a few years earlier would reveal some realizations of that pattern that have been sufficiently lexicalized to be considered worthy of listing. As for determining actual of degree of productivity based on dictionary comparison, two ratios were computed. The first ratio (R1) contrasts the number of neologisms in a pattern with the total number of realizations of that pattern within some category in the lexicon. It reflects that pattern's potential to 'regenerate itself' in the total lexicon, regardless of pattern size. The other ratio (R2) compares the number of neologisms in a pattern with the total number of neologisms in the semantic category concerned. It reflects the productivity of that pattern within that semantic category in the new lexicon, and consequently the mechanism most readily used by the synchronic innovator. In comparing the productivity of a pair of patterns, the primary ordering criterion is R2, but the measurement is viewed as more reliable when R1 ranking yields the same order.

A third method involves quantitative examination of texts, innovations by specific authors (e.g. Mor 1994), or innovations in specific genres, such as journalistic. An interesting measure currently in use (e.g. Baayen & Renouf 1996, Lieber 1992) exploits the inverse relationship between frequency and productivity (see also Bybee 1985, Schwarzwald 1981b). High frequency of use facilitates memorization of irregular forms and minor rules, and thus tends to protect them from undergoing productive, regular processes. Word formation rules are thus not available for forms stored in the mental lexicon. They do, however, apply in infrequent forms, which are not memorized in the lexicon, and are thus more amenable to processes of regularization, paradigmatic leveling, etc. *Geese* and *oxen*, for instance, are frequent enough to be memorized, and thus maintain their irregular plural forms, whereas *indices* and *appendices*, whose frequencies of occurrence are lower in everyday registers, are usually regularized as *indexes* and *appendixes*, respectively. Moreover, because recent neologisms take some time to get established, they are likely to have low frequency of occurrence in a given corpus. For example, while established *flexibility* will have high frequency, use of the productive suffix +*ness* in *flexibleness* is likely to be less common, until it takes hold. Or a neologism may turn out to be a nonce word (a word coined and used for a single occasion, like +*ly* neologisms such as *headmistressly* in Baayen & Renouf 1996), which by definition means low frequency. Thus, for a variety of reasons, there exists some correlation between low frequency and high productivity.

Based on these observations on the relationship between frequency and productivity, one method of measuring productivity of a particular morphological pattern is to divide the number of its *hapax legomena* occurrences in a large corpus (18 million words in the case of Lieber 1992) by the total number of tokens realized in that pattern.[2] A sufficiently large corpus is needed to lower the chance that *hapax legomena* are accidental rather than a true reflection of low frequency or of unestablished neologisms: in a big corpus, even rare words are likely to be repeated, whereas a true neologism is too new or too ephemeral to reoccur. This is not to say that rare or obsolete items will necessarily appear more than once in a large corpus; it is only argued that they are less likely to occur only once than single neologisms are. Unfortunately, no corpus of significant size is available for Modern Hebrew as yet, but examination of a small

---

[2] For alternative computations, and evaluation of what is actually measured, see Baayen & Renouf (1996).

corpus compiled for the purpose of this research suggests that even a limited corpus can work, at least for the major word formation patterns in Israeli Hebrew. While a good number of *hapax legomena* will clearly be accidental in a small corpus, some will nevertheless reflect recent neologisms, and at least preliminary ratios between infrequent and frequent realizations of a word formation pattern can be established. The status of *hapax legomena* as neologisms can be verified by dictionary check or by evaluating the transparency of the base as well as of the derivation process. Degree of productivity will be computed by a method similar to the one used for dictionary comparison, with the corpus representing the lexicon. Two ratios will be used: R1, the number of *hapax legomena* in a pattern to the total number of realizations of that pattern within some category in the whole corpus, representing its 'regeneration' in the total lexicon, and (b) number of *hapax legomena* in a pattern to the total *hapax* number in the semantic category concerned, representing that pattern's productivity in the new lexicon within that semantic category.

Three different methods of measuring and evaluating productivity of word formation are thus proposed: productivity tests (open-ended and judgment tasks), dictionary comparison, and the ratio of *hapax legomena* to tokens in corpora. Since none of these methods is totally reliable in itself, processes which score highly by all three criteria can safely be regarded as productive.

The Hebrew data reported on in this volume (from productivity tests, dictionary comparison, and frequency in corpora) will also support the claim by many (e.g. Baayen & Renouf 1996, Clark 1993, Bolinger 1975), that lexical formation is first and foremost semantically based and concept driven. Other factors, such as phonotactic constraints, preemption, or formal linguistic complexity,[3] are not the reason for selection of a word formation pattern; they only impose constraints on the derivation process, whose primary motivation is semantic. It will also be shown that the use of derivational patterns is constrained by a requirement for semantic or functional distinctiveness

---

[3] Van Marle (1985), for instance, argues that degree of lexical productivity decreases as the number of phonological, morphological, and semantic restrictions on a word formation rule increases. But as pointed by Baayen & Renouf (1996), the number of potential words removed by such restrictions vary widely; productivity varies depending on the nature on the base; and such method cannot incorporate any semantic consideration.

from already-existing forms (Clark's 1993 'contrast'). Furthermore, analysis of Hebrew word formation supports the claim made in Aronoff (1976) and in Baayen & Renouf (1996) that the productivity of a word formation pattern may vary significantly with the type of base from which it is likely to have been derived.

CHAPTER TWO

THE 'MECHANICAL' ASPECTS OF THE DERIVATIONAL MECHANISM

2.1   *The two 'mechanical' derivational strategies*

When innovating, speakers of Hebrew have to make two simultaneous choices. One choice is 'mechanical', as to the nature of the derivation mechanism proper. Speakers need to determine whether the derivation should be discontinuous or linear, and in the case discontinuous word formation, what the optimal phonological configuration would be. The discussion in this chapter focuses on the mechanics of derivation. Chapters 3–6 will deal with the more substantive choice, that of selecting a specific derivation pattern.

In English, the past and past participle forms of most verbs are derived by adding *+ed* (phonetically [t], [d], or [Id]) to the base form, which is linear derivation. For some special groups of verbs, however, the base undergoes predictable internal changes that are the same for all verbs concerned, as in (see Appendix I for an extensive list):

(1) **Discontinuous word formation patterns in the English verb system**
  a. *speak-spoke-spoken, freeze-froze-frozen, steal-stole-stolen, weave-wove-woven*
  b. *swim-swam-swum, drink-drank-drunk, shrink-shrank-shrunk, sing-sang-sung, sink-sank-sunk, ring-rang-rung, spring-sprang-sprung, stink-stank-stunk*
  c. *grow-grew-grown, blow-blew-blown, know-knew-known, throw-threw-thrown*
  d. *bind-bound-bound, find-found-found, grind-ground-ground, wind-wound-wound*
  e. *drive-drove-driven, write-wrote-written, ride-rode-ridden, rise-rose-risen, arise-arose-arisen, strive-strove-striven, smite-smote-smitten, bestride-bestrode-bestridden*
  f. *take-took-taken, shake-shook-shaken, forsake-forsook-forsaken*

There are at least 24 such groups, but their distribution is very restricted. The structure of verbs belonging to such groups may be looked at as a discontinuous (i.e. non-linear) fixed sequence of stem-internal vowels, plus possibly a suffix like *+en*. For the first subgroup, for instance, that sequence would be $C(C)\bar{\imath}C\text{-}C(C)\bar{o}C\text{-}C(C)\bar{o}C$. Onto this configuration, a variable string of consonants is mapped after it has been extracted from the base, e.g. *spk, frz, stl* in the first subgroup.

In Hebrew,[1] verbs can be structured only in this discontinuous fashion. Nouns and adjectives may be derived in the same way, but linear derivation patterns are also available. In discontinuous derivation, the consonantal skeleton is referred to as the 'root', and the discontinuous canonical pattern onto which it is applied to form an actual word is called *binyan* 'building, structure' in the verb system, and *miškal* 'metrical pattern' elsewhere. The discontinuous derivation device is a hallmark of Semitic word-formation (Goshen-Gottstein 1964).

There are essentially only five *binyanim* in Hebrew, but if quasi-automatic passives associated with two of them are also counted, the number becomes seven. Although every *binyan* has its own paradigm for each of the tenses, each *binyan* is named by the 3rd person singular masculine past tense form of a prototypical root. Sometimes *qtl* 'slay' is used for this purpose, but designations derived from *pˁl* 'act, do' are more common. The seven *binyanim* (in whose names *p*, *ˁ*, and *l* stand for the first, second, and third elements of the root, respectively) are thus called: *paˁal* (sometimes referred to as *qal* 'light'), *nifˁal, piˁel, puˁal, hitpaˁel, hifˁil,* and *hufˁal.* The 3rd person singular masculine past tense form is also used as a citation form to represent each *binyan* conjugation of a particular root (e.g., the root *grm* is cited in *paˁal* as *garam*, in *nifˁal* as *nigram*, etc.). There are roots whose conjugations are completely regular, referred to as *šlemim* 'whole, intact', but many involve deviations from the norm. Deviations are caused by the presence in the root of a guttural (*gronit*), a glide (*w* or *y*) that has been weakened to a vowel, a syllable-final *n* that assimilates, identical 2nd and 3rd consonants that merge, etc. Those are referred to as *gzarot* 'derived' (singular *gizra*). *gizra* may also be used to refer to the *šlemim*, which constitute zero derivation. The verb system is thus rigorously defined, limited to discontinuous derivation that can be effected by a small number of patterns, whose phonological structure is relatively fixed and therefore highly restrictive. Consequently, no foreign verbs can be borrowed directly. Consonants must be extracted out of existing foreign nouns, adjectives or verbs, then applied onto one of the seven patterns. But once that happens, such verbs behave like native ones.[2]

The derivational system for nouns and adjectives is far less con-

---

[1] The similarity between discontinuous formation in Semitic and the so-called 'strong' verb patterns in English is pointed out in Bolozky (1986, 1995) and in Spencer (1991).

[2] With some minor differences noted in Schwarzwald (1997).

strained than that of verbs. There exist a few hundred non-linear nominal and adjectival patterns, a number of linear ones, and a sizeable number of nouns and adjectives that do not fit into any pattern at all. The noun/adjective system is also more open to borrowing, and some of the patterns, be they discontinuous or linear, are quite productive. Linear patterns are particularly amenable to borrowing, since they leave the base essentially unaffected, and thus transparent. Many nouns are borrowed as they are, stress pattern included, regardless of whether they belong to an existing pattern or not. In fact, new linear derivation patterns for nouns and adjectives may be formed through the borrowing process. For example, after a significant number of nouns had been borrowed with the agentive suffix + *er*, + *er* suffixation began to apply to native stems as well (e.g. *širyon* 'armor' > *širyoner* 'soldier in armor corps', *bizayon* 'disgrace' > *bizyoner* 'one responsible for a disgrace').

In the following section we will be trying to show that the formation of any new lexical item, including discontinuous derivation by extraction (see Ornan 1983) of consonants to be applied onto a *binyan* or *miškal*, is based not on an abstract consonantal root, but on some formerly existing word, or more precisely lexeme (see Aronoff 1983, 1992, 1994). A lexeme is an uninflected form belonging to a major lexical category (noun, verb, adjective/adverb), that is not necessarily a free form and which may even be only potential. It will also be demonstrated that non-linear word formation is as productive as ever in Hebrew, and is no danger of losing ground to linear derivation under the influence of European languages. This is true not only in the verb, where non-linear derivation is still the only alternative, but in the noun system as well.

2.2   'Root-based' versus 'word-based' derivation

The notion of the abstract consonantal root has been axiomatic in grammars of Semitic languages since the Middle Ages. Yet it is not easy to find arguments for its actually playing a role in the process of word formation. One such argument is that there exist co-occurrence restrictions on consonant combinations in Semitic stems. The first and second consonants are generally neither identical nor homorganic. The same constraint applies (less stringently) to the first and third consonants. The second and third consonant can be identical, but not homorganic, again, with exceptions. Medieval linguists were aware of these restrictions, and in recent times relevant data from all Semitic languages were put together by J. H. Greenberg in his well known article in *Word* (1950), a seminal work that has served as a base for all subsequent research on this topic. The argument is simple: since the co-occurrence restrictions can only be stated in terms of stem consonants, while intervening vowels are irrelevant, there must be some level of representation at which speakers refer to the consonantal root as an independent entity. But this argument is not all that strong. These constraints are in fact a function of the likelihood of each pair of consonants actually co-occurring on the surface as a cluster, and the restriction is on identical or homorganic consonants occurring without an intervening vowel in the output of the phonological process (e.g. Schwarzwald 1974). Still, most speakers are aware of the root concept. In some circles, identifying the etymologically-correct root, or constructing neologisms on the basis of knowledge of root and normative *miškal*, is a mark of schooling as well as intellectual capacity. Innovations by experts (the Hebrew Language Academy, linguists, language educators, linguistically-oriented literati, etc.) may very well be root-based. However, there is little evidence, historical or system-internal, to support the common assumption of the 'classical' Semitic root playing a central role in word-formation among even educated speakers. Such evidence cannot be found in popular innovations of various sources, nor in wide but selective acceptance by the Hebrew-speaking community of certain new normative derivations. Rather, the evidence often suggests derivation (through extraction) from existing words rather than from roots.

The underlying assumption is that: (a) native speakers tend to derive new words from existing ones, (b) most innovators do not conceive of roots the way etymologists do. When native speakers do not derive by simple linear affixation, they extract sequences of consonants out of existing words, regardless of the 'etymologically-correct' roots underlying them, while trying to maintain some of the structure of the base (mostly consonant clusters). That Hebrew word formation is word-based supports the general claim made, that words are derived from other words rather than from morphemes. For Hebrew, this claim is also made by Bat-El (1986, 1989), whose extraction process is based on the prosodic theory of non-linear, discontinuous morphology, as in McCarthy (1979, 1981), McCarthy & Prince (1986).

2.3   The 'mechanical' derivation of verbs

The 'mechanical' derivation of verbs has implications to the issue of word vs. root-based derivation. Hebrew verbs can only be formed non-linearly, in some *binyan*. Even very young children know (Berman, to appear) that in verb formation, consonant sequences are extracted out of existing words to be reapplied unto discontinuous patterns, regardless of whether they correspond to traditional roots (see also Rosén 1977 and Bat-El 1989):

(2) **Illustrating extraction regardless of traditional root**

Denom. Verb	Gloss	Source N/Adj	Gloss
misper[3]	enumerate	*mispar*	number
mixšev	computerize	*maxšev*	computer
himxiš	make real	*muxaši*	real, tangible
himxiz	dramatize	*maxaze*	drama, play

In *misper* and *himxiš*, the etymological roots of the source nouns are *s.p.r* 'count' and *x.w.š* 'feel', respectively, and the *m* is prefixal. Had the new form been derived from historical root and pattern, only the root would have been extracted, without the prefix *m+*. One view is that the roots were restructured into *m.s.p.r* and *m.x.š*. In any case, we are no longer dealing here with the traditional root. Rather, speakers seem to extract whatever consonants they find in the source noun while maintaining the original order. The same is true of *tifked* 'function (V)' below, since the root of *tafkid* 'function (N)' is *p.k.d*; *t* is prefixal. Here is a sample list of such cases:[4]

(3) **Further illustrations of extraction regardless of traditional root**

	Denom. Verb	Gloss	Source Noun	Gloss
(a)	*tifked*	function	*tafqid*	function
	tirgel	exercise (tr.)	*targil*	exercise
	tidrex	brief	*tadrix*	briefing
	tixker	debrief	*taxkir*	debriefing
(b)	*tifʿel*	operate	*tifʿul*	operation
	tiskel	frustrate	*tiskul*	frustration
	tidlek	refuel	*tidluk*	refueling
	tizmen	call for appointment	*tizmun*	calling for appointment

---

[3] Stress is word-final, unless marked otherwise.

[4] For fuller lists of 'root expansions', including *š.p.ʿ.l*, see Schwarzwald & Neradim (1994/95). On semitic 'root augmentation' in general, see Goldenberg (1994).

A new sub-pattern of *pi^el* could be emerging (i.e. *tif^el*), since by now there are numerous similar *t*-initial cases. The (a)-cases above developed from related *t*-initial nouns that predated the verbs. All consonants are extracted, regardless of whether or not they belong to the stem. The same applies to the (b)-cases, except that those may have been realized in an already-established *tif^el* pattern, since there is no evidence of pre-existing related forms containing a *t+* prefix.

There are other affixes extracted from pre-existing nouns and reapplied in derived verbs, such as a glottal stop prefix:

(4) **Extraction from a stem with a glottal stop prefix**

Denom. Verb	Gloss	Source Noun	Gloss
'ixsen[4a]	store	*'/haxsana*	storage
'izker	refer, mention, cite	*'/hazkara*	mention (N); memorial
'ixzev	disappoint	*'axzava*	disappointment
'ivxen	diagnose	*'/havxana*	diagnosis; distinction

or an *+on/+an* suffix (see also Nir 1984):

(5) **Extraction from a stem with an *+on/+an* suffix**

Denom. Verb	Gloss	Source Noun	Gloss
sikren	a rouse curiosity	*sakran*	curious
digmen	work as model	*dugman*	model
xišben	calculate	*xešbon*	calculation
ximcen	oxidize	*xamcan*	oxygen

or an *+it/+a(t)* suffix:

(6) **Extraction from a stem with an *+it/+(at)* suffix**

Denom. Verb	Gloss	Source Noun	Gloss
tixnet	program (V)	*toxnit*	program
^ivret	Hebraize	*^ivrit*	Hebrew
xivret	socialize (tr.); pass (tr.) to public ownership	*xevra(t)*	society

There is some evidence at certain phases in the development of Modern Hebrew to suggest consonant extraction going beyond the tra-

---

[4a] Since the focus of this work is not phonetics, orthographic pre-vocalic *'* (*'álef*) and *^* (*^áyin*) are included, even when not realized phonetically. They are represented so as to signal an underlying consonantal slot, that will capture syllable-structure similarities with comparable regular forms in the same derivational pattern. Word-final *'* (*'álef*) is excluded, since its post-vocalic slot is of limited relevance to syllable structure, and because it is never realized, not even when contrastively stressed.

ditional root. Mirkin (1968a) discusses an early innovator, Y. Epstein, who proposed *tifked* 'function (V)' from *tafkid* 'function (N)', quoting *taram* 'contribute' from *truma* 'contribution' as precedent. Since the root of *truma* is *r.w.m*, and *t* is prefixal, like the *t* of *tafqid*, there is no doubt about it that Epstein specifically and consciously recommended consonant extraction that includes the affix. It illustrates how diachronic evidence can support system-internal synchronic claims. It also demonstrates that overall extraction (beyond the 'classical' root) is a general phenomenon, originating not only from colloquial tendencies, but extending to erudite innovation as well. Berman & Sagi (1981) report a similar derivation among children around age 10, using *tavas* 'defeat' instead of standard *hevis*, owing to the ready availability of the noun *tvusa* 'defeat (N)'.

The fact that consonant extraction refers to extended stems, which include what used to be affixes, itself indicates that the derivational process refers to existing words and not to abstract roots. It is not necessarily proof of the claim, since the original roots can always be extended into 'secondary' ones such as *'.b.t.x*, *s.k.r.n*, *t.x.n.t*, etc.

One can draw a stronger argument for the word rather than a root being the base for derivation from the general tendency to preserve as much as possible of the structure of the derivation base, primarily by maintaining the original consonant clustering. For example, a borrowed noun like *flirt*, whose expected realization as a verb is in *pi'el*, should have been transformed into the form **filret*. Instead, the final *t* is reduplicated, resulting in *flirtet* 'flirted', even though **filret* would satisfied the sonority constraints just as well (Bolozky 1978). This keeps the expected *binyan* choice, and at the same time preserves the transparency of the source. In some cases like this, the source vowels might also be preserved, since they happen to correspond to those of the verb pattern, but in general it is only the original consonant clusters that are maintained:

(7) **Original consonant clustering maintained by reduplication**

Source Noun	Gloss	Possible Form	Actual Form	Gloss
faks	facsimile	*fikes*	*fikses*	fax (V)
toxnit	plan	*tiken/tixen*	*tixnen/tixnet*	plan/program (V)
sifra	digit	*siper/sifer*	*sifrer*	assign digits
kod	code	*kived/kiyed*	*kided/koded*	codify
mana	portion	*mina*	*minen*	apportion

Even where other considerations apply, such as preemption by already-occupied slots (*siper* 'tell', *mina* 'appoint'), cluster preservation is still the determining factor. Similarly, the realization of *hišpric* 'squirt' in *hif'il* could have also been *hišpirc, but cluster preservation selects the former. Bat-El (1994) makes the same point, noting that although other configurations would have satisfied the sonority hierarchy just as well, the variants preserving the consonant clusters of the base for derivation are the form for which the innovator opts:

(8) **Consonant cluster preservation through syllable division in new *pi'el* forms**

Base	Gloss	Possible	Actual	Gloss
sandlar	shoemaker	*snidler	*sindler*	make shoes
praklit	lawyer	*pirklet	*priklet*	practice law
traklin	salon, parlor	*tirklen	*triklen*	make neat, tidy up
(*progres*	progress)	*pirgres	*prigres*	progress
gušpánka	approval, seal	*gišpnek	*gišpenk*	approve, seal
nostálgya	nostalgia	*nistleg	*nistelg*	be nostalgic

Since the derivation process must reference the base in order to form the denominative verb, Bat-El concludes that it is necessary to derive from existing words rather than from roots, and that there is no justification for an independent level at which an entity such as a consonantal root can be argued to exist. To relate between bases and derived forms, she proposes to transfer clusters through the use of a 'stem modification' mechanism, as proposed in Steriade (1988) and employed in McCarthy & Prince (1990) for some Arabic broken plurals and diminutives.

Extraction encompasses derivational affixes but not inflectional ones. There are some cases in which derivational affixes may be disregarded by extraction as well, as in:

(9) **Cases where derivational affixes are disregarded by extraction**

Etym. Root	Source Noun	Gloss	Denom. Verb	Gloss
z.m.r	*tizmóret*	orchestra	*tizmer*	orchestrate
g.b.r	*tigbóret*	reinforcement	*tigber*	reinforce

Bat-El (1986, 1989) suggests that the explanation lies in the bond between the stem and the affix, and that the more inflection-like the affix is (as is the suffix $+et$, compared with the prefix $ti+$), the more likely it will be ignored by extraction. When a new verb form is derived from an existing verb, it affects the stem proper, ignoring *binyan* as well as tense marking affixes (like $hi+$ or $mV+$). In a way, this is the only sense in which an argument can still be made for the 'psychological reality' of the root as distinct from a preexisting word upon which a new derivation will be based. While in general, derivational affixes are not excluded from extraction, they are never included in a derivation that is internal to the verb system. Thus, when Berman & Sagi (1981)[5] report children at ages 3–4 producing sentences like

(10) *ha-kosem*   *ʿilem*   *ʾet   ha-šafan*
     the-magician   make disappear acc. the-rabbit
     'The magician made the rabbit disappear'

    xibéti   lo   ʾet   ha-matana
    I hid   to him acc. the-present
    'I hid the present from him'

where *ʿilem* and *xibe* replace standard *heʿelim* and *hexbi*, respectively, it is clear that at that stage, all they could have heard before were *neʿelam* 'disappear' and *hitxabe* 'hide (int.)' as possible sources. The fact that they would never consider including the *n* of *nifʿal* or the *t* of *hitpaʿel* may be used as an argument for a root-like entity serving as a base for derivations that occur within the verb system proper.

    Child language appears to provide another possible argument for the verbal root. Berman (1990) shows that in general, children rely on triconsonantal roots as the least marked and most accessible when they form denominative verbs. Although they occasionally add a consonant (reduplicative or an unmarked one) to produce a quadriliteral form (e.g. *séfel* 'cup' > *mesaflel, panas* 'torchlight' > *mepansen, (ʾ)aron* 'cupboard' > *me(ʾ)arnet*), children can rarely recover all four consonants. They may ignore one (e.g. *safsal* 'bench' > *mesafel*), or they change a consonant by repetition or substitution (e.g. *(ʾ)argaz* 'box' > *megargez, (ʾ)ambatya* 'bath' > *me(ʾ)amben*). In addition to doubling the second consonant of two (*kise* 'chair' > *mekases* or *mekaskes, sal* 'basket' > *mesalel, mesalsel, maslil, kaf* 'spoon' > *mekafef*), they may also add a different consonant (*kise* 'chair' > *mekaset, sapa* 'sofa' > *mesapen, pax* 'trash can' > *mepaxen, kir* 'wall' > *mekaret*). In relying on

---

[5] For a rich array of data on children's acquisition of morphological marking of transitivity, with many illustrations, mostly of children ages 2–3 using morphologically-intransitive forms in transitive constructions, see Berman (1993a, b). However, the data from Berman & Sagi (1981) quoted above constitute a stronger argument for the root, since they involve non-standard creations that ignore affixal consonants found in forms these children have already acquired.

triconsonantal roots, they add consonants mainly at the end, with a
universal preference for coronals as the least marked consonants, or
they reduplicate. This is a generalization aimed at simplification too,
somewhat like the regularization of the *kfulim* (*sabóti* 'I turned' >
savávti, galóti 'I rolled, removed' > *galálti*). It regularizes the size of
the extracted consonant sequence to three, making it uniform and
thus easier to deal with, until the full adult mechanism is acquired.
However, as pointed out in Bat-El (1994), this kind of derivation
does not have to be interpreted as support for the root-base hypoth-
esis. It may simply suggest that children prefer the unmarked bi-
syllabic verb stem, which the enormous productivity of *pi'el* shows
to be the prevalent syllabic template for new verbs.

Finally, a simple argument can be made, that roots are unavoid-
able when no preexisting words can be found that could serve as a
possible base for more recent ones. It is very difficult, however, to
identify a neologism which has no possible base in an existing word.
Slang verbs such as *hikric* 'resourcefully obtain' or *kifer* 'disappoint,
cause despair' may constitute such examples, but undoubtedly someone would find a plausible source even for those.

Even if it can firmly be established that the base of neologism
must be a preexisting word, it should be remembered that in the
verb system, derivation continues to be strictly discontinuous. Consonant
clusters of the base may be preserved, but the mechanism is still of
extraction and reapplication. One scholar argues that new verbs may
also be derived linearly. Wexler (1990) assumes that the *binyan* system in general, and the semantic correlates of individual *binyanim* in
particular, have undergone drastic decrease in productivity. He attributes this development to a tendency in Slavic and Yiddish (of which
Modern Hebrew is a descendant, according to his theory) to contain conjugations with particular affixes that are devoid of semantic
functions (e.g. the Yiddish infinitival endings + *e(n), enen* or *even*). He
goes as far as to say that in Modern Hebrew (henceforth MH) the
binyan system is being completely restructured in the direction of the
Slavic practice of deriving compound verbs linearly by affixation.
hit+, he argues, is becoming a linear device for deriving denominative verbs by mere prefixation, without reference to the discontinuous consonant-vowel pattern of the base. As support for this claim
he cites *hitxaver* 'become friends (with)' alongside *hitxaber* 'join', and
the Yiddish use of the reflexive pronoun in translation equivalents:
xávern zix 'be associated with'. Since the second root radical in *hit-*

pa'el must be a stop, *hitxaver* could only have been derived from *xaver* 'friend'. Semiticists agree (see Goldenberg 1981, Kutscher 1969, 1982), that morphology is the most stable component of the grammar, and that non-linear word-formation, particularly in the verb system, is the safest criterion for Semitic typology. If Wexler could indeed prove that verb-formation is becoming linear, it would constitute strong support for his claim that from a typological point of view, MH is not Semitic.

However, his view is not tenable. *hitxaver* 'become friends (with)' is the only example Wexler cites to support his claim for linear derivation in the verb system. In fact, he could have added the following *hif'il* formations (noted in another context), which may be regarded as a consequence of merely affixing the *hif'il hi +* to a stem: *hišvic* 'sweat; brag', *hišpric* 'squirt' and *hiflik* 'slap', from *švic, špric* and *flik*, respectively. There are also some isolated literary instances like the poet Shlonsky's *hit'orvevu* 'be like a raven (pl.)' (quoted in Ephratt 1993).[6]

Such evidence for Wexler's analysis of the MH verb system is rare, and even for these few cases, he still needs to show that the identity between the source stem and the canonical pattern does not result from extraction and reapplication. Even if he were able to do that, there is no getting around the fact that in the vast majority of cases, the vowels of the stem do not correspond to the *binyan* vowels. Even in the case of *hištavec* 'have a stroke', often quoted alongside *hitxaver*, the source noun has two *a*'s: *šavac* 'stroke'; and *hiflic* 'pass wind, fart', associated with the *hišvic* group, is derived from *floc* 'fart (N)'. No representative sample of recent innovations, either spontaneous or from productivity tests, shows clear evidence for linearly derived verbs.

2.4   *Mechanical derivation of nouns and adjectives*

As noted above, derivation of nouns and adjectives is not as strictly constrained as verb formation is. New nouns and adjectives may be formed in numerous discontinuous patterns, as well as linearly. Nir

---

[6] It might be argued that the *o* of *hit'orvevu*, though clearly chosen because it preserves the transparency of the original *'orev* 'raven', is really the *o* used for a large class of verbs in *pi'el, pu'al* and *hitpa'el* in which the last two stem consonants are identical, e.g. *pocec* 'blow up' (coll. *picec*), *boded* 'isolate, insulate' (coll. *bided*).

(1984) lists several different linear formation patterns, including +*ut*, +*an*, +*iya*, +*on*, +*ay*, +*it* and +*ar* for nouns, and +*i*, +*a'i*, +*ni*, +*oni*, +*áli*, +*ísti* for adjectives:

(11) **List of linear formation patterns in Nir (1984)**
Nouns

Form	Gloss	Source	Gloss
N +*ut* (see 2.4.2, and 5.2 on abstract nominalizations)			
mahut	essence	ma	what
xazirut	behaving like a pig	xazir	pig
N +*an* (see 2.4.1, and 5.3 on agents)			
xalilan	flutist	xalil	flute
mizrexan	orientalist	mizrax	orient
N +*iya* (see 5.5 on locatives and 5.6 on groups)			
nagariya	carpenter's shop	nagar	carpenter
kartisiya	ride pass	kartis	ticket
N +*on* (see 5.7 on diminutives)			
yarxon	monthly	yérax	month
gišron	little bridge	géšer	bridge
N +*ay* (see 5.3 on agents)			
ʿitonay	journalist	ʿiton	paper, journal
xašmelay	electrician	xašmal	electricity
N +*it* (see 5.7 on diminutives)			
kosit	a little glass	kos	a glass
masaʾit	truck	masa	a load
N +*ar*			
sandlar	shoemaker	sandal	sandal
smartutar	rag dealer	smartut	rag

Adjectives

N +*i* (can be added to most types of bases; see Chapter 5)			
takcivi	budgetary	takciv	budget
pitʾomi	sudden (Adj.)	pitʾom	suddenly
If base ends with fem. +*a*, realized as +*ti*:			
taʿasiyati	industrial	taʿasiya	industry
yecirati	creative	yecira	creation
N +*aʾi* (see 5.3 on agents)			
ʿitonaʾi	journalistic	ʿiton	paper, journal
ʾakademáʾi	academic	académya	academy
N +*ni*			
bogdani	treacherous	boged	traitor
marokani	Moroccan	maróko	Morocco
N +*oni*			
civʿoni	colorful	cévaʿ	color
ʿironi	municipal; urban	ʿir	city, town
N +*áli* (borrowed)			
teʾatráli	theatrical	teʾatron	theater

(cont.)

Form	Gloss	Source	Gloss
maksimáli	maximal	*máksimum*	maximum
N+*isti* (borrowed)			
socyalísti	socialist	*socyalizm*	socialism
fašísti	fascist	*fašizm*	fascism

Recent types of linear word formation, some of which are not at all, or only marginally attested at earlier stages of the language (Nir 1978, 1984, 1990, 1993; Rosén 1977; Kutscher 1982; etc.), include: (a) lexemic prefix compounding, (b) appending foreign suffixes, (c) blends, (d) clippings. The prefixes of the first type, lexemic prefix compounding, are largely borrowed from Aramaic, and modeled on Graeco-Latin forms (see Kutscher 1982, Nir 1984, Ravid 1990), as in:

(12) **Illustrating lexemic prefix compounding**

Prefix	Gloss	Form	Gloss
du+	two	*du-sitri*	two-way; bilateral
kdam+	pre-	*kdam-cvaʾi*	pre-military
batar+	post-	*batar-mikraʾi*	post-Biblical
tat+	sub-	*tat-ʾenoši*	sub-human

Foreign suffixes can be appended to native stems, as in:

(13) **Illustrating appended foreign suffixes**

Prefix	Gloss	Form	Gloss
katan	small	*katánčik*	very small
baxur	young man	*baxúrčik*	nice young man (affectionate)
bizayon	disgrace; scandal	*bizyoner*	one responsible for disgrace/scandal
širyon	armor; armor corps	*širyoner*	soldier in armor corps

Blends involve merging of two independent lexical items into a new blended word (see Berman 1985, Berman & Ravid 1986). Some such blends have been part of the lexicon for quite a while, as in:

(14) **Illustrating well-established blends**

Stem	Gloss	Stem	Gloss	Blend	Gloss
kol	sound	*nóaᶜ*	movement	*kolnóaᶜ*	movie theater, movie making
rašam	record (V)	*kol*	sound	*rešam-kol*	tape-recorder
migdal	tower	*ʾor*	light	*migdalor*	lighthouse

Other blends are more recent, and Nir (1990) feels, probably correctly, that compounding will continue to increase, owing to its inherent transparency. Many recent compounds are 'clipped' blends (see Berman 1991, Berman & Ravid 1986, Ravid 1990, Bat-El 1996), i.e. with part of each (or part of only one) base being lost in the compounding process, as in:

(15) **Illustrating well-established blends**

Stem	Gloss	Stem	Gloss	Blend	Gloss
midraxa	sidewalk	*rexov*	street	*midrexov*	pedestrian mall
rakévet	train	*kével*	cable	*rakével*	cable car
péle	wonder	*télefon*	telephone	*pélefon*	cellular phone

This tendency seems to have gained considerable popularity in the media, particularly in commercial brand names used in advertizing (for a detailed description of 'language in the service of advertizing', see Nir 1984), as in:

(16) **Illustrating commercial blends generated by the media**

Stem	Gloss	Stem	Gloss	Blend	Gloss
'of	chicken	*muxan*	ready	*'ofxan*	chicken ready to cook
plada	steel	*délet*	door	*pladélet*	steel door
dlá'at	squash	*qaloryot*	calories	*dalorit*	a kind of squash

Such formations often draw from foreign examples (e.g. the recent *kapliya* 'caplet', from *kapsula* 'capsule' + *tavlit* 'tablet', pl. *tavliyot*). Ravid (1990) points out that clipped blends are not structure-preserving, since partial base loss is involved, and thus are by definition partly opaque as to their source nouns. They are usually invented by linguists or by clever advertisers; most speakers rarely generate such blends, nor are they always able to analyze and understand them. The common pronunciation of normative *rakével* 'cable car' as *raxval* or *raxbal* is a case in point. Instead of combining morphemes, most speakers simply realize the consonant sequence *rkvl* in the discontinuous pattern *CaCCaC*. . . . Blend formation is thus not particularly productive, certainly not clipped blends. The sophisticated mechanism it requires does not encourage further creative use by the average speaker.

Linear, 'continuous' derivation, compounding included, is clearly on the rise in MH. On the other hand, its expanded use does not affect the continued productivity of discontinuous derivation, as shown in empirical research by Berman and others. In Berman (1987), production test results indicate 3:2 ratio in favor of discontinuous formation, and non-linear derivation is reported to be strong in Berman & Sagi (1981), Ravid (1990), Walden (1982), etc. The observation that discontinuous derivation is as productive as ever is reinforced by evidence from aphasia (Barkai 1980), and from psycholinguistic experiments (e.g. Bentin & Feldman 1990, Feldman & Bentin, 1994, Ephratt 1997). Thus, the linear and the discontinuous strategies maintain their respective productivities. Since discontinuous derivation is alive and well in MH, it should clearly be regarded as morphologically Semitic.

Three derivation patterns from the MH noun system will be discussed below, to demonstrate that non-linear word-formation continues to be (very) productive. The first pattern comprises of nouns ending with the agentive suffix + *an*, the second of nouns with the nominalizing suffix + *ut*, and the third of the so-called segolate nouns.

2.4.1 *Mechanical derivation of nouns with the agentive suffix* + an

2.4.1.1   CaCCan *and* N + an *constituting a single entity*

Using the + *an* pattern as an illustration for the continued productivity of non-linear word formation is particularly appropriate. It allows both discontinuous and linear derivation, e.g. *kablan* 'contractor' (cf. *kibel* 'receive') vs. *'alxut* + *an* 'wireless operator' (*'alxut* 'wireless' + *an*), and the choice of device is not affected by semantic considerations. As reported in Bolozky (1985, 1986b), *CaCCan* and N + *an* are essentially identical (beyond the morpho-phonological difference). Semantically, both *CaCCan* and N + *an* tend to be agentive. Even when realizations are broken down further into more specific semantic classes, both *CCaCan* and N + *an* can be found in any group, clearly suggesting that *CaCCan* and linear N + *an* are realizations of the same category. Discontinuous *CaCCan* is illustrated in the left column, and linear N + *an* on the right in the examples below. Numbers are out of a data base of 1,090 items that reflects all relevant forms that could be drawn from the dictionaries of Even-Shoshan (1970), Alkalay (1965) and Barkali (1964):

(17) **Illustrating discontinuous and linear** + *an* **agentives from dictionaries and noun lists**

Characteristic activity or quality [849 instances]

batlan 'idler, loafer' (< *batel* 'idle')	*'alxutan* 'radio operator' (< *'al* 'no' + *xut* 'wire' + *an*)
kablan 'contractor' (< *kibel* 'receive')	*mikco'an* 'professional' (< *mikcóa'* 'profession' + *an*)
baxyan 'weeper, cry-baby' (< *baxa* 'cry')	*rexušan* 'capitalist' (< *rexuš* 'property' + *an*)
bayšan 'shy' (< *hitbayeš* 'be shy')	*xucpan* 'insolent' (< *xucpa* 'cheek' + *an*)

Plant- (or animal-) related forms, also normally denoting characteristic quality [96]

tavlan 'diver (water-bird)' (< *taval* 'dip')	*gdilan* 'thistle' (< *gdil* 'strand' + *an*)
navxan 'barker' (< *navax* 'bark')	*reyxan* 'basilicum' (< *re(y)áx* 'smell' + *an*)

navran 'rodent' (< *navar* 'burrow')   *xartoman* 'snipe (bird)' (< *xartom* 'beak' + *an*)
samkan 'red mushroom' (< *hismik* 'blush') *tikan* 'cockroach' (< *tik* 'bag, case' + *an*)

Substances [51]
xamcan 'oxygen' (< *xamac* 'be sour') *meyman* 'hydrogen' (< *máyim/meym* 'water' + *an*)
xankan 'nitrogen' (< *xanak* 'choke')   *coran* 'silicon' (< *cor* 'rock' + *an*)
zarxan 'phosphorus' (< *zarax* 'shine') *zxuxan* 'frit' (< *zxuxit* 'glass' + *an*)
paxman 'carbon' (< *pexam* 'coal')   *divkan* 'gluten' (< *dévek/divk* 'glue' + *an*)

Instruments [60]
mazgan 'air conditioner' (< *mazag* 'mix') *potxan* 'opener' (< *potéax* 'open' + *an*)
lavyan 'sattelite' (< *liva* 'accompany') *roxsan* 'zipper' (< *roxes* 'zip' + *an*)
halman 'mallet, hammer' (*halam* 'bang') *'aguran* 'crane, derrick' (< *'agur* 'crane' + *an*)
masran 'inductor' (*masar* 'hand over') *kolan* 'tuning fork' (< *kol* 'sound' + *an*)

Body parts [9]
dagdegan 'clitoris' (< *digdeg* 'tickle') *toseftan* 'appendix' (< *toséfet* 'addition' + *an*)
matxan 'tensor (muscle)' (< *matax* 'stretch') *pikan* > 'capitate bone' (< *pika* 'cap' + *an*)

Secondary kinship [4]
'axyan 'nephew (or dimin.?)' (< *'ax* 'brother') *dodan* 'cousin' (< *dod* 'uncle' + *an*)

Miscellaneous (locatives, unclassified) [21]
nadyan 'wash pond' (< *nida* 'impurity') *maxmecan* 'wash pit' (< *maxmeca* 'wash pit?' + *an*)

This parallelism in itself supports the claim that the two derivation strategies are different realizations of the same morpho-semantic pattern. Nor are the two strategies different in stylistic register. In the dictionary data used here, literary realizations outnumber colloquial and everyday ones by a ratio of at least 2:1 regardless of strategy. Typically, the *CaCCan* form reflects a transparent verb base, while N+*an*, by virtue of the linear derivation process, transparently preserves the source noun or adjective.

The etymology of +*ān* is unclear. There have been attempts (see Gross 1994 and references therein) to interpret it as mimation of the ancient accusative case in its adverbial use (as in *ḥinnām* 'free; in vain', *yōmām* 'during the day', *rēqām* 'empty-handed', etc.), or as a reflex of the pronominal ending +*nā*, but the evidence for either is slim. Generally in Semitic, +*ān* (or its +*ōn* variant) forms abstract nouns (some of which have become concrete), manifest in patterns such as *CiCaCon*, *CiCCon*, *CoCCan*, *CaCCan*, and adjectives that may also function as nouns and as agents. +*ān* may also serve as a plural marker, which probably constituted a separate morpheme to start with (see Gross 1994). Its productivity stems, according to Gross, from its capability to derive adjectives from nouns so as to denote related attributes, and from its transparent relationship to the base. If the adjective branched off from abstract nouns with +*ān* via semantic shift (from the gerund to its subject), then both readings, agentive adjectives and agentive nouns, were easily generated.

Essentially, both *CaCCan* and N + *an* started in Mishnaic Hebrew:[7]

(18) **CaCCan forms by origin**

Biblical	3	[.48%]
Mishnaic	108	[17.48%]
Medieval[8]	75	[12.14%]
Modern	432	[69.90%]
Total:[9]	618	[100.00%]

N +an forms by origin

Biblical	–	
Mishnaic	44	[13.46%]
Medieval	7	[2.14%]
Modern	276	[84.40%]
Total:	327	[100.00%]

Although the percentage of linear N+*an* innovations in MH is very high, there were significant precedents for it in Mishnaic Hebrew (MishH), and in spite of the fact that MH *CaCCan* cases are 'only' about 70%, their sheer number is overwhelming. In other words, both devices have coexisted from MishH, and are very productive in MH. The distribution of + *an* forms clearly does not support the claim that linear derivation is replacing discontinuous word-formation under the impact of European languages, or a 'hidden Slavic standard', as Wexler (1990) would argue.

Below are some instances of *CaCCan* and N + *an* by the period at which they were introduced into the language (even for MishH, gemination is not marked; see Blau's 1990 analysis below. Med = Medieval Hebrew):

(19) **Some CaCCan innovations, by period of introduction**
Mishnaic Hebrew

baṭlan 'idler, loafer'
  (< *baṭel* 'idle')
šaqran 'liar' (< *šiqer* 'lie')
qablan 'contractor'
  (< *qibel* 'receive')

dabran 'talkative, verbose'
  (< *diber* 'speak')
gazlan 'robber' (< *gazal* 'rob')
qamṣan 'miser' (< *qimeṣ* 'take handful; save')

Medieval Hebrew

'axlan 'glutton' (< *'axal* 'eat')
qabran 'gravedigger'
  (< *qavar/qiber* 'bury')
šadxan 'matchmaker'
  (*šidex* 'match')

badḥan 'joker' (< *bidaḥ* 'amuse')
lamdan 'learned man, scholar'
  (< *lamad* 'study')
salḥan 'forgiving, lenient'
  (< *salaḥ* 'forgive')

---

[7] Biblical Hebrew (BH) forms like *na'aman* 'pleasant, lovely', *barqan* 'briar, thorn', *'avdan* 'ruin' can only marginally be claimed to constitute realizations of *CaCC + an*, and those that look like BH N + *an* are probably realizations of discontinuous *CoCC + an* (*qorban* 'sacrifice', *'ovdan* 'ruin, destruction') and *CiCC + an* (*'inyan* 'matter', *qinyan* 'property, possession', *binyan* 'building', *kivšan* 'oven, furnace, kiln', *miškan* 'dwelling; temple').

[8] I have not been able as yet to distinguish the different sources for cases whose origin is medieval.

[9] The difference between the total data base 1,090 and the sum of *CaCCan* and

Modern Hebrew

'asfan 'collector' (< *'asaf* 'collect')　　*badran* 'entertainer' (< *bider*
　　　　　　　　　　　　　　　　　　　　　　　　　　　　　'entertain')

raḳdan 'dancer' (< *raḳad* 'dance')　　*rašlan* 'negligent, slovenly'
　　　　　　　　　　　　　　　　　　　　　　　　　　(< *hitrašel* 'be slovenly')

baxyan 'weeper, cry-baby'　　　　　　　*bazbezan* 'spendthrift' (< *bizbez*
　　(< *baxa* 'cry')　　　　　　　　　　　　　　'waste')

(20) **Some N + *an* innovations, by period of introduction**
Mishnaic Hebrew

dodan 'cousin' (< *dod* 'uncle' + *an*)　　*'eymatan* 'terrorist' (< *'eyma(t)*
　　　　　　　　　　　　　　　　　　　　　　　　　　'terror' + *an*)

leysan 'mocker, jester' (*leṣ*　　　　　　*reyqan* 'empty, vain' (< *reyq*
　　'mocker' + *an*)　　　　　　　　　　　　　　'empty' + *an*)

kotvan 'scribe' (< *kotev* 'write' + *an*)　　*duvšan* 'honey cake' (< *dvaš/duvš*
　　　　　　　　　　　　　　　　　　　　　　　　　　'honey' + *an*)

Medieval Hebrew

miṣran 'neighbor' (< *méṣer/miṣr* 'border' + *an*)
śimḥan 'happy person' (< *śimḥa* 'happiness' + *an*)
solḥan 'forgiving, lenient' (< *soleaḥ* 'forgive' + *an*)
ga'avtan 'boastful, haughty' (< *ga'ava(t)* 'pride' + *an*)

Modern Hebrew

rošan 'tadpole' (< *roš* 'head' + *an*)　　*coran* 'silicon' (< *cor* 'rock' + *an*)
'egrofan 'boxer' (< *'egrof* 'fist' + *an*)　　*yevu'an* 'importer' (< *yevu*
　　　　　　　　　　　　　　　　　　　　　　　　　　'import' + *an*)

maxširan 'tool operator'　　　　　　　*matiran* 'permissive' (< *matir*
　　(< *maxšir* 'tool' + *an*)　　　　　　　　'permit' + *an*)

2.4.1.2　*Verb-related* CaCCan *forms*

When *CaCCan* forms are related to verbs, the relationship is generally either to *pa'al* or to *pi'el*. Although one might be tempted to
derive such *CaCCan* forms linearly from their related *pa'al* or *pi'el*
bases, it will be argued below that such derivation is not appropriate, for methodological reasons. There is no doubt as for the relationships themselves, but the derivation process proper should be
discontinuous, not linear.

　　The *CaCCan* forms below are clearly related to existing *pa'al* or
pi'el stems,[10] as indicated by the difference in stop/fricative realization. p, *b* and *k* are maintained in *pi'el*-related forms, and their respective variants, *f, v* and *x*, point to relationship with *pa'al* verbs (the

---

N + *an* cases by origin, 945, is due to the absence of etymological information for
some of the forms found only in Alkalay or Barkali.

　[10] At least synchronically. Gross (1994) suggests that *CaCCan* was derived from
CaCeC, the *benoni* of (some) intransitive verbs in *pa'al*, which is the standard *benoni*

blocking of Spirantization in *pi'el*-related forms may be attributed to historical geminates, as in the *pi'el* forms themselves):

(21) *CaCCan* **forms, related to** *pa'al* **and** *pi'el* **bases**

Form	Gloss	Pa'al	Gloss	Pi'el	Gloss
dabran	talkative, verbose			*daber*	talk
kabcan	beggar, pauper			*kabec*	collect
kablan	contractor			*kabel*	receive
šabšan	one who makes errors			*šabeš*	confuse
tapsan	climber, alpinist			*tapes*	climb
vakxan	polemist			*(hit)vakéax*	argue
'axlan	glutton	*'axal*	eat		
baxyan	weeper, cry-baby	*baxa*	weep		
kafcan	jumper; leander	*kafac*	jump		
safdan	mourner	*safad*	mourn		
savlan	patient, long-suffering	*saval*	suffer		
navran	field mouse; rodent	*navar*	burrow		

The relationships are further supported by the frequency of related stems. Thus, when there is no related verb, realization would not occur in the associated pattern. The non-existent **sibel* accounts for *savlan* rather than **sablan*, **šabaš* accounts for *šabšan* rather than **šavšan*, etc. In other cases, the alternative option is marginally acceptable to the extent that a related verb can be shown to exist as an infrequent item. Thus, only *kablan* 'contractor' is attested since *kibel* 'receive' is so much more frequent than literary *kaval* 'complain', and only *'axlan* 'glutton' is attested because *'axal* 'eat' is so more frequent than literary *'ikel* 'consume'. Speakers do understand what potential forms like *kavlan* 'chronic complainer' (from literary *kaval* 'complain'), or *'aklan* 'corrosive' (from literary *'ikel* 'consume') would mean had they been attested, and this further emphasizes how productive the process is.

One more specific illustration of the effect of frequency of use is *kabran* 'gravedigger'. Originally from *kiber* 'bury',[11] it is universally replaced by *kavran* in colloquial Modern Hebrew. Today, *kiber* is quite obsolete, and the relationship of *kavran* to frequent *kavar* 'bury' (or *kéver* 'grave') is the most transparent.

There are also 'minimal-pair'-type *CaCCan* cases where the stop-fricative variation, supposedly from the same root, points to derivation from verbs as well as from nouns:

---

form for all *pa'al* verbs in Aramaic. Aramaic +*ān* must have had considerable impact on the development of comparable forms in Hebrew.

[11] Probably 'bury regularly', since one of the original meanings of *pi'el* was 'repeated action'.

(22) *tapsan* 'climber, alpinist' (< *tipes* 'climb') vs. *tafsan* 'mold maker' (< *tófes* 'mold')

xablan 'saboteur' (< *xibel* 'sabotage (V)') vs. *xavlan* 'rope maker/rigger' (< *xével* 'rope').

While *tapsan* could have only been derived from *tipes*, *tafsan* can only be related to the noun *tófes*, and while *xablan* is related to *xibel*, *xavlan* could have only been derived from the noun *xével*.

It should also be noted that the realization of the last radical in *CaCCan* also suggests derivation from existing, mostly verbal, bases. Since it follows the second radical with no intervening vowel, it should be a stop in the unmarked case. In fact, however, it usually turns out to be a fricative, since it is word-final in the base, and word-final alternating consonants are fricatives:[12]

(23) **CaCCan forms and related bases, where the third root radical is fricative in both**

Form	Gloss	Base	Gloss
'asfan	collector	*'asaf*	collect
xanfan	flatterer	*xanaf*	flatter
xasfan(it)	stripper	*xasaf*	expose
zayfan	forger	*zayef*	forge
sagfan	ascetic	*sagef*	torture, castigate
yaxfan	barefooted; hooligan	*yaxef*	barefoot
kalfan	gambler at cards	*klaf*	card
šax(a)fan	tuberculous	*šaxéfet*	tuberculosis
katvan(it)	typist	*katav*	write
yašvan	squatter; buttock	*yašav*	sit
nadvan	donor, benefactor	*nadev*	contribute
nakvan(it)	puncher of computer cards	*nakev*	punch
našxan	biter	*našax*	bite

---

[12] The only case I know of in which the stop resurfaces in stem-final position in normative Hebrew is *kalban* 'dog trainer, handler' < *kélev* 'dog', possibly because of the underlying segolate base, /*kalb*/, which is realized in the ·common common female conterpart, *kalba* 'bitch'. There are also two cases in which speakers' conception of what the normative form 'should be' causes a literary form to be replaced by a colloquial counterpart with a stop:

xalvan 'milkman' > *xalban* (in spite of *xalav* 'milk (N, V)')

calvan(im) 'crusader(s)' > *calban(im)* (in spite of *clav* 'cross (N)', and *calav* 'cross (V)')

Literary *xalvan* 'milkman' is invariably replaced by *xalban* in the colloquial, in spite of clearly-related *xalav* 'milk (N)' and *xalav* 'milk (V)', and the same applies to literary *calvan(im)* 'crusader(s)', which is universally pushed aside by *calban(im)*, in spite of the obvious relationship to *clav* 'cross (N)' and *calav* 'cross (V)'. I have also heard *sarban giyus* 'conscientious objector' (cf. *sarev* 'refuse') replacing *sarvan giyus* and *tokpan(i)* 'aggressive' for *tokfani*. But these are quite marginal; the norm is to preserve the fricative of the source.

(cont.)

Form	Gloss	Base	Gloss
carxan	consumer	carax	consume
šadxan	matchmaker	šadex	match
xasxan	thrifty	xasax	save
xayxan	smiler	xayex	smile

Since for the majority of verb-related cases, the relationship to a *paʿal* or *piʿel* stem is quite transparent, one might be tempted to suggest that speakers derive such forms from their related verbal stems in a simple linear fashion, followed by stem-vowel elision (e.g. /daber+an/ > dabran, /zayef+an/ > zayfan, /ʾaxal+an/ > ʾaxlan, /ʾasaf+an/ > ʾasfan) rather than by applying consonants extracted from the base onto the *CaCCan miškal*.

Though quite possible, this type of linear derivation is not very probable, particularly not in MH. In general, agentive nouns formed from verbs are derived from (or are identical to) the *benoni*, the present tense or the present participle, as in

(24) **benoni forms as agent nouns**

ʾofe 'bake (V); baker'	*yored* 'go down; emigrant from Israel'
šomer 'guard (V); guard (N)'	*šoxet* 'slaughter (V); ritual slaughterer'
menahel 'direct (V); director'	*meʾamen* 'train (V); trainer'
mefakéax 'inspect; inspector'	*metofef* 'drum (V); drummer'
malxin 'compose music; composer'	*marce* 'lecture (V); lecturer'
mazkir 'remind; secretary'	*maškif* 'observe; observer'

A direct relationship also exists between the *benoni* and verb-related +*an* forms. Colloquial +*an* agentives related to *hitpaʿel* and to *hifʿil* are clearly derived from the *benoni*[13] in a linear fashion (see also Bat-El 1989):

(25) **+an forms derived from the benoni of hitpaʿel**

Verb	Gloss	Root	Liter. N	Coll. N	Gloss
histagel	adapt	s.g.l	staglan	mistaglan	opportunist
histakel	observe	s.k.l	staklan	mistaklan	observer
hištamet	shirk	š.m.t	štamtan	mištamtan	shirker

(26) **+an forms derived from the benoni of hifʿil**

Verb	Gloss	benoni	Coll. form w/ +*an*	Gloss
hicxik	make laugh	macxik	macxikan	funny one
hirgiz	make angry	margiz	margizan	annoying person
hecic	peep	mecic	mecican	peeping Tom

---

[13] #*mV*+ marks the *benoni* of five of the seven verb patterns.

And finally, there is the *paʿal*-related sub-*miškal*, *CoCCan*, which in Mishnaic-Palestinian Hebrew served as a variant of Mishnaic-Babylonian *CaCCan*. If it is regarded as linear derivation, it will be derived from the *benoni* of *paʿal*, *CoCeC* (with concomitant deletion of *e*):[14]

(27) **Mishnaic-Palestinian *CoCCan* forms derived from the *benoni* of *paʿal***

Palestinian	Gloss	Benoni	Babylonian
kotvan	scribe, calligrapher	*kotev*	*katvan*
doršan	preacher, expositor	*doreš*	*daršan*
dorsan	hide tanner	*dores*	*darsan*
roṣʿan	cobbler	*roṣéaʿ*	*raṣʿan*
roṣhan	murderer	*roṣéaḥ*	*raṣhan*
ṭorḥan	bothersome	*ṭoréaḥ*	*ṭarḥan*
noqdan	pedant	*noqed*	*naqdan*

The above illustrations demonstrate that linear derivation of +*an* forms from a related stem should be based on the *benoni*. In the *paʿal*-related and *piʿel* related cases before us, however, it would be difficult to argue for linear derivation of *CaCCan* realizations from their respective *paʿal* or *piʿel benoni* bases. In *paʿal*-related forms, linear derivation would necessitate deriving from the past stem. In *piʿel*-related ones, the present/imperfect stem would be the correct one, but without the prefix *me*+, which is required for distinguishing the present/present participle *benoni* from the future/imperfect stem.[15] In other words, since *CaCCan* forms cannot be shown to be derived by linear affixation of +*an* to a *benoni* stem, as required for agents/agent attributes, they can only be generated discontinuously, in the *CaCCan miškal*.

---

[14] Linear derivation of *CoCC*+*an* realizations is not a certainty, particularly since in some cases there is no comparable *benoni paʿal* form from which it can be derived:

Palestinian	Gloss	Possible Base	Babylonian
boyšan	shy	*mevayyeš*	*bayšan*
godfan	curser, blasphemer	*megaddef*	*gadfan*
ʿoqman	tricky, insincere	*ʿaqom*	*ʿaqman*
košfan	magician	*mexaššef*	*kašfan*

[15] In MishH (see Gross 1994), one does find *meCaCCan*, as an alternant of *CaCCan* or of comparable *paʿal* forms, as in *dabran* 'talkative' ~ *medabran*, *qablan* 'contractor' ~ *meqablan*, *qaṣran* 'laconic' ~ *meqaṣran*, *hovlan* 'destructive' ~ *ḥablan* ~ *meḥablan*, *košfan* 'magician' ~ *kašfan* ~ *mexašfan*, but not in MH.

2.4.1.3   *Variations between* CaCCan *and* N+an

When trying to determine the relative productivity of word-forma-tion strategies involving the suffix +*an*, one also finds numerous cases whose historical origin is probably linear, but may no longer be lin-ear today. Speakers cannot tell from the surface form in these cases whether linear derivation or discontinuous realization of *CaCCan* is involved, since synchronically, both interpretations are possible. This is the case in forms like *ga'avtan* 'boastful' (*ga'ava* 'pride'), *parvan* 'fur-rier' (*parva* 'fur'), *ya'aran* 'forester' (*yá'ar* 'forest'), etc. Included are also forms in which a base vowel is elided, as in *safkan* 'skeptic' (*safek* 'doubt'), *psantran* 'pianist' (*psanter* 'piano'); or *e* is maintained or added for phonetic reasons, as in *pardesan* 'citrus grower' (*pardes* 'citrus grove'), *marpekan* 'aggressive, pusher' (*marpek* 'elbow'); or *a* is inserted in the environment of a historical guttural, as in *mahapxan* 'revolu-tionary' (/*mahpexa*/ 'revolution'). Also relevant are derivations from segolate bases, as in *raftan* 'dairy farmer' (/*raft*/ > *réfet* 'cowshed'), *yarkan* 'greengrocer' (/*yark*/ > *yérek* 'greens'). Occasionally, colloquial reduction, by now recognized as normative by the Academy, oblit-erates the distinction between strategies, as in literary *kalkalan* 'econ-omist' (*kalkala* 'economy') becoming *kalkelan* and *mada'an* 'scientist' (*mada'* 'science') turning into *mad'an*. There are ·also cases in which both strategies can be shown to have applied, and to be equally acceptable even at the literary register. For instance, both *taxbulan* and *taxbelan* 'resourceful person' are attested (*taxbula* 'ruse, strategem'), as are *taxsisan* and *taxsesan* 'strategist' (*taxsis* 'strategy'). In most instances of multiple realization, however, the colloquial *CaCCan* variant is clearly the preferred one. Thus, *yazman* 'initiator' is commoner than *yozman* (*yozma* 'initiative', or *yozem* 'initiate, *benoni* form'), *zalelan* 'glut-ton' is more frequent than *zolelan* (*zolel* 'devour food, *benoni* form'). Also, the presumably linear *CoCCan* cases derived from the *pa'al benoni* *CoCeC* (see *kotvan* 'scribe' etc. above) are often pushed aside today in favor of discontinuous *CaCCan* counterparts. Although *CoCCan* is maintained in daily or semi-formal use for instrumentals (*potxan* 'opener', *roxsan* 'zipper' and *'ogdan* 'file folder'), as well as in derived adjectives (*xovevani* 'amateurish', *xolmani* 'dreamy', *dorsani* 'destructive', *torfani* 'devouring', *tordani* 'bothersome'), the *CaCCan* variants are clearly preferred when both variants co-exist in MH. MH *CaCCan* variants are favored regardless of whether the *CoCCan* form origi-nated in MishH, as above, or in Medieval Hebrew:

(28) **benoni-derived CoCCan originating in Medieval Hebrew and CaCCan variant**

CoCC + an	Gloss	Benoni	CaCC + an
solḥan	forgiving, lenient	*soléaḥ*	*salxan*
zoᶜaman	always angry	*zoᶜem*	*zaᶜaman*

or in MH:

(29) **benoni-derived CoCCan originating in Modern Hebrew and CaCCan variant**

CoCC + an	Gloss	Benoni	CaCC + an
rotnan	grumbling, discontented	*roten*	*ratnan*
rotxan	hot-tempered	*rotéax*	*ratxan*
šoxexan	forgetful, oblivious	*šoxéax*	*šaxexan*
xomdan	covetous, lustful	*xomed*	*xamdan*

Productivity tests on children as well as on adults also support the claim that the two derivation strategies maintain their productivity, with a certain preference for discontinuous *CaCCan*, at an average ratio of 1.37:1 in open-ended coinage tests and 3:2 in judgment tasks (see Clark & Berman 1984, Berman 1987). As noted, linear derivation is commonly manifest in the adding of +*an* to a *benoni* form with a +*mV* prefix (e.g. *mistaklan* 'one who peeps' above), since such a prefix makes it easier to identify an agent. Children's focusing on +*an* is accounted for by noting that suffixes are acquired earlier than prefixes, owing to the centrality of the ends of words. *CaCCan* (supposedly substandard) was also preferred in a small judgment test, showing that literary *katalogan* 'cataloguer' tends to be reinterpreted as *katlegan*, *pulmusan* 'polemist, disputant' as *palmesan*, *sixletan* 'rationalist' as *sxaltan* or *saxletan*. It appears, then, that discontinuous *CaCCan* is alive and well, and is even further reinforced by linear derivation which on the surface looks like *CaCCan*. Furthermore, whenever both strategies are attested, or when speakers are given a productivity-measuring task, the *CaCCan* variant tends to be preferred.

Blau (1990) contains an interesting summary of the recent history of *CaCCan*. Since the first *a* is a *patax* and the second *kamac*, there were different views on how *CaCCan* forms should be realized. Some claimed that the schwa is quiescent, and thus the third root radical should always be a stop (e.g. *carkan* for 'consumer'). Some also argued that if the form is *piᶜel*-related, the second root radical should be a geminated stop (e.g. /*kabbᵉlan*/ 'contractor' > *kablan*). The Hebrew Language Academy pointed out that a *schwa meraxef* (a 'hovering' *schwa*, which counts as a *schwa mobile* but is not realized as such phonetically) is very common before the third radical. This led to the claim that there exists only one *miškal*, *CaCCan*, with both the second and third radical invariantly always fricative. Forms like *kablan* 'contractor' (cf. *kibel* 'receive'), which had already been rooted in speech based on related basic stems, were approved as exceptions. Blau notes that this is not a new phenomenon. The presence of *qorvan* 'sacrifice' in Ez 40:43 alongside standard *qorban* suggests similar dualism in earlier stages of the language, probably also under the influence of related stems. Blau's view is that exceptions like *kablan* do not mean a minor *CaC$_i$C$_i$^{e}Can* sub-pattern, nor another one in which the schwa is quiescent (for *xalban* etc.). Rather, there is one *CaCCan miškal* in which two separate sets of phonemes operate, stops and fricatives, instead of allophonic variants, as a result of the collapsing of Spirantization as a phonetically-motivated process. In other words, by the time these +*an* forms were created, Spirantization was no longer operational, and with two independent phonemes /b/ and /v/, both *kablan* 'contractor' and *kavlan* 'complainer' were straightforward realizations of *CaCCan*. The same applies to *'axlan* 'glutton' and *'aklan* 'corrosive', with /k/ and /x/ constituting two independent phonemes, and to *tapsan* 'alpinist' and *tafsan* 'mold maker', with independent /p/ and /f/. The same position is adopted here.

2.4.2   *Mechanical derivation of abstract nouns with the suffix +ut*

From formation of nouns with the suffix +*ut*, discussed in Bolozky & Schwarzwald (1992), one can also learn of the interplay between discontinuous and linear derivation. In general, formation of abstract nouns with the +*ut* suffix[16] has been viewed as linear derivation. The suffix +*ut* tends to attach itself to the inflected stem according to Sznejder (1929), or to allomorphs according to Rosén (1957).[17] Bolozky & Schwarzwald (1992) demonstrate that at least by lexical counts, there are strong methodological reasons to suggest that discontinuously-derived nouns with +*ut* outnumber linearly-derived ones by a

---

[16] In general, it appears that most forms with +*ut* were formed between the medieval and modern periods, and include medieval haphazard creations as well as recent innovations and Academy-introduced ones. On the whole, they tend to belong to the non-colloquial register, which children learn late.

[17] The inflected stem is typically the one resulting from vowel reduction; other allomorphs are often the segolate base stems.

ratio of almost 2:1. In their discussion, summarized below, they classify realizations of nouns with +*ut* into cases in which +*ut* suffixation is clearly linear; in-between cases which may be attributed to either strategy; and cases which are best described as discontinuous formations.

2.4.2.1 *Linearly-derived forms with* +ut

Unless specified otherwise, all +*ut* cases below will constitute abstract nominal counterparts of their related glossed stems. Linear +*ut* derivations may involve monosyllabic stems, as in:

(30) **Monosyllabic stem with +*ut***

ma 'what' > *mahut* 'essence'	*yeš* 'there is' > *yešut* 'presence'
kal 'easy, light' > *kalut*	*xad* 'sharp' > *xadut*
dak 'thin' > *dakut*	*lax* 'humid' > *laxut*
'on 'potency' > *'onut*	*bur* 'ignorant' > *burut*

or polysyllabic stems for which there exist no sufficient realizations of the same *miškal* (a non-linear derivation pattern) to justify further grouping, as in:

(31) **N +*ut* forms which clearly appear to be linearly derived**

'ezrax 'citizen' > *'ezraxut*	*'evil* 'fool' > *'evilut*
'umlal 'miserable' > *'umlalut*	*'enoš* 'man' > *'enošut*
biryon 'violent person' > *biryonut*	*gizbar* 'treasurer' > *gizbarut*
'efšar 'possible (Adv.)' > *'efšarut*	*'adrixal* 'architect' > *'adrixalut*

but the majority of linear +*ut* derivations involve adding +*ut* to words ending with a common suffix, most notably the adjectival +*i*. There exist numerous such cases; a few examples:

(32) **Linear derivation of +*i* +*ut* forms**

yalduti 'childish' > *yaldutiyut*	*'arci* 'earthly' > *'arciyut*
xaluci 'pioneering' > *xaluciyut*	*gašmi* 'physical' > *gašmiyut*
ma'asi 'pragmatic' > *ma'asiyut*	*xagigi* 'festive' > *xagigiyut*
dati 'religious' > *datiyut*	*'iti* 'slow' > *'itiyut*

2.4.2.2 *Forms with* +ut *that may be interpreted as either linear or discontinuous*

In other cases, which involve an unchanging *miškal* followed by +*ut*, it is difficult to tell whether linear or discontinuous derivation is involved. Either interpretation is possible, as in *CaCCanut* and *CaCaCut* realizations, for instance:

(33) **Illustrating** *CaCCanut* **and** *CaCaCut*

CaCCanut	*batlan* 'loafer' ~ *batlanut*	*kamcan* 'miser' ~ *kamcanut*
	ʿaclan 'lazy' ~ *ʿaclanut* ~ *ʿaclut*	*nadvan* 'donor' ~ *nadvanut*
	patpetan 'talkative' ~ *patpetanut*	*ravrevan* 'braggart' ~ *ravrevanut*
	gandran 'dude' ~ *gandranut*	*štaltan* 'dominant' ~ *štaltanut*
CaCaCut	*nagar* 'carpenter' ~ *nagarut*	*xayat* 'taylor' ~ *xayatut*
	tayar 'tourist' ~ *tayarut*	*xazan* 'cantor' ~ *xazanut*
	zaban 'sales person' ~ *zabanut*	*tabax* 'cook' ~ *tabaxut*
	balaš 'detective' ~ *balašut*	*sapar* 'barber' ~ *saparut*

The same holds for some nouns derived from the present participles of *nifʿal, piʿel, puʿal, hifʿil* and *hufʿal* (i.e. *niCCaCut, meCaCCut, meCuCaCut, maCCiCut* and *muCCaCut*, respectively), as in:

(34) **Illustrating Present Participle forms followed by** + *ut*

niCCaCut	*nifkad* 'absent' ~ *nifkadut*	*nivʿar* 'ignorant' ~ *nivʿarut*
	nirgan 'complaining' ~ *nirganut*	*nexmad* 'cute' ~ *nexmadut*
meCaCCut	*meyaled* 'obstetrician' ~ *meyaldut*	*mefaked* 'commander' ~ *mefakdut*
meCuCaCut	*meyuman* 'proficient' ~ *meyumanut*	*meyuxad* 'special' ~ *meyuxadut*
	mexuyav 'obliged' ~ *mexuyavut*	*meyutar* 'redundant' ~ *meyutarut*
maCCiCut	*mazkir* 'secretary' ~ *mazkirut*	*manhig* 'leader' ~ *manhigut*
	madrix 'guide' ~ *madrixut*	*malšin* 'informer' ~ *malšinut*
muCCaCut	*mugbal* 'restricted' ~ *mugbalut*	*mufraʿ* 'disturbed' ~ *mufraʿut*
	mufšat 'abtract' ~ *mufšatut*	*murkav* 'complex' ~ *murkavut*

and one could make the same argument where vowel deletion is involved, as in

(35) **Illustrating** + *ut* **forms which appear to have involved vowel deletion**

hitCaCeC ~ *hitCaCCut*

hitnaged 'object' ~ *hitnagdut*	*hitkanes* 'convene' ~ *hitkansut*
hitkadem 'advance' ~ *hitkadmut*	*hitnageš* 'collide' ~ *hitnagšut*

(le)hiCaCeC ~ *hiCaCCut*

(le)hikanes 'enter' ~ *hikansut*	*(le)hitakel* 'bump (into)' ~ *hitaklut*
(le)hinatek 'be disconnected' ~ *hinatkut*	*(le)hikalet* 'be absorbed' ~ *hikaltut*

CoCeC ~ *CoCCut*

soxen 'agent' ~ *soxnut*	*šoter* 'policeman' ~ *šotrut*
xonex 'trainer' ~ *xonxut*	*xoveš* 'dress wound' ~ *xovšut*

CaCeC ~ *CaCCut*

šaxen 'neighbor' ~ *šxenut*	*šalem* 'whole' ~ *šlemut*
davek 'attached, devoted' ~ *dvekut*	*bašel* 'ripe' ~ *bšelut*

CaCiC ~ CCiCut
pakid 'clerk' ~ *pkidut*	*šalíax* 'messenger' ~ *šlixut*
gamiš 'flexible' ~ *gmišut*	*dalil* 'thin' ~ *dlilut*

CiCeC ~ CiCCut
tipeš 'foolish' ~ *tipšut*	*xereš* 'deaf' ~ *xeršut*
giben 'hunchback' ~ *gibnut*	*'ilem* 'dumb, mute' ~ *'ilmut*

In these deletion-related cases, however, the scales are more in favor of discontinuous derivation, since these once-phonetically-natural deletion rules can hardly be motivated as actual phonetic processes today. It is more likely that each member in pairs like *hitnaged-hitnagdut*, *soxen-soxnut*, *tipeš-tipšut*, *šaxen-šxenut*, *pakid-pkidut* etc., is related to its counterpart in a non-linear relationship, not through appending-plus-deletion.

2.4.2.3 *Forms with* +ut *that should be derived discontinuously*

There are other reasons for characterizing 'deletion'-type derivations like the above as *miškalim* rather than as linear derivations with subsequent reduction. A sequence like *CCiCut* appears to be, and to have been, derived by affixation of +*ut* and reduction of the *a* in nouns and adjectives of the *CaCiC* type. But Bolozky & Schwarzwald (1992) show that in order to derive all realizations of *CCiCut* linearly, one would require a variety of *ad hoc* processes, since a variety of bases is involved:

(36) Bases required if linear derivation of *CCiCut* is assumed

CaCiC	*pakid* 'clerk' > *pkidut*	*šalíax* 'messenger' > *šlixut*
	gamiš 'flexible' > *gmišut*	*dalil* 'thin' > *dlilut*
CaCuC	*patúax* 'open' > *ptixut*	*racuf* 'successive' > *recifut*
	xaruc 'diligent' > *xaricut*	*kaful* 'double' > *kfilut*
CaCoC~CaCuC	*'arox* (~*'aruk*+) 'long' > *'arixut*	*'agol* (~*'agul*+) 'round' > *'agilut*
	matok (~*metuk*+) 'sweet > *metikut*	*ratov* (~*ratuv*+) 'wet' > *retivut*
CoCeC	*boded* 'lonely' > *bdidut*	
naCoC	*nafoc* 'widespread' > *neficut* (but also *nafic* 'explosive' > *neficut*)	
muCCaC	*mušxat* 'corrupt' > *šxitut*	
No clearly-identifiable base	*šrirut* 'arbitrariness' (*šarir* 'valid' is unrelated)	
	kritut 'divorce' (*karat* 'chop off' is only remotely related)	

The stems that underlie *CCiCut* are quite varied (the *pakid*, *patúax*, and *'arox* types, at least, as well as some other minor ones), and cannot all be derived by phonetically motivated processes. Nevertheless, in spite of the wide variation in stems underlying *CCiCut*, one would still want to capture the native speaker's intuition that all of these sub-groups are related by attributing them to one canonical pattern. The obvious solution is to derive them all non-linearly in a discontinuous *CCiCut* pattern, rather than by appending $+ut$ linearly to a variety of stems and arriving at the correct output by applying an array of *ad hoc* rules.

Arguments of this type also suggest that an independent non-linear $CaCC_iC_iut$ pattern will be required for the following group, in which reduplication is involved, normally suggesting diminution:

(37) $CaCC_iC_iut$ **forms involving reduplication**

’*adom* 'red' ~ ’*admumi* 'reddish' > ’*admimut* (~ ’*admumiyut*)
’*avir* 'air' ~ ’*avriri* 'airy' > ’*avrirut* (~ ’*avririyut*)
lavan 'white' ~ *lavnuni* 'whitish' > *lavninut* (~ *lavnuniyut*)
ʿ*agum* 'sad' ~ ʿ*agmumi* 'sort of sad' > ʿ*agmimut* (~ ʿ*agmumiyut*)
ʿ*akom* 'crooked' ~ ʿ*akmumi* 'somewhat crooked' > ʿ*akmimut* (~ ʿ*akmumiyut*)
ʿ*arum* 'cunning' ~ ʿ*armumi* 'crafty, wily' > ʿ*armimut* (~ ʿ*armumiyut*)
ʿ*arom* 'naked' > ʿ*armimut*

Had all of these forms been derived linearly from their assumed bases, a number of unmotivated processes would be required. Instead, it would be much simpler to assume a non-linear reduplicative pattern $CaCC_iC_iut$, possibly a variant of the *CCiCut miškal.*

It can be shown that as in the case of *CCiCut*, linear derivation of all *CaCCut* would also require a variety of underlying bases (including alternants of segolate nouns), as in:

(38) **Bases required if linear derivation of *CaCCut* is assumed**

CéCeC/ CaCC	*yéled* (~ *yald* +) 'child' > *yaldut*	*mélex* (~ *malk* +) 'king' > *malxut*
	ʿ*éved* (~ ʿ*avd* +) 'slave' > ʿ*avdut*	ʿ*écev* (~ ʿ*acv* +) 'sorrow' > ʿ*acvut*
CaCeC	*kašer* 'valid, Kosher' > *kašrut*	ʿ*acel* 'lazy' > ʿ*aclut*
	ʿ*arev* 'guarantor' > ʿ*arvut*	*xanef* 'hypocrite' > *xan(e)fut*
CaCoC	*gadol* 'big' > *gadlut* 'greatness'	*yatom* 'orphan' > *yatmut*
	ʿ*amok* 'deep' > ʿ*amkut*	’*adon* 'master' > ’*adnut* 'authority (lit.)'
	gavóah (</gavoh/) 'tall' > *gavhut*	*raxok* 'far' > *raxakut*
CaCaC/ CoCeC	*bagar/ boger* 'become adult' > *bagrut*	
	samax/ somex(/ musmax) 'rely' > *samxut* 'authority'	
	yanak/ yonek 'suck' > *yankut* 'babyhood'	
	kadar/ koder 'be dark' > *kadrut*	*šote* 'fool' > *šatyut*
	lavan 'white' > *lavnut*	*naval* 'villain' > *navlut*
	katan 'small' > *katnut*	*kacar* 'short' > *kacrut*
CaCuC	*baxur* 'young man' > *baxarut*	*pašut* 'simple' > *paštut*

Such *CaCCut* cases will have to be generated from at least the *yéled, kašer, gadol, bagar/ boger* and *baxur* base-types, which clearly argues against phonetically motivated derivation of $+ut$ and for simple non-linear pattern realization in *CaCCut.*

Similar arguments can be made regarding *CiCCut*, i.e. that its realizations will have to be derived from a variety of base-types if it is claimed that they are to be derived linearly, as well as with regard to some other, smaller +ut subtypes.

Yet another argument for the need for non-linear derivational patterns related to +ut alongside the linear strategy is the occasional simultaneous coexistence of derivations from the same base, one of which is linear and the other argued here to be non-linear,[18] as in:

(39) **Linear and discontinuous alternants of the same base, both containing +ut**

Form	Gloss	Linear	Non-linear	Gloss
ʾadon	master	ʾadonut	ʾadnut	authority
ʿašir	rich	ʿaširut	ʿašrut	riches
ʿarev	guarantor	ʿarevut	ʿarvut	guarantee
ʾem/ʾima	mother	ʾimahut	ʾamhut	motherhood
ʾav/ʾába	father	ʾavahut/ʾavut	ʾavhut	fatherhood
yatom	orphan	yetomut	yatmut	being an orphan
nocri	Christian	nocriyut	nacrut	Christianity

The simultaneous existence of such variants is easier to explain with two separate mechanical derivation devices rather than by inapplication or application of a reduction process, which normally does not tend to be optional.

Finally, Bolozky & Schwarzwald (1992) show that by dictionary counts (Even-Shoshan 1970), discontinuously-derived forms with +ut outnumber those derived linearly:

(40) **The distribution of +ut form by type of derivation, based on dictionary counts**

	Bibl	%	MshH	%	Med	%	Mod	%	Total	% Total
Clearly linear	16	23.2	65	37.4	199	34.2	907	39.4	1187	38.0
Miškalim[19]	31	45.0	84	48.2	366	62.9	1349	58.6	1830	58.5
Undetermined	22	31.8	25	14.4	17	2.9	46	2.0	110	3.5
Total	69	100.0	174	100.0	582	100.0	2302	100.0	3127	100.0

These figures are not fully accurate, in that Even-Shoshan (1970) lists only some of those borrowed adjectives ending with +i to which +ut can be appended. Since this linear word-formation pattern is very productive, the suggested preference for discontinuous derivation with +ut may be somewhat overstated. But there is no indication whatsoever that it might be less productive than linear derivation of +ut.

---

[18] The non-linear alternant is more literary, except for *nacrut* 'Christianity', which is common usage. *yatmut* 'being an orphane' is marginally literary.

[19] Some of them, as argued above, may also be regarded as linearly derived.

2.4.3   The segolates: linear or discontinuous derivation?

In Bolozky (1995a) it is argued that in Israeli Hebrew, the segolates and segolate derivatives should be described not on the basis of their historical underlying stems, but rather by the surface regularities that characterize them. For methodological reasons, these regularities must be stated in terms of canonical discontinuous noun formation patterns (*miškalim*). It was shown that for the majority of segolates and segolate derivatives, linear derivation cannot be motivated. The only plausible analysis is to assume pairing relationships between related discontinuous patterns without actually deriving one from the other in a linear fashion. The arguments for the position taken in Bolozky (1995a) are reproduced below.

2.4.3.1   On deriving segolates from their historical bases

The segolates, perhaps the largest noun pattern that does not involve an affix, are so termed because their final syllable is normally characterized by a *segol* (ε), or because in the largest segolate sub-group, the isolation form contains a *segol* in each of its two final syllables. Since Israeli Hebrew merges historical ε, e and ^{e} into a single e phoneme, the Israeli Hebrew segolates are best characterized by the penultimate stress that is the hallmark of the segolates, followed by e in the final syllable (or occasionally by a if a 'guttural' was involved historically, or i where y had been).

Historically, segolate formation was clearly linear. Diachronically (cf., for instance, Bauer & Leander 1922, Malone 1971), the final *segol* is not an underlying segment but an epenthetic vowel whose function is to split syllable-final consonant clusters, which Semitic languages tend to avoid. The assumption, based on evidence from alternating forms, is that historically the segolate bases were of the form /... CVCC/, with a stem vowel that could be a, i, o, u, and occasionally ε.[20] In isolation, i.e. when no suffix had been added, the impermissible word-final cluster in /... CVCC/ was split by ε. Later, a preceding non-round (or front) vowel was assimilated to that *segol*:

(41)   **The different types of segolate nouns**
(a)   /málk/ 'king' > málɛk > mélɛk > mélɛx > Israeli Hebrew mélex
mélex 'king' ~ malka 'queen' ~ malxut 'kingdom'

---

[20] Mostly in the environment of the velars g, k/x, and the gutturals.

yéled 'boy' ~ *yalda* 'girl' ~ *yaldut* 'childhood' ~ *yaldon* 'small child'
kélev 'dog' ~ *kalba* 'bitch' ~ *kalbon* 'small dog'
késef 'money' ~ *kaspi* 'monetary' ~ *kaspomat* 'ATM'
géver 'man' ~ *gavri* 'manly'
néfeš 'soul, spirit' ~ *nafši* 'spiritual, psychological'
réfet 'cowshed' ~ *raftan* 'person working at cowshed' (but *rifti* 'my
　　cowshed')

(b) (i)　/*bírk*/ 'knee' > *bírɛk* > *bérɛk* > *bérɛx* > Israeli Hebrew *bérex*
　　　　bérex 'knee' ~ *birkáim* '(two) knees'
　　　　kéves 'sheep' ~ *kivsa* 'ewe'
　　　　sémel (historically either *sémɛl* or *sémɛl*) 'symbol' ~ *simli*
　　　　　'symbolic'

　　(ii)　/*sípr*/ 'book' > *sípɛr* > *sépɛr* > *séfɛr* > Israeli Hebrew *séfer*
　　　　séfer (historically with *cere*) 'book' ~ *sifrut* 'literature' ~ *sifriya*
　　　　　'library'
　　　　šévet (historically with *cere*) 'tribe' ~ *šivti* 'tribal'
　　　　šéxel (historically with *cere*) 'brain, wisdom' ~ *šixli* 'of the brain'

(c) (i)　/*gódl*/ 'size' > *gódɛl* > Israeli Hebrew *gódel*
　　　　gódel 'size' ~ *godlo* 'his size'
　　　　xódeš 'month' ~ *xodší* 'monthly' ~ *xodšáim* 'two months'
　　　　móten 'hip' ~ *motnáim* '(two) hips'
　　　　córex 'need' ~ *corxey* 'the needs of'
　　　　šóreš 'root' ~ *šorši* 'deep-rooted'
　　　　kódeš 'holiness' ~ *kodšo* 'his holiness'

　　(ii)　*xómec* 'vinigar' ~ *xumco* 'his vinegar'
　　　　kómec 'a handful' ~ *kumco* 'his small quantity'
　　　　ʿókec 'sting' ~ *ʿukco* 'his sting'

(d)　/*négd*/ 'opposite, against' > *néged* > Israeli Hebrew *néged*
　　néged 'opposite, against' ~ *negdo* 'opposite him'
　　néxed 'grandson' ~ *nexda* 'granddaughter'
　　ʿéser 'ten' ~ *ʿesrim* 'twenty'
　　xémed 'grace, charm' ~ *xemda* 'desirable thing'

When the middle consonant is (or historically was) a glide, an underlying /*y*/ triggers the insertion of a homorganic *i*. No vowel copy is
involved. At the end of a syllable, /*ay*/ is reduced to *ey* and /*aw*/ to *o*:

(42) **Segolates with an underlying glide**
(a) /*báyt*/ 'house' > *báyit* ~ *beyti* 'domestic'
　　záyit 'olive' ~ *zeyti* 'olive-colored'
(b) /*máwt*/ 'death' > *máwet* > *máwɛt* > Israeli Hebrew *mávet* > *moto* 'his death'
　　gáven 'tint, hue' ~ *xad-goni* 'monochrome'

In addition to accounting for alternating forms being realized with
a /...*CVCC*/ stem, another advantage of this type of diachronic
derivation is in explaining the penultimate stress of unsuffixed segolates. In the original base, stress fell on the final syllable, which fol-

lows the Hebrew norm. The *segol* was inserted only later, when the location of stress had been established and would not be moved again to accommodate the new vowel. *Segol* insertion can also account for the penultimate stress in feminine singular present tense forms, as in:

(43) **Feminine singular present tense forms as segolates**

F.S. Present	Gloss	Assumed Base
kotévet	write	/*kotev* + *t*/
medabéret	speak	/*medaber* + *t*/
mitlabéšet	get dressed	/*mitlabeš* + *t*/

as well as in feminine nouns ending with the feminine suffix +*et*, regardless of whether they are deverbal or not:

(44) **Feminine Nouns Ending with +*et***

Noun	Gloss	Assumed Base	Alternant	Gloss
šotéret	policewoman	/*šoter* + *t*/		
merakézet	coordinator, (f.)	/*merakez* + *t*/		
mitnadévet	volunteer (f.)	/*mitnadev* + *t*/		
kotéret	headline	/*kotar* + *t*/	*kotarti*	of headline
miktéret	pipe	/*miktar* + *t*/	*miktarto*	his pipe
miflécet	monster	/*miflac* + *t*/	*miflacti*	monstrous
tizmóret	orchestra	/*tizmor* + *t*/	*tizmorti*	orchestral
bikóret	criticism	/*bikor* + *t*/	*bikorti*	critical
któvet	address	/*ktov* + *t*/	*ktovti*	my address
ʿacéret	rally	/*ʿacer* + *t*/		
kalétet	audio cassette	/*kalet* + *t*/		
kalévet	rabies	/*kalev* + *t*/		
zaméret	singer (f.)	/*zamer* + *t*/		
masóret	tradition	/*masor* + *t*/	*masorti*	traditional
makólet	grocery store	/*makol* + *t*/		
maskóret	salary, wages	/*maskor* + *t*/	*maskurto*	his salary
yaldónet	little girl	/*yaldon* + *t*/		
ktantónet	very little, (f.)	/*ktanton* + *t*/		

In Israeli Hebrew, should the segolates be derived from their bases (/*malk*/, /*sifr*/, /*xodš*/, etc.) by means of phonological processes? This would reflect the relationships with alternant forms (*malka*, *sifrut*, *xodši*, etc.) and account for the deviant assignment of stress. Alternatively, should they rather be described in terms of surface segolate patterns, with related forms merely associated instead of actually being derived by actual processes?

Deriving *mélex* from /*malk*/, *séfer* from /*sipr*/, etc. is rather complex, and it is very unlikely that a native speaker literally converts from base to output in this fashion. The processes required to do this would be *ad hoc* and without independent phonetic or phonological justification. Deriving in the opposite direction, i.e. from *mélex* to *malk + a* etc., would also be hard to motivate, although at least in part, it would make more sense in Israeli Hebrew than following the historical route: as shown in Bolozky & Schwarzwald (1990), the unstressed *e* of segolates is weak, more so in the *+ et* suffix but in frequent stems as well, and tends to be elided in fast and/or casual speech. But the vowel changes from *e* to *a* or *i* would be quite arbitrary. What is most likely to capture speakers' intuitions is a pairing relationship between surface segolate patterns and alternating stem patterns involving suffixes, both expressed in discontinuous canonical form.

One may state, then, the following surface generalizations describing the segolates:

(45) **Surface generalizations describing the segolates**
(a) Nouns ending in ... *CeCeC#* or ... *CoCeC#* that are not derived directly from the verb are penultimately stressed
(b) They often have alternants in the form of ... *CaCC* ... (*malka, miflacti*), and sometimes *CiCC* ... (*sifrut*), ... *CoCC* ... (*xodši, tizmorti*), ... *CuCC* ... (*kumco, maskurto*), or *CeCC* ... (*nexda*; alternants with *e* are the rarest)
(c) If the word ends with *+ et*, a *benoni* (present participle) form will also be penultimately stressed (i.e. not only *miktéret*, but *kotévet* as well)

The gutturals add some complexity to surface segolate sequences, owing to their historical preference for low vowels over high ones, and to their inability to cluster with another consonant within the same syllable, which resulted in the epenthesis of a vocalic nucleus so as to separate between them:

(46) **Segolate nouns with gutturals**

	Form	Gloss	Historical	Plural	Alternant	Gloss
(a)	ʾérec	land, earth	ʾéreṣ	ʾaracot	ʾarci	earthly
	ʾéven	stone, rock	ʾévɛn	ʾavanim	ʾavney	stones of
	xéder	room	ḥédɛr	xadarim	xadron	small room
	xélek	part	ḥélɛq	xalakim	xelki	partial
	ʿéved	slave	ʿévɛd	ʿavadim	ʿavdut	slavery
	ʿégel	calf	ʿégɛl	ʿagalim	ʿegla	fem. calf
	ʿérex	value	ʿérɛx	ʿaraxim	ʿerki	of value
	ʾécel	at someone's	ʾéṣel		ʾecli	at my place
(b)	náʿar	boy	náʿar	neʿarim	naʿara	girl
	páxad	fear	páḥad	pxadim	paxdan	coward
	náxal	river	náḥal	nexalim	naxlîʾéli	wagtail
	táʿam	taste	ṭáʿam	teʿamim	taʿami	my taste

(cont.)

Form	Gloss	Historical	Plural	Alternant	Gloss
mikláxat	shower	*miqláḥat*	*miklaxot*	*miklaxon*	shower unit
potáxat	open, f.s	*potáḥat*			
(c) *cévaᶜ*	color	*ṣévaᶜ*	*cvaᶜim*	*civᶜoni*	colorful
péle	wonder	*pélɛ*	*plaʾim*	*pilʾi*	wondrous
šévax	praise	*šévaḥ*	*švaxim*	*šivxo*	his praise

Again, actual derivations from bases with underlying gutturals, most of which are not even realized, would constitute unnecessary complication. It would make more sense to extend the surface patterns identified as penultimately stressed segolates:

(47) Surface Segolate Patterns Involving (ex-)Gutturals

(a) ... *Ca(ᶜ/x)aC#* (*ráᶜas* 'noise', *náxal* 'river', *mišmáᶜat* 'discipline', *mikláxat* 'shower', *šomáᶜat* 'hear, f.s', *šoláxat* 'send, f.s'), or phonetically ... *Ca(x)aC#*, since the ᶜ is normally not realized (*ráaš* etc.)

(b) *CeCe#* (*péle* 'wonder', *déše* 'lawn')

(c) *CeCa(ᶜ/x)#* (*tévaᶜ* 'nature', *kérax* 'ice'), or phonetically *CeCa(x)#*, since the ᶜ is normally not realized (*téva* etc.)

(d) *Co(ᶜ/x/ʾ)aC#* (*nóᶜar* 'youth', *dóʾar* 'mail', *šóxad* 'bribe'), or phonetically *Co(x)aC*, since these ᶜ and ʾ are not normally realized (*nóar* etc.)

Exceptions like *nahar* 'river', *naxaš* 'snake', *šana* 'year', *koxav* 'star', *geʾe* 'proud', *kehe* 'dark' are a minority, and would be marked as such.

It may thus be argued, that regardless of whether one deals with 'regular' segolates or with segolate sub-groups with ex-gutturals, it is hard to motivate deriving them linearly in Israeli Hebrew. Discontinuous derivation, on the other hand, is direct and simple, and does not require the use of abstract processes that are difficult to motivate. Speakers are aware of the relationship between ... *CeCeC#* and ... *CaCC...*, for instance, just as well as they know of the connection between the verb pattern *paᶜal* (*CaCaC*) and its abstract nominalization *CCiCa*.

2.4.3.2 *On deriving segolate plurals*

The argument against linear derivation of the segolate plural is even more compelling. Regular plural formation typically involves linear affixation of +*im* or +*ot*, with possible subsequent reduction. The plural of segolate nouns is different. It resembles what is termed in Arabic 'broken plural', i.e. a kind of *miškal* of its own, *CCaCim/ot*:

(48) **Regular plural forms of segolate nouns**

Sing.	Gloss	Plural	Sing.	Gloss	Plural
mélex	king	*mlaxim*	*yéled*	boy	*yeladim*
kélev	dog	*klavim*	*géver*	man	*gvarim*
réfet	cowshed	*refatim/ot*	*néfeš*	soul	*nefašot*
kéves	sheep	*kvasim*	*sémel*	symbol	*smalim*
séfer	book	*sfarim*	*ševet*	tribe	*švatim*
gódel	size	*gdalim*	*córex*	need	*craxim*
dófen	side	*dfanot*	*róved*	layer	*revadim*

A basic stem-initial *o* is maintained in some cases, i.e the sub-pattern *CoCaCim* is also an option:

(49) **Segolate plurals where a basic stem-initial *o* is maintained**

Sing.	Gloss	Plural	Sing.	Gloss	Plural
xódeš	month	*xodašim*	*šóreš*	root	*šorašim*
kódeš	holiness	*kodašim*	*'óren*	pine	*'oranim*

The plural *a* appears to correspond to the second, unstressed *e*. However, when that unstressed *e* constitutes part of the feminine suffix + *et*, the plural *a* corresponds to the basic, stem-final *é*:

(50) **Plural forms where the *a* corresponds to the basic, stem-final *e***

Sing.	Gloss	Plural	Sing.	Gloss	Plural
miflécet	monster	*miflacot*	*mazkéret*	souvenir	*mazkarot*
miktéret	pipe	*miktarot*	*maxtéret*	underground	*maxtarot*
maxbéret	notebook	*maxbarot*	*ktantónet*	very small (f.)	*ktantanot*
kotéret	headline	*kotarot*	*xotémet*	seal	*xotamot*
zaméret	singer (f.)	*zamarot*	*'acéret*	rally	*'acarot*

This suggests that there is no reasonable phonological way to actually derive the plural forms from their singular counterparts. All we have here is a surface discontinuous relationship, according to which the plural of segolate nouns is of the form . . . *aCim/ot*.

The class of segolate nouns is huge, and . . . *aCim/ot* accounts for the plural of most of them. A few deviant sub-patterns occur. A basic *o* at the end of the stem is maintained as *o*, resulting in . . . *oCot*, which may or may not be regarded as linear derivation:

(51) **Segolate plurals where a basic stem-final *o* is maintained**

Sing.	Gloss	Plural	Sing.	Gloss	Plural
tizmóret	orchestra	*tizmorot*	*malkódet*	trap	*malkodot*
maskóret	salary	*maskorot*	*bikóret*	criticism	*bikorot*
masóret	tradition	*masorot*	*któvet*	address	*ktovot*

Plurals of segolates with /y/ either lose their glide completely or maintain its reduced form:

(52)

Sing.	Gloss	Plural	Sing.	Gloss	Plural
báyit	house	*batim*	*záyit*	olive	*zeytim*

The alternation is not applicable to verbs, or nouns derived from verbs:

(53)

F.S. Form	Gloss	Plural	F.S. Form	Gloss	Plural
kotévet	write	*kotvot*	*šotéret*	policewoman	*šotrot*
merakézet	coordinator, f	*merakzot*	*mitnadévet*	volunteer (f.)	*mitnadvot*

So the vast majority of segolate nouns have corresponding ... *aCim/ot* plural form, and the relationship is not arrived at by derivation, but by associating between pairs of discontinuous patterns. The generalization involved could be something like:

(54) **Surface generalizations regarding segolate plurals**
(a) The plural of segolate forms is ... *aCim/ot*
(b) The plural of the largest subgroup, *CéCeC*, is *CCaCim/ot*
(c) The plural of *CóCeC* is either *CCaCim/ot* or *CoCaCim/ot*
(d) When *ó* is stem-final, the plural is ... *oCot* (which probably constitutes linear derivation)

Cases involving the glide *y* are few, and are probably memorized individually.

2.4.3.3 *On deriving the plural of 'feminine segolates' ending with* +a
Feminine segolates ending with +*et* are segolate in form and in stress-pattern. Many forms ending with the feminine suffix +*a* are segolate-related, demonstrating only some segolate characteristics. *yalda* 'girl' and *malka* 'queen' above are feminine counterparts of *yéled* 'boy' and *mélex* 'king', respectively. Some inanimate nouns of the form *CaCC*+*a* or *CiCC*+*a* can also be related to masculine segolate counterparts:

(55) **Feminine segolates with related masculine segolate counterparts**

Feminine	Gloss	Related masc.	Gloss
givʿaʿ	hill	*gévaʿ*	hill
ricpa	floor	*récef*	sequence, continuity
sidra	series	*séder*	order
cidpa	shell	*cédef*	shell (matter)
dimʿa	tear	*démaʿ*	tear (matter, situation)
šimša	pane	*šemeš*	sun

The relationship, however, is neither direct nor automatic, and many other *CaCC*+*a* or *CiCC*+*a* forms share some segolate characteristics even though there exists no masculine counterpart, e.g.

(56) **Feminine segolates without masculine counterparts**
  simla 'dress', *simxa* 'joyous occasion', *kilya* 'kidney', *šifxa* 'fem. slave',
    liška 'bureau',
  pisga 'summit', *pitma* 'nipple', *pinka* 'plate', *parsa* 'hoof', *'ašma* 'guilt'
  mišxa 'ointment', *bikta* 'hut', *minxa* 'gift', *sin'a* 'hate', *milga* 'scholarship'

The fact that these 'feminine segolates' are not segolate in form or stress pattern may account for their plural formation being somewhat opaque. Owing to this partial opacity, both discontinuous and linear derivations may apply, sometimes even to the same single form. A number of feminine segolate sub-groups may be distinguished. In one, the normative plural pattern *CCaCot* is also the form heard in the spoken register:

(57) **Normative *CCaCot* also used in speech:**

Singular	Gloss	Plural	Singular	Gloss	Plural
yalda	girl	*yeladot*	*'alma*	girl	*'alamot*
giv'a	hill	*gva'ot*	*dim'a*	tear	*dma'ot*
ricpa	floor	*recafot*	*simla*	dress	*smalot*
šimša	pane	*šmašot*	*kilya*	kidney	*klayot*
sidra	series	*sdarot*	*sifra*	digit	*sfarot*
cidpa	shell	*cdafot*	*cir'a*	wasp	*cra'ot*
simxa	joyous occas.	*smaxot*	*šifxa*	slave (f.)	*šfaxot*

In fact, the normative plural may even cause back-formation of a new, non-normative singular:

(58) **Non-normative back formation in feminine segolates**

Singular	Gloss	Plural	Alternative Coll. Sing.
šimša	pane	*šmašot*	*šmaša*
kilya	kidney	*klayot*	*klaya*
cidpa	shell	*cdafot*	*cdafa*

For this group, then, the plural counterpart is the discontinuous *CCaCot*, as is normally the case in segolates. In other forms, the spoken register contains both the normative pattern *CCaCot* and the non-normative *CVCCot*, which levels the plural form with the singular base as well as with the construct state plural form, with some variation due to historical spirantization. In other words, discontinuous and linear relationships coexist:

(59) **Non-Normative *CVCCot* alongside Normative *CCaCot* in speech:**

Singular	Gloss	Formal Pl.	Constr. Pl.	Cnstr. Col.	Col. Pl.
liška	bureau	*lešaxot*	*lišxot*	*liškot*	*liškot*
bik'a	valley	*bka'ot*	*bik'ot*	*bik'ot*	*bik'ot*

(cont.)

Singular	Gloss	Formal Pl.	Constr. Pl.	Cnstr. Col.	Col. Pl.
šixva	layer	*šxavot*	*šixvot*	*šixvot*	*šixvot*
pisga	summit	*psagot*	*pisgot*	*pisgot*	*pisgot*
pirca	breach	*pracot*	*pircot*	*pircot*	*pircot*
pitma	nipple	*ptamot*	*pitmot*	*pitmot*	*pitmot*
pinka	plate	*pnaxot*	*pinxot*	*pinkot*	*pinkot*

And yet in others, one never, or hardly ever, hears the normative *CCaCot* in speech:

(60) **Only Non-Normative *CVCCot* in speech:**

Singular	Gloss	Formal Pl.	Constr. Pl.	Cnstr. Col.	Col. Pl.
kalba	bitch	*klavot*	*kalvot*	*kalbot*	*kalbot*
malka	queen	*mlaxot*	*malxot*	*malkot*	*malkot*
darga	rank	*dragot*	*dargot*	*dargot*	*dargot*
parsa	hoof	*prasot*	*parsot*	*parsot*	*parsot*
'ašma	guilt	*'ašamot*	*'ašmot*	*'ašmot*	*'ašmot*
'asla	toilet seat	*'asalot*	*'aslot*	*'aslot*	*'aslot*
'arka	extension	*'araxot*	*'arxot*	*'arkot*	*'arkot*
mišxa	ointment	*mešaxot*	*mišxot*	*mišxot*	*mišxot*
milga	stipend	*melagot*	*milgot*	*milgot*	*milgot*
'imra	saying	*'amarot*	*'imrot*	*'imrot*	*'imrot*
bitna	lining	*btanot*	*bitnot*	*bitnot*	*bitnot*
bikta	hut	*bkatot*	*biktot*	*biktot*	*biktot*
tirxa	bother	*traxot*	*tirxot*	*tirxot*	*tirxot*
minxa	gift	*menaxot*	*minxot*	*minxot*	*minxot*
nikba	tunnel	*nekavot*	*nikvot*	*nikbot*	*nikbot*
nikra	crevice	*nekarot*	*nikrot*	*nikrot*	*nikrot*
kin'a	jealousy	*kna'ot*	*kin'ot*	*kin'ot*	*kin'ot*
ritma	harness	*retamot*	*ritmot*	*ritmot*	*ritmot*
šigra	routine	*šgarot*	*šigrot*	*šigrot*	*šigrot*
šidra	spine	*šdarot*	*šidrot*	*šidrot*	*šidrot*
sin'a	hate	*sna'ot*	*sin'ot*	*sin'ot*	*sin'ot*

Israelis sometimes over-generalize erroneously from the formal plural to the construct:

(61) **Erroneous hyper-correction in plurals of feminine segolates**

Sing.	Gloss	Formal Pl.	Cons. Pl.	Erron. Pl. Expres.	Gloss
xevra	company	*xavarot*	*xevrot*	**xavarot kaš*	fictitious companies
'emda	position	*'amadot*	*'emdot*	**amadot amemšala*	government positions

And to complicate matters even further, there also exist forms in which it is the 'non-broken' plural, manifest in linear suffix addition (i.e. *CVCCot/im*), that is actually the normative one:

(62) **Occasional linear affixation in feminine segolate plural that is normative**

Singular	Gloss	Plural
'ašpa	garbage; quiver	*'ašpot*
šikma	sycamore	*šikmim*
pišta	flax	*pištim*

Linear derivation also applies when the base vowel is *o* or *u* (except for *xorba* 'ruin' ~ *xoravot*):

(63) **Linear affixation in feminine segolate plural when the base vowel is *o* or *u***

Singular	Gloss	Plural
xoxma	wisdom	*xoxmot*
ʿorma	cunning	*ʿormot*
xumca	acid	*xumcot*

Occasionally, two linear strategies coexist, regular linear derivation, and alongside it alternative linear formation, in which *'aleph* is appended to the base under the influence of Aramaic:

(64) **Two alternative linear derivations of some feminine segolate plurals**

Singular	Gloss	Regular Pl.	Alter. Pl.
simta	alley	*simtot*	*simta'ot*
pitka	note	*pitkot*	*pitka'ot*
girsa	version	*girsot*	*girsa'ot*
tavla	table	*tavlot*	*tavla'ot*

In more complex cases of this type, the register distinction between formal discontinuous *CCaCot* and informal linear derivation may again be observed. Linear derivation with ' is somewhere in between the formal and informal:

(65) **Feminine segolate plurals with three variants**

Singular	Gloss	Formal Pl.	Informal Pl.	Alter. Pl.
piska	paragraph	*psakot*	*piskot*	*piska'ot*
kicba/kicva	pension	*kcavot*	*kicvot*	*kicba'ot/kicva'ot*

A related generalization is that if the first consonant and the following vowel constitute a prefix, they do not constitute feminine segolates, which accounts for the non-occurrence of **mecavot*, **mera'ot*, **txanot*, **tkavot* and **tkarot* below:

(66) **No *CcaCot* plural when the initial CV sequence is prefixal**

Singular	Gloss	Root	Plural
micva	commandment	*c.v.y*	*micvot*
mar'a	mirror	*r.'.y*	*mar'ot*
taxana	station	*x.n.y*	*taxanot*
tikva	hope	*k.v.y*	*tikvot*
tikra	ceiling	*k.r.y*	*tikrot*

2.4.3.4 *Segolates in the* miCCaCa *pattern*

It should also be noted that the construct state form of *mVC(C)aCa* is segolate *mVC(C)éCet*:

(67) **The construct state of feminine segolates**

Form	Gloss	Construct
milxama	war	*milxémet*
mištara	police	*mištéret*
miflaga	party	*mifléget*
memšala	government	*memšélet*
merkava	carriage	*merkévet*
mamlaxa	kingdom	*mamléxet*
mo'aca	council	*mo'écet*
mošava	settlement	*mošévet*

When some *miCCaCa* forms shift to *maCCeCa* in casual speech, they lose their 'segolate status', and consequently their construct form shifts from discontinuous *miCCéCet* to linearly derived *maCCeCat*, since the construct state *mVC(C)éCet* may only be formed for *mVC(C)aCa* forms:[21]

(68) **The colloquial construct state of feminine segolates in *miCCaCa***

Formal	Gloss	Constr.	Casual	Casual Constr.
mispara	hairdresser shop	*mispéret*	*maspera*	*masperat*
mixbasa	laundry shop	*mixbéset*	*maxbesa*	*maxbesat*
mištala	nursery	*mištélet*	*maštela*	*maštelat*

Even this particular case indicates that the segolates tend to be derived from a specific discontinuous *miškal* and not linearly from a given base.

---

[21] An over-generalization is probably responsible for *'ayéret pitúax* 'development town' instead of normative *'ayarat pitúax* (from *'ayara* 'small town'). Apparently, this is caused by analogy to (normative) *'aséret* 'the ten of', the construct state of *'asara* 'ten', as in *'aséret yemey tšuva* 'the ten days of repentance'.

2.4.3.5 *Deriving the segolates: conclusion*
It appears, then, that in Israeli Hebrew, the majority of segolates
and segolate derivatives should be accounted for by the pairing of
discontinuous canonical patterns, with the exception of one small
subgroup (with a stem-final *ó*). In 'feminine segolates' of the pattern
CaCC+*a* or *CiCC*+*a*, linear plural formation is an alternative device,
particularly in the colloquial register.

2.4.4 *Mechanical derivation of nouns and adjectives: conclusion*

It has been shown that discontinuous derivation continues to exist
productively alongside linear formation in both +*an*-related and +*ut*-
related forms, as well as in the large segolate class. Since there is
no significant communicative distinction associated with choice of
derivational device, there is little reason to believe that MH is gradually losing the Semitic (non-linear) character of its word-formation
component. This is not to say that the presence of the suffix is unim-
portant. On the contrary, there is no doubt that a linear suffix
increases the productivity of patterns like +*an* and +*ut*. Still, the
miškal itself has not weakened. This is clearly supported by the continued preference for *CaCCan* noted above, and its still being the
preferred realization for agentives in spite of the increase of linear
formation with +*an*. Also, discontinuous derivation of +*ut* forms is
at least as productive as linear +*ut* formation (Bolozky & Schwarzwald
1992), and the same applies to the huge class of segolate nouns. And
as noted earlier, the preference for discontinuous *miškal* derivation is
independently supported by Berman's (1987) findings in productivity tests. Of all forms whose mechanical derivation strategy could be
determined in open-ended productivity tests, 60% were discontinuous
and 40% linear, i.e. a 3:2 ratio in favor of non-linear derivation.

CHAPTER THREE

SELECTING DERIVATION PATTERNS:
THE VERB SYSTEM

3.1 *Analysis of data on verb formation from the '70s*

One way of measuring lexical productivity is by means of productivity tests, in which non-existing forms are created by speakers in given contexts. Such tests may be open-ended, or may involve selection from a number of options. Open-ended coinage tests, which elicit intuitive innovation, tend to reflect the most prominent, transparent patterns that easily come to mind through scanning of the new lexicon. Speakers tend to look for patterns that are associated with broad semantic clues, even when more normatively appropriate options are available in the broader lexicon. At the same time, open-ended tests may also reflect individual creativity, manifest in neologisms that may only occur in a single subject's mental lexicon. Thus, while selection of a pattern may center on the obvious default choice, it sometimes also varies widely, resulting in a broad array of forms, some of them quite unexpected. Judgment tasks offer a variety of options, of which the speakers may not have been aware had they not been pointed out to them, and thus represent a fuller, more complex lexicon, which includes the normative option. They therefore reflect a more specific, focused choice of derivation pattern. However, since the selection offered excludes some marginal alternants to start with, the presence of the most common form among the proposed alternatives may reinforce of what would have been an intuitive default choice in an open-ended productivity test anyway. Thus, judgment tasks exclude marginal forms of the type likely to surface in open-ended tests. Among the more common alternatives, judgment tests either broaden the variety of preferences, or focus the selection and favor the default choice even further. In either case, significant agreement between the results of the two types of tests facilitates determination of relative degree of productivity.

Unlike Wexler (1990), who argues that the *binyan* system has been declining from as early as BH, and that by now the *binyanim* have few semantic correlates, I believe that at least in productivity situations, the verb system exhibits remarkable regularity.[1] It is true that when the verb system is considered in its totality, the traditional meanings associated with the *binyanim* are a small minority, and the derivation process from one root realization to another is not automatic (Ornan 1971). As pointed out in Schwarzwald (1981b, 1982), the typical 'grammar book' generalizations on *binyanim* meanings tend to reflect relationships among the more frequent verbs. The prominence of these frequent verbs in daily use may indeed result in inappropriate assumptions as to their weight in the morphosemantic system as a whole. But when speakers innovate, they do not consider the total lexicon. In recent word-formation, as well as when productive innovation is induced by productivity tests (see Bolozky 1978, 1982, 1986a), speakers first appear to scan the newly formed component of the lexicon, looking for the broadest and most transparent generalizations. Their choice of pattern for the form to be realized thus conforms to general tendencies observable within the productive sub-system of recent innovations. In that recent lexicon, *binyan* choice is not arbitrary. It follows a procedure based on a broad semantic feature hierarchy, confirming the generalization (see Baayen & Renouf 1996, Clark 1993) that lexical formation is first and foremost concept driven. This is an intuitive, classificatory-global strategy. Relatively recent neologisms suggest that the majority of speakers first make the most general dichotomy between 'focus on the theme'[2] and 'focus on the agent'. If the focus is on the theme, and the target meaning is a true passive, the default passive counterparts of the relevant active *binyanim* are selected,[3] i.e. *pi'el* > *pu'al* and *hif'il* > *huf'al*:

---

[1] For the essential role of the *binyanim* in a description of the Hebrew verb system within a Functional Grammar framework, see Junger (1987). For analysis of the *binyanim* within sign-oriented linguistics, see Tobin (1995). An early analysis of the meanings of the *binyanim* in colloquial Hebrew can be found in Ariel (1972).

[2] 'Theme' is probably a more appropriate notion than 'patient', when we wish to cover both the 'entity undergoing the action' and the 'entity in a certain state or undergoing change of state'. 'Focus' is required primarily for reflexives, where the patient is the same as the agent, and for reciprocals, which involve an agent and a patient which alternate in roles. Since no agent is involved that is independent of the theme, the focus is on the theme.

[3] The active verb does not have to constitute an existing lexical entry; a potential form may suffice.

(1) *mimeš* 'realize (tr.), make real' > *mumaš* 'be realized'
 gimed 'make small' > *gumad* 'be made small'
 himxiz 'make into a play' > *humxaz* 'be made into a play'
 hitpil 'desalinate' > *hutpal* 'be desalinated'

However, in all other theme-centered neologisms, be they inchoative (i.e. 'become . . .', or 'begin a new state'), reflexive, or reciprocal, *hitpaʿel* is chosen:[4]

(2) *hit'azréax* 'become citizen'   *hitpager* 'die'   *hitgamed* 'become tiny'
 hitmameš 'become real'   *hitrakez* 'concentrate (int.)'   *hizdayen* 'copulate'
 hitpalmes 'argue (about)'

If the focus is on the agent (the 'instigator of the action'), speakers usually opt for *piʿel*:

(3) *biyel* 'stamp (an envelope)'   *siveg* 'assort'   *bilef* 'bluff'
 viset 'regulate'   *nitev* 'mark route'   *xiyeg* 'dial'
 flirtet 'flirt'   *fikses* 'send by fax'   *divax* 'report'

which accounts for its being the most productive *binyan*, with agentive verbs constituting the largest body of innovated verb forms. There is, however, a class of agentives that shows some preference for *hifʿil* realization, which for our purposes will be loosely referred to as 'causative'. This is a somewhat problematic term, since in a broad sense, all agentive verbs are causative: they cause new situations that affect the patient/theme.[5] For speakers of Hebrew, causatives usually mean causing the patient to do something (e.g. *he'exil* 'feed'), or causing an entity to be (or become) something (e.g. *xizek* 'strengthen', *higdil* 'enlarge, tr.'), the so-called 'factitives', or causing an entity to begin a new state (e.g. *hizkir* 'remind, i.e. cause to

---

[4] *nifʿal* also has an inchoative meaning, but in the productive lexicon it is manifest only occasionally, possibly because of 'interference' from the passive meaning of *nifʿal*, and because of the restricted semantic scope of *nifʿal* when compared with *hitpaʿel*. The innovator looks for the pattern that is semantically most general and most transparent. Alternatively, it could be claimed that *hitpaʿel* is chosen whenever the derived verb is intended to be intransitive. Judging from the way the system behaves as a whole, it appears, however, that choice of pattern for a new verb is semantically determined more than it is syntactic.

[5] Some would argue that the notion 'causative' should include any agentive verb which has an actual or potential 'resultative' adjective, i.e. since *nitev* 'mark route', for instance, would have a related adjectival *menutav* 'that has been marked (route)', it should be regarded as causative. This elasticity of causation as a component feature of agentivity is one of the reasons, it seems, for the increasing colloquial tendency for choosing *piʿel* as the realization of all agentive verbs, including some of the causatives that in literary Hebrew are reserved for *hifʿil*, as well as for the variations on the choice hierarchy described below.

remember'). Thus, the term causative will be used here only for cause-to-do verbs, for factitives, and for cause-a-new-state-to-begin verbs. In innovations observed in the '70s, such causatives showed relative preference for *hif'il*:

(4) *himxiš* 'make real'   *hitpil* 'desalinate'   *hincíax* 'eternalize'
    himxiz 'make into a play'   *hifnim* 'internalize'   *hikvič* 'squeeze (child lang.)'

Since the commonest base for new verbs is existing nouns and adjectives, borrowed as well as native, most causatives of this kind will be factitive.

These observations were supported by findings from productivity tests reported on in Bolozky (1978). An open coinage test and a judgment task were administered, with 50 different subjects in each test. Sentence frames contained blanks for potential verbs to be filled in. In the coinage test, base nouns and target meanings were read aloud; in the judgment task, suggested forms were also provided. Since it was taken for granted that passives are more-or-less automatically related to their active counterparts (i.e. *pi'el* > *pu'al* and *hif'il* > *huf'al*), even when the latter are only potential, passive formation was not included in the test design. Below are the percentages of the most preferred realizations for each target meaning,[6] by semantic category (Coin. = coinage, Judg. = judgment):

(5) **Most preferred verb realizations in productivity tests conducted in the '70**
I. Focus on patient/theme (non-passive) suggested
A. Non-agentive target meaning (mostly inchoative)

Noun	Gloss	Target meaning	Preferred	% Coin.	% Judg.
marks	Marx	become a Marxist	*hitmarkses* etc.[7]	100	100
šerif	sheriff	become sheriff	*hištaref*	90	100
šmalc	schmaltz	become schmaltzy	*hitšmalcec* etc.	96	100
vasal	vassal	become vassal	*hitvasel*	94	98
salóni	armchair revolutionary (< *salon* 'parlor')	become ...	*histalen*	94	96
snob	snob	become snobbish	*histaneb* etc.	92	98

B. Agentivity suggested, but agent not distinct from patient (reflexive, reciprocal)

Noun	Gloss	Target meaning	Preferred	% Coin.	% Judg.
šerif	sheriff	make/proclaim oneself sheriff	*hištaref*	100	100

[6] For a complete list of all realizations, see Bolozky (1978). Only data from the 1995/96 tests will be reported in full below.

[7] For a breakdown of variants within the same *binyan*, see discussion of structure-preserving and non-structure-preserving below, and Appendix II.

II. Agentive (if patient involved, it is distinct from agent)
A. Causative suggested

Noun	Gloss	Target meaning	Preferred	% Coin.	% Judg.
marks	Marx	make one a Marxist	*mirkses* etc.	90	98
šérif	sheriff	make one sheriff	*hišrif*	72	82
salóni	armchair revolutionary	make one ...	*hislin*	66	70
snob	snob	make one snobbish	*hisnib*	60	64
šmalc	schmaltz	make it schmaltzy	*hišmilc* etc.	64	60
vasal	vassal	make one a vassal	*hivsil*	60	52

B. General Agentive suggested

patent	patent	register as patent	*pitent* etc.	100	100
ʾasfalt	asphalt	cover with asphalt	*ʾisfelt* etc.	96	100
talk	talcum powder	spray with talcum	*tilkek* etc.	72	82
vasal	vassal	live as a vassal	*visel*	70	82
šérif	sheriff	serve as sheriff	*širef*	74	68
panel	panel	cover with panels	*pinel*	68	76
zbeng	blow	give a blow	*hizbing*	66	72
kéres	hook	fit with a hook	*keres*	66	70
sport	sport	engage in sports	*sportet* etc.	68	56
salóni	armchair revolutionary	speak like an ...	*hislin*	56	52

(6) **Average scores for *binyan* choice by semantic category, with all significant realizations included, even if not preferred for particular target meanings (N = 50)**

I. Focus on patient/theme (non-passive) suggested

	Binyan	% Coin.	% Judg.
A. Non-agentive (mostly inchoative)	*hitpaʿel*	94.33	98.67
B. Agentive, but agent indistinct from patient	*hitpaʿel*	100.00	100.00

II. Agentive (if patient involved, it is distinct from agent)

	Binyan	% Coin.	% Judg.
A. Causative	*hifʿil*	43.00	44.67
	piʿel	25.67	26.33
B. General Agentive	*piʿel*	61.40	63.40
	hifʿil	12.20	12.40

Scores for *binyan* realization in each semantic category are similar for both types of tests, and are systematically somewhat higher in the judgment tasks. One explanation is that in addition to those speakers who chose the default form in the open-ended test, others were 'reminded' of the most expected alternant when it was offered to them as an option, and realized that this would have been their intuitive choice had they thought of it on their own. As for semantic categories, note that *pinel* 'cover with panels' and *ʾisfelt* 'cover with asphalt', and possibly even *pitent* 'register as patent', would normally be regarded as causative. However, by limiting causative to include 'cause-to-do', 'factitive', and 'cause to begin' only, they will still be classified as general agentives. Agentives that are not clearly causative in that limited sense therefore constitute a very broad category, since they are the default realization of all verbs in which the agent exercises control over the action denoted by the verb. This includes most denominative verbs, a huge class. It also encompasses transitive as well as intransitive verbs, as long as the latter do not belong in the 'focus on the theme' category. Consequently, while *hitpaᶜel* is the most productive binyan for the latter, *piᶜel* takes precedence when the target verb is agentive. These findings are closely supported by data in Berman (1980, 1982, 1989, 1993a, b) and Berman & Sagi (1981) on child language acquisition of Hebrew. Even if children do not yet associate the particular adult *binyan* with a basic concept at an early stage (e.g. causation in *xibéti lo 'et hamatana* 'I hid the present from him', with a *piᶜel* form rather than the normative *hifᶜil*), those concepts can be shown to have already been acquired, since the child never crosses transitivity lines (i.e. will never say **hitxabéti lo 'et hamatana*). Later on, the adult system is used and overused (e.g. *hašemeš masrifᵓoti* 'the sun is burning me', selecting a typically-causative *binyan* instead of the standard basic *paᶜal* form). Children also demonstrate productive use of the *binyanim* in productivity tests, to a degree that approaches the adult mastery described in Bolozky (1978) and in Berman's work.

Thus, the basic verb-derivation strategy at the intuitive global stage is to distinguish between 'focus on the patient/theme', with passive, inchoative, and reflexive/reciprocal verbs on the one hand, and agentive verbs, subdivided into causatives and general agentives, on the other. This is the scheme used by the majority of speakers tested in Bolozky (1978). It is not the only possible hierarchy. Analysis of the 1978 data indicates the existence of variations to the hierarchy in minority groups. There appear to be two minority variations in which choice is not sporadic; the same speakers maintain each variation consistently. One minority group opts for *hitpaᶜel* for all (non-passive) intransitives (including some non-causative agentives, e.g. *hištaref* for 'serve as sheriff') and *piᶜel* for all transitives, an essentially syntactic choice. The other group, while opting for *hitpaᶜel* for theme-centered verbs like the majority, consistently assigns 'cause to be(come)' factitives to *piᶜel*, in addition to all other agentives being realized in it. The distinction between 'cause to do' causatives and 'cause to be(come)' factitives is reflected in the total lexicon and to some extent in the productive one as well. *hifᶜil* is the unmarked causative *binyan*, in which any causation may be realized, while one of the meanings of *piᶜel* is factitive (see Bolozky & Saad 1983). In Bolozky's (1978) pro-

ductivity tests, quite a few subjects preferred[8] to realize factitives in
pi'el rather than in *hif'il* (*širef/širef* 'make someone sheriff', *visel* 'make
someone a vassal', *silen* 'make someone an armchair revolutionary',
mirkses/mirkes 'make someone a Marxist'). Only 2%–4% realized
inchoative verbs in *nif'al* instead of *hitpa'el*, as in *nislan* for 'become
an armchair revolutionary' in Bolozky (1978) (see also *nifrak* 'fall
apart' in child language in Berman & Sagi 1981), which is accounted
for by the existence of *nif'al* inchoatives in the wider lexicon. A similarly minute minority (2%–4%) opted for inchoatives in *hif'il*, as in
hislin 'become an armchair revolutionary', *hivsil* 'become a vassal',
reflecting the observation that in the full lexicon, verbs like *hilbin*
'whiten, tr./intr'. are not only causative, but inchoative as well. Since
these are not the most prominent or most readily available realizations of inchoatives in the new lexicon, their role in productive innovation is minimal. There are also some isolated occurrences of general
agentives realized in *hif'il* (e.g. *hišrif* 'serve as sheriff', *hislin* 'behave/speak
like an armchair revolutionary'), but those were not consistent with
particular speakers. Perusal of the recent lexicon also reveals some
isolated cases of semantic split/differentiation determining agentive
verb realization in isolated items. For example, *hifšit* and *pišet* both
meant 'remove (usually clothes)' in BH; *pišet* was later used for 'simplify' (see 'preemption' below). All of these, however, constitute minor
deviations from the basic word-formation procedure outlined above.

One may conclude that productivity tests conducted on adults or
children portray certain general tendencies for classificatory-global
innovation that is semantically-based. The actual distribution of forms
realized in particular *binyanim* in the recent lexicon constitutes evidence for the proposed global hierarchy from the language itself.

The semantic-global considerations, as well as the focused-local
ones to be discussed presently, are subject to universal constraints:

(i) avoidance of unpronounceable clusters. *kimpleks* 'make complex,
complicate', for instance, could have been realized in *hif'il* as a
causative, but **hikmpliks* is clearly unpronounceable. *pi'el* resolves
the difficulty, since its base contains two syllables throughout the
paradigm, which means that it can accommodate six consonants,

---

[8] Generally between 16%–48%, depending on the item, and in one case,
mirkses/mirkes, 90% in open-ended coinage tests and 98% in judgment tasks.

and theoretically even more, provided that syllable division allows it.[9] Another illustration: *šlimper* 'make sloppy'; **hišlmpir* is unpronounceable.

(ii) preemption (see Clark & Clark 1979, Clark 1993). *yibe* 'import' and *yice* 'export' would have probably been realized in *hifꜥil* as causatives, but the appropriate slots are already occupied by *hevi* 'bring in' and *hoci* 'take out', respectively. Another illustration: *pišet* 'simplify'; *hifšit* 'remove clothes; make abstract' is already taken. Actually, as noted above, *pišet* did exist, in the sense of 'remove clothes' (BH), as well as 'stretch out; smooth out' (MishH), but at the formal/literary register only. In the everyday lexicon, the slot was free.

Though universal, these constraints are not at the top of the pattern selection hierarchy. The phonetic constraint does not determine, for instance, that any root be automatically realized in *piꜥel* if it is quadriliteral or longer. Rather, if the target meaning is a general agentive verb, it is realized in *piꜥel*, and *piꜥel* will indeed accommodate it if it is quadriliteral or longer, but not because of its phonological complexity. If the target meaning suggests *hifꜥil* realization, but the result would be unpronounceable, the form is realized in *piꜥel*, the semantically-closest *binyan* in which it can be pronounced.

Independently of the semantic classificatory-global selection, innovators fine-tune pattern selection based on focused-local considerations. These involve a variety of more specific realization options provided by the total lexicon (rather than just the 'new' one), and are more evident in judgment tests, where such options are offered and speakers are requested to make a choice. The proposed options 'remind' speakers of other available choices that may not have occurred to them spontaneously. The selection tasks may trigger more normative options that do not necessarily occur at the initial intuitive stage. At the same time, they may reinforce what would have been the natural intuitive selection, by juxtaposing it with other

---

[9] Theoretically, there could be more: three in the onset of the first syllable, three in the coda of the second, and a variable number shared by the coda of the first syllable and the onset of the second. In practice, there seem to be no more than six. Schwarzwald (1996) suggests that the productivity of *piꜥel* is enhanced by its not being subject to phonological restrictions on root radicals. But as she points out in her earlier work (Schwarzwald 1974), the absence of a restriction in *piꜥel* on identical or homorganic first and second radical is actually phonetic, resulting from *piꜥel* always having a vowel between these two consonants.

options and helping the subject realize that it is the most appropriate one. This is apparently what tends to happen in the verb system. The general tendency is for the judgment test results to reinforce the findings from the coinage tests, often with even larger percentages. The preference for *hitpaʿel* as the preferred *binyan* for inchoatives is consistently higher than in the coinage tests. The same is essentially true of the other categories, but not with the same consistency, probably because of the somewhat-vague border between 'true' causatives and other agentives. There is one aspect in which the selection tests markedly differ; they demonstrate a clearly-stronger tendency to preserve the transparency of the source, e.g. *flirtet* 'flirt (V)', from *flirt*, normally by maintaining the original consonant clustering of the source noun (see also Chapter 2). **hiflirt* would have been pronounceable, but is not opted for. To allow realization in *piʿel*, where this form belongs semantically, and still preserve the original clustering, the last consonant is reduplicated to produce *flirtet* rather than the expected **filret* (which would have been equally pronounceable.) The same is true of recent *fikses* 'fax (V)'; there is no phonetic reason to prevent **fikes* or **hifkis*. The reduplication strategy has also been shown to be productive in productivity tests, as seen in Bolozky (1978) and Berman (1990). Note that in some forms, cluster preservation and preemption operate simultaneously. *Sifrer* 'assign digits' results from preservation of the source clusters of *sifra* 'digit', as well as from the fact that the *siper* 'tell, recount' slot is already occupied. Similarly, *tixnen* 'plan' preserves the consonant clustering of *toxnit* 'plan (N)', and makes up for the *tiken* 'measure, set, prearrange (lit.)' being already taken.

Below are specific realizations in Bolozky (1978), where some variants emerge within particular *binyanim*. In each case, at least one variant preserves the clustering of the base. Included are only forms whose base contains consonant clusters. Although *šeref/širef* reflects the CV structure of *šérif* better than *hišrif*, bases without clusters are not considered. It appears that the speaker's target verb pattern can broadly be characterized as a structure composed of three expandable slots (a term like *šoršan* may be used for such a slot), corresponding to the three radicals of the root. What makes the base most opaque is splitting its original consonant clusters between these slots by means of a vowel. Thus, *šeref/širef* or *hišrif*, with *š*, *r* and *f* slots, are regarded as equally transparent; the "loss" of the vowel between *š* and *r* in *šérif* is of no consequence. On the other hand, deriving

*filret from a base form like *flirt* would assign the consonants to a
f-lr-t pattern, splitting the *fl* and *rt* clusters of the base, which the
derived *flirtet* maintains. In the case of *špric* 'a squirt', which results
in *hišpric* 'squirt (V)', it is not obvious where the first radical slot
ends and the second begins, but it does not really matter as long as
the *špr* sequence is maintained. Similarly, if *'iptent* from *patent* 'patent'
occurs (see below), the result is still cluster-preserving, since only a
basic vowel is discarded, and the *nt* cluster remains intact.

(7) **Some Cluster-Preserving and Non-Cluster-Preserving Realizations in the Verb Productivity Tests reported in Bolozky (1978)**
(N subjects = 50, N bases = 11. CCP = Consonant Cluster Preservation;
CP = Cluster-Preserving; NCP = Non-Cluster-Preserving; Co. = Coinage
tests; Ju. = Judgment tests. For details, see Appendix II)

Base	Target Meaning		Binyan	Realization	CCP.	% Co.	% Ju.
'asfalt 'asphalt'	cover with asphalt		*pi'el*	*'isfelt*	CP	88	98
				'isflet	NCP	8	2
marks 'Marx'	make one a Marxist		*pi'el*	*mirkses*	CP	62	80
				mirkes	NCP	28	18
			hif'il	*himriks*	NCP	8	2
patent 'patent'	register as patent		*pi'el*	*pitent*	CP	56	68
				pitnet	NCP	44	32
			hif'il	*hisfilt*	CP	4	–
sport 'sports'	engage in sports		*pi'el*	*sportet*	CP	56	50
				spirtet	CP	10	4
				sipret	NPS	2	2
			hitpa'el	*hitsportet*	CP	22	36
				hitspartet	CP	4	4
				histportet	NCP	2	4
				histapret	NCP	4	–

(8) **Averages of scores (N bases = 11)**

	% Coin.	% Judg.
Structure-preserving	72.55	80.55
Non-structure-preserving	26.00	19.27

Structure-preserving variants are commonly opted for in both types
of tests, and with the exception of *sportet*, the preference for them
increases further in the judgment tests.[10] Speakers whose first intuition does not include the reduplication device are reminded of its
availability, and of other opportunities to preserve the base, and are
therefore more likely to make their choice in that direction. That is

---

[10] The small decline in *sportet* is due to competition with a related structure-
preserving form, *hitsportet*, which may be explained by interpretation of the latter as
a focus-on-the-theme verb, with identical agent and theme.

why the reduplication device is more common in judgment tasks than it is in coinage productivity tests.

It is important to note, however, that like the pronounceability and preemption constraints, structure-preserving considerations are secondary to the primary global-semantic ones. The first consideration in the hierarchy of *binyan* choice is a broad semantic (and possibly syntactic) assignment as outlined above. Normally, other factors play a role within the semantic classification without violating it. *flirtet* and *fikses* are realized in *pi'el* as general agentives. Reduplication allows them to remain in the appropriate *binyan* and still maintain the transparency of the derivation base. If cluster preservation were the primary consideration, it could account for *fikses*, since **hifkis* breaks the original cluster, but not for *flirtet*, since **hiflirt* would have preserved the transparency of the source just as well. Furthermore, had the semantic considerations not been primary, *hitpa'el* could equally be chosen, since **hitflartet* and *hitfakses*[11] also preserve the transparency of the source noun. *kimpleks* and *šlimper* cannot be realized phonetically in *hif'il*, but this is not the primary reason for their being assigned to *pi'el*. Their realization in *pi'el* fits one variation on the semantic hierarchy, in which factitive causatives are realized in *pi'el* (while 'cause-to-do' ones opt for *hif'il*), as well as the increasing tendency to realize all agentives, causative and otherwise, in *pi'el*. One cannot place the cluster-preservation constraint at the head of the global phase, basing *binyan* choice on it as the primary consideration, nor give precedence to the phonetic constraint, stating that with four consonants or more in the base, *pi'el* should be automatically selected. Over-stressing the preemption constraint would also be in error, since avoidance of homonymity is a tendency, not an absolute rule.

Occasionally, the semantic factor may be outweighed. *hišpric* 'squirt', *hiflik* 'hit', and *hišvic* 'sweat; brag' should have been realized in *pi'el* as **šiprec*, **pilek* (or *filek*), and **šivec*, respectively, if not for preservation of transparency of source which prevailed. Apparently, the complete identity between the original stem and that of *hif'il* was too hard to resist. In the case of the latter two, analogy with *hirbic* 'hit, beat' must have played a role as well. The same holds for bilingual children (Hebrew-English) in utterances like *hu hitrik oti* 'he played a

---

[11] In this case, *hitfakses* actually exists, but with a different target meaning, the reciprocal 'fax each other'.

trick on me', or even bilingual adults, as in *lidrop 'et hakurs* 'to drop the course'.[12] These, however, are marginal cases. The preferred option is choice of a *binyan* on broad semantic grounds, provided that the general constraints are not violated and that the source remains as transparent as possible. Even when cluster preservation takes precedence, it is very unlikely to cross the 'focus-on-agent'/'focus-on-theme' boundary, i.e. no inchoative will be realized in *pi'el*,[13] or causatives in *hitpa'el*.

3.2 Analysis of data on verb formation from the '80s and '90s

3.2.1 Recent productivity tests on verb formation

Productivity tests were also conducted in 1995/96, mostly at two Israeli teacher training colleges[14] and some at Ben-Gurion University of the Negev. Fifty subjects were involved in the coinage tests and the same[15] 50 in comparable judgment tasks. All subjects were specializing in Hebrew language study or Hebrew language teaching.[16] One hundred and nine identical sentence frames were included in both types of tests, covering a variety of structures, including verbs, nouns, and adjectives. In the coinage tests, subjects were given questionnaires in which they were instructed to fill in the gap within

---

[12] In a way, these are the only convincing data in support of Wexler's argument for linear derivation of new verbs. But as noted above, they are too few for making a strong case for it.

[13] Inchoatives, however, may occasionally be realized in *hif'il*, since similarly to English *blacken*, *widen*, etc., there exists a group of verbs in *hif'il*, mostly related to colors and certain human qualities (see Bolozky 1978) that may function as either causative or inchoative, like *hilbin* 'make/become white', *hišxim* 'make/become brown', *hišmin* 'make/become fat'. But they are marginal in the new lexicon, and thus hardly function in the innovating process.

[14] Dr. Dorit Ravid of Tel Aviv University and Dr. Emanuel Allon of Beit Berl College assisted in administering these productivity tests.

[15] Whether it is desirable to use the same speakers for both types of experiments involving identical stimuli is, of course, debatable. Bolozky (1978), for instance, used different subjects for each type. The advantage of using different groups of subjects for very similar tests is in avoidance of bias in the selection task created by prior exposure to the same stimuli in the coinage test. However, testing the same subjects in a different mode eliminates the effect of variables such as age, sex, educational background, military service, etc. on possible outcomes of the two types of tests.

[16] Future tests should be conducted on non-students, or at least on students who do not specialize in language teaching, to eliminate a possible normative bias.

each sentence, by coining a word. This new word, in their opinion, would have been the most likely one in the given context based on a given target meaning. They were told to fill in a single word only, using the underlined item within the definition of the target meaning provided, and to employ vocalization marks in a manner that will unambiguously specify what form they had in mind. They were given to understand that it is not the normative vowel marking that is requested, just some basic notation that will distinguish ambiguous forms. In the judgment tasks, speakers were provided with the same sentence frames, and were asked to circle what they would consider the most appropriate item from a selection of alternatives offered underneath the blank in each sentence. Since the meaning might not always be self-evident, or the context could allow a number of options, the desired target meaning was provided in the selection tasks as well. Here is a one-sentence illustration for each type of test:

(9) (a) **Coinage**

géri   kúper   lo   raca   lihyot   šérif;   tošavey   ha-ʿir _____ *ʾoto   be-xóax*
Gary Cooper not want to be Sheriff; the residents of the-town _____ him by-force

(*ʿasu   ʾoto   le-šérif*)   'Gary Cooper did not want to be sheriff; the town's residents
(made him to-sheriff)_____ him by force (made him sheriff)

(b) **Judgment**

géri kúper lo raca lihyot šérif; tošavey ha-ʿir _____ *ʾoto be-xóax* (*ʿasu ʾoto le-šérif*)
[*šarfu   hišrífu   šerfu*]

Below are the scores for invented verb forms, in percentages. The totals are less than 100%, either because a slot was left blank, or because a subject did not follow instructions in constructing a proposed form (e.g. when filling in a suppletive form, or re-introducing the base noun instead of creating a verb form. For full details, see Appendix III):

(10) **I. Focus on patient/theme suggested**, N subjects = 50 (Co. = Coinage, Ju. = Judgment)
i. Non-agentive target meaning (mostly inchoative), N subjects = 50, N bases = 9

Binyan	% Co.	% Ju.	Illustrations
hitpaʿel	70.00	85.33	*magad* 'battalion commander' > *hitmaged* 'become battalion commander'
			zálman 'sloppy dresser' > *hizdalmen* 'become sloppy'
puʿal	6.44	3.56	*magad* 'battalion commander' > *mugad* 'become battalion commander'
			šérif 'sheriff' > *šoraf* 'become sheriff'
hifʿil	3.33	3.11	*snob* 'snob' > *hisnib* 'become snobbish'

(cont.)

Binyan	% Co.	% Ju.	Illustrations
			žlob 'crude/big/strong man' > *hižlib* 'become crude/big/ strong man'
hufʿal	2.67	2.44	*šerif* 'sheriff' > *hušraf* 'become sheriff'
			magav 'border police' > *humgav* 'become a member of the border police'
nifʿal	2.44	2.22	*šerif* 'sheriff' > *nišraf* 'become sheriff'
			magad 'battalion commander' > *nimgad* 'become battalion commander'
paʿal	.22	.44	*snob* 'snob' > *sanab* 'become snobbish'
			yóram 'nerd' > *yaram* 'become nerdy'

ii. Agentivity suggested, but agent not distinct from patient (reflexive, reciprocal) N subjects = 50, N bases = 3

hitpaʿel	68.67	76.00	*búnker* 'bunker' > *hitbanker* 'hide self in bunker'
			šerif 'sheriff' > *hištaref* 'make/proclaim oneself sheriff'
			pitka 'note' > *hitpatkeʾu* 'send each other notes'
hifʿil	5.33	8.00	*šerif* 'sheriff' > *hišrif* 'make/proclaim oneself sheriff'
puʿal	3.33	1.33	*šerif* 'sheriff' > *šoraf* 'make/proclaim oneself sheriff'
hufʿal	3.33	1.33	*šerif* 'sheriff' > *hušraf* 'make/proclaim oneself sheriff'
nifʿal	.67	–	*šerif* 'sheriff' > *nišraf* 'make/proclaim oneself sheriff'

iii. Passive, N bases = 7

puʿal	52.00	52.86	*panel* 'panel' > *punal* 'be covered with panels'
			talk 'talcum powder' > *tulak/tulkak* 'be sprayed with talcum powder'
			matax 'foreign currency' > *mutax* 'be invested in/turned into foreign currency'
hufʿal	22.57	28.29	*šerif* 'sheriff' > *hušraf* 'be made sheriff'
			kéres 'hook' > *hukras* 'be fitted with a hook'
			magad 'battalion commander' > *humgad* 'be made battalion commander'
hitpaʿel	8.00	6.86	*šerif* 'sheriff' > *hištaref* 'be made sheriff'
			magad 'battalion commander' > *hitmaged* 'be made battalion commander'
nifʿal	4.00	6.29	*šerif* 'sheriff' > *nišraf* 'be made sheriff'
			bagac 'high court' > *nivgac* 'be presented to high court'
hitpuʿal	.57	–	*panel* 'panel' > *hitpunal* 'be covered with panels'
paʿul	–	.86	*talk* 'talcum powder' > *taluk* 'be sprayed with talcum powder'
hifʿil	–	.29	*kéres* 'hook' > *hikris* 'be fitted with a hook'

II. Agentive
a. Causative suggested (N subjects = 50, N bases = 9)

piʿel	73.78	72.44	*marks* 'Marx' > *mirkses/mirkes* 'make one a Marxist'
			naxs 'bad luck' > *nixes/nixses* 'cause to be unlucky'
			ʾafro 'afro hair style' > *ʾifrer/ʾifer* 'make (hair) afro . . .'
hifʿil	20.89	25.33	*snob* 'snob' > *hisnib* 'make one snobbish'
			šerif 'sheriff' > *hišrif* 'make one sheriff'
paʿal	1.11	.44	*ʾafro* 'afro hair style' > *ʾafar* 'make (hair) afro . . .'

b. General Agentive suggested (if patient involved, it is distinct from agent) (N subjects = 50, N bases = 14)

Binyan	% Co.	% Ju.	Illustrations
pi'el	78.71	77.86	*talk* 'talcum powder' > *tilek/tilkek* 'spray with talcum powder'
			'asfalt 'asphalt' > *'isfelt/'isflet* 'cover with asphalt'
			pincéta 'tweezers' > *pincet* 'tweeze'
hif'il	9.57	4.43	*kéres* 'hook' > *hikris* 'fit with a hook'
			zheng 'a blow' > *hizhing* 'give a blow'
			matax 'foreign currency' > *himtíax* 'invest in foreign currency'
hitpa'el	2.43	3.00	*sport* 'sport' > *hispartet/hitsportet* 'engage in sports'
pa'al	2.71	2.43	*magad* 'battalion commander' > *magad* 'serve as battalion commander'
nif'al	.14	.43	*šérif* 'sheriff' > *nišraf* 'serve as sheriff'

The '90s tests basically repeated the earlier tests, except that passive formation was also examined. The dominance of *pu'al* among passive neologisms is a direct corollary of the massive productivity of *pi'el*, its active counterpart. *Huf'al* passives come second, reflecting the preference noted above for causatives in *hif'il, huf'al*'s active counterpart. This constitutes further support for the claim (e.g. in Aronoff 1976 and Baayen & Renouf 1996) that degree of productivity of a word formation pattern is often a function of the type of base from which it is, or may be argued to be, derived. Essentially, the rest of the data reinforce findings from the '70s, but some differences also emerge. Except for passives, the preferred pattern for 'focus on the theme' verbs (inchoative, reflexive, reciprocal) is again *hitpa'el*. Also, as expected, the percentage of subjects using *hitpa'el* is greater in the judgment tasks than it is in the coinage tests. In the judgment test, speakers are 'reminded' of the *hitpa'el* form being the most appropriate pattern for inchoatives, reflexives, reciprocals. On the other hand, the *hitpa'el* scores for all 'focus on the theme' cases are generally lower in the recent data than in the early ones. In the '70s tests, the *hitpa'el* scores generally ranged around 90% in the coinage tests and close to 100% in the judgment tasks. In the '90s tests scores ranged from 60%–80% *hitpa'el* cases in the coinage tests and 70%–90% in judgment tasks (see appendix III for details). The higher judgment scores are expected. The question is why the lowest scores for *hitpa'el* are that much lower. The subjects were students at teacher training college in both cases, the only difference being that in the recent tests, these students were specializing in Hebrew language. Perhaps greater awareness among the latter of 'more educated' alternatives, such as *hif'il* for inchoatives,[17] accounts for more subjects opting for non-*hitpa'el* variants, in both types of tests. Also, passive options made available in the recent tests may have drawn some of the scores that could have gone to *hitpa'el*.

A more significant difference is in the realization of causatives, where the earlier tests indicated preference for *hif'il* over *pi'el*. The preference was not as strong as for *hitpa'el* in 'focus on the theme' cases, but was still significant. In the later tests, however, *pi'el* clearly takes over as a causative marker, except for *hisnib* 'make one snobbish', where the wish to preserve the source transparently favors *hif'il*. A similar tendency will be observed in dictionary comparison below. Currently, it appears that *pi'el* is the preferred option for all agentives in which the agent is distinct from the patient, including causatives, for a number of reasons. As noted earlier, *pi'el* has always incorporated cause-to-be(come) causatives (i.e. factitives). Also, the border between causatives and general agentives is fuzzy since all agentives may be regarded as causatives, and *pi'el* is the unmarked, default realization for agentive verbs. Furthermore, some nouns can be realized as agentive verbs only in *pi'el* for phonetic reasons. When a large enough number of 'exceptions' are formed, there increases the likelihood of additional formations following suit by a sort of analogy. Again, as expected, the judgment tests reconfirm the tendencies observed in the coinage tests, except for some decline in *žileb* etc. 'make one big/crude' and *nixes* 'cause to be unlucky' (see Appendix III), probably because *hižlib* and *hinxis* preserve the source more transparently.

As in the earlier tests, general agentives clearly prefer *pi'el,* and the tendency is usually stronger in the judgment tests than in the coinage ones, except for some decline where *hif'il* preserves the base more effectively, as in *hizbing* 'give a blow', *hikrip* 'install crepe-like material on shoe sole' (see Appendix III). *hif'il* is also occasionally favored where the sentence frame provided could give rise to either general agentive or specific causative interpretation (*kerep/hikrip* 'install crepe-like material on shoe sole/make shoe "creppy"', *mitax/himtíax* 'invest in/turn into foreign currency', *bigec/hivgic* 'present to high court/subject to high court ruling', see Appendix III).

---

[17] As in *hilbin* 'whiten' being either causative or inchoative, or *hišmin* meaning either 'fatten (tr.)' or 'grow fat'.

A mixed picture emerges when ones considers the preservation of the transparency of the base while maintaining binyan choice. Below are some illustrations. Included are only forms whose base contains consonant clusters:

(11) **Illustrations of Structure-Preserving and Non-Structure-Preserving Configurations in the 1995/96 Verb Productivity Tests** (N subjects = 50, N bases = 23. Conf. = Configuration; Co. = Coinage tests; Ju. = Judgment tests; CP = Structure-Preserving; NCP = Non-Structure-Preserving. For details, see CP and NCP Status in Appendix III)

Base	Target Meaning	Binyan	Realization	Conf.	% Co.	% Ju.
'asfalt 'asphalt'	cover with asphalt	*pi'el*	*'isfelt*	CP	84	74
			'ispelt	CP	4	–
			'isflet	NCP	12	24
patent 'patent'	register as patent	*pi'el*	*pitent*	CP	56	50
			pintent	CP	12	14
			'iptent	CP	–	4
			pitnet	NCP	20	22
			pintet	NCP	4	–
			pinten	NCP	2	–
		hif'il	*hiptint*	NCP	–	8
zbeng 'blow'	give a blow	*pi'el*	*zibeng*	NCP	28	24
			zibneg	NCP	10	16
			zinbeg	NCP	10	4
			zimbeng	NCP	10	2
			zinbeng	NCP	4	–
			zimbeg	NCP	2	–
			zbineg	NCP	2	–
			zbingeg	CP	4	12
			tizbeng	CP	–	2
		hif'il	*hizbing*	CP	22	38
naxs 'bad luck'	cause to be unlucky	*pi'el*	*nixes*	NCP	70	52
			nixnes	NCP	2	–
			'inxes	NCP	–	8
			minxes	NCP	–	8
			nixses	CP	14	12
			nixsen	CP	4	2
			nixser	CP	2	–
		hif'il	*hinxis*	NCP	8	16

(12) **Summary of Structure-Preserving and Non-Structure-Preserving by Base** (see all relevant forms in Appendix III. N subjects = 50, N bases = 23)

Base	Target Meaning	%CP/Co	%CP/Jud	%NCP/Co	%NCP/Jud
pincéta 'tweezers'	tweeze	100	98	–	–
búnker 'bunker'	hide self in bunker	98	98	–	–
pitka 'note'	send each other notes	98	94	–	2
zálman 'sloppy dresser'	become sloppy dresser	88	92	–	4
'asfalt 'asphalt'	cover with asphalt	88	74	12	24
buldózer 'bulldozer'	bulldoze	72	96	2	–
patent 'patent'	register as patent	68	76	26	22
marks 'Marx'	become a Marxist	68	78	10	22
marks 'Marx'	make one a Marxist	72	78	24	22

(cont.)

Base	Target Meaning	%CP/Co	%CP/Jud	%NCP/Co	%NCP/Jud
'áfro 'afro hair style'	make hair afro-style	62	58	24	42
sport 'sports'	engage in sports	60	72	22	24
snob 'snob'	make one snobbish	60	60	36	38
blond(i(ni)) 'blond'	make blond	48	60	44	38
šmalc 'schmaltz'	make it schmaltzy	40	62	58	38
žlob 'big/crude'	make one big/crude	28	52	70	48
krep 'crepe-like material'	install this material on shoes	24	36	72	62
zbeng 'blow'	give a blow	26	52	66	46
snob 'snob'	become snobbish	22	22	62	78
žlob 'big/crude'	become big/crude	22	12	58	82
naxs 'bad luck'	cause to be unlucky	20	14	80	84
talk 'talcum powder'	spray with talcum	14	16	78	84
šmalc 'schmaltz'	become schmaltzy	12	28	66	72
talk 'talcum powder'	be sprayed w/talcum	6	14	86	80

(13) **Averages of scores (N bases = 23)**	**% Coin.**	**% Judg.**
Structure-preserving	52.00	58.35
Non-structure-preserving	38.96	39.65

The earlier tests indicated general preference for cluster-preserving variants. That preference is maintained in the later tests when the scores are averaged, but is not as dominant. When individual bases are considered, only in slightly more than half of the 23 bases do cluster-preserving variants constitute a majority. Also, whereas the earlier judgment test scores were almost always higher for forms preserving the consonant clustering of the base, this is not always the case in the recent tests. On the whole, cluster preservation is still the preferred option, particularly when the base lends itself to structure-preserving syllabic division that does not require the introduction of additional devices (e.g. *pitent* is preferred to *pitnet*, *'isfelt* to *'isflet*, *bildzer* to *blidzer*). When cluster preservation requires reduplication of the final consonant to maintain the clustering of the base, the NCP variant usually prevails (e.g. *tilek* over *tilkek*, *nixes* over *nixses*, *sineb* over *snobeb*). The reduplicated form is preferred only where it is supported independently. For example, in verbs derived from *marks*, the additional *s* is "supported" by the second *s* of *marksist* 'Marxist', *sportóto* 'proper name for a sports lottery' suggests an extra *t* in verbs based on *sport*, and *'afruri* 'grayish' may be claimed to play a role in adding an extra *r* to verbs from similarly-sounding *'áfro*. It appears that the cluster preservation principle continues to apply, but there may be some reluctance to maintain it at the price of reduplication. This difference from the earlier tests, in which reduplication was reinforced in the judgment tasks, may have something to

do with the later subjects specializing in Hebrew. The subjects' awareness of traditional grammatical norms may have been responsible
for the apparent preference for normative standards over innovative
transparency-preserving strategies such as reduplication.[18] Additional
tests involving non-students might throw more light on this question.
Note that decreased reduplication does not preclude the introduction of extra consonants not originating from the base. Just as Berman
(1990) reports on children adding consonants not found in the base
(see Chapter 2), so do our adult subjects on occasion (e.g. *šmilcen*
and *šmilcet* from *šmalc* rather than *šmilcec*, or *'ifren* and *'ifret* from *'áfro*
rather than *'ifrer*). *t* and *n* are preferred for insertion, as the least
marked consonants. Occasionally, subjects may even reduplicate or
simply add a consonant for no phonetic or cluster-preservation reason (e.g. *bigcec* from *bagac* or *žilben* from *žlob*). Such cases are relatively rare.

3.2.2 *Verb formation as reflected in dictionary comparison*

This section will deal with *binyan* productivity as reflected in comparisons between a newer and an earlier dictionary, or by analyz-
ing neologisms extracted from recent dictionary supplements. Of
recent verbs[19] listed in the Ben-Amotz & Ben-Yehuda (1972, 1982)
colloquial/slang dictionaries, 174[20] were not found in an earlier edition of Even-Shoshan (1970) published in 1963. Some of them were
already in existence in 1963, and their being excluded from the 1963
edition was due to their colloquial register, but the majority do constitute relatively-recent neologisms formed within a few decades preceding the publication of the Ben-Amotz/Ben-Yehuda dictionaries.
Although objections might be raised to the use of evidence from
slang, it has been shown (e.g. in Bolozky 1994b) that slang, being a
colloquial phenomenon, is characterized by the same word formation mechanisms operating on the general colloquial component of
the language. Appendix IV provides illustrations, incorporating about
a third of the data. Below is a sample:

---

[18] As already noted, the earlier group of subjects was composed of teacher trainees
as well, but not ones specializing in Hebrew language teaching.
[19] Actual new formations, not including the numerous new usages of existing verbs.
[20] Or 181, when forms that can be either theme-centered or agentive, e.g. *hilbin*
'whiten (tr. or intr.)', are regarded as separate entries, and thus counted twice.

(14) **Examples of recent verbs in the Ben-Amotz/Ben-Yehuda (1972, 1982) dictionaries that are not listed in Even-Shoshan (1963)**

I. FOCUS ON THE THEME
i. *Non-agentive (mostly inchoative)*

Form	Gloss	Source[21]	Gloss
hitpaʿel:			
hitfašel	fail (int.)	*fášla*	failure, flop; disappointment (Ar.)
hištafen	get scared	*šafan*	rabbit
nifʿal:			
nikvač	get squeezed, crumpled	*kveč*	soft, mushy matter (Ger.)
paʿal:			
xarap	(fall a)sleep soundly	*xrop*	(deep) sleep (Yid.)

ii. *Agentive, where agent is not distinct from patient (reflexive, reciprocal, etc.)*

hitpaʿel:			
hitbareg	squeeze (self) in	*bóreg*	screw
histalbet	indulge oneself in pleasure	*stam + batala*	mere + doing nothing
hictalcel	phone each other	*cilcel*	ring

iii. *Passive*

hufʿal:			
hoʿozav	be caused to leave, to resign	*ʿazav*	leave
hitpuʿal:			
hitputar	be made to resign	*hitpater + putar*	resign + be fired

II. INCHOATIVES/GENERAL AGENTIVES

hitpaʿel:			
hitbardek	be messed up; shirk work	*bardak*	chaos (< brothel (Trk.))
hitparxéax	become/behave like a hoodlum	*pirxax*	hoodlum

III. AGENTIVES
i. *Causatives*

hifʿil:			
higlič	cause one to slip	*glič/galaš*	skid, slip (Yid.)/slide (V)
hilxic	cause one to be tense	*laxac*	press, pressure (V)
piʿel:			
mistel	cause to be drunk	*mastul*	intoxicated, drugged (Ar.)
pindrek	over-spoil (child, etc.)	*mefunak + drek*	spoilt + disgusting thing/person (Ger.)

---

[21] Note that the sources/bases proposed are on occasion "best guesses;" the etymological information provided by the dictionaries concerned, if any, is not always reliable.

ii. *General agentives (if patient is involved, it is distinct from agent)*

Form	Gloss	Source	Gloss
pi'el:			
birber	speak nonsense	*diber* + onom.	speak + onomatopoeia
firgen	compliment others	*fargínen*	not begrudge (Yid.)
hif'il:			
hiknis	fine	*knas*	fine (N)
hisnif	snuff in cocain	*snaf*	snuff (Eng.)
hitpa'el:			
hit'agner	ignore	*'ignor*	ignore (Eng.)
hitparper	shirk duty; be unfaithful to one's spouse	*parpar*	butterfly
pa'al:			
gamaz	evaluate very negatively	*gámzu*	name of vitriolic Israeli critic

iii. *General agentives/causatives*

pi'el:			
fišel	mess up (tr. & int.)	*fášla*	failure, flop; disappointment (Ar.)

Here is the distribution of the total number of verbs in Ben-Amotz/Ben-Yehuda ('72/'82) that are not found in the 1963 edition of Even-Shoshan (N = 174; total verbs in Ben-Amotz/Ben-Yehuda = 304):

(15) Totals of verbs in Ben-Amotz/Ben-Yehuda '72/'82 not found in Even-Shoshan 1963

	hitpa'el	*hif'il*	*pi'el*	*nif'al*	*huf'al*	*pa'al*	*hitpu'al*
Focus on theme							
Non-agentive (mostly inch.)	35	–	–	2	–	1	–
Agentive (agent = patient . . .)	5	–	–	–	–	–	–
Passive	–	–	–	–	1	–	2
Inchoative/agentive	7	–	–	–	–	–	–
Agentive							
Causative	–	8	28	–	–	–	–
Agentive (if pat, not = agent)	8	8	64	–	–	1	–
Agentive/causative	–	–	4	–	–	–	–
total:	55	16	96	2	1	2	2

As in the productivity tests, *hitpa'el* is the preferred realization of focus-on-the-theme verbs, and agentive verbs tend to be realized in *pi'el* (even causatives). A similar picture emerges from analysis of new verb forms in the 1993 Hebrew and Army Slang Lexicon that are not found in Ben-Amotz/Ben-Yehuda ('72/'82), some of which are listed below (see Appendix V for more illustrations, incorporating about half of the data):

(16) **Some recent verbs in the Hebrew and Army Slang Lexicon (1993) that are not listed in Ben-Amotz/Ben-Yehuda (1972, 1982)**

I. FOCUS ON THE THEME

i. *Non-agentive (mostly inchoative)*

Form	Gloss	Source	Gloss
hitpa'el:			
hitbarber	get lost	? *hitbalbel*	get confused, mixed up
hitxarbeš	get messed up	*xára + xerbon +*	excrement (Ar.) + mess up (N) +

ii. *Agentive, where agent is not distinct from patient (reflexive, reciprocal, etc.)*

hitpa'el:			
hitfakes	focus oneself	*fókus*	focus
hitkaséax	fight with and confront someone verbally	*kásax*	sweeping, cleaning out (Ar. *kásaḥ*)

II. AGENTIVES

i. *Causatives*

hif'il:			
hišviz	depress, exhaust (tr.)	*šavur + záyin*	broken + penis
pi'el:			
fidéax	embarrass	*fādíḥa*	misfortune, calamity (Ar.)
šifcer	improve, strengthen[22]	*šiper + bicer*	improve + fortify

ii. *General agentives (if patient is involved, it is distinct from agent)*

pi'el:			
dija	work as DJ	*díjey*	disc jockey (Eng.)
pilfen	call by cellular phone	*pélefon*	cellular phone ('wonder phone')
milcer	work as a waiter	*melcar*	waiter
nifes	smoke pot	*náfas*	puff; smoking pot (Ar.)
hitpa'el			
hištanker	inform (on someone)	*štínker*	informer; stinker (Yid.)

The new data in the 1993 slang dictionary can be summarized in the following table (N = 44; total verbs in this dictionary = 786):

(17) **Totals verbs in the 1993 slang dictionary not found in Ben-Amotz/Ben-Yehuda '72/82**

	hitpa'el	*hif'il*	*pi'el*	*pa'al*
Focus on theme				
Non-agentive (mostly inch.)	8	–	–	–
Agentive (agent = patient . . .)	6	–	–	–
Agentive				
Causative	–	2	6	–
Agentive (if pat, not = agent)	4	1	15	2
total:	18	3	21	2

---

[22] This verb's meaning must have changed with time, since in Ben-Amotz/Ben-Yehuda (1982) it is glossed as 'speak too much, speak a lot of nonsense'.

As noted above, identifying neologisms through dictionary comparison is not limited to juxtaposing an older and a newer dictionary; the data may also be derived by counting new forms in a supplement to a dictionary. The 167 new verbs in the 1983 supplement to the 1970 edition of Even-Shoshan are distributed as follows (N = 167; total verbs in Even-Shoshan '83 = 332):

(18) **Totals of new verbs in the '83 supplement to Even-Shoshan (1970)**

	hitpaʿel	*nifʿal*	*puʿal*	*hufʿal*	*hifʿil*	*piʿel*	*paʿal*
Focus on theme							
Non-agentive (mostly inch.)	18	–	–	–	–	–	–
Passive	–	2	47	7	–	–	–
Agentive							
Causative	–	–	–	–	11	39	2
Agentive (if pat, not = agent)	2	–	–	–	–	39	–
total:	20	2	47	7	11	78	2

Below are some illustrations of realizations of new verbs in the different categories (for a more detailed list, see Appendix VI, which incorporates about a third of the data):

(19) **Some new verbs in the 1983 supplement to Even-Shoshan (1970)**

I. FOCUS ON THE THEME
i. *Non-agentive (mostly inchoative)*

Form	Gloss	Source	Gloss
hitpaʿel:			
hištaklel	become balanced	*šakul*	balanced
hitʾangel	become English	*ʾangli*	English

ii. *Passive*

nifʿal:			
nitmar	be permuted	*hitmir*	permute
nigmaz	be criticized severely	*gámaz*	criticize severely (< *gámzu*, see above)
puʿal:			
muxšav	be computerized	*mixšev*	computerize (< *maxšev* 'computer')
ʾuzrar	be divided into zones	*ʾizrer*	zone (V) (< *ʾezor* 'region')
hufʿal:			
hudran	be given as gift	*hidrin*	give as gift (< *doron* 'gift')

II. AGENTIVE

i. Causative

Form	Gloss	Source	Gloss
pi'el:			
mixšev	computerize	*maxšev*	computer
nirmel	normalize	*normáli*	normal
hif'il:			
he'egid	form a concern	*ta'agid/'igud*	concern/union
hitri	make fresh, freshen	*tari*	fresh

ii. General agentives (if patient is involved, it is distinct from agent)

pi'el:

kiter	complain	*kúter*	cat (Yid.)
ri'ayen	interview	*re'ayon*	interview (N)
hitpa'el:			
hištaxcen	become arrogant	*šaxcan*	arrogant; arrogant person

The predominance in productivity tests of *hitpa'el* for realization of theme-centered verbs and of *pi'el* for general agentives are strongly supported by the distribution of neologisms listed in all of these recent dictionaries or dictionary supplements. Similarly, reconfirming the trend suggested by scores of productivity tests conducted in the '90s, dictionary comparison also shows that *pi'el* is becoming the preferred marker of all agentive verbs, causatives included, pushing *hif'il* down the causative-marking hierarchy. Thus the relative scarcity of *hif'il* causatives compared with the number of causatives in *pi'el*. We do find a sizable number of *hif'il* causatives when an existing form acquires a new meaning, as in:

(20) **Form**	**Original Gloss**	**More Recent Gloss**
hiškiv	put down (usually to bed)	cause to have sex; cause to laugh
higniv	smuggle	cause wonder, admiration
hicníax	cause to parachute	appoint from outside

but only a few in actually-new forms.

That *pi'el* is gradually pushing *hif'il* aside as the preferred realization for causatives as well as all other agentives is also suggested by longtitudinal study of innovation through time. Examination of new *hif'il* forms listed in the supplement to Even-Shoshan (1963), which according to the introduction must have been completed in 1967 or 1968, indicates that *hif'il* continues to function as a productive causative pattern more in the literary register than in the everyday one, and is almost non-existent in exclusively-colloquial style, as shown below (totals and illustrations):

(21) **Totals of new *hif'il* verbs in the supplement to Even-Shoshan 1963**

	literary	colloq. only	everyday lexicon
causatives:	8	1	2
non-caus agentives:	1	–	1
causative/inchoatives:	1	–	2
Total:	10	1	5

(22) **Illustrating new *hif'il* verbs in the supplement to Even-Shoshan (1963) (1967 or 1968)**

Form	Gloss	Source	Gloss
LITERARY AND LITERARY-RARE:			
causatives:			
hitxiv	make damp	*ratov*	wet
hicpif	cause to be crowded	*cafuf*	crowded
general agentive:			
hivhin	walk on tiptoe	*bóhen*	toe
causatives/inchoative:			
hindir	make rare; become rare	*nadir*	rare
COLLOQUIAL ONLY:			
causative:			
hislik	cache, conceal	*slik*	cashe (N) < *silek* 'remove'?
EVERYDAY LEXICON:			
causatives:			
higmiš	make (more) flexible	*gamiš*	flexible
hifnim	internalize	*pnim*	interior
general agentive:			
hex(e)ri	defecate	*xára*	excrement (Ar.)
causatives/inchoatives:			
he'efir	make grey; turn grey	*'afor*	grey
hivgir	make into adult; become adult	*boger/ mevugar*	adult

Similar distribution emerges from *hif'il* forms in the Sivan/Levenston dictionary of 1967/77 that are not found in the 1963 edition of Even-Shoshan (illustrations immediately follow):

(23) **Totals of *hif'il* verbs in Sivan/Levenston 1967/77 not found in Even-Shoshan (1963)**

	literary	colloq. only	everyday lexicon
causatives:	10	–	4
general agentive:	1	–	1
causative/inchoative:	1	–	–
inchoatives:	1	–	–
Total:	13	0	5

(24) *hif'il* verbs in Sivan/Levenston (**1966/67**) that are not listed in Even-Shoshan (**1963**)

Form	Gloss	Source	Gloss
LITERARY AND LITERARY-RARE:			
causatives:			
he'ešir	make happy	*me'ušar*	happy
higxix	cause to smile	*gixex*	smile, chuckle
general agentives:			
hivrid	cover with hail, hail	*barad*	hail
causatives/inchoatives:			
higbin	make/become (like) cheese	*gvina*	cheese
inchoative:			
he'eziv	become covered with moss	*'ezov*	moss
EVERYDAY LEXICON:			
causatives:			
he'eziv	cause to leave	*'azav*	leave
hifrit	privatize	*prati*	private
general agentives:			
hivriš	clean with brush	*mivréšet*	brush

The number of new *hif'il* causatives declines even further in the 1983 supplement to the 1970 edition of Even-Shoshan (see above, and Appendix VI). There are only 12 new *hif'il* realizations. Although all of them are causative, they are also all literary or literary-rare.

It appears that the productivity of *hif'il* as a causative pattern is maintained to some extent in the literary register, but keeps declining in colloquial and everyday usage. As noted above, *pi'el* taking over may also be due in part to speakers frequently being unable to draw a distinction between causatives and other agentives. Most agentive verbs do involve a degree of causation; it is only for clarity of presentation that 'causative' is restricted in our discussion to 'cause to be/come' factitives and to 'cause to do'. The earlier preference for *hif'il* in causative realization among many of the subjects in tests from the '70s suggests that *hif'il* may still have been reasonably productive in the everyday lexicon when those tests were run. The *hif'il* preference may also be attributed to a more prescriptive, normative approach by the teachers of those student subjects characteristic of that period. During the two decades between the tests, recognition of the legitimacy of colloquial Hebrew has gained ground among language teachers. By the mid '90s, the preference for *hif'il* as a causative pattern had eroded, even for Hebrew language students and teacher trainees.

At first glance, the Ben-Amotz/Ben-Yehuda (1972/1982) list above appears to suggest that *hif'il* is becoming an alternative to *pi'el* for realization of new general (non-causative) agentives in the colloquial, but the number is misleading. Of the eight non-causative agentives, choice of *hif'il* for six of them allows preservation of the initial consonant cluster in the source stem, and in some cases the whole stem:

(25) **Form**   **Gloss**   **Source**   **Gloss**

Form	Gloss	Source	Gloss
hiknis	fine	*knas*	fine (N)
hiflic	pass wind, fart	*floc*	fart (N), passing wind (Yid.)
hiflik	hit	*flik*	a blow (Yid.)
hišpric	squirt	*špric*	squirt (N) (Yid.)
hišvic	brag; sweat	*švic*	bragging; sweat (Yid.)
hisnif	snuffed in cocain	*snaf*	snuff (N) (Eng.)

Original cluster preservation would not have been possible in the expected *pi'el*, which would have yielded **kines*, **filec*, **filek*, **šiprec*, **švec*, and **sinef* respectively. Apparently, cluster preservation considerations took precedence in these cases, in order to maintain the transparency of the base. These forms should not be interpreted as evidence for *hif'il* becoming a significant alternative to *pi'el* as a marker of non-causative agentive verbs.

As in the productivity tests, dictionary comparison also shows that although *hitpa'el* focuses on the theme, it may occasionally also be agentive. New *hitpa'el* agentives are found mostly in the slang dictionaries. As noted in the productivity tests, this is not unexpected. While *pi'el* is almost exclusively agentive, *hitpa'el*'s focus on the theme also incorporates reflexives and reciprocals, which involve the theme as well as an agentive element, though one that is not distinct from the patient/theme. Reflexives incorporate an agent that is one and the same as the patient/theme, and reciprocals involve two arguments with shifting agent and patient roles (or possibly even two agents, one of which is 'more patient-like'). The development of *hitpa'el* agentives is thus natural: a verb like *hitfaléax* 'sneak in without paying', for instance, may be viewed as a basic reflexive, 'sneaking oneself in', which has developed from an agent = patient predicate to a fully agentive verb. *hizdangef* 'walk around on Dizengoff St.' can be regarded as 'bringing oneself to be on Dizengoff St.', subsequently acquiring full agentive status. Most of these agentive *hitpa'el* verbs involve adopting some behavior, like *hitparper* 'shirk work; be unfaithful to wife', *hitbardek* 'be messy; shirk work', *hit'agner* 'ignore', *hitgases* 'use foul language'. They may all have started with a reflexive-type verb, meaning something like 'causing oneself to behave in a certain way', whose agentive aspect took over (i.e. the focus is no longer on the patient). Even-Shoshan (1970) itself contains about 150 agentive verbs in *hitpaʿel*, which suggests that there is a base for this realization in the established lexicon as well. Thus, while realization of agentive verbs in *hitpaʿel* is marginal, it is not insignificant, and in the future could perhaps even expand further, particularly in the colloquial register.

How should one rank patterns for productivity based on dictionary comparison? Since there exist patterns whose domain is limited to start with, but which within that domain can be quite productive, one would not want to measure productivity by absolute numbers only. Therefore, the number of innovations in a particular pattern should be considered in relation to its scope within the lexicon. However, as noted above, while the dictionary contains the total lexicon, speakers usually rely on its recent/new component, which is the most salient and most readily available model for further neologism. As both the total lexicon and its recent sub-component are relevant for the process of innovation, both should be taken into account. Below, 'ratio 1' (= R1) is the proportion of innovations in a particular pattern, within some semantic category (e.g. agentive), to the pattern's share of that category in the Even-Shoshan (1970) (= ES) base (e.g. all agentives in that pattern listed in ES). It is intended to measure the productivity of a pattern in capturing some semantic target meaning, relative to its size in the total lexicon (as reflected, with as much reliability as might be expected, in ES), in proportion to size rather than in absolute numbers. R1 thus characterizes 'internal' productivity within a morphological pattern, the degree to which a pattern 'regenerates itself' relative to its share within some semantic category in the total lexicon. 'Ratio 2' (= R2) is the proportion of the neologisms in a pattern to the total number of innovations in all patterns within the category concerned. By calculating the percentage of pattern realizations among all recent neologisms in a particular category, one captures the sense that productivity is to a large extent also dependent on speakers' awareness of how that category is realized in the recent, new lexicon, and that pattern's prominence in it. R2 thus reflects productivity of a pattern within some semantic category at the moment of innovation, which is what we are trying to characterize here. Thus patterns will be ranked for relative degree of productivity by R2, with secondary ordering by R1. If for two patterns ordered by relative R2 size, R1

exhibits the same relative ranking, it will mean that for that particular semantic category, the higher productivity of the first pattern
within the recent lexicon is reinforced by that pattern's propensity
to regenerate itself. It will also mean that speakers base their pattern choice in word formation not only on pattern salience in the
recent lexicon, but also on knowledge of what patterns are likely to
regenerate themselves in a particular category within the total lexicon. If for a pair of patterns, R1 ranking does not agree with R2
ordering, it could be attributed to a number of reasons, but all other
things being equal, it might signal a productive pattern whose scope
within the category concerned is limited to start with, but which still
maintains a high degree of productivity within that restricted scope.
In such a case, one might argue for ranking rearrangement if the
R1-to-R1 ratio of the second pattern to the first is higher than the
R2-to-R2 ratio of the first pattern to the second (henceforth 'ratio
weighting'). Such rearrangement, however, is only an indication of
ranking that would have applied had the category scope been confined
to the limits normally associated with the second pattern to start
with, resulting in higher R2 for the second pattern. Below are the
totals for dictionary comparison data on new verbs, where each column represents additional, new forms for a particular dictionary that
were not listed in the previous one.

(26) **Productivity ranking of verb patterns based on dictionary
comparison** (ES = Even-Shoshan 1970; ES '83 = ES 1983 Supplement;
BABY = Ben-Amotz/Ben-Yehuda 1972/1982;[23] PHAS = Prolog's Hebrew
and Army Slang Lexicon 1993. Verbs which are either focused on the
theme or agentive are counted twice).

FOCUS ON THEME
PASSIVE

R2 Ranking	ES	ES '83	BABY	PHAS	New	R1	R2	R1 Ranking	Alt. Order?
pu'al	1,595	47	–	–	47	.0295	.7833	hitpu'al	
huf'al	784	7	1	–	8	.0102	.1333	pu'al	{hitpu'al}
nif'al	480	2	2	–	4	.0083	.0667	huf'al	
hitpu'al	1	–	1	–	1	1.0000	.0167	nif'al	
			Total new:		60				

---

[23] In Chapters 4 and 5, the Ben-Amotz/Ben-Yehuda dictionary will be compared
with Even-Shoshan (1970). For verbs, the 1963 edition was used, to increase the
scope of the data.

NON-AGENTIVE (MOSTLY INCHOATIVE)

R2 Ranking	ES	ES '83	BABY	PHAS	New	R1	R2
hitpaᶜel	711	18	19	8	45	.0633	.9574
nifᶜal	547	–	2	–	2	.0037	.0426
paᶜal	276[24]	–	–	–	–		
hifᶜil	77	–	–	–	–		
piᶜel	65	–	–	–	–		

Total new: 47

AGENTIVE, WHERE AGENT IS NOT DISTINCT FROM PATIENT

R2 Ranking	ES	ES '83	BABY	PHAS	New	R1	R2
hitpaᶜel	228	–	11	6	17	.0746	1.0000
nifᶜal	138	–	–	–	–		
piᶜel	10	–	–	–	–		

Total new: 17

AGENTIVE

CAUSATIVE

R2 Ranking	ES	ES '83	BABY	PHAS	New	R1	R2
piᶜel	456	39	28	6	73	.1601	.7935
hifᶜil	949	11	5	2	18	.0190	.1957
paᶜal	56	1	–	–	1	.0179	.0109

Total new: 92

GENERAL AGENTIVE (IF PATIENT INVOLVED, IT IS DISTINCT FROM AGENT)

R2 Ranking	ES	ES '83	BABY	PHAS	New	R1	R2	R1 Ranking
piᶜel	1,462	39	44	15	98	.0670	.7538	*hitpaᶜel*
hitpaᶜel	148	2	15	4	21	.1419	.1615	*piᶜel*
hifᶜil	154	–	7	1	8	.0519	.0615	*hifᶜil*
paᶜal	1,036	–	1	2	3	.0029	.0231	*paᶜal*

Total new: 130

Patterns in which no basis for comparison exists were not considered. When ordering the patterns by R2, the productivity ranking is basically the same as the one established through the productivity tests:

---

[24] ES also contains over 400 entries of 'focus-on-the-theme' cases in *paᶜal* which do not fit either the inchoative category nor the reflexive/reciprocal one. They are, however, taken in account when the verb system is evaluated independently of semantic category in Chapter 6 below.

(27) **Summary of productivity ranking of verb patterns based on dictionary comparison**
    Focus on the Theme
        Passive: *pu'al, huf'al, nif'al*
        Non-agentive (inchoative): *hitpa'el, nif'al*
        Agentive, where agent is not distinct from patient: *hitpa'el*
    Agentive
        Causative: *pi'el, hif'il, pa'al*
        General Agentive: *pi'el, hitpa'el, hif'il, pa'al*

The only significant difference is that while in the productivity tests, *hif'il* is more productive in general agentive realization than *hitpa'el*, the latter is more productive according to dictionary comparison. This is probably a reflection of the increasing colloquial tendency noted above, manifest primarily in the slang dictionaries, for some agentives to be realized in *hitpa'el* in analogy with 'legitimate' *hitpa'el* agentives (reflexives and reciprocals). Actually, R1 of *hitpa'el*, its rate of internal 'regeneration' in the agentive category, is even higher than that of *pi'el* by dictionary comparison; the relative newness of this phenomenon means that the established ES base for *hitpa'el* agentives is comparatively small. But R2 for *pi'el* agentives is so much higher, that there is no doubt as to its ranking as the most productive pattern for this category. Another case in which R1 ranking does not agree with that of R2 ranking is in *hitpu'al* passives—again a reflection of the newness of the phenomenon, which means that the ES base for it is very limited. In this particular case, the ratio weighting method described above (reordering when the R1-to-R1 ratio of the second pattern to the first is higher than the R2-to-R2 ratio of the first pattern to the second) suggests that *hitpu'al* be raised to second position to precede *huf'al*, but such reordering would apply only if the category scope is severely restricted: *hitpu'al* is a relatively new hybrid between *hitpa'el* and *pu'al*, used exclusively for a reflexive action forced by an outside agent, e.g. 'being forced to resign' or 'being forced to volunteer'. Had the target semantic scope been restricted in this manner to start with, *hitpu'al* would have been at least second in ranking, perhaps even first. The tentative nature of this hypothetical reordering is indicated by bracketing.

3.2.3   *Data from a limited corpus on verb formation*

Limited corpora scanned by graduate students at Ben-Gurion University of the Negev indicate that the number of *hapax legomena* in *pi'el* is greater than those realized in *pa'al*,[25] which in itself already suggests that the former is more productive. The two corpora they used were merged, and combined with another small corpus, which resulted in a 132,000-word body of data, of which 65,000 were journalistic, 67,000 literary. The journalistic component of the corpus included two complete weekend issues of the afternoon papers *Ma'ariv* and *Yedi'ot 'axaronot* from January 1996. Selected articles from the morning papers *Ha'arec* and *Davar Rišon* from 1995/96, and to a lesser extent from the afternoon papers mentioned above, were also used. The literary component consisted of excerpts from novels by Aharon Meged, Me'ir Shalev, Dorit Abusch, Hayim Tal, Hasida Reti, and Revital Beck.

In a very large corpus, most *hapax legomena* will reflect productive innovation, since as noted above, innovative neologisms have not yet been sufficiently established to be repeated. There is no guarantee, of course, of the same happening in a small corpus. To nevertheless make a small corpus usable as a means of measuring productivity, one needs to ascertain that at least a portion of the *hapax* cases are relatively recent, reflecting productive tendencies that are current, not yet frozen by usage. To ensure that, we will only consider patterns in which a portion of the *hapax* forms are relatively recent, and require that at least one of these recent forms be a proven neologism. A proven neologism will be defined as an item that is not listed in Even-Shoshan (1970). Our 132k corpus does include a good number of relatively recent verb forms among the *hapax legomena* in all categories, notably in *pi'el* and in *hitpa'el*, as well as in *hif'il* (see Appendix VII for illustrations), and virtually none in *pa'al* or in *nif'al*. There are also four *bona fide* proven neologisms, three of which are not found in any dictionary (only *histalbet* is, in the slang dictionaries):

(28) **Very recent *hapax legomena* verbs in a 132k-word corpus**

FOCUS ON THEME
Agentive, where agent is not distinct from patient
Form   Gloss   Source   Gloss
hitpa'el:
hit'adken   updated oneself   *'idken*   update (tr.)
histalbet   indulge oneself in pleasure   *stam + batala* mere + doing nothing (sl.)
histaleb   variant of *histalbet*? (sl.)

---

[25] In Treivish & Matiash (1996), a journalistic corpus of 44,000 tokens contained 80 *hapax legomena* in *pa'al* out of 1,444 tokens (5.5%), while in *pi'el* the ratio was

(cont.)
AGENTIVE
General (non-causative) Agentive

Form	Gloss	Source	Gloss
pi'el:			
divšeš	pedal (V)	*davša*	pedal

Relative productivity based on corpus data will be calculated by a method similar to the one used in dictionary comparison. The total number of tokens for each pattern within a particular category in the corpus will represent the pattern's share in the total lexicon for that category, and the total number of *hapax legomena* for that category (at least some of which will constitute neologisms) will stand for the new lexicon. We will again calculate two ratios for each semantic category: (a) the ratio of the *hapax legomena* in a particular *binyan* within some category to the total number of its tokens within that category in the corpus (Ratio 1 = R1), and (b) the ratio of the *hapax legomena* in a particular *binyan* within some category to the total number of *hapax* verbs within that category in the corpus (Ratio 2 = R2). Below are the rankings, with ratios for patterns that do not qualify (in the absence of proven neologisms) placed between brackets:

(29) **Totals and ratios for *hapax legomena* verbs in a 132k-word corpus**

FOCUS ON THEME
PASSIVE

R2 Ranking	Tokens	*hapax*	R1	R2
pu'al	461	69	[.1497	.5188]
huf'al	347	49	[.1412	.3684]
nif'al	454	15	[.0330	.1128]
	Total *hapax*:	133		

NON-AGENTIVE TARGET MEANING (NON-PASSIVE), MOSTLY INCHOATIVE

R2 Ranking	Tokens	*hapax*	R1	R2	R1 Ranking
hitpa'el	717	55	[.0767	.3793]	*hitpa'el*
nif'al	551	36	[.0653	.2483]	*nif'al*
pa'al	2,861[26]	36	[.0126	.2483]	*pi'el*

---

almost double: 49 out of 523 tokens (9.4%); In Tsafrir (1995), where a 18,000 token literary sample was examined, 170 *hapax legomena* out of 1226 tokens were found in *pa'al* (13.9%), and 92 out of 288 in *pi'el* (32%, almost triple).

[26] As in the case of dictionary comparison, there were a significant number of

(cont.)

R2 Ranking	Tokens	*hapax*	R1	R2	R1 Ranking
hifʿil	705	10	[.0141	.0690]	*hifʿil*
piʿel	268	8	[.0299	.0552]	*paʿal*

Total *hapax*: 145

AGENTIVITY SUGGESTED, BUT AGENT NOT DISTINCT FROM PATIENT (REFLEXIVE, RECIPROCAL)

R2 Ranking	Tokens	*hapax*	R1	R2
hitpaʿel	443	42	.0948	.8571
nifʿal	213	7	[.0329	.1429]

Total *hapax*: 49

AGENTIVE

CAUSATIVE

R2 Ranking[27]	Tokens	*hapax*	R1	R2	R1 Ranking
hifʿil	1,049	52	[.0496	.7324]	*piʿel*
piʿel	85	19	[.2235	.2676]	*hifʿil*

Total *hapax*: 71

GENERAL AGENTIVE (IF PATIENT INVOLVED, IT IS DISTINCT FROM AGENT)

R2 Ranking	Tokens	*hapax*	R1	R2	R1 Ranking
piʿel	1,980	148	.0747	.6167	*piʿel*
paʿal	4,104	46	[.0112	.1917]	*nifʿal*
hifʿil	1,345	37	[.0275	.1542]	*hifʿil*
nifʿal	87	5	[.0575	.0208]	*hitpaʿel*
hitpaʿel	188	4	[.0213	.0167]	*paʿal*

Total *hapax*: 240

Since only two patterns, one for each major category, qualify for evaluation in this small corpus, we will not go into the details of the ranking. Strictly speaking, we can only say that corpus data support earlier findings that *hitpaʿel* is the most productive category for 'focus on the theme' realizations, and *piʿel* for general agentives. However, since the corpus does contain a good number of *hapax* forms that are new, albeit not very recent (see Appendix VII), we will tenta-

---

'focus-on-the-theme' cases in *paʿal* which did not fit either the inchoative category nor the reflexive/reciprocal one. These cases will be taken in account when the verb system is evaluated independently of semantic category in Chapter 6 below.

[27] There were also 27 causative realizations in *paʿal*, but none of them was a *hapax legomenon*.

tively ignore the brackets and consider all patterns within the general categories. In that case, we can show that productivity ranking based on corpus data, reflected in R2, generally corresponds to ranking by productivity tests and by dictionary comparison, with a few exceptions. The most notable difference is the relatively high ranking of *paʿal* for both inchoatives and general agentives, which probably reflects the significant number of *paʿal* realizations for these categories in the established lexicon: the corpus was too small to repeat rare *paʿal* items, which resulted in a relatively large number of *paʿal hapax* forms. Note that in both *paʿal* cases, the 'internal regeneration' rate, reflected by R1, is comparatively very low, as expected. In general agentives, R1 of *hifʿil* is 2.46 times that of *paʿal*'s, while R2 of the latter is only 1.24 times that of the former. It might be argued that since in a literary/journalistic corpus, *hifʿil* is still characteristically causative, it would have ranked higher than *paʿal* had the two been compared for causative realization only. A similar claim can be made for *hifʿil* and *piʿel* for causatives, where R2 is higher in *hifʿil*: while R2 of *hifʿil* is 2.7 times that of R2 of *piʿel*, R1 of the latter is 4.5 times R1 of the former. In a non-colloquial corpus, *piʿel* is still characteristically restricted to 'factitive' causatives; had the category been limited to factitives, *piʿel* would have outranked *hifʿil*. There are other cases where R1 ranking does not agree with R2 ranking, but there is no reason to believe that they are related to restricted scopes (the unexpectedly high R1 for *piʿel* among non-agentive, mostly inchoative, verbs is all due to highly literary forms). The ranking of *hitpaʿel* agentives is as low as it is in the productivity tests. Its higher position in ranking by dictionary comparison may be due to its higher frequency in slang, reflected in the two recent slang dictionaries.

We have shown that quantitative evidence from corpora, even when limited, supports findings from productivity tests and from dictionary comparison for the relative productivity of the various patterns in the modern Hebrew verb. In the next two chapters, the three evaluation methods will be applied to adjectives and to nouns, for the purpose of determining the extent to which the productivity rankings resulting from each one agree with those of the others.

CHAPTER FOUR

SELECTING ADJECTIVAL DERIVATION PATTERNS

A common way of forming new adjectives is by linearly appending the attributive suffix $+i$ ('having the characteristic of . . .'), often referred to by the Arabic term *nísba*. Such adjectives are generally derived from nominal bases (Ravid & Shlesinger 1987, Mor 1996), but derivation from base adjectives (e.g. *xiconi* 'external' from *xicon* 'external', *muxaši* 'tangible' from *muxaš* 'tangible'), or from adverbs (e.g. *miyadi* 'immediate' from *miyad* 'immediately', *mamaši* 'real' from *mamaš* 'really') is also possible. Derivation from adjectival bases is rare because it would be tautological, i.e. there is no real semantic need for it.[1] It does often apply to borrowed bases, though, because such bases are not regarded as adjectival to start with (e.g. *normal* > *normáli, puritan* > *puritáni*). The derivation is usually linear. Suppletion/ reduction may be involved (e.g. *mikre* 'event' > *mikri* 'accidental', *šlila* 'negation' > *šlili* 'negative'), or redupliction[1a] (e.g. *xag* 'holiday, cele-bration' > *xagigi* 'festive'), but few discontinuous *miškalim* are involved.[2]

However, as shown in Werner (1983) and Muchnik (1997), dis-continuous derivation of adjectives is equally common. If the form is directly related to a particular verb, adjectives are likely to be realized in the participial *benoni* forms. Deverbal adjectives that are identical to the passive participle (the so-called endstate 'resultative' adjectives, like closed, written, etc. in English), are nonconcatena-tively derived in *miškalim*. There four possible sources for resultatives: the verb patterns *CaCaC, niCCaC, CuCaC* and *huCCaC*, yielding *CaCuC, niCCaC, meCuCaC* and *muCCaC*, respectively. Other participial forms,

---

[1] Some exceptions: the *tipeš* 'a fool; foolish' > *tipši* 'foolish' group, as well as adjectives derived from ordinal numbers, as in *rišon* 'first' > *rišoni* 'primary, primeval; preliminary' (O. Schwarzwald, personal communication).

[1a] Cf. Neradim (1995).

[2] Neradim (1995, pp 58–60) notes a number of cases that might be attributed to *miškalim*, e.g. *gamloni* 'large and tall' from *gamal* 'camel' instead of the expected *gmaloni*. O. Schwarzwald (personal communication) also notes *CCiCi*, as in *plili* 'crim-inal,' *recini* 'serious.'

the 'active' ones (*meCaCeC, maCCiC, mitCaCeC, CoCeC*), can also function as adjectives, but since those tend to be agentive adjectives, and
are sometimes indistinguishable from their agentive noun counterparts, they will be discussed in the section on agents (Chapter 5).
The same applies to +*an* forms. Of the non-deverbal *miškalim*, one
salient pattern is *CaCiC*, used primarily for '+able'-type adjectives.

4.1   *Productivity tests on adjective formation*

The productivity tests described in Chapter 3 were conducted in
1995/96 at two Israeli teacher training colleges and at Ben-Gurion
University of the Negev. The same 50 subjects involved in the coinage
tests and comparable judgment tasks, were also given sentence frames
designed to elicit new adjectival formation, or were offered choices
from a variety of potential adjectives. When the suggested target
gloss centered on a verb, the breakdown of results was as follows
(see Appendix VIII (i) for details):

(1) **Tests where the suggested (adjectival) meaning involved a verb**
(N subjects = 50, N bases = 5. Co. = Coinage, Ju. = Judgment)

Pattern	% Co.	% Ju.	Illustrations
meCuCaC	75.2	76.4	*'anténa* 'antenna' > *me'unténet* 'equipped (f.) with antenna'
			xóken 'enema' > *mexukan* 'one given an enema'
			bagac 'high court' > *mevugécet* 'presented (f.) to high court'
muCCaC	7.6	4.8	*gril* 'grill' > *mugral* 'done on a grill'
			kével 'cable' > *muxbal/muxval* 'connected to cable'
CaCuC	4.8	7.6	*gril* 'grill' > *garul* 'done on a grill'
			kével 'cable' > *kavul* 'connected to cable'
niCCaC	.8	.4	*kével* 'cable' > *nixval* 'connected to cable'
			bagac 'high court' > *nivgécet* 'presented (f.) to high court'
mitCaCeC	–	.4	*'anténa* 'antenna' > *mit'anténet* 'equipped (f.) with antenna'
maCCiC	.4	–	*gril* 'grill' > *magril* 'done on a grill'
+*i*	5.6	4.0	*bagac* 'high court' > *bagácit/bagacístit* 'presented (f.) to high court'.
			gril 'grill' > *grili* 'done on a grill'
CaCiC	.8	.8	*gril* 'grill' > *garil* 'done on·a grill'

When the suggested adjectival meaning included a verb, the predominant pattern was the resultative *meCuCaC*, since its verbal source,
pu'al, is the automatic counterpart of the very productive *pi'el*. The

other endstate resultatives, *muCCaC* and *CaCuC*, follow far behind. Realizations in *niCCaC* were rare, partly because of the low productivity of *niCCaC* in general, and also because many of its realizations are not passive. *mitCaCeC* and *maCCiC* are marginal because they are never passive. +*i* is also marginal for such adjectives, and *CaCiC* even more so. The judgment tasks data confirm the findings of the open ones. When the suggested gloss of the form to be derived did not involve a verb, the default attributive adjectival form ending with +*i* was the first choice, as predicted, but resultatives occur as well, again with *meCuCaC* as the preferred option, and *muCCaC* and *CaCuC* far behind (see Appendix VIII (ii) for details):

(2) **Tests where the suggested (adjectival) meaning did not involve a verb** (N bases = 10)

Pattern	% Co.	% Ju.	Illustrations
+*i* and variants			
+*i*	64.4	60.6	*mexdal* 'criminal negligence' > *mexdalit* 'criminally negligent (f.)'
			kabaret 'cabaret' > *kabaréti/kabarti/kavarti* 'of cabaret'
			motel 'motel' > *motélit* 'of motel (f.)'
			búldog 'bulldog' > *búldogi* 'bulldog-like'
+*a'i*	3.4	11.0	*xárake* 'wild driving' > *xaraka'it/xarake'it* 'wild (f.) (driving)'
			sálmon 'salmon' > *salmona'i* 'of salmon'
+*an*+*i*	3.6	3.4	*mis'ada* 'restaurant' > *mis'adanit* 'of restaurant (f.)'
+*ist*+*i*	1.2	.6	*xárake* 'wild driving' > *xarakístit* 'wild (f.) (driving)'
+*ik*+*i*	1.6	–	*šabak* 'security police' > *šabáknikit* 'of security police (f.)'
+*on*+*i*	.6	.8	*mis'ada* 'restaurant' > *mis'adonit* 'of restaurant (f.)'
+*an*+*ér*+*i*	.2	–	*šabak* 'security police' > *šabakanérit* 'of security police (f.)'
Other adjectival patterns			
meCuCaC	15.2	18.6	*búldog* 'bulldog' > *mevuldag* 'bulldog-like'
			sálmon 'salmon' > *mesulman* 'of salmon'
			brezent 'tarp' > *mevurzant/mevruzant/mevurzan/mebruzant/mevorzan*
muCCaC	–	2.4	*xárake* 'wild driving' > *muxréket* 'wild (f.) (driving)'
			šabak 'security police' > *mušbéket* 'of security police (f.)'
CaCiC	.2	.8	*xárake* 'wild driving' > *xarika* 'wild (f.) (driving)'
CaCuC	.4	–	*xárake* 'wild driving' > *xaruka* 'wild (f.) (driving)'
+*ist*	.2	–	*búldog* 'bulldog' > *buldogist* 'bulldog-like'
+*on*	.2	–	*búldog* 'bulldog' > *buldogon* 'bulldog-like'

As we shall see in the section on agentives (Chapter 5), +*a'i* is normally an agent attribute, and in the colloquial it is often also used for the agent noun itself. For the purpose of determining broad adjective formation, its adjectival manifestation will be regarded here as a variant of +*i*. When all forms ending with +*i* are combined (including +*a'i*), the distribution is as follows:

(3) Tests where the suggested (adjectival) meaning did not involve a verb (N bases = 10)

Pattern	% Co.	% Ju.
+*i*	75.0	76.4
meCuCaC	15.2	18.6
muCCaC	–	2.4
CaCuC	.4	–
CaCiC	.2	.8
+*ist*	.2	–
+*on*	.2	–

There were two problems with the test design where the suggested adjectival meaning did not involve a verb. No '+able'-type target meanings were suggested that would have properly evaluated the productivity of the *CaCiC* pattern for adjectives, and the productivity of *muCCaC* for such adjectives cannot be reliably determined, since in a number of cases the given base would not have been pronounceable in a *muCCaC* configuration. In either case, evidence for productivity will be drawn from dictionary comparison and from corpus data. As for *CaCCan*, its productivity for adjective formation will be measured in the section on nouns, since native speakers find it difficult to distinguish between agentive nouns realized in this pattern and agentive adjectives associated with them.

The productivity test data on adjective formation again support the generalization that lexical formation tends to be semantically based and concept driven (Baayen & Renouf 1996, Clark 1993), as well as the claim that the productivity of a word formation pattern may vary significantly with the type of base from which it is likely to have been derived (Aronoff 1976 and Baayen & Renouf 1996). If the target meaning involves a verb, the nominal base from which the subject is requested to form an adjective is apparently no longer a noun. Rather, it is the unrealized intermediate stage of a passive verb form derived from it (e.g. *'anténa* 'antenna' > *'untan* 'be equipped with antenna'), which is then transformed into the passive participial adjectival resultative form (*me'untan*). If no verb is involved, the preferred adjectival realization is +*i*-affixation. One can look at this dichotomy in two ways: semantically, as a choice between adjectives expressing 'the result of a process' and mere attributive formation; or morphologically, between derivation from essentially verbal bases and truly nominal ones.

4.2   *Adjective formation as reflected in dictionary comparison*

Dictionary comparison, as outlined above, independently confirms
the relative productivity of adjective formation patterns manifest in
the productivity tests.[3] Below are some illustrations (ES = Even-
Shoshan 1970; BABY = Ben-Amotz/Ben-Yehuda 1972/1982; PHAS =
Prolog's Hebrew Army and Slang Lexicon 1993); for more detailed
lists, see Appendices IX–XI):

**(4) New adjectives in the 1983 ES Supplement (not found in ES
1970 proper)**

Form	Gloss	Source	Gloss
meCuCaC:			
medupras	depressed	*dipres*	depress (< *diprésya* 'depression')
memuxšav	computerized	*muxšav*	be computerized (< *maxšev* 'computer')
muCCaC:			
mulad	inborn, innate	*hulad*	be caused to be born (< *yalad* 'give birth')
mo'ošar	enriched	*ho'ošar*	be enriched (< *'ašir* 'rich')
CaCuC:			
dafuy	imperfect, flawed	*dófi*	fault, flaw
xašuy	secretive, clandestine	*xaša'i*	secret
niCCaC:[4]			
nirhav	majestic	*marhiv*	majestic
+*i* Adjectives:			
btixuti	of safety	*b(e)tixut*	safety
mimsadi	of the establishment	*mimsad*	establishment
CaCiC:			
'axif	enforceable	*'axaf*	enforce
hafix	reversible	*hafax*	turn over, reverse
CaCeC:			
cadek	legitimate	*cadak*	be right

**(5) New adjectives in BABY '72/'82 not found in ES 1970 (or its
'83 supplement)**

Form	Gloss	Source	Gloss
mevurdak	disorganized	*bardak*	brothel (Trk.)
memustal	drunk, drugged	*mastul*	intoxicated, drunk (Ar.)

---

[3] Of the established adjectival patterns that are clearly no longer productive
(except, perhaps, in the realm Hebrew Language Academy innovations), only *CaCeC*
realizations have been scanned for our purposes here. Although one could have
included other patterns, even ones that tend to be associated with specific semantic traits (e.g. *CaCoC/CaCuC*, used mostly for colors and shapes, *CiCeC*, often referring to physical defects, *CaCaC*, etc.), their very limited productivity would have
made such exercise rather redundant.

[4] There are also some 'resultative' nouns in *niCCaC* in ES '83: *nišgar* 'consignee',
nimxe 'assignee'.

(cont.)

Form	Gloss	Source	Gloss
muCCaC:			
muštan	humiliated; of little value	šéten/ hištin	urine/urinate
CaCuC:			
faclu(a)x	useless; ugly (not obvious that belongs to this pattern)		
niCCaC:			
nexcac	ugly	?xacac	gravel
+*i* Adjectives:			
cahali	of the Israeli army	cáhal	I.D.F (Israel Defense Army) (acronym of *cva hagana le-yisra'el*)
davka'i	stubborn	dávka	in spite of, on the contrary
CaCiC:			
xatix	hunk	xatixa	attractive girl

(6) **New adjectives in PHAS '93 not found in BABY or ES (or its '83 supplement)**

Form	Gloss	Source	Gloss
meCuCaC:			
memuna‘	mobile (with car)	manóa‘	motor, engine
mevo'as	depressed	bá(')asa	misery, distress (Ar. *ba'sā'*)
muCCaC:			
mutraf	exceptional, exciting	hitríf	drive crazy (< *metoraf* 'crazy')
CaCuC:			
šavuz	devastated, disgusted feeling	šavur + záyin	broken + penis
+*i* Adjectives:			
xalavi	indecisive	xalav	milk
CaCiC:			
[yaziz	partner (sex and friendship w/o marriage)	yadid + záyin	friend + penis]

Below are the totals for data on adjective formation derived from dictionary comparison, ranked for relative productivity in the manner used in Chapter 3 for ranking verb patterns for relative productivity:

(7) **Productivity ranking of adjective formation patterns based on dictionary comparison**

R2 Ranking	ES	ES '83	BABY	PHAS	New	R1	R2	R1 Rank	Alt Order
+*i* Adj.	2,690[5]	120 (247)[6]	72	3	195	.0725	.5945	+*i* Adj.	
meCuCaC	1,320	56	20	6	82	.0621	.2500	*CaCiC*	

---

[5] Including borrowings; of those, 2,003 are native Hebrew adjectives. Although it might be argued that suffixes like + *ívi* (*'impulsívi*, *'eksklusívi*, etc.), + *áli* (*frontáli, monumentáli*, etc.) should be treated separately, they were all included under +*i* here, since it appears that they were generally borrowed into Hebrew as 'atomic' adjectival units ending with +*i*.

[6] As noted above, one expects some of the forms in a supplement to a dictionary

(cont.)

R2 Ranking	ES	ES '83	BABY	PHAS	New	R1	R2	R1 Rank	Alt Order
CaCiC	297	17 (16 lit.)	2(4)[7]	1?	20	.0673	.0610	meCuCaC	
CaCuC	1,132	10 (9 lit.)	1?	3	14	.0124	.0427	niCCaC	muCCaC
muCCaC	376	5	4	1	10	.0266	.0305	muCCaC	CaCuC
niCCaC	104	4 (all lit.)	1	–	5	.0481	.0252	CaCeC	
CaCeC	98	2 (1 lit.)	–	–	2	.0204	.0061	CaCuC	

Total New: 328

Based on these calculations, +*i*-adjective formation appears to be the most productive adjective formation device, regardless of base. *meCuCaC* is second in the general ranking, and its status as the most productive of the verb-related patterns is confirmed. *CaCuC* and *muCCaC* are lower than *meCuCaC*, as expected. But their relative ordering with respect to each other is not what the productivity tests predict, and an argument can be made for reversing it: 9 of the 10 *CaCuC* innovations are literary, which weakens the pattern's claim for productivity. Also, R1 for *muCCaC* is more than double the R1 of *CaCuC*, whereas R2 of the latter is only 1.4 times that of *muCCaC*. These considerations support a *muCCaC—CaCuC* ordering for dictionary comparison, consistent with findings from the productivity tests. R1 of *niCCaC* is also relatively high, but *niCCaC* should not be ranked higher, since most of its new forms are literary. The relatively-high ranking of *CaCiC* in third place is expected, and would probably have been higher had the category been limited to '+able-type' adjectives, but its R2 is significantly lower than that of *meCuCaC*. The positioning of *CaCeC* as the least productive adjective formation pattern is also expected.

Back to the internal distribution of resultatives, Mirkin (1968)[8] esti-

---

to constitute omissions, but the proportion of omissions is quite low when compared with actual innovations (or colloquial items that have been standardized). In this case, however, their percentage is high: about half of the 247 occurrences are well-established borrowed adjectives, as well as gentilic adjectives (*'angli, rusi*, etc.), which for some reason were not included in the earlier version of the dictionary. Only 120 are *bona fide* relatively-recent additions.

[7] It is 4 if borrowed *xafif* 'light, casual' and *tawil* 'tall, long' (both from Arabic) also count as belonging to this same *miškal*.

[8] Mirkin (1968b) disagrees with Rosén (1956), who argues for separation between 'verbal' *meCuCaC* and 'nominal' *meCuCaC* (which have not been included in this study). Mirkin argues that *meCuCaC* forms are either automatically both 'verbal' and

mates that there are about 2,500 realizations in *meCuCaC*, while only a bit over 1,300 were found in Even-Shoshan (1970). The rest may be either forms that were 'too automatic' or too colloquial for Even-Shoshan to list, or literary innovations of particular authors which Even-Shoshan chose not to list or of which he was not aware.

The strong preference for *meCuCaC* over the other resultative patterns is due to a number of reasons:

* The relationship to the very productive *CiCeC* or *hitCaCeC* patterns. All transitive *CiCeC* verbs may have related *meCuCaC* adjectives, which accounts for a very large number of forms, and many *hitCaCeC* verbs have related *meCuCaC* adjectives as well.

* Stems with four, five, or even six consonants, which are so common among recent innovations based on borrowings, can only be realized in *meCuCaC* for phonetic reasons. As noted above, each *C* may also stand for a cluster of consonants extracted from the base. The trisyllabic structure of *meCuCaC* thus maximizes the number of consonants that may be incorporated.

* *meCuCaC* is more transparent than *muCCaC*. The present participle prefix *me+* is clearly separated from the stem, in which the *u_a* pattern characterizing the passive is fully transparent. In *muCCaC*, on the other hand, it is not obvious to the speaker/hearer that *m+* and not *mu+* is the present participle prefix; if *mu+* is regarded as the carrier of the present participle, the *u_a* passive pattern marker loses some of its transparency.

* Most of *CaCuC* slots are already occupied, which restricts the number of innovations in it. There are many new uses for existing *CaCuC* forms, as in the following (taken from the slang dictionaries), but relatively few actual morphological neologisms can be found in *CaCuC*.

(8) **Some existing *CaCuC* forms whose meaning changes in slang usage**

Form	Regular Meaning	Slang Usage
daluk (*'al*)	lighted	enthusiastic (about), admiring
karúaʿ (*'al*)	torn	very much in love (with)

'nominal', or they exist independently of preexisting verbs. He also emphasizes the relationship of *meCuCaC* to the 'heavy' *binyanim*, particularly *CiCeC*, and notes that while being essentially passive, *meCuCaC* is not always perfective.

(cont.)

Form	Regular Meaning	Slang Usage
xalud	rusted	very old (person)
xafur	dug (in)	in a very bad mood
maxuk	erased	exhausted; not worthy of attention
ganuv	stolen	very nice, very desirable
šafut (ʿal)	judged	desperately in love (with)
harus (ʿal)	destroyed	desperately in love (with)

As for adjectives that are not verb-related, +*i* suffixation is quite dominant, and *CaCiC* realizations are typically literary. As noted above, there are many new entries with +*an*, but since most of them function as nouns as well as adjectives, they will be discussed in the section on innovations in the noun system (Chapter 5).

4.3   *Evidence from corpora on adjective formation*

Mor (1994, 1995, to appear) notes that in the writings of authors like David Vogel, as well as in current journalistic writing, new verb-related resultative adjectives are formed, and that the preferred order of distribution among the patterns again seems to be *meCuCaC-muCCaC-CaCuC*.

To ascertain that the number of resultative *hapax legomena* is also correlated with recently formed neologisms (which are also infrequent, mostly because they have not existed long enough), a 3,750,000 journalistic corpus was (manually) examined by Mor. It comprised of samples collected from news stories, articles, economic sections and sports published in the Israeli press (*Haʾárec, Maʿariv* and *Yedíʿot ʾaxaronot, Davar Rišon, Sfarim, Haʿir, Sofšavuaʿ, Mišor, Ha-Kibuc*) in the period between the end of February, 1995 to the end of May, 1996. Only resultative adjectives were counted. Below are the *hapax legomena* found:

(9) **hapax legomena resultative adjectives in a 3,750k journalistic corpus (Mor)**

Form	Gloss	Source	Gloss
meCuCaC:			
mepluntar	entangled (recent)	*plónter*	a tangle
megumgam	stammered, incoherent	*gimgem*	stammer
mefohak	drowsy; dreary/empty; wide	*pihek*	yawn
memugan	armored, bullet-proof	*magen*	shield

(cont.)

Form	Gloss	Source	Gloss
mekutav	in complete contradiction	*kitev/kótev*	polarize/pole
mesuxak	well-played; appealing	*sixek*	play, act
muCCaC:			
mulhat	red hot (recent)	*hilhit/lohet*	make very hot/ red hot
muchar	declared	*hichir*	declare
mugmar	finished	*gamar/gimer*	finish
CaCuC:			
saxuf	swept, carried away, dragged	*saxaf*	sweep

The *hapax*-to-token and *hapax*-to-total *hapax* ratios are as follows (token numbers are rounded up; note that only adjectival occurrences are counted):[9]

(10) **Productivity ranking of resultative adjectives in Mor's data**

R2 Ranking	Tokens	*hapax*	R1	R2
meCuCaC	17,625	6	.0000340	.6000
muCCaC	9,750	3	.0000308	.3000
CaCuC	14,250	1	.0000070	.1000
	Total *hapax*:	10		

Thus the corpus confirms that *meCuCaC* is the most productive resultative adjective, followed by *muCCaC*. But since the Mor data did not cover adjectives that are not derived from verbs, an additional journalistic/literary corpus was scanned, consisting of about 112,000 words (only about a half of which overlapped the corpus used for verbs in Chapter 3). When a corpus is this small, *hapax legomena* may very well be accidental, reflecting neither low frequency nor recent innovation. To eliminate some of the arbitrariness involved, we will again constrain the evaluation of productivity in a small corpus, and only measure the relative productivity of patterns in which a portion of the *hapax* forms are relatively recent, and where at least one form is a proven neologism, which for our purposes will refer to an item that is not listed in Even-Shoshan (1970). Once at least one neologism has been identified, the pattern will be categorized as productive. Relative productivity will be determined only with respect to other patterns in which at least one neologism has been found. Below

---

[9] Additional realizations when the relevant forms were used as inflected verbs (and occasionally as nouns): *meCuCaC* about 7,200, *muCCaC* approximately 6,000, *CaCuC* about 7,500.

is the list of *hapax legomena* in the corpus that are clearly new, at least in the sense that they do not appear in ES (1970):

(11) **Recent innovations in a 112k corpus**

Form	Gloss	Source	Gloss
+*i*-Adjectives			
ʿarisati	of the crib	ʿarisa	crib
ʿatidi	of the future	ʿatid	future
btixuti	of safety	b(e)tixut	safety
cahali	of the Israeli army	cáhal	I.D.F (Israel Defense Army) (acronym of *cva hagana le-yisra'el*)
derugi	scaled	derug	scaling
késtneri	of (Erich) Kästner	Kästner	German author of children's lit.
sarsuri	of pimp; of go-between	sarsur	pimp; go-between
siʿudi	requiring assistance (especially when disabled)	siʿud/sáʿad	assistance, welfare
šikumi	of rehabilitation	šikum	rehabilitation
tluti	dependent	tlut	dependency
yamtixoni	Mediterranean	ha-yam ha-tixon	the Mediterranean sea
'elizabetáni	Elizabethan	'elízabet	Elizabeth
'ekológi	ecological	ekológya -	ecology
bitni	of the stomach	béten	stomach, belly
kfiyati	compulsive	kfiya	complulsion
mimuši	tangible, made real	mimuš	realizing, making real
míti	mythical	mítos	myth
narkisísti	narcissistic	narkis	Narcissus
kartézyáni	Cartisian	kartézyus	de Cartes
siloni	like a jet	silon	jet
šimši	sunny; of the sun	šémeš	sun
šivuki	of marketing	šivuk	marketing
telavívi	of Tel Aviv	telaviv	Tel Aviv
tikšorti	of the media	tikšóret	communications; media
wóspi	WASPy	wósp	WASP (Eng.)
yelidi	native	yelid	native (N)
CaCiC:			
šafir	not malignant	šafar	be good
zaniáx	negligible	zanax	neglect
meCuCaC:			
metuskal	frustrated	tiskel	frustrate
meyusam	applied	yisem	apply (< *sam* 'put, place')

The distribution of adjectives in the limited corpus was as follows:

(12) **Productivity ranking of adjective formation patterns based on a 112k corpus**

R2 Ranking	Tokens	*hapax*	R1	R2	R1 Ranking
+*i* Adj.	1,982	252	.1271	.4818	*meCuCaC*
meCuCaC	691	101	.1462	.1940	+*i* Adj.

(cont.)

R2 Ranking	Tokens	*hapax*	R1	R2	R1 Ranking
CaCiC	525	21	.0400	.0401	CaCiC
muCCaC	173	25	[.1445	.0478]	
CaCuC	1,015	102	[.1005	.1950]	
niCCaC	228	10	[.0438	.0191]	
CaCeC	554	12	[.0217	.0229]	
CaCaC/ CaC	369	–			

Total *hapax*: 523

Only three of the patterns concerned (those whose ratios are not placed within square brackets) fulfill the recent component requirement, and R2 ranking confirms the expected productivity order: +*i*—*meCuCaC*—*CaCiC*. Although R1 of *meCuCaC* is 1.15 times larger than R1 of +*i*-adjectives, the latter's R2 is 2.48 times that of the former, which more than adequately justifies their relative ordering.

Thus, corpus data reinforce other findings showing that the preferred patterns for deriving adjectives are *meCuCaC* for verb-related bases and +*i* suffixation otherwise, which makes the latter the default adjective-formation device. 'Able'-type adjectives tend to be realized in *CaCiC*.

4.4   *A productive, borrowed adjective formation pattern?*

The slang dictionaries of Israeli Hebrew include a significant number of words in *maCCuC* that are borrowed from Arabic *maCCūC*, as in:

(13) **Form**	**Gloss**	**Form**	**Gloss**
mabsut	happy, satisfied	*majnun*	crazy
mastul	drunk, drugged	*maxruk*	'burnt' in love, enthusiastic
maꞩun	wicked and cunning	*(ꞌaxul-)manyuk*	'bastardy' (affectionate)

The above have clear Arabic counterparts (category A). Other realizations in this pattern originate from an Arabic root, but Arabic has no *maCCūC* counterparts (category B), and there are innovations in *maCCuC* that are totally unrelated to any existing Arabic source (category C). Items in category A are borrowed as individual items, and by themselves do not prove the existence of a new pattern in Hebrew. It is items in categories B and C, as in the table below, that will determine whether Israeli Hebrew has adopted *maCCuC* as a productive pattern (all realizations quoted are from the 1972/1982 Ben-Amotz/Ben-Yehuda slang dictionary):

(14) *maCCuC* forms in Israeli Hebrew, according to Ben-Amotz/Ben-Yehuda '72/'82

Form	Gloss	Arabic Counterpart	Gloss	Possible Hebrew Source	Gloss
mabʿus	depressed	*bāʾis*	wretched		
		báʾsāʾ	wretchedness		
maxlu	disgusting; corrupt	*maxlūʿ*	wild; immoral; outcast; coward	*maxli*	sickening
manfus	drugged from smoking hash	*náfas*	puff of smoke		
maskun	poor, miserable	*miskīn*	poor, miserable	*misken*	miserable
maltux	stupid	*láṭix*	dirty, impure		
		lúṭaxa	ass; stupid		
maxnut(a)	ugly	*muḥánnaṭ*	mummified	*xanut*	mummified
mafluc(a)	disgusting			*miflécet*	monster
masrux	stinking			*masríax*	stinking
masxut	exhausted			*saxut*	exhausted

Israeli Hebrew slang has clearly borrowed the discontinuous Arabic *maCCūC* as a productive adjectival pattern. What is yet unclear is the extent of this phenomenon and the degree to which it is still productive today. Although this word-formation device belongs in the slang register, slang often reflects productive innovative trends that may in turn show up in the standard register as well. However, the distribution of the relevant forms is unclear even within the realm of slang. Except for *maxlú(a)* 'disgusting; corrupt', the critical words of categories B and C (i.e. those illustrated in the above table), all included in the Ben-Amotz/Ben-Yehuda dictionary, are not re-listed in the 1993 Prolog slang dictionary. The question, then, is whether the new *maCCuC* pattern constitutes a temporary phenomenon, originating from the 'Palmach (1948) generation' and currently losing its productive quality (and in fact, pointing out to decrease in the influence of Arabic on Israeli Hebrew owing to its declining prestige value). Another possibility is that the Prolog dictionary simply fails to reflect a current reality in which *maCCuC* continues to be productive today, owing to contact with the Palestinian population, and/or innovations originating from second generation of speakers of Judeo-Arabic in the Army. In 1994, a pilot study was conducted. Thirty two speakers, chosen randomly, were presented with the above items, and they were asked to explain the meaning of the ones with which they are familiar, and add forms in the same word-formation pattern that were not included in the sample. When direct borrowings from Arabic were excluded, the data for subjects (out of a 32) who understood each particular form were as follows:

(15) **Findings from a random sample of 32 speakers** (yes = understand/use the form, out of 32)

Form	Gloss	Source	Gloss	Yes
maskun	poor, miserable	*misken*	poor, miserable	27
mab'us	depressed	*mevo'as*	depressed	24
			(< Ar. *ba'sā'* 'misery')	
masrux	stinking	*masríax*	stinking	23
maxlúa/ maxlu	disgusting; corrupt	*maxli*	disgusting	16
maflúc(a)	disgusting	*miflécet*	monster	12
masxut	exhausted	*saxut*	wrung out, exhausted	11
manfus	drugged from smoking (hash)	*náfas*	puff of smoke (Ar.)	7
maxnut(a)	ugly	*xanut(a)*	mummified	5
maltux	stupid	*lúṭaxa*	ass; stupid (Ar.)	2

A number of additional forms offered by individuals:

(16) **Additional forms offered by individuals (among the 32 above)**

Form	Gloss	Source	Gloss	Yes
magnuv	wonderful, attractive	*magniv*	wonderful, attractive	21
mag'ul	disgusting	*mag'il*	disgusting	3
madluk	enthusiastic	*madlik*	causing enthusiasm	1
maftúxa	no longer a virgin	*ptuxa*	open	1
man'ul	pent up, not open	*na'ul*	locked	1

A small sub-group of the 32 speakers surveyed noted that they actively use some or most of these forms. Such speakers tended to be older and to have some knowledge of, or background in, Arabic. The majority of those who identified items, and even some of those who proposed additional ones, stated that they heard the forms but rarely use it themselves, except for *magnuv* 'wonderful, attractive' (< *magniv*) and *maxlúa/ maxlu* 'disgusting; corrupt', which appear to be used generally. So as a creative pattern, *maCCuC* seems to be only marginally productive in current Israeli Hebrew. At the same time, however, speakers did offer additional forms in *maCCuC* not borrowed directly from Arabic and not listed in any dictionary, which suggested that additional tests would be useful.

In January 1995, 17 students from the Hebrew Language department of Ben-Gurion University were presented with an extended questionnaire containing dictionary items as well as all those added by earlier subjects. Again, note that this was still an inquiry of a preliminary nature, not a proper psycholinguistic experiment, and that most speakers appear to have passive knowledge of these forms. Only a minority report that they would use (some of) them actively:

(17) **January 1995 questionnaire filled in by 17 Hebrew Lang. students at Ben-Gurion U**

Form	Gloss	Source	Gloss	Yes
maxlúa/maxlu	disgusting; corrupt	*maxli*	disgusting	8
maftúxa	no longer a virgin	*ptuxa*	open	7
mab'us	depressed	*mevo'as*	depressed	6
			(< Ar. *ba'sā'* 'misery')	
maskun	poor, miserable	*misken*	poor, miserable	5
magnuv	wonderful, attractive	*magniv*	wonderful, attractive	4
masrux	stinking	*masríax*	stinking	4
mag'ul	disgusting	*mag'il*	disgusting	4
madluk	enthusiastic	*madlik*	causing enthusiasm	2
manfus	drugged from smoking (hash)	*náfas*	puff of smoke (Ar.)	1
maltux	stupid	*lútaxa*	ass; stupid (Ar.)	1
maftúc(a)	disgusting	*miflécet*	monster	1
masxut	exhausted	*saxut*	wrung out, exhausted	1
maxlul	hollow-headed	*xalul*	hollow	1

As in previous surveys, speakers feeling more comfortable with these items were older students and/or ones with knowledge of Arabic. On the other hand, no additional forms (beyond the ones added by speakers surveyed earlier) were offered by this group, which suggests that the productivity of this pattern is limited.

This is probably the only instance of a discontinuous word-formation pattern having been borrowed into Israeli Hebrew. Even if similar borrowing ever occurred at some earlier phase of the language, it must have been rare. But with the decline in the role and in the prestige value of Arabic in Israeli life, the productivity of *maCCuC* is clearly decreasing. The pre-existing small group of native Hebrew nouns in *maCCuC* neither impedes the reception of the *maCCuC* pattern from Arabic nor does it enhance it, since native *maCCuC* is not productive. The number of native *maCCuC* occurrences is very limited (about 15), and with the exception of

(18) *man'ul* 'lock'   *maslul* 'lane'
     malbuš 'piece of clothing'   *macpun* 'conscience'

they are all literary-rare. Also, it is a noun pattern, whereas the borrowed one is a resultative adjectival pattern. Apparently, the immense productivity of *meCuCaC* (and the relative productivity of *muCCaC* and to a lesser extent *CaCuC*) constitutes appropriate background for the reception of *maCCūC* from Arabic as an additional passive participle used for adjectives. At the same time, however, the limited productivity of the new *maCCuC* is in part due to the fact that it does not seem to be associated with any particular class of verbs, whereas *meCuCaC*, for instance, can be realized as the passive participle of almost any transitive verb in *piᶜel*.

CHAPTER FIVE

SELECTING NOMINAL DERIVATION PATTERNS

5.1 *Nominal pattern formation: an overview*

We have seen that both adjectives and nouns can be derived from verbs. Passive participial *benoni* yields endstate resultative adjectives (e.g. *memuxšav* 'computerized', *medupras* 'depressed', see Chapter 4). Active participles yield agent nouns (e.g. *šomer* is 'guard/a guard', *menahel* is 'manage/manager', *mitnadev* is 'volunteer/a volunteer', *madrix* is 'guide/a guide'), or adjectives (e.g. *bolet* 'prominent', *meša'amem* 'boring', *mitkadem* 'progressive', *macxik* 'funny'). However, adjective formation differs from agentive noun formation. The very productive +*i*-suffixation, which serves as the unmarked choice for adjectives derived from non-verb-related bases, allows resultative patterns like *meCuCaC* to take precedence in verb-associated forms. On the other hand, verb-based agent-formation patterns like +*an* and +*a'i* directly compete with the active participle. As for deriving nouns from verbs, Berman (1978) distinguishes between the infinitive absolute, functioning in adverbial constructions (e.g. *'im rédet haxašexa* 'with the fall of darkness', *besaymo* 'upon his completing') or in nominal ones (e.g. *bo'o* 'his coming', *šuvo* 'his return') which she identifies as the gerund, and the abstract derived nouns associated with the *binyanim*. The infinitive absolute, which is mostly a feature of BH, will not be discussed here. In Israeli Hebrew it is found in the literary register and in journalistic style, and its productivity is rather limited. Our analysis will concentrate on other *binyan*-related nominalizations. The 'default' associations of abstract nominalizations with particular *binyanim*, as even the most basic grammar books recognize, are:

(1) **The basic abstract nominalization patterns associated with particular *binyanim***

CaCaC (*pa'al*)-CCiCa[1]   niCCaC (*nif'al*)-hiCaCCut
CiCeC (*pi'el*)-CiCuC   hitCaCeC (*hitpa'el*)-hitCaCCut
hiCCiC (*hif'il*)-haCCaCa and/or *heCCeC*

---

[1] There are few manifestations of *CCiCa* in Biblical Hebrew. It is mostly a feature of Mishnaic Hebrew, carried over to Modern Hebrew.

Other patterns may also be associated with particular *binyanim*. For *paʿal*, for instance, there are additional patterns like:

(2) **Secondary nominalization patterns associated with *pa'al***
  CCeCa (*gneva* 'stealing, theft')   CCaCa (*de'aga* 'worrying, worry')
  CCuCa (*ge'ula* 'salvation')   tCuCa (*tkuma* 'revival')
  CiCCa (*sin'a* 'hate')   CCiCut (*ptixut* 'openness')

and there are also secondary nominalization patterns associated with *pi'el*:

(3) **Secondary nominalization patterns associated with *pi'el***
  CaCaCa (*bakaša* 'request')   CiCaCon (*nicaxon* 'victory')
  miCCaC (*misxak* 'playing, game')

In some of these, the secondary form coexists alongside the default one, with a more restricted meaning (e.g. *kima* 'getting up' vs. *tkuma* 'revival', also cf. Ben-Asher 1973 and Berman 1978, p. 347). There are also relatively-minor patterns involving the present participle followed by +*ut* in other *binyanim* (see Chapter 2 and discussion below). On the whole, the relationships between *binyanim* and their default nominal realizations are fairly regular, but there are gaps and suppletion-type pairings, as well as semantic idiosyncracies. Gaps are common, for example no **gniva* from *ganav* 'steal', no **nekima* from *nakam* 'take revenge'.[2] There are also realizations in unexpected patterns. The nominalization of *kibes* 'launder' is normally *kvisa* rather than the expected *kibus*, that of *lamad* 'learn' is *limud* in common usage, the expected *lemida* usually being reserved for 'acquisition'.[3] The nominalized form may function as the directly related verbal noun, or it can refer to a more specific offshoot reading of it (e.g. *hagdara* is 'defining' as well as 'definition', *haxnasa* is 'bringing in' as well as 'income').

In the case of two *binyanim*, the default abstract nominalization contains the suffix +*ut*, which is also the most common choice in deriving abstract nominalizations that do not involve verbs. As in the case of +*i* adjectives, +*ut* suffixation involves minimal semantic

---

[2] There is *gimur* 'finish (of product)', but no underlying verb **gimer* (except perhaps in slang, cf. Chapter 3). *rugaz* is a highly literary base for everyday *merugaz* 'angry'. *korem* 'vine grower' does not have a **karam* counterpart, nor does *yogev* 'farmer' have **yagav*. *matun* 'slow, moderate' has no related **matan*.

[3] The normal counterpart of *'asar* 'forbid; arrest' is *'isur* for 'forbidding'. The expected *'asira* is used only in the sense of 'arresting' (i.e. no **'iser*). *knisa* 'entry, entrance' is a more common nominalization of *nixnas* 'enter' than the expected *hikansut* is.

change, the sole function of which is to assign the stem to which it is attached the status of an abstract noun, 'being...', 'the state of...' (see Rosén 1977). Abstract nominalization that does not entail any semantic deviation from the base other than the abstraction itself goes to +*ut* by default. Consequently, +*ut* is conceived of as transparent and global, capturing the broadest nominal category, and is therefore highly preferred at the intuitive derivation phase. Children already use +*ut* productively at the age of four (Berman & Sagi 1981: *cmi'ut* 'thirst', *mazi'ut* 'sweating', *ke'evut* 'being in pain', *ra'ut* 'wickedness', *kosmut* 'magic'), and adults prefer it to any other derivational pattern for abstract nominalization. *CiCuC* is also productive in verb-related nominalization, owing to the productivity of its verb base *pi'el*. One should also note the colloquial use of the infinitive as abstract nominalization, as in:

(4) *'ani yoter tov miménu belixtov*
   I   more good than-him in-to-write
   'I'm better than him in writing'

   ... *belecayer*
   ... in-to-draw
   '... in drawing'

   hu ma'avir et kol hayom belehistovev
   he passes acc. all the-day in-to-walk around
   'He passes the whole day (in) walking around'

Mor (1996) notes that use of the infinitive as noun is on the increase in the written language as well, as a replacement for the (generally) more formal infinitive absolute (= gerund, in Berman 1978's terminology). It generally follows *be+* 'in', as above, and occasionally *šel* 'of', as in:

(5) *ze pri ha-hašqa'a šel laléxet...*
   this fruit of the-investment of to go
   'This is the fruit of the investment of going...'

At the intuitive derivation stage, appending +*on* is the preferred device for forming diminutives out of nominal or adjectival bases. In the colloquial register, +*čik* often fulfills a similar function. The intuitively-preferred location marker is +*iya*. +*an* is the most productive agentive pattern, and when no distinction is drawn between an instrument and an agent, +*an* may also be used as a default marker for both.

Beyond these generalizations, there seem to be no clear preferences in the intuitive/global derivational hierarchy of noun formation. There are only tendencies. Some abstract nouns are found in marked patterns such as *miCCaC/miCCaCa*, *CiCaCon*, *CaCeCet*, or *CóCeC*, following a specific semantic correlate or simply by analogy. A sizeable group of instruments are assigned to *maCCeC/maCCeCa*, but some of them are shifted to the *benoni* of *pi'el*, *meCaCeC(et)*, a similar pattern serving as the unmarked 'performer' of the action. A significant number of location nouns not marked by +*iya* are realized in *miCCaC/miCCaCa*, but at the same time there are shifts from *miCCaCa* to *maCCeCa*, a similar pattern that is more salient semantically, and less marked phonetically (*a* being the unmarked Hebrew vowel). Semantic saliency also accounts for local shifts from *CiCCon* to *CiCaCon*. Local shifts involving back-formation exemplify the principle of paradigm leveling for the purpose of simplification and reduction of alternation.

5.2 *Selection of abstract nominalization pattern*

The most common realization of abstract nominalization is the +*ut* pattern, and there are many more cases ending with +*ut* that involve a *miškal* than one might expect. Two of the *binyanim*, *hitpa'el* and *nif'al*, have +*ut* as part of their nominalization pattern, and there are also patterns involving the present participle followed by +*ut* (see Chapter 2):

(6) **Nominalizations ending with +*ut***

hitCaCCut:	*hitkadem* 'advance' > *hitkadmut*	*hitnageš* 'collide' > *hitnagšut*	
hiCaCCut:	*(le)hikanes* 'enter' > *hikansut*	*(le)hitakel* 'bump (into)' > *hitalkut*	
CoCCut:	*xonex* 'trainer' > *xonxut*	*xoveš* 'dress wound' > *xovšut*	
niCCaCut:	*nifkad* '(be) absent' > *nifkadut*	*niv'ar* 'ignorant' > *niv'arut*	
meCaCCut:	*meyaled* 'obstetrician' > *meyaldut*	*mefaked* 'commander' > *mefakdut*	
meCuCaCut:	*mexuyav* 'obliged' > *mexuyavut*	*meyutar* 'redundant' > *meyutarut*	
maCCiCut:	*mazkir* 'secretary' > *mazkirut*	*manhig* 'leader' > *manhigut*	
muCCaCut:	*mugbal* 'restricted' > *mugbalut*	*mufra'* 'disturbed' > *mufra'ut*	

The default nominalizations for *binyanim* that do not end with +*ut* are:

(7) **Default nominalizations not ending with +*ut***

CCiCa:	*katav* 'write' > *ktiva* 'writing'	*sagar* 'close' > *sgira* 'closing'	
CiCuC:	*tipel* 'treat' > *tipul* 'treating; treatment'	*bišel* 'cook' > *bišul* 'cooking'	

(cont.)

haCCaCa:	*hifʿil* 'operate' > *hafʿala* 'operating'	*hirxiv* 'broaden' > *harxava* 'broadening'	
[*heCCeC*:	*hisbir* 'explain' > *hesber* 'explanation'	*hirkiv* 'compose' > *herkev* 'composition']	

5.2.1 *Productivity tests on formation of abstract nominalizations*

As in the case of adjectives, data from productivity tests on abstract nominalization depends on whether an underlying verb is implied by the proposed base. In the tests described previously, involving 50 subjects taking coinage as well as judgment tests, the following distribution pertains to abstract nominalizations. Again, some items were left blank. Also, marginal single forms and some irrelevant ones will not be quoted. For details, see Appendix XII.

(8) **Productivity tests on abstract nominalization where a verb base was implied** (N subjects = 50, N bases = 16. Co. = Coinage, Ju. = Judgment)

a. Target meaning focuses on patient/theme—inchoative, reciprocal (N bases = 5)

Pattern	% Co.	% Ju.	Illustrations
hitCaCCut	63.60	75.20	*yóram* 'nerd' > *hityarmut* 'becoming nerdy' *magad* 'battalion commander' > *hitmagdut* 'becoming battalion commander' *pitka* 'note' > *hitpatkeʾut/ hitpatkut* 'sending each other notes' *zálman* 'sloppily dressed man' > *hizdalmenut* 'dressing self sloppily'
Other +*ut*	13.20	12.40	*pitka* 'note' > *pitkaʾut* 'sending each other notes'
CiCuC	10.80	7.60	*yóram* 'nerd' > *yerum* 'becoming nerdy'
hiCaCCut	2.80	2.80	*šérif* 'sheriff' > *hišarfut* 'becoming sheriff'
haCCaCa	3.20	1.60	*šérif* 'sheriff' > *hašrafa* 'becoming sheriff'
meCuCaCut	1.20	–	*šérif* 'sheriff' > *mešorafut* 'becoming sheriff'
niCCaCut	.80	–	*šérif* 'sheriff' > *nišrafut* 'becoming sheriff'
muCCaCut	.40	–	*šérif* 'sheriff' > *mušrafut* 'becoming sheriff'
+*iyáda*	.33	–	*zálman* 'sloppily dressed man' > *zalmaniyáda* 'dressing self sloppily'

b. Target meaning focuses on patient/theme—passive (N bases = 3)

Pattern	% Co.	% Ju.	Illustrations
meCuCaCut	54.67	59.33	*panel* 'panel' > *mefunalut/ mepunalut* 'being covered with panels'

(cont.)

Pattern	% Co.	% Ju.	Illustrations
			matax 'foreign currency' > *memutaxut* 'being turned into foreign currency'
muCCaCut	26.67	30.67	*kéres* 'hook' > *mukrasut* 'being fitted with a hook'
			matax 'foreign currency' > *mumtaxut* 'being turned into foreign currency'
CiCuC	11.33	6.00	*panel* 'panel' > *pinul/pinlul* 'being covered with panels'
hitCaCCut	4.00	3.33	*kéres* 'hook' > *hitkarsut* 'being fitted with a hook'
haCCaCa	2.00	–	*matax* 'foreign currency' > *hamtaxa* 'being turned into foreign currency'
niCCaCut	1.33	.67	*kéres* 'hook' > *nikrasut* 'being fitted with a hook'

c. Target meaning involves causation (N bases = 2)

Pattern	% Co.	% Ju.	Illustrations
CiCuC	48.00	53.00	*snob* 'snob' > *sinub* 'making one snobbish'
			šérif 'sheriff' > *šeruf* 'making one sheriff'
haCCaCa/	46.00	47.00	*snob* 'snob' > *hasnaba* 'making one snobbish'
'aCCaCa			*šérif* 'sheriff' > *hašrafa* 'making one sheriff'

d. Target meaning involves general agentivity (non-causal)
(N bases = 6)

Pattern	% Co.	% Ju.	Illustrations
CiCuC	58.67	61.33	*panel* 'panel' > *pinul* 'covering with panels'
			bagac 'high court' > *biguc* 'presenting to high court'
			čárter 'charter' > *čirtur* 'organizing charter flights'
			šnórkel 'snorkel' > *šnirkul* 'diving with snorkel'
+ut	7.00	19.67	*zálman* 'sloppily dressed man' > *zalmaniyut* 'dressing self sloppily'
			brezent 'tarp' > *brezenta'ut* 'manufacturing tarp'
haCCaCa/	13.33	8.33	*bagac* 'high court' > *havgaca* 'presenting to high court'
'aCCaCa			*'anténa* 'antenna' > *'antana* 'setting up an antenna'
+iya	5.33	1.33	*čárter* 'charter' > *čarteriya* 'organizing charter flights'
hitCaCCut	2.33	4.00	*'anténa* 'antenna' > *hit'antenut* 'setting up an antenna'
CCiCa	.67	1.33	*bagac* 'high court' > *bgica* 'presenting to high court'
+izm	.67	–	*čárter* 'charter' > *čarterizm* 'organizing charter flights'
+a	.67	–	*brezent* 'tarp' > *brezenta* 'manufacturing tarp'
+ácya	.33	–	*brezent* 'tarp' > *brezentácya* 'manufacturing tarp'
+érya	.33	–	*brezent* 'tarp' > *brezentérya* 'manufacturing tarp'

(9) **Productivity tests on abstract nominalization where no verb base was implied** (N subjects = 50, N bases = 5. Co. = Coinage, Ju. = Judgment)

Pattern	% Co.	% Ju.	Illustrations
+ut	46.80	66.80	*šérif* 'sheriff' > *šéifiyut/šérifut* 'a sheriff's occupation'
			kosem 'magician' > *kosmut* 'the magician's occupation'
			'axam 'V.I.P' > *'axamiyut* 'V.I.P status'
+izm	14.00	13.20	*máčo* 'macho' > *mačo'izm* 'the macho quality'
CiCuC	13.20	13.60	*masaž* 'massage' > *misuž* 'massage art'
			kosem 'magician' > *kisum* 'the magician's occupation'
CCiCa	.80	1.60	*'axam* 'V.I.P' > *'axima* 'V.I.P status'
+ológya	1.60	.80	*masaž* 'massage' > *masažológya* 'massage art'
CéCeC/CóCeC	.80	.80	*'axam* 'V.I.P' > *'óxem* 'V.I.P status'
haCCaCa	.80	–	*kosem* 'magician' > *haksama* 'the magician's occupation'
+ácya	.80	–	*masaž* 'massage' > *masižácya* 'massage art'
+iya	.40	–	*máčo* 'macho' > *mačiya* 'the macho quality'
miCCaC	–	.40	*kosem* 'magician' > *miksam* 'the magician's occupation'

In some of the target meaning definitions, underlying verbs were implied through the use of gerunds like 'becoming . . .', 'being . . .+ Past Participle', 'making/causing . . .', 'setting . . .', 'organizing . . .', 'manufacturing. . . .' One may argue that such verbs (*become, cause, set, organize*) serve as bases in the formation of nominalized forms. When a verb is thus implied in the definition of the target meaning, preference is given to the default nominalization associated with that potential verb (or its related resultative adjective). Take, for instance, 'becoming battalion commander'. The most likely verb form for 'become battalion commander' would have been *hitmaged, hitpa'el* being the preferred realization for inchoatives. Therefore, the nominalization pattern opted for is *hitCaCCut*, the default nominalization of *hitpa'el*, i.e. *hitmagdut*. Similarly, *meCuCaCut* is the preferred pattern for nominalizations whose base would have been a participial resultative adjective in the pattern *meCuCaC*, which is directly related to the passive verb pattern *CuCaC*. *CuCaC* is the somewhat automatic passive counterpart of the very productive *CiCeC*, which makes it productive too, and by implication its participial adjective and its nominal counterpart *meCuCaCut* as well. Where the target meaning involves causation, both *CiCuC* and *haCCaCa* are productive, with some advantage for the former. This is what one would expect from related *pi'el* and *hif'il* competing for the position of preferred realization for causative verbs, and the current stronger preference for *pi'el*. And finally, when the nominal target meaning involves general agentivity that is not clearly causal, *CiCuC* takes precedence, reflecting the preference of general (non-causative) agentive verbs for *pi'el*, the base of *CiCuC*. These preferences are even stronger in the judgment tasks, where the suggested form 'reminds' the subject of what would have been the default realization of the implied verb, and consequently of what its nominalized counterpart should be. But the scores of other realizations may also be boosted, prompted by an array of choices.

When the target meaning does not involve a verb base, realizations ending with +*ut* prevail. Other options are +*izm* or *CiCuC*. Presumably, *CiCuC* is chosen when the borders between a verb-based and non-verb-based reading are ambiguous. For example, the gloss and sentence frame for 'massage art' could suggest either 'massaging art', or 'doing massage'. The claim that productivity is affected by the type of base from which the innovation is derived is again supported by the Hebrew data.

5.2.2 *Abstract nominalization formation as reflected in dictionary comparison*

Below are some data to illustrate the distribution of new abstract nominalizations as emerging from dictionary comparison (for more detailed lists, see Appendices XIII–XV):[4]

(10) **New abstract nominalizations in the 1983 supplement to Even-Shoshan (1970)**

Form	Gloss	Source	Gloss
CCiCa (all literary):			
'arisa	becoming betrothed	*'aras/'arus*	betroth/betrothed
driga	grading, gradation	*déreg/dereg*	grade, echelon/grade (V)
CiCuC:			
'imut	confrontation	*'imet*	confront; juxtapose
'išrur	ratification	*'išrer*	ratify (< *'išer* 'confirm')

---

[4] Note that minor nominalization patterns like *miCCaC*, *CiCaCon* or *CóCeC* are not included in the dictionary comparison counts or the in corpus statistics for abstract nominalization, because of their negligible productivity as demonstrated by the productivity tests. Although Even-Shoshan (1983) lists a number of nominalization innovations in *miCCaC*, they are all literary rare (except for *mimsad* 'establishment'). Other than these, and occasional realization in child language (see above), no innovations in these patterns have been observed.

(cont.)

Form	Gloss	Source	Gloss
haCCaCa:			
ha'acava	causing sorrow	*he'eciv*	cause sorrow (< *'acuv* 'sad, sorry')
hagmada	major reduction	*higmid*	reduce significantly (< *gamad* 'dwarf')
heCCeC:			
hegev	reaction; reactance	*hegiv*	react
hevreg	screw-type connection	*hivrig*	screw (V) (< *bóreg* 'screw (N)')
hitCaCCut:			
hit'ašpezut	being hospitalized	*hit'ašpez*	be hospitalized (< *'išpez* 'hospitalize')
histal'ut	becoming rock	*séla'*	rock
hiCaCCut:			
hita'amut	being parallel; accommodation	*hit'im/ta'am*	fit, match
CoCCut:			
'oyvut	being enemy	*'oyev*	enemy
niCCaCut:			
nivxarut	being chosen	*nivxar*	be chosen
meCaCCut:			
mexabrut	authorship	*mexaber*	author
meCuCaCut:			
mexuyavut	commitment	*mexuyav*	committed
muCCaCut:			
mušlamut	being perfect	*mušlam*	perfect

Other + *ut* (i.e. not obviously associated with a verb-related *miškal*):

niciyut	hawkishness	*nici*	hawkish (< *nec* 'hawk')
kraviyut	being combatant	*kravi*	combatant (< *krav* 'combat, fight')
'elitízm	elitism	*'elíta/'ilit*	elite
stalinízm	Stalinism	*stálin*	Stalin

(11) **New abstract nominalizations in Ben-Amotz/Ben-Yehuda '72/'82**

Form	Gloss	Source	Gloss
CiCuC:			
fisfus	missing	*fisfes*	miss
xirbun	shitting; ruin(ing)	*xirben*	shit (V)/mess up
hitCaCCut:			
hitfalxut	sneaking in	*hitfaléax*	sneak in
hitfašlut	failing	*hitfašel*	fail (int.) (< *fášla* 'failure, flop' (Ar.))
Other + *ut*:			
fáyteriyut	being a fighter	*fáyter*	fighter (Eng.)
póciyut	arrogance	*poc(i)*	arrogant person, arrogant

(cont.)

Form	Gloss	Source	Gloss
+*izm*:			
bitxonízm	emphasis on security	*bitaxon*	security

(12) **New abstract nominalizations in the 1993 Prolog Dictionary**

Form	Gloss	Source	Gloss
CiCuC:			
be'us	disgust, despair	*mevo'as*	in despair (< *básā'* 'misery' (Ar.))
fištun	urinating	*fišten*	urinate (< *hištin* 'urinate')
***meCuCaCut*:**			
menumasut	being polite	*menumas*	polite
Other +*ut*:			
xelma'ut	stupidity	*xelma'i*	stupid (< *xelm* 'town notorious for fools')

Summary of total dictionary innovations in table form (with 'total +*ut*' in brackets, since it incorporates specific patterns with +*ut* listed below):

(13) **Productivity ranking of nominalization patterns based on dictionary comparison**

R2 Ranking	ES	ES '83	BABY	PHAS	New	R1	R2	R1 Ranking	Alt Ord
[Total +*ut*	3,699	145	43	3	191	.0516	.4548]	*meCuCaCut*	{*CiCuC*}
Non-V-rel+*ut*	2,291	117	34	2	153	.0668	.3643	N+*izm*	
CiCuC:	1,652	99 (47 lit.)	29	7	135	.0817	.3214	*muCCaCut*	{Total +*ut*}
N+*izm*	158	30	4	–	34	.2152	.0809	*CoCCut*	
haCCaCa:	883	34 (19 lit.)	–	–	34	.0385	.0809	*meCaCCut*	{*meCuCaCut*}
CCiCa:	1,347	18 (all lit.)	1?	1?	20	.0148	.0476	*niCCaCut*	{*haCCaCa*}
hitCaCCut:	974	9 (6 lit.)	9	–	18	.0185	.0428	*CiCuC*	{*CoCCut*}
meCuCaCut:	18	6	–	1	7	.3888	.0167	Non-V+*ut*	{*muCCaCut*}
heCCeC:	169	6 (4 lit.)	–	–	6	.0355	.0143	Total +*ut*	{*hitCaCCut*}
CoCCut:	32	5 (2 lit.)	–	–	5	.1562	.0119	*haCCaCa*	{*niCCaCut*}
muCCaCut:	16	3	–	–	3	.1875	.0071	*heCCeC*	{*CCiCa*}
niCCaCut:	30	3	–	–	3	.1000	.0071	*hitCaCCut*	{*heCCeC*}
meCaCCut: {*meCaCCut*}	8	1	–	–	1	.1250	.0024	*CCiCa*	
hiCaCCut:	321	1	–	–	1	.0031	.0024	*hiCCaCut*	

Total New: 420

Based on R2 ranking, +*ut* (regardless of whether it forms part of a verb-related *miškal* or not) and *CiCuC* are at the top of the list, with productivity rates that are close. *CiCuC* is the most productive verb-related nominalization, a function of the productivity of *pi'el*. Verb-related nominalization follows the default pattern associated with the relevant *binyan*, even if that verb is only potential, i.e. cannot be attested as an actually occurring form. The speaker 'knows' the relationship, even if a base verb does not exist, just as English speakers 'know' that *aggression* could have been derived from unattested **aggress*. *+ut* and *CiCuC* are followed by *+izm*. Of *+ut* patterns involving a present participle, *hitCaCCut* and *meCuCaCut* are the most productive, reflecting the great productivity of *hitCaCeC*, as well as of *meCuCaC* resultatives demonstrated above (Chapter 4). As for cases in which ordering by R1 does not confirm ordering by R2, one might argue for potential ranking rearrangement by 'ratio weighting' (if the R1-to-R1 ratio of the second pattern to the first is higher than the R2-to-R2 ratio of the first pattern to the second) for most of the patterns involved. The category covered is any nominalization; had it been only verb-related nominalizations, *CiCuC*, *meCuCaCut* etc. would have ranked higher, in which case even Total *+ut* would be pushed down. The curly brackets indicate that this reordering would apply only if we narrowed down the category scope to verb-related nominalizations.

5.2.3   *Quantitative evidence from corpora on abstract nominalizations*

Examination of all abstract nominalization tokens in our 112,000-word corpus reveals that only six nominalization patterns contained *hapax legomena* that were also proven recent innovations:

(14) **Recent *hapax legomena* nominalizations**

Form	Gloss	Source	Gloss
CiCuC:			
ri'anun	refreshening	ri'anen	refreshen (< ra'anan 'fresh')
si'ud	assisting (esp. the disabled)	si'ed	assist (< sá'ad 'assistance, welfare')
tigbur	reinforcing	tigber	reinforce (< gavar 'get stronger')
divšuš	pedaling	divšeš	pedal (V) (< davša 'pedal' (N))
haCCaCa:			
haklada	entering data on keyboard	hiklid	key in (< klid 'key (in compter etc'.)
hitCaCCut:			
hitxašbenut	settling accounts	hitxašben	settle accounts (< xešbon 'account')

(cont.)

Form	Gloss	Source	Gloss
hiCaCCut:			
hisardut	survival[5]	*sarad*	survive
meCuCaCut:			
mexuyavut	commitment	*mexuyav*	committed (< *xayav* 'obliged')
Other +ut:			
ʾobsesíviyut	obsessiveness	*ʾobsesívi*	obsessive
hafganatiyut	clear demonstration of intention	*hafganati*	demonstrative (< *hafgana* 'demonstration')
xromátiyut	chromaticism	*xromáti*	chromatic
naʿariyut	youthful appearance	*naʿari*	youthful (< *náʿar* 'youth, boy')
ʾíniyut	being 'in', fashionable	*ʾin*	'in', fashionable (Eng.)
xadqiyumiyut	unique existence	*xadkiyumi*	unique (< *ʾexad* 'one'+ *qiyum* 'existence')
kovlanut	chronic complaining	*kovlan*	complainer (< *kaval* 'complain')
ratnanut	grumbling	*ratnan*	grumbler (< *ratan* 'grumble')
vizuʾáliyut	visualness	*vizuʾáli*	visual

The numbers and ratios are as follows (patterns with no proven innovations are bracketed):

(15) **Corpus data on formation of abstract nominalization**

R2 Ranking	Tokens	*hapax*	R1	R2
Total +*ut*	1,102	174	.1579	.3473
CiCuC	1,469	153	.1041	.3054
Non-V-rel+*ut*	825	124	.1503	.2475
heCCeC	121	14	[.1157	.0279]
CCiCa	1,089	ˑ87	[.0799	.1736]
haCCaCa	644	71	.1102	.1417
hitCaCCut	230	40	.1739	.0798
hiCaCCut	4	4	1.0000	.0080
meCuCaCut	6	3	.5000	.0060
N+*izm*	2	2	[1.0000	.0040]
CoCCut	9	2	[.2222	.0040]
niCCaCut	6	1	[.1667	.0027]
muCCaCut	12	1	[.0833	.0020]
	Total *hapax*:	501		

---

[5] The status of *hisardut* is unclear. Although it might be new, it is hard to tell how recent it is. It may have been omitted from ES because the author regarded it as substandard. There is no **nisrad*, and since *hisardut* is part of a split paradigm with *sarad* 'survive', ES may have considered it illegitimate.

The relative productivity of the six qualifying patterns will be as follows:

(16) **Productivity ranking of abstract nominalization patterns based on corpus data**

R2 Ranking	Tokens	*hapax*	R1	R2	R1 Ranking	Alt. Order
[Total +*ut*	1,102	174	.1579	.3473]	*hiCCaCut*	
CiCuC	1,469	153	.1041	.3054	*meCuCaCut*	
Non-V-rel+*ut*	825	124	.1503	.2475	*hitCaCCut*	
haCCaCa	644	71	.1102	.1417	Total +*ut*	
hitCaCCut	230	40	.1739	.0798	Non-V-rel+*ut*	
hiCaCCut	4	4	1.0000	.0080	*haCCaCa*	drop *hiCaCCut*?
meCuCaCut	6	3	.5000	.0060	*CiCuC*	

CiCuC and non-verb-related +*ut* are the most productive, presumably the former for verb-related nominalizations, the latter for other nominalizations. +*ut* is also the most productive pattern for the whole category once all its realizations are considered, including verb-related nominalizations. The relative ordering of the last four patterns is the same as by dictionary comparison, except that the ordering of the last two is reversed.: *meCuCaCut*'s position is lower than its standing according to dictionary comparison. A single form, *hisardut* 'survival', qualified *hiCaCCut* for ranking. If it turns out not to be a new form (see footnote above), *hiCaCCut* will not be included in ranking.

Measurements based on all three criteria thus suggest that *CiCuC* is the most productive pattern for verb-related nominalization, while +*ut* is the default one for all other abstract nominalizations. Overall, total +*ut* is somewhat more productive than *CiCuC* for the category as a whole.

5.3   *Agent (and agent attribute) selection*

Agents can be realized in a number of patterns. There is the *CaCaC* (historically *CaC$_i$C$_i$aC*) pattern of professionals, and there are also many agent nouns and agent attributes that are identical to the active participle. Occasionally, agents may also be realized in nominal patterns like *CaCiC* (e.g. *pakid* 'clerk'), and through originally-borrowed +*ist* and +*er* suffixation. In the colloquial, the normally-diminutive (see below) +*čik* may mark agents as well. The most frequent realization for agents or agent attributes, however, seems to be the +*an* pattern, followed by N+*a'i* (normatively N+*ay* for agents, e.g. *'itonay* 'journalist', N +*a'i* for attributes, e.g. *'itona'i* 'journalistic').[6] Two obvious reasons for their exceptional productivity immediately come to mind. One is that unlike the other patterns, which mostly refer to agents/occupations, +*an* and +*ay*/+*a'i* denote agent attributes just as often as they refer to agent nouns. This is an advantage, because when the agent is characterized by an attribute or quality (as in *šakran* 'liar'), the borders between the agent and the adjectival agent attribute are blurred. A second reason is that both +*an* and +*a'i* are semantically transparent and semantically specific, whereas the active participles with which they compete as agent markers 'hover' between the verb and the nominal agent. Another factor working for +*an* is that when realized as *CaCCan*, it is transparently related to verb bases in *pa'al* and in *pi'el*, just as the active participial agents are, while *CaCaC*, *CaCiC* and N+*ay*/+*a'i* generally are not. Thus, at the global level of the productive lexicon, +*an* is preferred to all alternatives by children as well as by adults. According to Berman & Sagi (1981), children prefer patterns that are marked with an affix, using it as a carrier for the feature for which they are looking. Younger ones tend to use active participles as agents, since zero derivation has the advantage of simplicity of form (see Clark 1993), in that alternation is minimized. Older children, like many adults, prefer linear suffixation of +*an* (or the *CaCCan miškal*), since its transparency (compare English +*er*) facilitates acquisition. There is also certain preference for suffixes over prefixes, owing to generally stronger focusing on the end of words, particularly in a language like Hebrew, with its predominantly final stress. Since +*a'i*/+*ay* is normally acquired later, children often opt for +*an* as an agent marker:

(17) **Children's use of +*an* as agent marker**

Form	**Gloss**	**Source**	**Gloss**
'azran	one who helps a lot	*'azar*	help
barxan	one who escapes a lot	*barax*	escape
katvan	one who writes a lot	*katav*	write
banyan	one who builds well	*bana*	build
zarkan	one who throws a lot	*zarak*	throw

and even when a *benoni* form with *mV*+ is chosen, they still add an +*an* suffix as in:

---

[6] In the colloquial, +*a'i* is often used for both agents and agent attributes. Occasionally, +*ay* may also be used for either an agent noun or an adjective.

(18) **Children's adding of +an to benoni forms with mV+**

Form	Gloss	Source	Gloss
marbican	one who hits	*marbic*	hit, beat, spank
mamci'an	inventive	*mamci*	invent(or)
mekarseman	one who gnaws	*mexarsem*	gnaw (coll. *mekarsem*)
mecalman	photographer	*mecalem*	photograph (V)

This *marbic > marbican*-type formation is linear, just as a child would form *mixtavan* 'mailman' by adding the agentive +*an* to *mixtav* 'letter'. Preference for agentive realization by appending +*an* to the *benoni* is characteristic of adult speech as well:

(19) **Adult usage of verb-related agentive forms with +an**

Form	Gloss	Source	Gloss
mecican	one who peeps, peeping Tom	*mecic*	peep
mistaklan	one who peeps, peeping Tom	*mistakel*	watch, observe
margizan	an annoying person	*margiz*	annoy
(mi)staglan	one who adjusts easily	*mistagel*	adjust

In productivity tests reported on in Clark & Berman (1984) and Berman (1987), there was 83% preference for +*an* realizations for agentives in open-ended tasks and 50% in judgment tasks, where other potential patterns were made available.[7] As noted above (and in Berman 1987), in addition to the greater prominence of the +*an* pattern due to the extra prominence of a suffix, it also benefitted from having become the unmarked pattern for both occupations and attributes. *CaCaC* is essentially used just for occupations, as shown below (based on data in Gerber 1992):

(20) ***CaCaC* agentives in the total lexicon**   ***CaCaC* agentives in common usage**

Semantic Feature	Total Number	Total Number
Occupation	214	76
Quality	38	7
Animal/plant	11	6
Instrument	19	4
Misc.	9	–
Total:	291	93

---

[7] Interestingly enough, when speakers were asked to make a list of typical occupations they know, *CaCaC* was the preferred agentive, followed by different *benoni* forms, with +*an* and +*ay* only in third place. According to Berman (1987), when

CaCaC is also made opaque by the common stem of *pa'al*, since in MH the two are pronounced identically.

The preference for +*an* as an agentive marker thus constitutes a case of broadening of semantic scope, with +*an* forms being identified with both features of agent-doer and agent attribute. This semantic expansion is very helpful to the innovator, who looks for a general, prominent form-and-meaning correlation as a clue to realization in a particular derivation pattern. It has made +*an*, basically, the unmarked agentive pattern.

In spontaneous derivation, the +*an* pattern is also commonly used for instruments. There are some recent +*an*-instruments in adult speech, such as

(21) **Recent +*an* instruments in adult speech**

Form	Gloss	Source	Gloss
mazgan	air-conditioner	*mizeg*	mix, moderate
lavyan	satelite	*liva*	accompany

and for most children, the following are interpreted as either a human agent or an instrument (see Clark & Berman 1984):

(22) **Children's use of +*an* for both agents and instruments**

Form	Gloss	Source	Gloss
cayran	artist; a painting instrument	*ciyer*	draw, paint
mašxan	one who pulls; an instr. for pulling	*mašax*	pull
parkan	agent/instr. derived from 'pull apart'	*perek*	pull apart
mafxidan	agent/instr. derived from 'scare'	*mafxid*	scary
matxilan	agent/instr. derived from 'start'	*matxil*	start

The adult innovator, like the child, may also see in occurrences of +*an* not only an occupation or agent-attribute, but a parallel instrument as well (see Clark & Berman 1984):

(23) **Adult use of +*an* for both agents and instruments**

Form	Gloss	Source	Gloss
badkan	one who examines a lot/instr. that examines	*badak*	examine
dax(a)fan	a pushy person/instrument for pushing	*daxaf*	push

---

subjects draw a list, it reflects the established 'old'-word lexicon vs. the potential-productive one which comes out in open-ended productivity tests and to a lesser degree in judgment tasks.

(cont.)

Form	Gloss	Source	Gloss
nakdan	a person assigning vowels/ dot-making tool	*niked*	vowel (V) (< *nekuda* 'dot')
nakvan	puncher (person or instrument)	*nikev*	make holes
pazran	spendthrift/instrument that scatters matter	*pizer*	scatter
tarteran	one who nags/noise-making tool	*tirter*	make noise
matxan	a practical joker/a stretching instrument	*matax*	stretch

5.3.1 *Productivity tests on agent formation*

In our productivity tests (50 coinage, 50 judgment), the agent preferences were as follows (for details, see Appendix XVI):

(24) **Productivity tests where the target meaning was an agent**: (N subjects = 50, N bases = 8. Co. = Coinage, Ju. = Judgment)

Pattern	% Co.	% Ju.	Illustrations
+*an*	21.00	37.00	*'omlet* 'omelette' > *'omletan/'amletan* 'one making omelettes'
			čárter 'charter' > *čarteran* 'charter flights specialist'
+*ay*/+*a'i*	22.25	31.00	*básta* 'vendor stall' > *basta'i/bastay* 'stall vendor'
			'anténa 'antenna' > *'antena'i/'antenay* 'one who assembles antennas'
+*ist*	14.00	8.25	*čárter* 'charter' > *čarterist* 'charter flights specialist'
			šrimps 'shrimp(s)' > *šrimpist* 'shrimp fisherman'
+*er*	10.00	7.25	*básta* 'vendor stall' > *bastoner/bastyoner* 'stall vendor'
			gril 'grill' > *gríler* 'one who grills'
meCaCeC	10.50	6.00	*'omlet* 'omelette' > *me'amlet* 'one making omelettes'
			'anténa 'antenna' > *me'anten* 'one who assembles antennas'
meCuCaC	5.50	–	*nagmaš* 'APC' > *menugmaš* 'APC-borne troop'
			tóšba' 'Jewish oral law' > *metušba'* 'oral law specialist'
+*nik*	2.00	3.00	*nagmaš* 'APC' > *nagmášnik* 'APC-borne troop'
maCCiC	1.00	.50	*gril* 'grill' > *magril* 'one who grills'
mitCaCeC	1.00	–	*čárter* 'charter' > *mitčarter* 'charter flights specialist'
CaCaC	1.00	–	*čárter* 'charter' > *čartar* 'charter flights specialist'
+*ar*	1.00	–	*šrimps* 'shrimp(s)' > *šrimpar* 'shrimp fisherman'
+*čik*	.50	.25	*nagmaš* 'APC' > *nagmáščik* 'APC-borne troop'

(cont.)

Pattern	% Co.	% Ju.	Illustrations
+*on*	.75	–	*šrimps* 'shrimp(s)' > *šrimpson* 'shrimp fisherman'
+*olog*	–	.50	*šrimps* 'shrimp(s)' > *šrimpsolog* 'shrimp fisherman'
+*átor*	.25	–	*'omlet* 'omelette' > *'omelátor* 'one making omelettes'
+*men*	.25	–	*gril* 'grill' > *grílmen* 'one who grills'
CoCeC	.25	–	*gril* 'grill' > *gorel* 'one who grills'

The productivity tests confirm the productivity of +*an* for agent nouns, but also suggest that +*ay*/+*a'i* is at least as productive. Averaging the coinage and judgment scores gives +*an* a slight advantage over +*ay*/+*a'i*. Although one would have expected stronger preference for +*an* in the open-ended coinage tests, reflecting the subject's first intuition, +*an* scores are actually higher in the judgment tasks. As pointed out earlier, comparison with alternatives may 'remind' subjects of what would have been their natural preference, but escaped them in the absence of a trigger. The explanation for +*ay*/+*a'i* choice might lie in the test design as well as in the subject population. Since it was difficult to formulate a relationship between base and target meaning that would suggest both an agent and an agent attribute at the same time, the target meanings centered on occupations. Furthermore, the particular subjects, Hebrew teacher trainees, still maintain the somewhat more formal preference for +*ay*/+*a'i* to denote occupations.[8] Borrowed +*ist* and +*er* are fairly productive. *CaCaC* is seldom chosen. Of verb-related agents, *meCaCeC* is fairly productive for agents, certainly more than other *benoni* patterns like *mitCaCeC*, *maCCïC* or *CoCeC*, again owing to the productivity of related *pi'el*. But *meCaCeC* is never the first choice among all agentive patterns.

5.3.2 *Agent formation as reflected in dictionary comparison*

Below are some data illustrating the distribution of innovations in agent and agent attribute realizations based on dictionary comparison (for more details, see Appendices XVII–XIX):

---

[8] Although they might not follow the normative distinction between +*ay* for agents and +*a'i* for agent attributes, which is usually adhered to only by purists.

(25) **New agents and agent attributes in the 1983 supplement to Even-Shoshan (1970)**

Form	Gloss	Source	Gloss
+ *an*: agents or agent-attributes:			
tilan	soldier launching missiles	*til*	missile
*mis*ʿ*adan*	restaurant proprietor	*mis*ʿ*ada*	restaurant
mafsidan	loser	*mafsid*	lose (pr. part.)
+ *ay*/+*a*ʾ*i*: [9]			
gimlay	retiree living on pension	*gimla*	pension
handasay	technician	*handasa*	engineering
palestinay	a Palestinian	*palestína*	Palestine
meCaCeC:			
*me*ʾ*ahévet*	lover (f.)	ʾ*ihev* (lit.)	make love (< ʾ*ahav* 'love')
*me*ʾ*aper*	makeup person	ʾ*iper*	makeup (V)
mesagseg	thriving	*sigseg*	thrive
CoCeC:			
ʾ*ocer*	curator	ʾ*acar*	safe keep, collect (< ʾ*ocar* 'treasure')
ʾ*ohed*	fan	ʾ*ahad*	like, sympathize
*go*ʿ*eš*	stormy, agitated	*ga*ʿ*aš*	be stormy
+ *ist*: [10]			
*bicu*ʿ*ist*	a no-nonsense hands-on doer	*bicúa*ʿ	performance, execution of task
šminist	12th grader	*šminit*	eighth; 12th grade
+ *er*:			
blófer	liar	*blof*	lie (< Eng. *bluff*)
konterrevolucyoner	a counterrevolutionary	Rus.	
+ *čik*:			
ʾ*aparátčik*	operator; a "doer" (derog.); party activist	Rus.	
maCCiC:			
maršim	impressive	*hiršim*	impress (< *róšem* 'impression')
*ma*ʿ*aliv*	insulting	*he*ʿ*eliv*	insult

---

[9] Most +*ay*/+*a*ʾ*i* innovations in the 1983 supplement to ES reflect the normative distinction between +*ay* as an agent noun marker and +*a*ʾ*i* as its adjectival counterpart.

[10] Forms with +*ist* are often borrowed with the suffix already an integral part of the word, as, for instance, in ES '83 ʾ*elitist* 'elitist', *fundamentalist* 'fundamentalist', *perfekcyonist* 'perfectionist'; but there are natively-formed creations as well, as in the two forms above. In other cases, the base may still be borrowed, but the alternant with +*ist* is formed after the base was borrowed.

(cont.)

Form	Gloss	Source	Gloss
mitCaCeC:			
mitnaxel	settler	*hitnaxel*	settle
CaCaC:			
capan	one who encodes	*cófen*	code
sayaᶜ	collaborator	*siyaᶜ*	help, assist, support

(26) **New agents and agent attributes in BABY 1972/82 not in 1983 ES supplement**

Form	Gloss	Source	Gloss
+*ist*:			
bitxonist	security-conscious person	*bitaxon*	security, safety
šekemist	P.X. worker	*šékem*	Israel's P.X.
sipuxist	annexationist	*sipúax*	annexation
+*an*:			
smolan(i)	leftist	*smol*	left
zablan/ zbalyan	one who talks too much	*zibel*	talk too much (< *zével* 'garbage')
mamci'an	resourceful person	*mamci*	inventor
+*ay*/+*a'i*:			
dugra'i	straightforward, very frank	*dúgri*	straight, frankly Ar. (< *dúγri*)
mikva'i	from Mikve Israel (N/Adj)	*mikve yisra'el*	name of agricutural school
k(i)yoska'i	kiosk owner	*kiyosk*	kiosk (esp. for cold drinks, candy)
+*er*:			
širyoner	oldier in armor corps	*širyon*	armor
bizyoner	one responsible for disgrace	*bizayon*	disgrace
+*čik*:			
tikúnčik	handyman	*tikun*	repair
napolyónčik	one with superiority complex	*napolyon*	Napoleon
meCaCeC:			
metamtem	wonderful	*timtem*	make stupid, stupefy (senses)
megameret	reaching orgasm (f.)	*gimer*	finish, conclude
maCCiC:			
matrif	wonderful	*hitrif*	drive mad
malxic	causing stress	*hilxic*	cause stress (< *laxac* 'press')
mitCaCeC:			
mithapex	gay	*hithapex*	turn over
mitromem	gay	*hitromem*	rise up
CoCeC:			
mokem	radar operator	*makam*	radar

(cont.)

Form	Gloss	Source	Gloss
CaCaC:			
bašal	cook (N)	bišel	cook (V)

(27) **New agents and agent attributes in PHAS 1993 not found in BABY 1972/82**

Form	Gloss	Source	Gloss
+ *an*			
balyan	always having a good time	bila	have a good time
barzelan	officer (army slang)	barzel	iron (here in insignia)
maški‘an	one who invests great effort	maškía‘	invest (pr. part.)
+ *er*:			
fantazyoner	one who fantasizes	fantázya	fantacy
protekcyoner	well-connected person	protékcya	connections
+ *ist*:			
čuparist	one enjoying special benefits	čupar	special benefit or pleasure
šušu’ist	intelligence worker	šúšu	hush hush (onomatopeic?)
***meCaCeC*:**			
meraxef	with no firm hold on reality	rixef	hover
meva’es	causing despair	be’es	cause despair (< *básā’* 'misery (Ar.)')
***maCCiC*:**			
madlik	wonderful, exciting	hidlik	light up (tr.)
+ *ay*/+ *a’i*:			
šeynkina’i	Israeli yuppie (N/Adj.)	šéynkin	name of a trendy Tel Aviv street

Below is a summary of the dictionary data on the distribution of agents and agent attributes:

(28) **Productivity ranking of agentive patterns based on dictionary comparison**

R2 Ranking	ES	ES '83	BABY	PHAS	New	R1	R2	R1 Ranking
+*an*	1,090	71	18	10	99	.0908	.4041	+*er*
+*ay*/+*a’i*	233	38	10	1	49	.2103	.2000	+*ist*
+*ist*	98[11]	2[12]	24[13]	2[14]	28	.2857	.1143	+*ay*/+*a’i*

---

[11] All borrowed.
[12] Plus 4 borrowings.
[13] Plus 6 borrowings.
[14] Plus 1 borrowing.

(cont.)

R2 Ranking	ES	ES '83	BABY	PHAS	New	R1	R2	R1 Ranking
+er	22[15]	2[16]	7[17]	5[18]	14	.6364	.0571	mitCaCeC
meCaCeC	142	10	2	2	14	.0986	.0571	meCaCeC
CoCeC	212	10	1	–	11	.0519	.0449	+an
CaCaC	415	9	1[19]	–	10	.0241	.0408	maCCiC
+čik	–	1	8	–	9		.0367	CoCeC
maCCiC	116	4	3	1	8	.0690	.0326	CaCaC
mitCaCeC	30	1	2	–	3	.1000	.0122	

Total New: 245

Only Ratio 2 was computed for + *čik*, since there are no ES occurrences of it on which Ratio 1 could be based. Most suffixed patterns (+*ay*/+*a'i*, +*an*, +*er*, and +*ist*) are highly productive for agents, and are close to each other in degree of productivity (*čik* is somewhat lower; it more commonly functions as a diminutive suffix—see below). The suffixless agentive group is significantly less productive. The prominence, transparency and simplicity of associating a suffix with agentivity enhances its productivity to start with (see also Berman & Sagi 1981, Clark & Berman 1984, Berman 1987). Since the four top suffixes are almost uniquely associated with agents and agent attributes, it is no surprise that as a group, the suffixed patterns are more productive than the unsuffixed ones. Four of the five patterns without suffixes are present participles which also function as agents, and consequently less specialized and less specific semantically. The comparative productivity would have been different if forms borrowed together with the agentive suffix were counted as neologisms. +*er* and +*ist* would have been at the top of list, in this order. But since such borrowings were not formed as neologisms in Israeli Hebrew, they are discounted, and +*an* and +*ay*/+*a'i* are ranked as the most productive agentive patterns. This is exactly what was found in the productivity tests. In a number of cases, ranking by R1 does

---

[15] All borrowed, and all colloquial.

[16] Plus 8 borrowings. Since they were borrowed with +*er* as atomic units, it is difficult to determine whether they reflect a productive derivation process. For the purpose of this study, borrowed items would constitute part of the base upon which neologism occurs, but would not count as neologisms.

[17] Plus 65 borrowings, mostly from Yiddish, some from English.

[18] Plus 2 borrowings.

[19] There are also at least 21 *CaCaC* forms borrowed from Arabic (like *falax* 'peasant; simple person', *nayak* 'fucker', *'awar* 'one with poor eyesight', *xašaš* 'hashish smoker', *jabar* 'strong, violent') and another 5 Arabic *'aCCaC* forms (like *'ahbal* 'stupid', *'akbar* 'great') that may be regarded as manifestations of *CaCaC*, but Hebrew speakers may not conceive of them as such.

not agree with R2 ranking. Ratio weighting would suggest that *CaCaC* and *maCCiC* exchange positions: R1 of the latter is almost 3 times that of the former, while R2 of *CaCaC* is only 1.25 times that of *maCCiC*. But there does not seem to be any independent reason to do so.

5.3.3   *Quantitative evidence from corpora on agent formation*

In the 112,000 word corpus, the following are agent or agent attribute realizations among the *hapax legomena* that were not listed in ES (1970):

(29) **Relatively recent agents and agent attributes in the 112k corpus**

Form	Gloss	Source	Gloss
meCaCeC:			
mehamer	gambler	*himer*	gamble
mexasel	annihilator	*xisel*	annihilate
meta'em	coordinator	*te'em*	coordinate
me'aveš	rustling	*'iveš*	rustle (V) (< *'wša* 'a rustle')
mera'anen	refreshing	*ri'anen*	refresh (< *ra'anan* 'fresh')
+*an*:			
macxikan	comedian	*macxik*	funny, causing laughter
šolfan	one who acts spontaneously	*šolef*	draw (gun etc.) (pres. part.)
+*ay*/+*a'i*:			
gimlay	retiree living on pension	*gimla*	pension
tunisa'i	Tunisian	*tunis(ya)*	Tunis(ia)
maCCiC:			
maf'il	operator; agent	*hif'il*	operate
maflig	extreme	*hiflig*	exaggerate; sail
mitCaCeC:			
mitmoded	contender (for position, title)	*hitmoded*	contend, face

Two new +*ist hapax* forms (*'otist* 'autistic person', *ta'o'ist* 'Taoist') were also found, but they must have been borrowed as atomic units, and thus do not count. The ratios of *hapax legomena* to tokens and to the total *hapax* count among agent nouns are as follows:

(30) **Productivity ranking of agentive patterns based on corpus data**

R2 Ranking	Tokens	*hapax*	R1	R2	R1 Ranking
+*an*	157	47	.2994	.2765	+*an*
meCaCeC	169	31	.1243	.1823	*maCCiC*
CoCeC	858	27	[.0315	.1588]	*meCaCeC*

(cont.)

R2 Ranking	Tokens	*hapax*	R1	R2	R1 Ranking
maCCiC	180	26	.1444	.1529	*+ay/+a'i*
+ay/+a'i	148	16	.1081	.0941	*mitCaCeC*
+ist	13[20]?	11?	[.8461]	.0647]	
+er	5	5	[1.0000	.0294]	
CaCaC	546	5	[.0091	.0294]	
mitCaCeC	57	2	.0351	.0118	

Total *hapax*: 170

Five agent formation patterns meet the condition postulated for determining relative productivity in a limited corpus, i.e. that a portion of the *hapax* forms be recent, and that at least one of them be a proven recent formation. The ratios for the others are put in brackets, and not evaluated. A comparison of *hapax*-to-token (and *hapax*-to-total-*hapax*) ratios among the five patterns that qualify suggests *+an* as the most productive device, followed by *meCaCeC*, with *maCCiC* coming next. The only difference from findings through other measures is in that *+ay/+a'i* is placed too low, certainly with respect to *maCCiC* and possibly when compared with *meCaCeC* as well. This might still be one consequence of using a limited corpus. The differences between R1 and R2 in the *meCaCeC-maCCiC* pair do not justify reordering.

Results of all three measurements suggest that *+an* is the most productive agentive pattern. It is followed by *+ay/+a'i* according to productivity tests and dictionary comparison. *meCaCeC* is not as productive as anticipated, in spite of its transparency as the agent pattern directly derived from *pi'el*. Apparently, it is superseded by suffixed patterns like *+er* and *+ist*, which enjoy some advantage owing to the prominence of the suffix, which is uniquely associated with agents.

5.4   Selection of patterns for instruments

Traditionally, the instrumental patterns *par excellence* have been *maCCeC* and *maCCeCa*, but as noted earlier, the typically-agentive *meCaCeC* and *+an* can also be instrumental. In fact, most of the patterns denoting agent nouns may also have an instrumental reading, as will be shown below.

---

[20] All borrowed.

126   CHAPTER FIVE

5.4.1 *Productivity tests on instrument formation*

In our productivity tests (50 coinage, 50 judgment), the distribution of instruments was as follows (see Appendix XX):

(31) **Productivity tests where the target meaning was an instrument**: (N subjects = 50, N bases = 5. Co. = Coinage, Ju. = Judgment)

Pattern	% Co.	% Ju.	Illustrations
+*iya*	23.60	14.80	*kúskus* 'couscous' > *kuskusiya* 'couscous-making instrument' *kótej* 'cottage cheese' > *kotejïya* 'instrument for producing cottage cheese'
meCaCeC	15.60	13.60	*pláster* 'band aid' > *meflaster* 'instrument for applying band aid' *xúmus* 'hummus' > *mexames* 'hummus processing instrument'
maCCeC [if N base = 4,	14.00 17.50	11.60 14.50]	*srox* 'shoelace' > *masrex* 'shoelace tying instrument' *kótej* 'cottage cheese' > *maktej* 'instrument for producing cottage cheese'
+*an*	9.20	14.00	*pláster* 'band aid' > *plasteran* 'instrument for applying band aid' *kúskus* 'couscous' > *kuskusan* 'couscous-making instrument'
+*on*	8.80	4.80	*pláster* 'band aid' > *plasteron* 'instrument for applying band aid' *kúskus* 'couscous' > *kuskuson* 'couscous-making instrument'
maCCeCa [if N base = 4,	3.60 4.50	13.60 17.00]	*xúmus* 'hummus' > *maxmesa* 'hummus processing instrument' *kúskus* 'couscous' > *maksesa* 'couscous-making instrument'
+*er*	2.80	9.60	*kúskus* 'couscous' > *kúskuser* 'couscous-making instrument' *xúmus* 'hummus' > *xúmuser* 'hummus processing instrument'
+*omat*	.80	6.00	*xúmus* 'hummus' > *xumusomat* 'hummus processing instrument'
+*prosésor*	.40	2.80	*xúmus* 'hummus' > *xumusprosésor* 'hummus processing instr.'

At least according to these tests, there appears to be no single pattern that is predominantly associated with instruments. Somewhat surprisingly, the +*iya* suffix, which is considered to be more characteristic of locations (see 5.5) and of groups/collectives (see 5.6), is comparatively the most productive.[21] Possibly, the instrument associated with the base item is also regarded as the location in which it is processed or stored for use (e.g. *kuskusiya* as an instrument for processing couscous is also the 'location' in which it is processed). As expected, *meCaCeC* is fairly productive. Speakers tend to regard it as a 'performer' pattern, regardless of whether a human agent or an instrument is involved. Since the base *pláster* does not allow *maCCeC* or *maCCeCa* formation for phonetic reasons, one could calculate their productivity on the base of N = 4 rather than N = 5, which would place *maCCeC* higher than *meCaCeC* on the productivity scale. What is somewhat unexpected is that these tests do not show +*an* to be as productive as it appears to be in child speech and in informal adult speech. Also, when speakers are 'reminded' of options like *maCCeCa* and +*er* for instruments, their selection scores rise significantly in the judgment tasks, but for some reason, the same does not apply to *maCCeC*.

5.4.2   *Instrument formation as reflected in dictionary comparison*

The distribution of innovative instrumental formation emerging from dictionary comparison is illustrated by the following:

(32) **New instrumentals in the 1983 supplement to Even-Shoshan (1970)** (for a more detailed list, see Appendix XXI):

Form	Gloss	Source	Gloss
maCCeC:			
macnem	toaster	*canum*	thin, shrunken
mavzek	flash light	*hivzik*	flash (V)
maCCeCa:			
magzera	paper cutter	*gazar*	cut (V)
makrena	projector	*hikrin*	project (V)
CaCaC: (historically with a geminated middle consonant):			
nagad	resistor	*nagad*	be against, opposite
kabal	condenser	*kibel*	receive
meCaCeC:			
mefaléset	grader; snow plough	*piles*	level (V), smooth flat
mexacec	rock crusher (to gravel)	*xacac*	gravel
+***an***:			
xaygan	dialer	*xiyeg*	dial (V) (< *xug* 'circle')

---

[21] The somewhat lower +*iya* scores in the judgment task are a consequence of +*iya* alternants erroneously not having been offered as an option in two of the five items.

(cont.)

Form	Gloss	Source	Gloss
xišan	sensor	*xiša*	sensing (< *xaš* 'sense' (V))

+ *on*:

ʾašpaton	garbage receptacle	*ʾašpa*	garbage
halixon	walker	*halixa*	walking (< *halax* 'walk')

+ *er* (all borrowed with suffix):

blénder	blender	Eng.
bóyler	boiler	Eng.

CoCeC:

kocev (lev)	(heart) pacer	*kacav*	allocate; provide rhythm
gorer(et)	towing vehicle	*garar*	tow (V)

+ *iya*:

mixtaviya	briefcase (loc./ instrumental)	*mixtav*	letter

(33) **New instrumentals in Ben-Amotz/Ben-Yehuda 1972/82**

Form	Gloss	Source	Gloss

+ *er* (22 items, all borrowed with suffix):

blínker	signaling light	Eng.
stárter	starter	Eng.

maCCeCa (1 item):

magleča	slide board' (loc./instr.)	*glič*	slide (Yid.)

+ *an* (1 item):

šadxan	stapler	*šadxan*	matchmaker (*šidex* 'make a match')

+ *iya* (1 item, borrowed with suffix):

bateríya	battery	Fr., Eng., etc.	

(34) **New instrumentals in PHAS 1993** (all occurrences)

Form	Gloss	Source	Gloss

+ *er*:

kvéčer	stapler	*kveč*	squeeze (Yid.)
špricer	water-spraying device	*špric*	squirt, spray (Yid.)

Here is the distribution of the totals in the various instrumental patterns:

(35) **Productivity ranking of instrumental patterns based on dictionary comparison**

R2 Ranking	ES	ES '83	BABY	PHAS	New	R1	R2	R1 Ranking
maCCeC:	207	26	–	–	26	.1256	.3939	*CaCaC*
maCCeCa:	76	16	1	–	17	.2237	.2576	+ *on*
CaCaC:	23	7	–	–	7	.3043	.1061	*maCCeCa*

(cont.)

R2 Ranking	ES	ES '83	BABY	PHAS	New	R1	R2	R1 Ranking
+*an:*	60	4	1	–	5	.0833	.0758	+*er*
+*on:*	11	3	–	–	3	.2727	.0455	*CoCeC*
meCaCeC:	45	3	–	–	3	.0667	.0455	*maCCeC*
+*er:*	9	8[22]?	22[23]?	2	2	.2222	.0303	+*an*
CoCeC:	11	2	–	–	2	.1818	.0303	+*iya*
+*iya:*	24	1	1[24]?	–	1	.0833	.0152	*meCaCeC*

Total New: 66

According to these data, *maCCeCa, maCCeC* and *CaCaC* maintain a considerable degree of productivity. One may also argue for some reordering of the patterns below them based on ratio weighting. However, the instrumental innovations listed above do not provide a reliable picture of actual usage. They concentrate heavily in the 1983 supplement to ES, and except for the +*er* borrowings, are all from a high/literary register, mostly generated by the Hebrew Language Academy. The slang dictionaries suggest that only +*er* suffixation enjoys a high degree of productivity in the colloquial, but even that cannot be ascertained, since most of the relevant items were borrowed with the suffix already an integral part of an atomic unit. Observation of the colloquial scene does reveal, however, at least one notable tendency: some *maCCeC* cases, primarily MH ones, shift into *meCaCeC*, as in:

(36) **Colloquial variants in *meCaCeC* of *maCCeC* instrumentals**

Instrumental—Literary	Colloquial Variant
macnen 'cooler'	*mecanen*
maghec 'iron'	*megahec*
makcec 'cutter'	*mekacec*
makrer 'refrigerator'	*mekarer*
mantek 'interrupter (teleph.)'	*menatek*
mafcéax 'nutcracker'	*mefacéax*
marsek 'masher'	*merasek*
marses 'sprayer'	*merases*
mašger 'launcher'	*mešager*
maxšev 'computer'	*mexašev*

---

[22] All of these +*er* cases are borrowed, and may have already entered the language as atomic units with the suffix already incorporated. Since their relevance here may thus be questioned, they will not be counted as neologisms.

[23] Again, all of these realizations have probably been borrowed with the suffix already incorporated.

[24] Already borrowed with suffix.

Shifts from *maCCeCa* (the feminine counterpart of *maCCeC*) to *meCaCeCet* (the feminine of *meCaCeC*) show that the partial merger cannot be attributed to orthographic similarity alone. The different suffixes clearly mark the two morphological patterns as orthographically distinct:

(37) *maxsexa* 'mower' > *mekasáxat*   *matxexa* 'clod crusher' > *metaxáxat*

Some *maCCeC* > *meCaCeC* shifts can be reversed as a result of frequent normative use, as in the case of *maxšev* 'computer', which by now is used as frequently as *mexašev*, but in most cases the *meCaCeC* variant has actually taken over. In fact, even the Academy recognizes *mekarer* 'refrigerator' as a legitimate variant of *makrer*. So in addition to competition with other patterns used to refer to instruments in forming new instrumentals, *maCCeC* also ends up losing some existing realizations to a competing *miškal*. The partial merger can be attributed to a variety of factors. *meCaCeC* is preferred because there is a transparent relationship between *meCaCeC* and related verbs, *meCaCeC* being the present participle of *pi'el*. In turn, *pi'el* is also the most productive *binyan* in MH. It is also well-motivated on semantic grounds. Speakers apparently feel that inanimate performers, i.e. instruments, are not that different from animate performers (see also comments on +*an* as agent-or-instrument in 5.3 above). As shown by Bolozky & Jiyad (1989, 1990), Schlesinger (1989), Berman & Sagi (1981), Clark (1993) and others, it is an expected phenomenon. Instruments can function syntactically as agents when there is no human agent, when the human agent is unknown or not on the scene, or when attention is drawn to the instrument by means of which an action is performed and away from its human instigator. A similar shift to the semantically-unmarked pattern occurs in Iraqi Arabic (Bolozky & Jiyad 1989, 1990), when instruments are realized with a typically-agentive *mu*+ prefix instead of the typically-instrumental *mi*+ prefix, as in *mukayyifa* 'air conditioner', *mujaffifa* 'dryer', *mubarrida* 'cooler'. So at least for the cases concerned, the two categories of agentive and instrumental can be said to have been extended into a general 'performer', or 'agent-causal', category, realized in the less marked and more general agentive form. The direction of the shift from instrumental to agentive is thus expected, as a shift from a marked to an unmarked semantic feature. The partial pattern merger and expansion of the semantic scope of the unmarked category is part of the generalization and simplification process typical of the productive lexicon. However, there is no indication that *meCaCeC* is about to take over as the unmarked pattern for instrumentals, either from the data reported on here, or from other research. In production tests reported in Berman (1987), there were more instrumentals realized in +*an* than in either *maCCeC, maCCeCa* or *meCaCeC* (25%–19%–15%–7%, respectively). This reflects the status of +*an* as the unmarked agentive pattern, or perhaps as the 'performer' category, including both instruments and agents. Only in judgment tasks, where other options were available, did *maCCeC* emerge at the head in Berman's tests (e.g. in *madgem* 'a sampling instrument') with about a third of the realizations (32% vs. 14% in the *benoni*, 11% in *maCCeCa*, e.g. in *maršema* 'a writing tool', and 11% in +*an*). When subjects were requested to list any instrumentals that come to mind, *maCCeC* and *maCCeCa* together came up in 28.5% of the instances, and the *benoni* (*meCaCeC*) in 25.5%.

5.4.3   Quantitative evidence from corpora on instrument formation

In our 112,000-word corpus, only 3 of the instruments that are *hapax legomena* are also new:

(38) **Instruments that are *hapax legomena* in a 112k corpus**

Form	Gloss	Source	Gloss
+*an*:			
kolfan	peeler	*kolef, mekalef*	peel (Pres. Part.)
motxan	thriller[25]	*motéax*	stretch, thrill (Pres. Part.)
+*on*:			
mešivon	answering machine	*mešiv*	answer (Pres. Part.)

Ratio computation results in the following ranking:

(39) **Productivity ranking of instrumental patterns based on corpus data**

R2 Ranking	Tokens	*hapax*	R1	R2
maCCeC	23	5	[.2174	.3333]
+*an*	5	3	.6000	.2000
+*on*	29	3	.1034	.2000
+*iya*	9	2	[.2222	.1333]
maCCiC	19	1	[.0526	.0667]
maCCeCa	24	1	[.0417	.0667]
meCaCeC	6	–		
CoCeC	13	–		

Total *hapax*: 15

---

[25] Though not strictly an instrument, it fits better in this category than in the agent class.

+*an* emerges as the most productive instrumental pattern by this criterion, but with the limited number of tokens and the scarcity of *hapax legomena* that are new, our corpus is clearly too small to evaluate instrumental realizations.

The three measurements thus do not agree on which is the most productive pattern for instruments. The productivity tests suggest +*iya*, dictionary comparison points to *maCCeC/maCCeCa*, and corpus data to +*an*. The next section suggests combining the instrumental category with the semantically related agentive one as a means of resolving the difficulty.

5.4.4   *Combine instrumentals with agents?*

Since the distinction between agents and instruments are often blurred, owing to their significant overlap as 'performers', one possibility is to simply analyze data combined for both categories. One may try to do so for the productivity tests, but it is not clear that the emerging picture will be reliable, since target meanings were geared specifically to either human agent or to instruments, not to a combined 'performer' category. If the scores are nevertheless coalesced, the following distribution results:

(40) **Scores where target meaning was agent or instrument** (N subjects = 50, N bases = 13)

Pattern	% Coinage	% Judgment
+*an*	16.46	28.46
+*ay/*+*a'i*	13.69	19.08
+*iya*	9.08	5.69
meCaCeC	7.85	8.92
+*er*	7.23	8.15
+*ist*	8.62	5.08
maCCeC	5.38	4.46
maCCeCa	1.38	5.23
+*on*	3.85	1.85

Some of the very minor patterns were not included. The value of combining these scores is somewhat in doubt, since +*iya* and *maCCeC/maCCeCa* are hardly ever chosen for agent realization, and +*ay/*+*a'i* and +*ist* are rarely chosen for instruments (though note *galay* 'detector', as in *galay mokšim* 'mine detector'). However, +*an*, *meCaCeC* and +*er* are indeed used for both categories, as expected, and +*an* is at the top of the list for 'performers'.

Dictionary comparison and corpus data may be coalesced more reliably, it seems. Note that *meCaCeC* is listed twice: once as in the dictionary totals, and once with *meCaCeC* innovations that constitute colloquial variants of *maCCeC*. The combined dictionary comparison would yield the following results:

(41) **Productivity ranking of agent/instrument patterns based on dictionary comparison**

R2 Ranking	ES	ES '83	BABY	PHAS	New	R1	R2	R1 Ranking
+*an*	1,150	75	19	10	104	.0904	.3152	+*er*
+*ay*/+*a'i*	233	38	10	1	49	.2103	.1485	+*ist*
meCaCeC	187	13	2	2	[17][26]			
with 19 coll. variants of *maCCeC* included					36	.1925	.1091	+*on*
+*ist*	98	2[27]	24[28]	2[29]	28	.2857	.0848	*maCCeCa*
maCCeC:	207	26	–	–	26	.1256	.0788	+*ay*/+*a'i*
maCCeCa:	76	16	1	–	17	.2237	.0515	*meCaCeC* +
meCaCeC	187	13	2	2	[17][30]	.0909	.0515	*maCCeC*
CaCaC	438	16	1[31]	–	17	.0241	.0515	*mitCaCeC*
+*er*	31	2[32]	7[33]	7[34]	16	.5161	.0485	*meCaCeC*
CoCeC	223	12	1	–	13	.0519	.0394	+*an*
+*čik*	–	1	8	–	9		.0273	*maCCiC*
maCCiC	116	4	3	1	8	.0690	.0242	*CoCeC*
+*on*	11	3	–	–	3	.2727	.0091	+*iya*
mitCaCeC	30	1	2	–	3	.1000	.0091	*CaCaC*
+*iya*	24	1	–[35]	–	1	.0417	.0030	

Total New: 330

Dictionary comparison suggests that +*an*, +*ay*/+*a'i*, *meCaCeC* and +*ist*, are the most productive patterns for 'performers', and R1–R2 discrepancies do not justify reordering them. As noted above, the reasons for the predominance of the suffixed patterns are in their semantic transparency and in being clearly identified with the agent/performer category. However, *meCaCeC* is quite productive in the colloquial as well, as manifest in normative *maCCeC* forms shifting to it. 19 such cases were observed in Bolozky & Jiyad (1989,

---

[26] Incorporated in the number that includes colloquial variants of *maCCeC*.
[27] Plus 4 borrowings.
[28] Plus 6 borrowings.
[29] Plus 1 borrowing.
[30] Incorporated in the number that includes colloquial variants of *maCCeC*.
[31] Plus 21 borrowed from Arabic.
[32] Plus 16 borrowings.
[33] Plus 87 borrowings.
[34] Plus 2 borrowings.
[35] One borrowed item listed.

1990). Had they been incorporated in either the 1983 supplement to ES or in the slang dictionaries, the productivity of *meCaCeC* for 'performers' would have been evident. R1–R2 differences derived from ratio weighting would suggest raising +*er* to precede +*ist*, raising *maCCeCa* to precede *maCCeC*, raising +*on* to precede *CoCeC* or *čik*, and lowering *CaCaC* below *maCCiC*. However, there appear to be no independent reasons for doing so.

Combining the corpus data for a 'performer' category yields a distribution in the 112k corpus that is not that different from the one for agentives, owing to the generally-small number of instrumental tokens:

(42) **Productivity ranking of agentive/instrumental patterns based on corpus data**

R2 Ranking	Tokens	*hapax*	R1	R2
+*an*	162	50	.3086	.2703
meCaCeC	175	31	.1771	.1676
maCCiC	199	27	.1357	.1459
CoCeC	871	27	[.0301	.1459]
+*ay*/+*a'i*	148	16	.1081	.0865
+*ist*	13[36]?	11?	[.8462	.0595]
+*er*	5	5	[1.0000	.0270]
maCCeC:	23	5	[.2174	.0270]
CaCaC	546	5	[.0091	.0270]
+*on*	29	3	.1034	.0162
+*iya*	9	2	[.2222	.0108]
mitCaCeC	57	2	.0351	.0108
maCCeCa:	24	1	[.0417	.0054]

Total *hapax*: 185

Only patterns in which at least one recent *hapax* has been found are considered. Of those, +*an* is the most productive, which is consistent with the results of other evaluations of 'performer'-formation productivity. It is followed by *meCaCeC*; +*ay*/+*a'i* is placed higher by the two other criteria.

Thus, in the combined 'performer' category, +*an* is the most productive pattern by all criteria. Though the rankings are not fully parallel, +*ay*/+*a'i* and *meCaCeC* occupy second and third positions, not necessarily in that order.

---

[36] All borrowed.

5.5 *Selection of location patterns*

According to Hebrew textbooks, the patterns denoting location are *miCCaC* and *miCCaCa*, but in fact those are not locative patterns *par excellence*, particularly not in the colloquial, and in *miCCaC* perhaps not even in normative Modern Hebrew, since *miCCaC* has more abstract nouns than it has locations (140–150 vs. 80–90 in Even-Shoshan 1970). The colloquial tendency to shift locatives from *miCCaCa* to *maCCeCa* further reduces its semantic transparency. The ending +*iya* is emerging as a prominent marker of location, particularly in the colloquial register. Another location marker is +*iyáda* (borrowed from Greek. For detailed discussions of +*iya* and +*iyáda*, see Almagor 1993, 1994).

5.5.1 *Productivity tests on locative formation*

In our productivity tests (50 open, 50 selection), the distribution of locatives was as follows (for details see Appendix XXII):

(43) **Productivity tests where the target meaning was a location:**
(N subjects = 50, N bases = 8. Co. = Coinage, Ju. = Judgment)

Pattern	% Co.	% Ju.	Illustrations
+*iya*	64.50	74.50	*kariš* 'shark' > *k(a)rišiya* 'place where sharks are held'
			'omlet 'omelette' > *'omletiya* 'place where they make omelettes'
			nagmaš 'APC' > *nagnašiya* 'APC repair shop'
maCCeCa	5.00	6.50	*xitul* 'diaper' > *maxtela* 'diaper factory'
miCCaCa	3.25	6.50	*xitul* 'diaper' > *mixtala* 'diaper factory'
+*iyáda*	3.25	4.50	*'asla* 'toilet bowl' > *'asliyáda* 'toilet bowl factory'
miCCaC	2.25	.75	*kariš* 'shark' > *mixraš* 'place where sharks are held'
+*it*	1.75	.75	*kariš* 'shark' > *k(a)rišit* 'place where sharks are held'
+*(i)yum*	.75	2.75	*kariš* 'shark' > *krišáryum* 'place where sharks are held'
+*a*	2.50	.50	*'asla* 'toilet bowl' > *'aslata* 'toilet bowl factory'
+*on*	1.50	.50	*'omlet* 'omelette' > *'omleton* 'place where they make omelettes'
+*an*	1.25	–	*'asla* 'toilet bowl' > *'aslan* 'toilet bowl factory'
maCCeC	.25	.75	*'asla* 'toilet bowl' > *ma'asel* 'toilet bowl factory'
+*er*	.50	–	*šnícel* 'schnitzel' > *šníceler* 'schnitzel place'

An appended +*iya* is clearly the most preferred marker of locatives, at least in the sense of 'place where something is made/sold/repaired'.

The 'classical' *miCCaCa* and *miCCaC* are far behind, even in the selection tasks. *maCCeCa* is more productive for locatives than either (see explanation below).

5.5.2 *Locative formation as reflected in dictionary comparison*

The distribution of innovative locatives according to dictionary comparison is illustrated below:

(44) **New location nouns in ES '83** (for more details, see Appendix XXIII)

Form	Gloss	Source	Gloss
+*iya*:			
ma'adaniya	delicatessen shop	ma'adan	delicacy
steykiya	steak house	steyk	steak
miCCaC:			
micmat	junction	cómet	juncture, node, crossroads
mircaf	platform (bus gate, etc.)	racif	platform, quay (< ricef 'pave')
miCCaCa:			
misrafa	garbage burning place	saraf	burn (V)
mifxama	coal production place	pexam	coal
+*iyáda*:			
tremp(i)yáda	arranged hitchhiking spot	tremp	a ride

(45) **New location nouns in Ben-Amotz/Ben-Yehuda '72/'82** (all occurrences)

Form	Gloss	Source	Gloss
+*iya*:			
kambaciya	operations officer's post	kambac	operations officer (acron. from kcin 'officer of' + mivca'im 'operations')
kačkiya	girls' quarters'[37]	káčke	duck (Yid.)
+*iyáda*:			
kačkiyáda	girls' quarters'[38]	káčke	duck (Yid.)
steykiyáda	steak house	steyk	steak
miCCaCa:			
mizlala	small restaurant	zalal	devour

The data can be summarized as follows:

(46) **Productivity ranking of locative patterns based on dictionary comparison**

R2 Ranking	ES	ES '83	BABY	PHAS	New	R1	R2
+*iya*	53	11	2	–	13	.2453	.3714
miCCaCa	80	11 (10 lit.)	1	–	12	.1500	.3428

---

[37] As well as a group of girls chattering.
[38] As well as a group of girls chattering.

(cont.)

R2 Ranking	ES	ES '83	BABY	PHAS	New	R1	R2
miCCaC	92	7 (all lit.)	–	–	7	.0761	.2000
+*iyáda*	–[39]	1	2	–	3		.0857

Total New: 35

Most of the innovations are in ES '83, but while those in *miCCaC* and *miCCaCa* belong to a high register, realizations in +*iya* tend are found at all language registers. Thus, the greater productivity of +*iya* is supported by both productivity tests and dictionary comparison. +*iyáda*'s placement is based on R2 alone, for the lack of an ES base.

Similarly to the colloquial shift from *maCCeC* to *meCaCeC* described above, a strong tendency can be observed for *miCCaCa* locatives to merge with *maCCeCa*, as in:

(47) **Literary Locatives**   **Colloquial Variants**

(a) *mixbasa* 'laundry (room)'   *maxbesa*
    mispara 'barber's shop'   *maspera*
    mištala '(plant) nursery'   *maštela*
    mištana 'urinal'   *maštena*
    mišxata 'slaughterhouse'   *mašxeta*
    mitpara 'sewing workshop'   *matpera*
    mighaca 'ironing shop'   *magheca*
    mispana 'docks, shipyard'   *maspena*
    miglafa 'zincography shop'   *maglefa*
    miltaša 'diamond polishing plant'   *malteša*
    maxlava 'dairy, dairy shop'   *maxleva*
    maxšaša 'hashish smokers' den'   *maxšeša*
    mixtava 'desk'   *maxteva*
    miglaša 'slide'   *magleša* (slang *magleča*)
(b) *midraxa* 'sidewalk'   *madrexa/midraxa*
    mirpa'a 'clinic'   *marpe'a/mirpa'a*
    mizbala 'garbage dump'   *mazbela/mizbala*
    mizraka 'water fountain'   *mazreka/mizraka*
    mizlala 'small restaurant (slang)'   *mazlela/mizlala*

In subgroup (a), 14 locatives are shifted from literary *miCCaCa* to colloquial *maCCeCa*. In subgroup (b), 5 occurrences of normative *miCCaCa* are allowed to be realized either in *miCCaCa* or in *maCCeCa* in the colloquial register. The direction of the shift, from *miCCaCa*

---

[39] Except for borrowings like *'otostráda* 'expressway' or *promenáda* 'promenade', which were borrowed as atomic units.

to *maCCeCa* and not vice versa, can also be explained in terms of transparency. In the total lexicon (based on dictionary counts), if *miCCaC* and *miCCaCa* on the one hand, and *maCCeC* and *maCCeCa* on the other, are indeed conceived of as related pairs by native speakers, then the former pair is less transparent semantically than the latter. While the majority of forms in both *maCCeC* and *maCCeCa* in ES are instrumental, only the majority of *miCCaCa* realizations are locative, and only about a quarter of *miCCaC* cases can be characterized as locative. *miCCaC* is more prominently used for a group of established abstract nouns, as, for instance, in the following (for a longer list, see Appendix XXIV):

(48) **Abstract nouns in *miCCaC***

Form	Gloss	Source	Gloss
mivdak	checkup, test	*badak*	check, examine, test
mifgaš	meeting, assembly	*pagaš*	meet
ma'asar	arrest	*'asar*	arrest; forbid
ma'ase	deed	*'asa*	do

Thus, semantically, the *miCCaC(a)* pattern is not sufficiently transparent for locatives, which allows *maCCeCa*, the more prominent pattern semantically to start with, to become a 'haven' for both instrumentals and locatives. This is facilitated by the prior existence of a number of *maCCeCa* realizations that could be characterized as either instruments or locations (*ma'afera* 'ashtray', for instance, is both an instrument for collecting ash, and a place for ash):

(49)

Form	Gloss	Source	Gloss
ma'afera	ashtray	*'efer*	ash
makpeca	spring-board	*kafac*	jump (V)
matxena	mill	*taxan*	grind, mill (V)
madrega	stair	*darga, dereg*	step, grade (V)

So generally, *maCCeC(a)* is more productive than *miCCaC(a)*. Its relatively greater productivity is also supported by productivity tests in Berman (1987). In her open-ended coinage tasks, *maCCeC(a)* occupied second place in instrument realization (after +*an*, see above), and a rank equal to that of *miCCaC(a)* in location realization (20% vs. 21%, respectively).[40] *miCCaC(a)* locatives are more common than

---

[40] I.e. *mislak* and *maslek* are equally likely as realizations of 'a place to be driven away to' (< *silek* 'remove, drive away'), *mixlama* and *maxlema* are just as common as 'place to dream in' (< *xalam* 'dream' (V)).

maCCeCa ones in Berman's data only in judgment tasks (45%–28%, respectively).[41] Berman also proposes a more general account of the instability of locative realizations: while agents are highly individuated and instruments semantically restricted, locatives can accommodate a variety of semantic features, which allows them to shift more easily from one pattern to another, or alternatively, to overlap with other semantic categories.

There is another possible explanation for the *miCCaCa* > *maCCeCa* shift. It may simply be a phonetically-motivated change, from a marked vowel (in this case *i*) to the unmarked vowel, *a*. This possibility seems to be supported by data from Iraqi Arabic (see Bolozky & Jiyad 1989, 1990), where the typically-instrumental *mi+* shifts to the typically-locative *ma+*, as in instrumentals such as *mibzal* 'tool for washing rice' > *mabzal, mijhar* 'microscope' > *majhar, midfaʿ* 'cannon' > *madfaʿ*. Since this is the opposite of what happens in MH, the phonological explanation is the only one that can account for both phenomena. *a* has been shown to be the unmarked vowel in Modern Hebrew (Plada 1958/59, Bolozky 1990b), and the same can probably be demonstrated for Arabic.

In view of this, we could add colloquial locatives and locative/instrumentals in *maCCeCa* to the table of locative distribution by dictionary comparison, and correct our statistics accordingly:

(50) **Productivity ranking of loc. and loc./instr. patterns based on dictionary comparison**

R2 Ranking	ES	ES '83	BABY	PHAS	New	R1	R2	R1 Ranking	Alt Ord
+*iya*	53	11	2	–	13	.2453	.3171	+*iya*	
miCCaCa	80	11 (10 lit.)	1	–	12	.1500	.2927	*maCCeC(a)*	{*maCCeC(a)*}
miCCaC	92	7 (all lit.)	–	–	7	.0761	.1707	*miCCaCa*	
maCCeC(a)	14	3	3[42]	–	6	.4286	.1463	*miCCaC*	
+*iyáda*	–[43]	1	2	–	3		.0732		

Total New: 41

---

[41] E.g. *mitpas* 'place where one is caught' (< *tafas* 'catch'), *mimtaka* 'place with sweets' (< *mamtak* 'candy').

[42] Only 3 of the 19 *maCCeCa* variants are listed in the slang dictionaries. Although we know there are more, we will go by the actual listing.

[43] Except for borrowings like *'otostráda* 'expressway' or *promenáda* 'promenade', which were borrowed as atomic units.

A high R1 and ratio weighting suggest that had the category been
restricted only to locatives that can also function as instrumentals,
maCCeC(a) would have ranked at least second in productivity. In
either case, the ranking is consistent with the rest of our findings,
as well as with Berman's (1987) data, where the relative percentages
in open-ended coinage tests for places were +*iya* 25%, and *miCCaC(a)*
and *maCCeCa* about 20% each.

5.5.3   *Quantitative evidence from corpora on locative formation*

The 112,000 word corpus was probably too small for determining
the relative productivity of locatives:

(51) **Productivity ranking of locative patterns based on corpus data**

R2 Ranking	Tokens	*hapax*	R1	R2
miCCaC	308	9	[.0292	.5000]
miCCaCa	66	5	[.0757	.2777]
+*iya*	28	2	[.0714	.1111]
+*iyáda*	1	1	[1.0000	.0555]
maCCeC(a)	15	1	[.0667	.0555]

Total *hapax*:   18

None of the *hapax* locative realizations was found to be recent. Our
evaluation of locative formation productivity will only draw from
productivity tests and dictionary comparison, which clearly point to
+*iya* as the most productive locative pattern and as the default realization for this category.

5.6   *Selecting a collection/group/system*

Some nominal derivation patterns may also denote a group, a collection, or a system:

(52) **Patterns that may denote a group, a collection, or a system**

Pattern	Form	Gloss	Source	Gloss
+*iya*	*sifriya*	library; a book collection	*séfer*	book
	zimriya	convention of choirs	*zémer*	song
miCCaC	*migvan*	array, variety	*gáven*	color, hue
	ma'ahal	emcampment	*'óhel*	tent
miCCaCa	*mitkafa*	offensive (= set of attacks)	*takaf*	attack
	mignana	a system of defenses	*g.n.n*	defend

(cont.)

Pattern	Form	Gloss	Source	Gloss
+*on*	*še'elon*	questionnaire (= set of questions)	*še'ela*	question
	mexiron	price list	*mexir*	price
CaCéCet	*tayéset*	squadron (air)	*tas*	fly
	kartéset	card collection (rollerdex etc.)	*kartis*	card

Since there seems to be no pattern whose primary function is to characterize collections or groups, we will examine the productivity of group/collection formation by the three criteria.

5.6.1 *Productivity tests on collective formation*

The distribution of forms denoting groups/collections in the productivity tests (50 coinage, 50 judgment) was as follows (for details see Appendix XXV):

(53) **Productivity tests where the target meaning was a group/collection/system:** (N subjects = 50, N bases = 4. Co. = Coinage, Ju. = Judgment)

Pattern	% Co.	% Ju.	Illustrations
+*iya*	38.00	32.50	*xérek* 'insect' > *xarakiya* 'insect collection'
+*iyáda*	17.00	22.00	*xatul* 'cat' > *xatuliyáda* 'group of cats'
+*on*	10.00	10.00	*matbéaʿ* 'coin' > *matbeʿon* 'coin collection'
miCCaCa	–	15.00	*xérek* 'insect' > *mixraka* 'insect collection'
maCCeCa	2.00	12.50	*váʿad* 'committee' > *mavʿeda* 'set/system of committees'
miCCaC	–	2.50	*váʿad* 'committee' > *mivʿad* 'set/system of committees'
maCCeC	1.00	1.00	*váʿad* 'committee' > *mavʿed* 'set/system of committees'
+*it*	1.00	1.00	*váʿad* 'committee' > *vaʿadonit* 'set/system of committees'

The preferred pattern in this category is +*iya*, followed by +*iyáda*, then +*on*.

5.6.2 *Collective formation as reflected in dictionary comparison*

The distribution of innovative group terms according to dictionary comparison is illustrated below:

(54) **New group nouns in the 1983 supplement to ES** (all occurrences)

Form	Gloss	Source	Gloss
+ *on*:			
ʾeruᶜon	list of events (in program)	*ʾeruáᶜ*	event
matʾimon	concordance	*matʾima*	corresponding, parallel (here, words)
meydaᶜon	compendium of information	*meydaᶜ*	information
sidron	serial	*séder*	order
taᶜarifon	price list	*taᶜarif*	price
zmiron	collection of chants/songs	*zémer, zmirot*	chant/song, chants
***miCCaC*:**			
mimsad	establishment (= system of institutions)	*mosad*	institution
mikšat	arcade (a set of arches)	*késet*	arch
mitᶜal	canal system	*teᶜala*	canal
+ *iyáda*:			
ʾuniversiyáda	muli-university sports event	*ʾunivérsita*	university
susiyáda	popular horse race	*sus*	horse
+ *iya*:			
makabiya	convention of Makabi teams	*makabi*	Jewish sports organization
***miCCaCa*:**			
mislaᶜa	planting area with rocks (locative/group)	*sélaᶜ*	rock
+ *it*:			
xešbonit	list of goods given to customer	*xešbon*	account, invoice

(55) **New group nouns in Ben-Amotz/Ben-Yehuda '72/'82** (all occurrences)

Form	Gloss	Source	Gloss
+ *iya*:			
kačkiya	group of girls chattering (or their location)	*kácke*	duck (Yid.)
+ *iyáda*:			
čaxčaxiyáda	the underprivileged in Israel	*čáxčax*	north African Israeli Jew
kačkiyáda	group of girls chattering (or their location)	*kácke*	duck (Yid.)

Here is the summary of group/collection neologisms in the various dictionaries:

(56) **Productivity ranking of collective/group patterns based on dictionary comparison**

R2 Ranking	ES	ES '83	BABY	PHAS	New	R1	R2	R1 Ranking
+on	18	6	–	–	6	.3333	.3524	miCCaC
+iyáda	–	2	2	–	4		.2353	+on
miCCaC	8	3	–	–	3	.3750	.1765	+iya
+iya	10	1	1	–	2	.2000	.1176	miCCaCa
miCCaCa	5	1	–	–	1	.2000	.0588	
+it	–	1	–	–	1		.0588	

Total New: 17

Dictionary neologisms suggest that +on is the most productive group marker, followed by +iyáda. miCCaC is quite productive as well, but its small R1 advantage over +on cannot be compared with +on's R2 size. However, all innovations upon which the above productivity ranking is based are quite literary, except for mimsad 'establishment'. When colloquial innovations are considered separately, +iya and +iyáda emerge as the most productive group patterns, as suggested by the productivity tests above.

5.6.3 *Quantitative evidence from corpora on collective formation*

For groups, as for locatives, the 112,000 word corpus was too small for determining relative productivity:

(57) **Productivity ranking of collective/group patterns based on corpus data**

R2 Ranking	Tokens	hapax	R1	R2
+on	4	2	[.5000	.4000]
miCCaC	11	1	[.0909	.2000]
+iyáda	1	1	[1.0000	.2000]
CaCéCet	1	1	[1.0000	.2000]
+it	–	–		

Total hapax: 5

None of the hapax group/collection realizations was found to be recent. Basing our productivity ranking on the two other criteria, it seems that in the colloquial, +iya and +iyáda are the preferred group patterns, whereas in the literary register, +on and miCCaC are the most productive ones.

5.7   *Selecting a diminutive pattern*

A detailed description and analysis of diminutive formation devices
in Modern Hebrew is provided in Bolozky (1994a), and will be summarized below. Bolozky (1994a) starts with a review of an article by
M. Z. Segal (1925) on diminution in early Modern Hebrew. Although
Segal mentions the diminutive role of suffixes like +*on*[44] and +*it*, as
well as the role of reduplication, his data on those are too marginal
for current Israeli Hebrew. The patterns themselves are discussed
only in passing, as part of a list of many other patterns which are
not productive at all today. Segal's data are particularly interesting
when he suggests that feminine suffixes are often associated with
diminution. In the early stages of language formation, the marking
of gender appears to have been intended to distinguish not sex, but
rather size and/or connotative value. In languages which distinguish
'masculine', 'feminine' and 'neuter', 'neuter' was preferably used for
lifeless things. Since the latter were considered inferior to living organisms, neuter also tended to carry some depreciatory or belittling sense
(cf., for instance, Jespersen 1924), even when it actually applied to
humans and animals. In languages without 'neuter', the 'feminine'
suffix denoted particularly lifeless objects (cf. Hetzron 1967) or objects
of small size, such as grain and fruit (e.g. *xita* 'wheat', *te'ena* 'fig'), or
an individual member of a mass noun (e.g. *'oni* 'ships, fleet' ~ *'oniya*
'ship'), or borrowed meanings (e.g. *yarex* 'thigh' ~ *yarka/yerexa* 'side'),
or narrowing down from the general to the particular (e.g. *malon* 'a
place to stay over' ~ *meluna* 'a temporary structure for sleeping in
the field', *xélek* 'part' ~ *xélka* 'a plot of land'). Only because sex in
living organisms was so evident (and because living organisms were
so central) did it later become the main criterion for gender distinction. It was the initial 'primitive' conception of the suffixed forms
as smaller or subordinate that gave rise to some diminution by means
of 'feminine' suffixation:

(58) **Diminution through feminine suffixation (Segal 1925)**

Base	Gloss	Base + Fem. suff.	Gloss
dag	fish	*daga*	small fish
'ec	wood, tree	*'eca*	small trees
xéres	clay, clay container	*xarsit*	fractions of clay; clay matter

---

[44] See also Gross (1994) on the very marginal role of +*on* as a diminutive device
in BH and in MishH.

In current Hebrew, however, it appears that the somewhat-productive use of +*it* and +*iya* for diminution is associated with these particular endings as suffixes, and has little to do with their feminine gender *per se*. Today's speakers do not conceive of the shift from masculine to feminine in itself as involving diminution.

5.7.1   *Minor diminutive patterns in Modern Hebrew*

There appear to be three relatively-minor diminutive formation devices in current Israeli Hebrew, reduplication, and the appending of +*it* and +*iya*. Another two diminutive patterns, +*čik* and +*iko*, are confined to the colloquial/informal register.

Redupulication applies to some nouns as well as to some adjectives, mostly ones denoting colors and some physical characteristics. To the extent that the diminution of nouns through reduplication continues to be productive, its productivity is confined to the higher registers. Of the occurrences listed in Even-Shoshan (1970), a few are familiar (note that the reduplicated form gloss of 'Noun' is always 'little Noun' in this section):

(59) **Diminution of nouns through reduplication: illustrations from everyday usage**

Noun	Gloss	Redupl.	Noun	Gloss	Redupl.
kélev	dog	*klavlav*	*xatul*	cat	*xataltul*
xazir	pig	*xazarzir*	*dag*	fish	*dagig*
kof	monkey	*kofif*	*zanav*	tail	*znavnav*
safam	moustache	*sfampam* (coll. *sfamfam*)	*zakan*	beard	*zkankan*
šafan	rabbit/hyrax	*šfanpan* (coll. *šfanfan*)			
géver	man	*gvarbar* (coll. *gvarvar*)			

All other instances of diminution through reduplication are literary/rare, and although they are not opaque, and would probably be understood when encountered, they are hardly ever used:

(60) **Diminution of nouns through reduplication: illustrations from the literary register**

Noun	Gloss	Redupl.	Noun	Gloss	Redupl.
'agam	lake	*'agamgam*	*clav*	cross	*clavlav*
xéder	room	*xadardar*	*xérek*	insect	*xarakrak*
kanaf	wing	*knafnaf*	*kares*	belly	*krasras*
kétem	spot	*ktamtam*	*péleg*	stream	*plaglag*
makdéax	drill	*kdaxdax*	*kémet*	wrinkle	*kmatmat*
šérec	bug, insect	*šracrac*	*taraf*	leaf	*trafraf*
'égev	flirt	*'agavgav*	*'anaf*	branch	*'anafnaf*

Formation of diminutivized adjectives through reduplication, however, is relatively common. The reduplicated form sort of 'attenuates' color and some attributes, similarly to English '. . . ish', as in 'reddish':

(61) **Diminution of adjectives through reduplication**

Adjective	Gloss	Redupl.	Redupl. F.
ʾadom	red	ʾadamdam	ʾadamdama
kaxol	blue	kxalxal	kxalxala
yarok	green	yerakrak	yerakraka
cahov	yellow	cehavhav	cehavhaba
katan	small	ktantan	ktantana
šamen	fat	šmanman	šmanmana
ʿagol	round	ʿagalgal	ʿagalgala
xamuc	sour	xamacmac	xamacmaca
xalak	smooth	xalaklak	xalaklaka

At least insofar as colors are concerned, any speaker would easily construct (or interpret) the reduplicated alternant that 'attenuates' a color even if s/he has not come across such form before.

Diminution by feminine suffixation also maintains a certain degree of productivity. But as noted above, it is a corollary of the suffix itself, not of its being feminine. One type of realization involves +*it* suffixation to inanimate[45] noun stems, as in:

(62) **Diminution through +*it* suffixation**

Noun	Gloss	Noun+*it*	Gloss
kaf	tablespoon	kapit	teaspoon
kos	glass	kosit	wineglass
mapa	tablecloth	mapit	napkin, small tablecloth
kar	pillow	karit	small pillow
pax	can, tin	paxit	small can
cnon	radish	cnonit	small radish
mapúax	bellow	mapuxit	harmonica
mila	word	milit	(small) function word
xameš	five	xamišit	fifth [and for any other fraction]
ʾulpan	Hebrew school/class	ʾulpanit	small/provisional Hebrew class
beyca	egg	beycit	ovum
buʿa	bubble	buʿit	small bubble
cinor	pipe, tube	cinorit	thin tube; catheter
xalil	flute	xalilit	recorder

---

[45] +*it*-suffixation to animate nouns usually involves gender change only, e.g. *student* '(male) student' ~ *studéntit* 'female student'. Note, however, that not all realizations of inanimate nouns with *it* involve diminution, e.g. *xavit* 'barrel', *zavit* 'angle', etc.

(cont.)

Noun	Gloss	Noun + *it*	Gloss
kadur	ball	*kadurit*	small ball; (red or white) cell
masor	saw	*masorit*	small saw
pasuk	phrase, verse	*psukit*	half-phrase, hemistich
ke'ara	dish	*ka'arit*	small dish
karon	wagon, train car	*kronit*	small wagon/car

One of the semantic correlates of the +*iya* suffix is 'a unit, or realization, of some matter', as in:

(63) +*iya* as 'unit'

Noun	Gloss	Noun + *iya*	Gloss
sukar	sugar	*sukar(i)ya*	candy
beyca	egg	*beyciya*	fried egg
ša'ava	wax	*ša'avaniya*[46]	waxed tablecloth

Occasionally, this 'unit' may also constitute a diminutive:

(64) **Diminution through** +*iya* **suffixation**

Noun	Gloss	Noun + *iya*	Gloss
naknik	sausage	*naknikiya*	frankfurter, hot dog
'uga	cake	*'ugiya*	cookie
maca	unleavened bread	*maciya*	cracker
néšef	ball	*nišpiya*	small ball, party
gúmi	rubber	*gumiya*	rubber band
léxem	bread	*laxmaniya*	(bread) roll
ma'ase	deed, tale	*ma'asiya*	a (?little) tale
néšef	ball, formal party	*nišpiya*	small ball/party

Two other non-major diminutive suffixes found in Israeli Hebrew are mostly characteristic of casual (or lower) registers, +*čik* and +*íko*. Both also tend to involve expression of affection. +*čik* is borrowed from Russian:

(65) **Diminution through** +*čik* **suffixation**

Form	Gloss	Form + *čik*	Gloss
baxur	young man	*baxúrčik*	nice young man
katan	small	*katánčik*	very small
šamen	fat	*šaménčik*	affectionate/forgiving modification of 'fat'
xayal	soldier	*xayálčik*	young/little soldier (affectionate)

+*íko* is borrowed from Judeo-Spanish (usually more affectionate than diminutive *per se*):

---

[46] Alternatively, *ša'avanit.*

(66) **Diminution through +*iko* suffixation**

Base	Gloss	Base+*iko*	Gloss
xaver	friend	*xaveríko*	friend (affectionate)
kof	monkey	*kofíko*	little monkey (affectionate)
moše	Moshe	*mošíko*	little Moshe (affectionate)
xayal	soldier	*xayalíko*	young/little soldier (affectionate)

Both +*čik* and +*iko* suffixations are colloquial phenomena, restricted to marginally-standard contexts. +*čik* seems to be fairly productive.

5.7.2   +*on-suffixation as a marker of diminution in Modern Hebrew*

There are approximately 680 forms ending with *on* in Even-Shoshan (1970), most of which are not morphologically transparent. Of those that are, we have already seen that +*on* suffixation may occasionally be used for instrumental marking, as in:

(67) **+*on* as an instrument marker**

Form	Gloss	Base	Gloss
'ašpaton	garbage container	*'ašpa*	garbage
halixon	walker	*halixa*	walking
mešivon	answering machine	*mešiv*	answer (v., pres.)

and we will also be dealing below (Chapter 7) with the *CiCCon* (e.g. *šilton* 'regime; government', *dimyon* 'imagination; similarity') and *CiCaCon* (e.g. *zikaron* 'memory', *kišalon* 'failure') patterns for abstract nouns. As noted above, a small +*on* sub-group refers to 'group' or 'collection', as in:

(68) **+*on* as a group marker**

Form	Gloss	Base	Gloss
xidon	quiz	*xida*	riddle
mexiron	price list	*mexir*	price
ta'arifon	price list	*ta'arif*	price
še'elon	questionnaire	*še'ela*	question
širon	song collection	*šir*	song
takanon	code	*takana*	ordinance

Another sub-group refers to 'events or entities related to time-units, especially publications':

(69) **+*on* as a marker of entities related to time units**

Form	Gloss	Base	Gloss
yomon	daily	*yom*	day
šavu'on	weekly	*šavúa'*	week
mekomon	local paper	*makom*	place

Very specialized +*on* denotations are 'temporary structures (made of . . .)':

(70) +*on* as a marker of temporary structures

Form	Gloss	Base	Gloss
badon	cloth structure	*bad*	cloth
paxon	tin structure	*pax*	tin
'azbeston	asbestos structure	*'azbest*	asbestos

statistical terms:

(71) +*on* as a marker of statistical terms

Form	Gloss	Base	Gloss
xecyon	50% section	*xéci*	half
'asiron	10% section	*'éser*	ten
me'on	1% section	*me'a*	hundred

and geological terms:

(72) +*on* as a marker of geological terms

Form	Gloss	Base	Gloss
šlišon	third of geological period	*šliš*	third
revi'on	fourth of geological period	*réva'*	quarter

However, the bulk of transparent +on derivatives, about 130 in the Even-Shoshan (1970) dictionary, are diminutives. Of all diminution devices available to the contemporary speaker of Hebrew, linear suffixation with +*on* is the most productive. It appears that any noun that may have a diminutive version in the real world either already has a diminutive alternant with +*on*, or could potentially have one. When such a form is introduced for the first time, be it by a normative authority, an author, or any 'lay' innovative speaker, it will be used, or understood, as a diminutive alternant of its base. In animate nouns, for which male and female entities coexist in the natural world, masculine is marked as diminutive by the suffix +*on*, and the feminine by further concatenation of +*et*, yielding +*ón*+*et*, as in (all unglossed diminutive N's below are 'small N'):

(73) **Diminution of animate nouns by +*on* suffixation**

Base N.	Gloss	M. Dimin.	F. Dimin.
yéled	boy	*yaldon*	*yaldónet*
baxur	young man	*baxuron*	*baxurónet*
sus	horse	*suson*	*susónet*
pišpeš	bug	*pišpešon*	*pišpešónet*
barvaz	duck	*barvazon*	*barvazónet*
kélev	dog	*kalbon*	*kalbónet*
xatul	cat	*xatulon*	*xatulónet*

Inanimate masculine nouns are diminutivized by +on-suffixation.
Below are a few illustrations from the numerous instances of inanimate +on diminutives found in the Even-Shoshan (1970) dictionary:

(74) **Diminution of inanimate masculine nouns by +on suffixation**

Noun	Gloss	Noun+on	Noun	Gloss	Noun+on
'af	nose	'apon	'arnak	purse	'arnakon
'argaz	crate	'argazon	tapúax	apple	tapuxon
bakbuk	bottle	bakbukon	gavía‘	cup	gvi‘on
gaviš	crystal	gvišon	géšer	bridge	gišron
pinkas	notebook	pinkason	pésel	statue	pislon
caríax	tower	crixon	crif	shack	crifon

Inanimate feminine nouns are also marked by +on, and their gender
is preserved by the same +et found in animate feminine ones, yielding +ón+et:

(75) **Diminution of inanimate feminine nouns by +ón+et suffixation**

F. Noun	Gloss	N+ónet	F. Noun	Gloss	N+ónet
giv'a	hill	giv'ónet	simla	dress	simlónet
dira	apartment	dirónet	mizvada	suitcase	mizvadónet
tipa	drop	tipónet	medina	state	medinónet
mimxata	handkerchief	mimxaónet	nešika	kiss	nešikónet
mis‘ada	restaurant	mis‘adónet	psi‘a	step	psi‘ónet
prusa	slice	prusónet	xavit	barrel	xaviyónet

The difference from diminutivized masculine nouns is that no free-
standing +on-forms like *simlon, *diron, *mizvadon are allowed, since
such inanimate feminine nouns have no masculine counterparts in
the natural world. In any case, regardless of the type of base noun
involved, the 'default' manner of forming new diminutives that are
not found in any dictionary involves adding the suffix +on to a masculine base, and +ónet to a feminine one. Thus, for instance, ze'ev
'wolf' can only be diminutivized as ze'evon, and this is how the form
will immediately be interpreted when heard for the first time. The
diminutive of ze'eva 'she-wolf' will most likely be realized as ze'evónet,
and will be understood as such. Similarly, the diminutive of ma‘ader
'hoe' will be ma‘aderon, and the form ma‘aderon can only be understood as 'small hoe'. mesiba 'party' will be dinimutivized as mesibónet,
and so on.

The diminutive suffix +on, in Modern Hebrew as in other languages, also serves to express either affection or depreciatory tinge
when attached to adjectives and to nouns embodying the qualities

concerned. Such emotive expressions may also involve diminution, but not necessarily:

(76) **Affectionate or depreciatory** +*on* **suffixation (may also be diminutive)**

Base	Gloss	Base+*on*	Base+*ónet*
xamud	cute, nice	*xamudon*	*xamudónet*
caʕir	young	*ceʕiron*	*ceʕirónet*
tamim	naïve	*tmimon*	*tmimónet*
tipeš	a fool, foolish	*tipšon*	*tipšónet*
misken	poor, miserable	*miskenon*	*miskenónet*

Whether the emotive +*on*/+*ónet* diminution is affectionate or derogatory may be determined either by context, or by whether the base noun carries positive or negative connotation to start with. In the following, for instance, the diminutives are based on negative readings of *yehudi* and *pakid*:

(77) **Derogatory** +*on* **suffixation when base itself has derogatory reading**

Base	Gloss	Base+*on*	Gloss
yehudi	Jew(ish)	*yehudon*	Jew boy (with all racist connotations)
pakid	clerk	*pkidon*	small(-minded) clerk

The strongest evidence for the productivity of the +*on* diminutive suffix is its distribution in forms that have already incorporated other diminutive morphemes. Even though the reduplicated forms below have alternants with +*on* appended directly to the base, it is also possible to add +*on*/+*ónet* to the reduplicated forms themselves, particularly in animate nouns, as in:

(78) **Diminutive** +*on* **affixed to forms diminutivized by reduplication**

Base	Gloss	Redup.	Base+*on*	Redup.+*on*	Redup.+*ónet*
kélev	dog	*klavlav*	*kalbon*	*klavlavon*	*klavlavónet*
xatul	cat	*xataltul*	*xatulon*	*xataltulon*	*xataltulónet*
xazir	pig	*xazarzir*	*xaziron*	*xazarziron*	*xazarirónet*

It is also possible to add +*on* to (inanimate) forms ending with the diminutive suffix +*it*. Since nouns ending with +*it* are all feminine, so are the further diminutions, which all end with +*ón*+*et*:

(79) **Diminutive** +*on* **affixed to forms diminutivized by** +*it*

Base	Gloss	Base+*it*	Base+*i(t)*+*ón*+*et*
pax	can	*paxit*	*paxiyónet*
kar	pillow	*karit*	*kariyónet*

(cont.)

Base	Gloss	Base + *it*	Base + *i(t)* + *ón* + *et*
kaf	tablespoon	*kapit*	*kapiyónet*
mapa	tablecloth	*mapit*	*mapiyónet*

The same applies to +*iya* diminution:

(80) **Diminutive +*on* affixed to forms diminutivized by +*iya***

Base	Gloss	Base + *iya*	Base + *iy* + *ón* + *et*
naknik	sausage	*naknikiya*	*naknikiyónet*
ʿuga	cake	*ʿugiya*	*ʿugiyónet*
maca	unleavened bread	*maciya*	*maciyónet*
maʿase	deed, tale	*maʿasiya*	*maasiyónet*

In lower registers, + *čik* often demonstrates similar capability:

(81) **Diminutive +*on* affixed to forms diminutivized by *čik***

Form	Gloss	Dimin.	Dimin. + *čik*
yéled	boy	*yaldon*	*yaldónčik*
dov	bear	*dubon*	*dubónčik*
gag	roof	*gagon*	*gagónčik*
kétem	stain	*kitmon*	*kitmónčik*
kélev	dog	*klavlav*	*klavlávčik*
klavlav	doggy	*klavlavon*	*klavlavónčik*
xatul	cat	*xataltul*	*xataltúlčik*
xataltul	kitty	*xataltulon*	*xataltulónčik*

and to some extent, the same may apply to + *íko*:

(82) **Diminutive +*on* affixed to forms diminutivized by +*íko***

Base	Gloss	Dimin. Variant	Base + *íko*
kélev	dog	*klavlav*	*klavlavíko*
šamen	fat	*šmanman*	*šmanmaníko*

But the 'double diminutives' with + *íko* are more like one-time innovations than stable creations, and are usually limited to vocative uses. In the colloquial, + *čik* is clearly more productive than + *íko*. Both, however, are quite marginal when compared with + *on*.

In its capability to append itself 'on top of' other diminutive suffixes, +*on* demonstrates partial similarity to 'Class II' English suffixes, whose relationship to the base is less tight than that of typical derivational suffixes of 'Class I' (see also Chapter 1). The dichotomy was proposed by Siegel (1979), who made use of the difference in 'boundedness with the stem' between the + and # boundaries proposed by Chomsky & Halle (1968): Group A (+*ion*, +*ity*, +*y*, +*al*, +*ic*, +*ate*, +*ous*, +*ive*; *re*+, *con*+, *de*+, *sub*+, *pre*+, *in*+, *en*+, *be* +), and Group B (*#ness*, *#less*, *#hood*, *#ful*, *#ly*, *#like*; *re#*, *sub#*, *un#*, *non#*, *de#*, *semi#*, *anti#*). There are a number of phonological distinctions in the behavior of the two affix classes: while Class I tend to cause the stress assignment in the base to shift, Class II do not. Class I affixes undergo non-automatic phonological processes (e.g. *prodúctive* ~ *productívity*); Class II affixes do not. What concerns us here, however, is the morphological difference. With some exceptions, a suffix of Class II can generally be added to the base after a suffix from Class I has already been appended, but not vice versa (e.g. *nervousness*, *nervously*, but not **beautifulity*). Consequently, Class II affixes tend to be more productive.[47] The uniqueness of +*on* as a diminutive device is that it may even be appended to an earlier occurrence of itself (for instance, in *gagon* 'little roof; awning' > *gagonon* 'very small roof/awning' in the productivity tests below), which is a powerful indication of productivity.

Thus, the unmarked diminutive-formation device in Modern Hebrew is +*on* suffixation. Feminine diminutives use the same marker, as well as the feminine +*(e)t*, and the stress stays (or falls) on the +*on* syllable. A reliable criterion for determining the productivity of particular diminution devices relative to others is the extent to which they can be applied successfully to the consequences of earlier diminution. By this criterion, the most productive diminution device in Modern Hebrew is suffixation with +*on*. In the colloquial, it suggests preference for +*čik*. The essentially-linear character of such derivational devices makes the relationship to the base quite transparent, which facilitates discrimination of those forms with +*on* that constitute diminution from other forms with *on* that do not.

5.7.3 *Productivity tests on diminutive formation*

The productivity tests (50 open, 50 selection) included six potential diminutive realizations. The bases for two of them were already the

---

[47] But not necessarily so. See for instance Clark (1993), Cutler (1980), where it is pointed out that as long as the base has not been distorted, Class I affixes may be just as productive; that Class I affixes may be more productive than comparable Class II in particular domains; that Class II compounding may or may not be productive; and so on.

result of a diminutive formation process. Below are the results (for details, see Appendix XXVI):

(83) **Productivity tests where the target meaning was a diminutive:** (N subjects = 50, N bases = 6. Co. = Coinage, Ju. = Judgment)

Pattern	% Co.	% Ju.	Illustrations
+*on*	67.33	75.66	*mexdal* 'criminal negligence' > *mexdalon* 'minor act of negligence' *'omlet* 'omelette' > *'omleton* 'small omelette'
+*it*	4.66	10.66	*xataltula* 'kitten' > *xataltulit* 'tiny kitten'
+*čik*	4.66	8.33	*gagon* 'little roof; awning' > *gagónčik* 'very small roof/awning'
+*íko*	–	2.00	*gagon* 'little roof; awning' > *gagoníko* 'very small roof/awning'
+*ik*	1.66	1.00	*'omlet* 'omelette' > *'omletik* 'small omelette'
+*iya*	1.66	–	*pasaž* 'commercial corridor area' > *pasažiya* 'small commercial corridor area'
+*an*	1.66	–	*'omlet* 'omelette' > *'omletan* 'small omelette'
Reduplication	.33	.33	*pasaž* 'commercial corridor area' > *psažsaž* 'small commercial corridor area'

Clearly, +*on* dominates diminutive pattern choice. +*it* and +*čik* are seldom used. Their occurrence increases a bit in the selection tasks, when speakers are made aware of their existence. Reduplication is rare. 'Double diminutives' generally occur when the first diminutive is already supplied with the base (more in judgment tasks, once the option is made available). The preferred option is to add +*on(et)* then, even if the base ends with a diminutive +*on* to start with. Other configurations are also possible [see Appendix XXVI. Note that the percentages in Co(inage) and Ju(dgment) tasks are for the particular item, not for the whole category]:

(84) **Further diminution of a diminutive base**	% Co.	% Ju.
xataltula 'kitten (f.)' (< *xatula* 'cat (f.)') > *xataltulónet* 'tiny kitten (f.)'	40	62
gagon 'small roof; awning' > *gagonon* 'very small roof/awning (< *gag* 'roof')'	40	52
gagon 'small roof; awning' > *gagónčik* 'very small roof/awning (< *gag* 'roof')'	18	18
xataltula 'kitten (f.)' (< *xatula* 'cat (f.)') > *xataltulit* 'tiny kitten (f.)'	8	28
gagon 'small roof; awning' > *gagonit* 'very small roof/awning (< *gag* 'roof')'	10	24
xataltula 'kitten (f.)' (< *xatula* 'cat (f.)') > *xataltulonit* 'tiny kitten (f.)'	–	10
gagon 'small roof; awning' > *gagoniko* 'very small roof/awning (< *gag* 'roof')'	–	6
gagon 'small roof; awning' > *gagoniya* 'very small roof/awning (< *gag* 'roof')'	2	–
xataltula 'kitten (f.)' (< *xatula* 'cat (f.)') > *xataltúlet* 'tiny kitten (f.)'	2	–
xataltula 'kitten (f.)' (< *xatula* 'cat (f.)') > *xataltélet* 'tiny kitten (f.)'	2	–

Occasionally, double diminutives may occur even when subjects are presented with a non-diminutive base, in which case the second diminutive morpheme would tend to be either +*on* or +*čik* [see

Appendix XXVI. Again, note that the percentages in Co(inage) and Ju(dgment) tasks are for the particular item, not for the whole category]:

(85) **Double diminution of a non-diminutive base**	% Co.	% Ju.
mexdal 'criminal negligence' > *mexdalónčik* 'minor act of negligence'	2	6
gamad 'dwarf' > *gmadmadon* 'very tiny dwarf' (Redup. +*on*)	–	8
gamad 'dwarf' > *gamadonon* 'very tiny dwarf'	2	–
gamad 'dwarf' > *gmadmádčik* 'very tiny dwarf' (Redup. +*čik*)	–	2
ʾomlet 'omelette' > *ʾomletónčik* 'small omelette'	–	2

Thus the realizations of double diminutives in productivity tests provide additional evidence for the status of +*on* as the primary diminution device.

5.7.4   *Diminutive formation as reflected in dictionary comparison*

The distribution of new diminutives according to dictionary comparison is illustrated below:

(86) **New diminutives in ES '83** (for a more detailed list, see Appendix XXVII)

Form	Gloss	Source	Gloss
+*on(+et)*:			
ʾekdaxon	small pistol	*ʾekdax*	pistol, handgun
maklon	small stick	*makel*	staff, stick
misʿadónet	little restaurant	*misʿada*	restaurant
+*it*:			
koxavit	asterisk (small star)	*koxav*	star
markolit	minimarket	*markol*	supermarket
Reduplication			
bcalcal	small onion/bulb	*bacal*	onion; bulb
sgalgal	sort-of violet	*sagol*	violet

(87) **New diminutives in BABY 1972/1982** (all occurrences)

Form	Gloss	Source	Gloss
+*on(+et)*:			
pargiyónet	young, inexperienced girl	*pargit*	young chicken
tiptipónet	a very tiny bit	*tiptipa*	a tiny bit (< *tipa* 'drop')
+*čik*:[48]			
baxúrčik	young man (affectionate)	*baxur*	young man

---

[48] The first two forms are not that new. Even-Shoshan must have excluded them owing to their low register. They are still included in the count, for consistency. The other two are also agent attributes (see above).

(cont.)

Form	Gloss	Source	Gloss
katánčik	very small	*katan*	small
napolyónčik	with superiority complex ('a little Napoleon')	*napolyon*	Napoleon
pišalónčik	inexperienced novice; useless person	Yid.	
+íko:			
xayalíko	young soldier (affectionate)	*xayal*	soldier

The distribution of new diminutives by dictionary comparison:

(88) **Productivity ranking of diminutive patterns based on dictionary comparison**

R2 Ranking	ES	ES '83	BABY	PHAS	New	R1	R2	R1 Ranking
+*on(+et)*	130	31	2	–	33	.2538	.6470	Reduplication
Reduplication	28	9	–	–	9	.3214	.1765	+*on(+et)*
+*čik*	–	–[49]	4	–	4		.0784	+*it*
+*it*	22	4	–	–	4	.1818	.0784	
+*íko*	–	–	1	–	1		.0196	
+*iya*	9	–	–	–	–			

Total New: 51

+*on(+et)* is clearly shown to be the most productive diminutive pattern. Reduplication appears to be more productive than +*it*, which is not supported by the productivity tests. It is apparently a reflection of greater preference for reduplication at the higher registers reflected by ES '83. Its R1 advantage is too small to compete with R2 of +*on(+et)*. +*čik* and +*íko* are ranked based on R2 alone, owing to the absence of ES bases for them.

A word of caution here. As noted in Chapter 1, dictionary data should be used with care. Lexicographers often fail to note the most productive forms, since they consider them to be 'too automatic'. This could be the reason for the total absence of diminutives from the PHAS dictionary. For dictionary comparison to constitute a reliable measure of productivity, a number of chronologically-ordered dictionaries should be included. Thus, if a new dictionary does not list automatic formations in some pattern, an earlier dictionary is likely to include recent realizations of this pattern that have been sufficiently lexicalized to be noted by the compiler.

---

[49] Here and particularly in the slang dictionaries, *čik* is an agent marker (e.g. *balátčik* 'tile layer', from *baláta* 'tile (from Ar.)') more often than it is diminutive.

5.7.5   *Quantitative evidence from corpora on diminutive formation*

There are only three new diminutives that are *hapax legomenon* in the 112,000 word corpus:

(89) **New diminutives that are *hapax legomena* in the 12k corpus**

Form	Gloss	Source	Gloss
+ *on(+ et)*:			
kupidon	cupid (diminutive)	*kúpid*	cupid
garbon(im)	panty hose	*gérev*	hose, sock
+ *it*:			
pilpelit	'peppery' young female	*pilpel*	pepper

The ratios of *hapax legomena* to tokens and to the total *hapax* count among diminutives in the corpus are:

(90) **Productivity ranking of diminutive patterns based on corpus data**

R2 Ranking	Tokens	*hapax*	R1	R2
+ *on(+ et)*	14	5	.3571	.3333
+ *it*	34	4	.1176	.2667
Reduplication	47	5	[.1064	.3333]
+ *iya*	3	1	[.3333	.0667]
	Total *hapax*:	15		

Although the corpus is clearly too small for this category, it still shows that + *on(+ et)* is the most productive diminutive pattern, in support of findings from productivity tests as well as from dictionary comparison. It also shows that + *it* is next on the productivity scale, but it is not clear whether the corpus is substantial enough to determine that. In fact, the combined results of all three criteria are insufficient to determine the relative productivity of diminution devices other than + *on(+ et)*.

5.8   *Selecting nominal derivation patterns: conclusion*

The three criteria, productivity tests, dictionary comparison and corpus analysis, have enabled us to establish the following for selection of derivation patterns in the noun system:

• In forming abstract nominalizations, *CiCuC* is the most productive patterns when a verb is implied, owing to the great productivity of its verb counterpart *pi'el*.

- +*ut* is the default pattern for all other abstract nominalizations.
- The most productive agentive pattern is +*an*. +*ay/a'i* is a close second.
- +*an* is also the most productive realization pattern for the performer category, which combines agents with instruments.
- +*iya* is the default pattern for locatives.
- +*on* is the default pattern for diminutives.

These are the patterns speakers would intuitively select when forming new nouns, based on salient form-meaning relationships they readily observe in the new everyday lexicon.

CHAPTER SIX

SELECTING DERIVATION PATTERNS
ACROSS SEMANTIC CATEGORIES

So far, we have tried to evaluate relative productivity of the various
noun and adjective derivation patterns as manifest in their selection
to denote particular semantic categories. While doing so, we also
noted that certain patterns cover more than one semantic type. In
some of those, one could simply expand the category concerned, for
instance in collapsing agents and instruments into a general performer
class. In other cases, one cannot do so in a straightforward manner.
It would be interesting, therefore, to find out how productive each
pattern is across the board, regardless of semantic category. This is
in no way intended to diminish the role semantics plays in new word
formation. On the contrary, all data and analysis of every category
investigated above clearly indicate that neologism is semantically
based. All we will attempt to do in this chapter is to point to those
morphological patterns which may be argued to constitute default
choices within very broad domains, once semantic characterization
is ambiguous. By ranking productivity across semantic categories we
will also identify the most automatic and the most general patterns
in the morphological system.

6.1   *Selecting derivation patterns across semantic boundaries*
in the verb system

Evaluating relative productivity of derivation patterns regardless of
semantic classification is reasonably straightforward, insofar as dictionary
comparison and corpus data are concerned. There are measurable
bases for comparison, such as the total number of lexical realizations
of each category as reflected in a particular dictionary, total number
of neologisms listed for each type, number of tokens for each class in
a corpus of definite size. It is problematic, however, in the case of
productivity tests, where there is no such base to start with. Percentages of potential realizations of patterns can only be computed and

compared within a category. There is no way of comparing across categories, since speakers had to be presented with specific target meanings. One cannot elicit a neologism without suggesting some semantic goal, albeit very broad. The only sense in which productivity tests may point to productivity beyond semantic categories is by demonstrating that some pattern or patterns constitute the default choice for neologism in a particular large domain, say within the verb system. Even then, however, there is no single pattern that will qualify as the default choice for any verb, though *pi'el* comes closest. It is the default choice for all agentive verbs, causatives included. But inchoatives still prefer *hitpa'el*, and passive ones usually opt for *pu'al*. So, there is no way to determine absolute productivity for verbs across semantic categories based on productivity tests alone. All one can do is establish productivity ranking within broader semantic categories.

Thus, description of innovation across semantic boundaries in the verb system is mostly based on dictionary comparison and on corpora. If we wish to capture the 'absolute' productivity of each *binyan*, regardless of semantic subcategory, in comparison with that of others as reflected in dictionary neologisms, the following picture emerges, generally corresponding to the findings in Sivan (1976):

(3) **Total number of new verbs by *binyan*, by number of verbs added in each dictionary**

R2 Ranking	ES	ES '83	BABY	PHAS	New[1]	R1	R2
pi'el	1,993	78	72	21	171	.0858	.4957
hitpa'el	1,087	20	45	18	83	.0764	.2406
pu'al	1,595	47	–	–	47	.0295	.1362
hif'il	1,180	11	12	3	26	.0220	.0754
huf'al	784	7	1	–	8	.0102	.0232
nif'al	1,165	2	4	–	6	.0052	.0174
pa'al	1,814	1	1	2	4	.0022	.0116

Total new: 345

This is more-or-less the expected relative order of productivity once semantic considerations are set aside. *pi'el* is the most productive, followed by *hitpa'el*. *pu'al* is in third place owing to the great productivity of its active counterpart, *pi'el*. It is not favored in the colloquial, judging from the absence of new *pu'al* forms in the slang dictionaries.

---

[1] A reminder: 'new' is defined as verbs that first appear in dictionaries published later than Even-Shoshan (1970), 'ES', counting only verbs that are not listed in an earlier one.

Still, it appears that use of the passive is not as uncommon as is generally claimed.

The corpus data, out of a 132,000 words corpus, yield the following ranking:

(4) **R2 Ranking**	**Tokens**	*hapax*	**R1**	**R2**
pi^{c}el	2,333	175	.0750	.2787
hitpa^{c}el	1,348	101	.0749	.1608
hif^{c}il	3,099	99	[.0319	.1576]
pa^{c}al	7,457	72	[.0097	.1146]
pu^{c}al	461	69	[.1497	.1099]
nif^{c}al	1,305	63	[.0483	.1003]
huf^{c}al	347	49	[.1412	.0780]

Total *hapax*: 628

The first two positions are occupied by the same *binyanim*, regardless of whether dictionary comparison or corpus analysis is used: *pi^{c}el* and *hitpa^{c}el*. Pragmatically, *pi^{c}el*'s predominance suggests that when the target meaning is hard to characterize, *pi^{c}el* is most likely to be the default choice. Of the other patterns ranked, relative ordering varies, but rough correspondence is maintained—except for the unexpectedly high position of *pa^{c}al* in the across-the-board corpus analysis. Because of limited corpus size, the *hapax* group in *pa^{c}al* included many non-recent words that were infrequent enough not to be repeated. If R1–R2 differences are taken into account, *pu^{c}al* and *huf^{c}al* would be raised above *hif^{c}il*, in that order, and the positions of *pa^{c}al* and *nif^{c}al* will be reversed, resulting in ranking that more closely resembles the ordering arrived at through dictionary comparison. But there is no independent justification for doing so.

6.2   *Selecting derivation patterns across semantic boundaries*
in adjectives and nouns

As in the case of verbs, productivity tests cannot be used to determine relative productivity of noun and adjective derivation patterns regardless of semantic category. All one can do is broaden the scope of semantic coverage and point to default choices for broader categories. +*i* is chosen for adjectives that are not verb-related, *meCuCaC* for those that are. Each *binyan* is associated with a default nominalization pattern; all other abstract nominalizations use +*ut*. +*iya* is the default pattern for locatives, +*on* for diminutives, +*an* for 'performers'.

Dictionary comparison of new adjectives and nouns regardless of semantic category provides the following distribution. Note that in some cases, the ES numbers are larger than those quoted for particular patterns above, since for this purpose, all realizations of each pattern were counted:

(5) **Productivity ranking of all noun and adjective patterns based on dictionary comparison**

R2 Ranking	ES	New	R1	R2	R1 Ranking
+*i* Adj.	2,690	195	.0725	.1651	+*ist*
Total +*ut*	3,699	191	.0516	.1617	+*on*
CiCuC	1,652	135	.0817	.1143	+*izm*
+*an*	1,150	104	.0904	.0881	+*ay*/+*a'i*
meCuCaC	1,320	82	.0621	.0694	+*er*
+*ay*/+*a'i*	233	49	.2103	.0415	+*meCaCeC*
+*on*	178	42	.2360	.0356	*maCCeCa*
meCaCeC	193	36	.1865	.0305	*maCCeC*
+*izm*	158	34	.2152	.0288	*miCCaCa*
haCCaCa	883	34	.0385	.0288	*mitCaCeC*
+*ist*	101	28	.2772	.0237	Reduplication
maCCeC	241	26	.1079	.0220	+*an*
CaCiC	297	20	.0673	.0169	*CiCuC*
CCiCa	1,347	20	.0148	.0169	+*iya*
maCCeCa:	115	17	.1478	.0144	+*i* Adj.
CaCaC	438	17	.0241	.0144	*maCCiC*
+*er*	81	16	.1975	.0135	*CaCiC*
+*iya*	201	16	.0796	.0135	*meCuCaC*
CaCuC	1,132	14	.0124	.0119	*CoCeC*
miCCaCa	123	13	.1057	.0110	Total +*ut*
CoCeC	223	13	.0519	.0110	*niCCaC*
+*čik*	–	13		.0110	*haCCaCa*
miCCaC	342	10	.0292	.0085	*heCCeC*
muCCaC	376	10	.0266	.0085	*miCCaC*
Reduplication	99	9	.0909	.0076	*muCCaC*
maCCiC	116	8	.0690	.0068	*CaCaC*
+*iyáda*	–	7		.0059	*CaCeC*
heCCeC:	169	6	.0355	.0051	*CCiCa*
niCCaC	104	5	.0481	.0042	*CaCuC*
+*it*	524	5	.0095	.0042	+*it*
mitCaCeC	30	3	.1000	.0025	
CaCeC	98	2	.0204	.0017	
+*íko*	–	1		.0008	

Total new: 1,181

When looking at nouns and adjectives irrespective of semantic category, the ratios produced by dictionary comparison suggest that overall, formation of adjectives by +*i*-suffixation is the most productive device in the noun/adjective system. Total +*ut* (including verb-related *miškalim*) is a close second. At least the next six positions are also expected: *CiCuC*, + *an*, *meCuCaC*, + *ay*/ *a'i*, + *on*, and *meCaCeC*. There is no point in considering R1–R2 discrepancies, since we are measuring productivity across the board, i.e. no narrowing of category will be of relevance. At this level, only the 'default' patterns matter.

Corpus data, out of 112,000 words, yields the following distribution of noun and adjective patterns when no semantic classification is made. Note the combining of related patterns in *maCCeC(a)* and *miCCaC(a)*:

(6) **Nouns and adjective distribution in a 112k corpus, across semantic boundaries**

R2 Ranking	Tokens	*hapax*	R1	R2	R1 Ranking
+*i* Adj.	1,982	252	.1271	.1913	+*an*
Total +*ut*	1,102	174	.1579	.1321	*meCaCeC*
CiCuC	1,469	153	.1041	.1162	Total +*ut*
meCuCaC	691	101	.1467	.0767	*meCuCaC*
haCCaCa	644	71	.1102	.0539	*maCCiC*
+*an*	162	50	.3086	.0380	+*i* Adj.
meCaCeC	175	31	.1771	.0235	+*it*
maCCiC	199	27	.1357	.0205	*haCCaCa*
+*on*	628	27	.0430	.0205	+*ay*/*a'i*
CaCiC	525	21	.0400	.0159	*CiCuC*
+*ay*/+*a'i*	148	16	.1081	.0121	+*on*
+*it*	34	4	.1176	.0030	*CaCiC*
mitCaCeC	57	2	.0351	.0015	*mitCaCeC*
CaCuC	1,015	102	[.1005	.0774]	
CCiCa	1,089	87	[.0799	.0660]	
maCCeC(a)	255	39	[.1529	.0296]	
miCCaC(a)	1,278	35	[.0274	.0266]	
CoCeC	871	27	[.0310	.0205]	
muCCaC	173	25	[.1445	.0190]	
heCCeC	121	14	[.1157	.0106]	
CaCeC	554	12	[.0217	.0091]	
+*ist*	13	11	[.8461	.0083]	
niCCaC	228	10	[.0438	.0076]	
+*iya*	80	9	[.1125	.0068]	
+*er*	5	5	[1.000	.0038]	
Reduplication	47	5	[.1064	.0038]	
CaCaC	846	5	[.0059	.0038]	
(historically with a geminated medial consonant)					
+*izm*	2	2	[1.000	.0015]	

Total *hapax*: 1,317

Some of the patterns are excluded from consideration because none of the *hapax legomena* can be proven to be new. The excluded patterns were placed at the bottom of the list. Although it is possible to rank them internally, as shown in brackets, the ranking is not reliable, because their *hapax legomena* are not very likely to represent recent formations. Of the qualifying patterns, the ranking of the first four is expected: +*i*-adjectives, (total) +*ut*, *CiCuC*, and *meCuCaC*. +*an*, *meCaCeC*, +*on*, *CaCiC*, and +*ay*/+*a'i* are also more-or-less where they should be. The ranking of *haCCaCa* and of *maCCiC* are higher than expected, but at least position of the former is partly supported by its ranking by dictionary comparison.

Here is a summary of the first thirteen most productive noun/adjective patterns regardless of semantic category by the two measurable criteria:

(7) | Pos. | Dict. Comp. | Corpus Data |
|---|---|---|
| 1 | +*i* | +*i* |
| 2 | +*ut* | +*ut* |
| 3 | *CiCuC* | *CiCuC* |
| 4 | +*an* | *meCuCaC* |
| 5 | *meCuCaC* | *haCCaCa* |
| 6 | +*ay*/+*a'i* | +*an* |
| 7 | +*on* | *meCaCeC* |
| 8 | *meCaCeC* | *maCCiC* |
| 9 | +*izm* | +*on* |
| 10 | *haCCaCa* | *CaCiC* |
| 11 | +*ist* | +*ay*/+*a'i* |
| 12 | *maCCeC* | +*it* |
| 13 | *CaCiC* | *mitCaCeC* |

If we only consider derivation patterns appearing on both lists, and assign weight to their respective positions in each list, the following productivity ranking emerges:

(8) | Final Rank | Pattern | Positions | Pos. Sum |
|---|---|---|---|
| 1 | +*i* | 1+1 | 2 |
| 2 | +*ut* | 2+2 | 4 |
| 3 | *CiCuC* | 3+3 | 6 |
| 4 | *meCuCaC* | 5+4 | 9 |
| 5 | +*an* | 4+6 | 10 |
| 6 | *meCaCeC* | 8+7 | 15 |
| 7 | *haCCaCa* | 10+5 | 15 |
| 8 | +*on* | 7+9 | 16 |
| 9 | +*ay*/+*a'i* | 6+11 | 17 |
| 10 | *CaCiC* | 13+10 | 23 |

These are probably indeed the ten most productive noun/adjective patterns, and their relative productivity, regardless of semantic category, seems to be reasonably correct (with the possible exception of *haCCaCa?*). In absolute terms, +*ut* is less productive than +*i* because it has to compete with another very productive nominalization pattern, *CiCuC*. *CiCuC*'s high productivity is of course due to its being the default nominalization of *pi'el*, the most productive verb pattern for the huge class of agentive verbs, including causatives. The main 'competitor' of +*i*, *meCuCaC* is productive as well, as the default realization of verb-related adjectives, but in absolute terms, it is less productive than *CiCuC*, which 'leaves more room' for +*i*. The position of +*an* is due mostly to its serving in a number of functions, for agents/agent attributes, instruments, and collectives/groups, and that of +*on* to its status as the default diminutive pattern. *meCaCeC*'s ranking is due to its transparent relationship to *pi'el*, as its active participle, and to its colloquial standing in capturing the 'performer' category, which may refer to either an agent or an instrument. *CaCiC* would have probably ranked much higher had productivity tests been designed specifically for the sub-category of 'able-type' adjectives, and had other measurements been restricted that way as well.

We already established independently that +*i* is the default adjective formation pattern, particularly when the base is not verb-related; that abstract nominalizations are mostly realized in *CiCuC* when verb-related and take +*ut* otherwise; that +*an* is preferred for 'performers', and +*on* for diminution. What the ranking tells us is that +*i* suffixation is the most automatic and most general morphological device in the adjective/noun system, but it is not clear what the pragmatic importance of this observation is. In new verb formation, the overall predominance of *pi'el* may suggest that when the target semantic characterization is borderline or ambiguous, *pi'el* would be chosen as the default choice, but such semantic ambiguity seldom arises in the noun/adjective system.[2]

---

[2] This kind of ambiguity does arise in the colloquial, as shown above, for nouns and adjectives ending with +*an* and with +*a'i*, but the fact that some types of forms are used as either nouns or adjectives does not mean that the innovator's target meaning is ambiguous as to syntactic category. Within verb system, on the other hand, it is possible to aim at a target meaning which is ambiguous for agentivity or theme-status.

6.2.1 *Interaction between the most productive suffixes in the noun/adjective system*

In Chapter 5, it was shown that the diminutive suffix + *on* is so productive that it can even be appended to an earlier occurrence of itself, for further diminution. That further diminution be involved is a must, since, as pointed out by Ravid & Shlesinger (1987), deriving an adjective from another adjective without change in meaning is a tautology, excluded for pragmatic reasons. The same principle applies more generally when any suffix is appended to a stem. The derived form must be semantically or functionally distinct from the base.[3]

The capability of a suffix to be attached to a base where another suffix has already been appended may be understood as an indication of productivity, but not necessarily so, since there are some significant exceptions.[4] Bearing in mind that multiple suffixation is a useful, though not always reliable criterion of productivity, we should briefly look now at how the most productive noun/adjective suffixes concatenate. Since such concatenations were not aimed for in the productivity tests, the data will be taken from dictionaries and from the corpus. It will be shown that the degree to which affixes can concatenate with others is a function of a variety of factors, some of which go beyond the properties of the particular suffixes concerned. The suffixes looked at, taken from the final ranking list above, are + *i*, + *ut*, + *an*, + *ay*/+ *a'i*, and + *on*, in this order. The discussion will proceed in reverse order, starting from + *on*.

6.2.1.1   + on *and other suffixes*

+ *on* is very productive in diminutive formation, but far less in other configurations. It hardly ever appends to stems ending with any of the other affixes (with some exceptions like *zehuton* 'personal data list'). When it is followed by an affix like + *i* or + *ut*, Even-Shoshan (1970) lists 80 + *oni* cases, 27 + *onut* ones. In some instances, the suffix sequence in such cases has already been merged into an 'atomic' single entity, + *oni* or + *onut*, as can be seen in:

---

[3] See Clark's (1993) 'contrast', drawn from early linguistic work on historical change (Bréal 1897, de Saussure 1916/1968, etc.).
[4] See Chapter 5 in reference to the two classes of suffixes in English.

(9)

Base	Gloss	+*on* Base?	+*oni*/+*ut*	Gloss
céva‘	color	?*civ‘on*[5]	*civ‘oni*	colorful
pérax	flower	**pirxon*[6]	*pirxoni*	flowery
cémax	plant	**cimxon*[7]	*cimxoni*	vegetarian
cémax	plant	**cimxon*	*cimxonut*	vegetarianism
		*kim‘on	*kim‘oni*	of retail
		*kim‘on	*kim‘onut*	retail
‘ir	town, city	**‘iron*	*‘ironi*	municipal
’adom	red	**’admon*	*’admoni*	reddish

Another possibility is that +*on* constitutes an integral part of an established non-linear *miškal*, in which it is probably not perceived as a separate morpheme, e.g.

(10)

Base	Gloss	Base *miškal*	+*oni*/ +*onut*	Gloss
dimyon	imagination	*CiCCon*	*dimyoni*	imaginary
šwyon	equality	*CiCCon*	*šwyoni*	egalitarian
kiš(a)ron[8]	talent	*CiC(a)Con*	*kišroni*	talented
bitaxon	security	*CiCaCon*	*bitxoni*	of security
‘ikaron	principle	*CiCaCon*	*‘ekroni*	of principle
timahon	amazement	*CiCaCon*	*timhoni*	eccentric
‘elyon	superior	*CiCCon*	*‘elyonut*	superiority
timahon	amazement	*CiCaCon*	*timhonut*	eccentricity

A third possibility is that +*on* is not part of a *miškal*, but is still not very transparent as a separate morpheme, since by now it is 'fused' with the stem:

(11)

Base	Gloss	+*on* Stem	Gloss	+*oni*/ +*onut*	Gloss
roš	head	*rišon*	first	*rišoni*	primary
roš	head	*rišon*	first	*rišonut*	priority
xuc	outside (N)	*xicon*	external (lit.)	*xiconi*	external
mila	word	*milon*	dictionary	*miloni*	lexical
‘et	time, period	*‘iton*	newspaper	*‘itonut*	press

Even-Shoshan (1970) also lists 22 cases of +*oniyut*, as in:

(12) **Illustrating realizations of +*oniyut* in Even-Shoshan 1970**

Base	+*on*	+*oni*	+*oniyut*
céva‘ 'color'	**civ‘on*	*civ‘oni* 'colorful'	*civ‘oniyut* 'being colorful'
	higayon 'logic'	*hegyoni* 'logical'	*hegyoniyut* 'being logical'

---

[5] In literary Hebrew, *civ‘on* is 'hue, tint', but very few speakers are aware of it.
[6] Except for potential 'small flower'.
[7] Except for potential 'small plant'.
[8] *Kišron* is normative, *kišaron* colloquial.

(cont.)

Base	**+ *on***	**+ *oni***	**+ *oniyut***
xuc 'outside (N)'	*xicon* 'external (lit.)'	*xiconi* 'external'	*xiconiyut* 'outward appearance'
xol 'non-sabbath day'	**xilon*	*xiloni* 'secular'	*xiloniyut* 'secularity'
kec 'end'	**kicon*	*kiconi* 'extreme'	*kiconiyut* 'being extreme'
šave 'equal'	*šivyon* 'equality'	*šivyoni* 'egalitarian'	*šivyoniyut* 'egalitarianism'

Of the frequent ones among those, a significant number have no free-standing + *on* form, which as already noted suggests the existent of atomic + *oni* alongside + *on* + *i*. In the 112k corpus, there were few occurrences of + *onut* (one of *ribonut* 'sovereignty' and 8 of *ʿitonut* 'press'), and none of + *oniyut*. In Even-Shoshan (1970), + *onut* and + *oniyut* groups are about the same size, 27 and 22, respectively. Most + *oniyut* cases are fairly common. Although the illustrations for + *onut* above are common as well, the majority of the 27 + *onut* cases are quite literary.[9] All + *onut* cases below are literary:

(13) **Some iterary + *onut* forms**

Base	**Gloss**	**+ *on*/+ *oni***	**Gloss**	**+ *onut***	**Gloss**
basar	meat	*bisroni*	meat-eating (Adj.)	*bisronut*	meat-eating (N)
		ʾevyon	pauper	*ʾevyonut*	being a pauper
		ʾegron	lexicon	*ʾegronut*	lexicography
		bitron	gorge, ravine	*bitronut*	full of gorges, uneven
cafrir	light wind	*cifroni*	capricious	*cifronut*	capriciousness
gáxam	caprice	*gimxon*	capricious	*gimxonut*	capriciousness
xuš	sense	*xišoni*	capable of feeling	*xišonut*	capability to feel

The difference in register between the two groups is best manifest when both use the same base. As stated above, two similar devices may exist simultaneously only when each member of a pair is semantically or functionally distinct from the other. In this case, either there is a difference in meaning, or the two forms differ in register, the + *oniyut* alternant being the colloquial variant:

(14) **+ *onut* and + *oniyut* appended to the same base**

+ *on*/+ *oni*	**+ *onut***	**Gloss**	**+ *oniyut***	**Gloss**
civʿoni 'colorful'	*civʿonut*	colorfulness (lit.)	*civʿoniyut*	colorfulness (coll.)

---

[9] A characterization reinforced by some of them having originated in Medieval Hebrew, in which base + *ut* was a common word formation device.

(cont.)

+on/+oni	+onut	Gloss	+oniyut	Gloss
hegyoni 'logical'	*hegyonut*	being logical (lit.)	*hegyoniyut*	being logical (coll.)
gamloni 'overlarge'	*gamlonut*	being overlarge (lit.)	*gamloniyut*	being overlarge (lit./coll.)
kadmon(i) 'ancient'	*kadmonut*	being ancient (lit.)	*kadmoniyut*	being ancient (lit./coll.)
timhoni 'eccentric'	*timhonut*	eccentricity (lit.)	*timhoniyut*	eccentricity (coll.)
dimyon 'imagination'	*dimyonut*	capability to imagine (lit.)	*dimyoniyut*	capability to imagine (lit./coll.)
dimyoni 'imaginary'			*dimyoniyut*	being imaginary
ga'on 'relig. leader'	*ge'onut*	position of religious leader		
ga'on 'a genius'	*ge'onut*	being a genius (lit.)		
ge'oni 'genius (Adj.)'			*ge'oniyut*	being a genius
rišon 'first'	*rišonut*	priority		
rišoni 'primary'			*rišoniyut*	primary nature; originality

An informal survey suggests that even when the +*onut*/+*oniyut* distinction is restricted to a register difference, the +*onut* variant is more general and connotatively neutral, whereas +*oniyut* is more specific and/or connotatively loaded. Thus, some feel that *timhoniyut* suggests 'more eccentricity' than *timhonut*; that *hegyoniyut* conveys 'more logic' than *hegyonut*; that *civ'oniyut* suggests greater variety of color than *civ'onut*. . . . Needless to say, such intuitions require testing. The register difference and/or semantic distinctions is probably triggered by the fact that +*onut* is more likely to be derived directly from the nominal ending with +*on*, whereas +*oniyut* is more directly related to the adjectival +*oni*.

None of the dictionaries lists any realizations of +*onuti*. None were found in the 112k corpus either.

Dictionary comparison yield the following productivity ranking for +*on* + other suffixes, indicating that +*oniyut* is somewhat more productive than +*onut*:

(16) **Productivity of +*on* + other suffixes according to dictionary comparison**

R2 Ranking	ES	ES '83	BABY	PHAS	New	R1	R2
+*oni*	80	4	–	–	4	.0500	.6667
+*oniyut*	22	–	1	–	1	.0455	.1666
+*onut*	27	1	–	–	1	.0370	.1666
				Total new:	6		

The corpus contain no occurrence of +*oniyut*.

(17) **Productivity of +*on* + other suffixes according to data from the 112k corpus**

R2 Ranking	Tokens	*hapax*	R1	R2
+*oni*	29	11	[.3793	.9167]
+*onut*	9	1	[.1111	.0833]
+*oniyut*	–	–		
	Total *hapax*:	12		

Since none of the *hapax legomena* is recent, the corpus data will not be used here. But at least by dictionary comparison, +*oni* is the most productive +*on* + suffix sequence, followed by +*oniyut*.

6.2.1.2   +ay/+a'i *and other suffixes*

+*ay*/+*a'i* does not frequently concatenate with other suffixes, nor does it generally append to bases ending with other suffixes. As for other suffixes being appended to it, the tautology constraint discourages combinations with the other agentive suffix, +*an*, which like +*ay* can be either an agent or an agent attribute, and with +*i*, which is functionally identical to +*a'i*. But Even-Shoshan (1970) lists 62 combinations with +*ut*:

(18) **Illustrating realizations of +*a'ut* in Even-Shoshan 1970**

Base	Gloss	+*ay* Stem	Gloss	+*a'ut*	Gloss
bul	stamp	*bulay/bula'i*	stamp collector[10]	*bula'ut*	stamp collecting
		xaklay/xakla'i	farmer/farm worker	*xakla'ut*	agriculture
bana	build (V)	*banay/bana'i*	builder	*bana'ut*	builder's occupation
kiba	put out fire	*kabay/kaba'i*	fire fighter	*kaba'ut*	fire fighting
pizmon	song	*pizmonay/pizmona'i*	song composer	*pizmona'ut*	song composing
malon	hotel	*melonay/melona'i*	hotelier	*melona'ut*	hotel industry
šaxmat	chess	*šaxmetay/šaxmeta'i*	chess player	*šaxmeta'ut*	chess playing

In some cases it is hard to tell whether the +*a'ut* form is from the +*ay*/+*a'i* stem, or from its nominal base:

(19) +*a'ut* **cases in which alternative bases can be assumed**

Base	Gloss	+*ay* Stem	Gloss	+*a'ut*	Gloss
bama	stage	*bamay*	director	*bama'ut*	directing
mexona	machine	*mexonay/mexona'i*	mechanic	*mexona'ut*	mechanic's work
xava	farm	*xavay*	farmer	*xava'ut*	farming
'afsanya	supply	*'afsenay/'afsena'i*	storekeeper	*'afsana'ut*	storekeeping

---

[10] As noted above, in normative Hebrew, +*ay* is reserved for agent nouns, +*a'i* for related adjectives. In the colloquial, +*a'i* is typically used for both agents and related adjectives.

Even-Shoshan (1970) lists only four $+a'iyut$ realizations, one of which has an $+a'ut$ alternant:

(20) **Illustrating realizations of $+a'iyut$ in Even-Shoshan 1970**

Base	Gloss	$+ay$ Stem	Gloss	$+a'iyut$	Gloss
próza	prose	prozá'i	prosaic	prozá'iyut	prosaicness
		xašay/xaša'i	secret	xaša'iyut	secrecy
		keday/keda'i	worthwhile	keda'iyut	worthwhileness
		vaday/vada'i	certainly/certain (adj.)	vada'ut	certainty (lit./coll.)
				vada'iyut	certainty (coll.)

As for dictionary comparison, 4 new $+a'ut$ cases were listed in ES '83, 2 in BABY, and 1 in PHAS, but no $+a'iyut$ in any of them, so there is no need for comparison to determine that the former is more productive. In the 112k corpus, 11 occurrences of $+a'ut$ were found, 9 of them tokens of vada'ut 'certainty', and 4 occurrences of $+a'iyut$, all of them keda'iyut 'worthwhileness'. The two hapax legomena were not recent, which rules out computing relative productivity by corpus data in this case. There were no $+a'uti$ cases, either in the dictionary or in the corpus. So at least based on dictionary comparison, $+a'ut$ is more productive than $+a'iyut$.

6.2.1.3 $+an$ and other suffixes

With few exceptions (e.g. tarbutan 'cultural officer (lit.)'), $+an$ does not append to bases ending with other suffixes, but it very frequently serves as a base for productive affixes appended to it. Even-Shoshan (1970) lists 633 lexical items ending with $+ani$. Of those, there are cases of $+ani$ with no free-standing intermediate $+an$ stage, suggesting atomic $+ani$ rather than $+an+i$. Also, although the $+an$ forms are first and foremost agent nouns, they may occasionally also function, especially in the colloquial, as agent attributes, i.e. as adjectives.[11] Below are a few illustrations:

(21) **Illustrating realizations of $+ani$ in Even-Shoshan (1970)**

Base	Gloss	$+an$ Stem	Gloss	$+a'ni$	Gloss
ragaz	be angry	ragzan	angry person; angry	ragzani	angry
šamar	preserve	šamran	conservative (N)	šamrani	conservative (Adj.)

---

[11] The degree to which an $+an$ form can also function colloquially as an adjective can be determined by the extent to which it can be modified by adverbs like me'od 'very', nora 'awfully', and kol kax 'so . . .' Bona fide adjectives take all, e.g. šakdan me'od 'very diligent', nora šakdan 'awfully diligent', kol kax šakdan 'so diligent'. Forms that are somewhat less likely to function as adjectives readily take the latter two, e.g. nora kamcan 'awfully stingy', and kol kax kamcan 'so stingy' are normal. kamcan me'od is somewhat less acceptable.

(cont.)

Base	Gloss	+*an* Stem	Gloss	+*a'ni*	Gloss
kibel	receive	kablan	contractor	kablani	of contractor
kimec	be thrifty	kamcan	miser; miserly	kamcani	miserly
xucpa	impudence	xucpan	impudent person; impudent	xucpani	impudent, cheeky
smol	left	smolan	leftist person	smolani	leftist (Adj.)
harpatka	adventure	harpatkan	adventurer	harpatkani	adventurous
rexuš	capital	rexušan	capitalist	rexušani	capitalistic
matir	allow(ing)	matiran	a permissive person	matirani	permissive
rúax	spirit	*ruxan		ruxani	spiritual
kol	sound	*kolan		kolani	loud
kóax	power, force	*koxan		koxani	aggressive; potential
xolem	dream (V)	*xolman		xolmani	dreamy
géza'	race	*giz'an		giz'ani	racist (Adj.)
le'om	nation	*le'uman		le'umani[12]	nationalistic
boged	betray	*bogdan		bogdani	treacherous
sof	end	*sofan		sofani	terminal

Even-Shoshan (1970) lists 454 realizations of +*anut* and only 19 of +*aniyut*. In the 112k corpus, 51 occurrences of +*anut* were found, and 1 of +*aniyut*. Abstract nominalization of +*ani* adjectives is usually derived by appending +*ut* to the +*an* base rather than to the +*ani* one (see Schwarzwald, to appear). Thus, for the majority of forms listed in the previous table, the derived abstract nominals end with +*anut*. +*aniyut* is more likely when no independent +*an* form exists, but such cases may still end with +*anut*:

(22) +*anut* and +*aniyut* realizations of +*ani* forms in previous table

+*an* Stem	+*a'ni*	+*anut*	+*aniyut*	Gloss
ragzan	ragzani	ragzanut		being angry
šamran	šamrani	šamranut		conservatism
kablan	kablani	kablanut		contracting
kamcan	kamcani	kamcanut		being miserly
xucpan	xucpani	xucpanut		being cheeky
smolan	smolani	smolanut		being leftist
harpatkan	harpatkani	harpatkanut		being adventurous
rexušan	rexušani	rexušanut		capitalism
matiran	matirani	matiranut		permissiveness
*ruxan	ruxani		ruxaniyut	spirituality
*kolan	kolani		kolaniyut	being loud
*koxan	koxani		koxaniyut	aggressiveness; potentiality
*xolman	xolmani		xolmaniyut	being dreamy

---

[12] *le'umi* is the connotationally-neutral 'national'.

(cont.)

+*an* Stem	+*a'ni*	+*anut*	+*aniyut*	Gloss
giz'an	giz'ani	giz'anut[13]		racism
le'uman	le'umani	le'umanut		nationalism = chauvinism
bogdan	bogdani	bogdanut		treachery

The generalization that +*aniyut* would be preferred where there exists no independent +*an* form is reinforced by additional forms from the 19 +*aniyut* cases listed by Even-Shoshan (1970):

(23) **Additional illustrations of +*aniyut* in Even-Shoshan 1970, where no +*an* form exists**

Base	Gloss	+*an*	+*ani*	Gloss	+*aniyut*	Gloss
xole	sick	*xolan	xolani	sickly, ailing	xolaniyut	being sickly, ailing
guf	body	*gufan	gufani	physical, corporal	gufaniyut	corporeality
xuš	sense	*xušan	xušani	sensual	xušaniyut	sensuality
móax	brain	*moxan	moxani	cerebral	moxaniyut	being cerebral
réax	smell	*reyxan	reyxani	fragrant	reyxaniyut	being fragrant

In other +*aniyut* cases, both variants can be found even in normative Hebrew:

(24) **Additional illustrations of +*anut*/+*aniyut* pairs in Even-Shoshan 1970**

+*an*/+*ani*	+*anut*	+*a'niyut*
'askan 'public figure/worker'	'askanut 'public service'	
'askani 'always busy'		'askaniyut 'being always busy'
sixletan 'rational'	sixletanut 'rationalism'	sixletaniyut 'being rational'

As in the case of +*onut*/+*oniyut*, speakers seem to feel that when +*anut* and +*aniyut* are only minimally different, +*anut* is more neutral and general, +*aniyut* more loaded and more specific. It pertains particularly to those cases in which the +*aniyut* alternant is non-normative, and therefore not even listed in Even-Shoshan (1970). Thus, some speakers claim that *le'umaniyut* 'nationalism = chavinism' suggests greater chauvinism than *le'umanut*, which they believe refers to the general doctrine as such, and is less judgmental. *giz'aniyut* 'racism' is conceived of as connoting greater racism than *giz'anut*, which is more descriptive of the concept. *reykanut* 'emptiness' (from *reyk* 'empty' ~ *reykan(i)*) covers any emptiness, whereas *reykaniyut* is usually reserved to the empty-headedness of humans. Some feel that even well-established *CaCCanut* cases may have *CaCCaniyut* alternants constituting 'intensified'

---

[13] Actually, in the last three cases, both variants may be attested in the colloquial, i.e. *giz'aniyut*, *le'umaniyut* and possibly *bogdaniyut* are acceptable as well.

versions, e.g. *šamraniyut* 'conservatism' suggesting greater conservatism than *šamranut*.

Further tests would be required in order to establish the degree of productivity of + *anut* vs. + *aniyut*. By dictionary counts, however, the former is far more productive than the latter, particularly when a related free-standing + *an* form exists. This is confirmed by summary of neologisms through dictionary comparison:

(26) **Productivity of + *an* + other suffixes according to dictionary comparison**

R2 Ranking	ES	ES '83	BABY	PHAS	New	R1	R2
+ *anut*	454	24	5	–	29	.0639	.5273
+ *ani*	633	26	–	–	26	.0411	.4727
+ *aniyut*	19	–	–	–	–		

Total new: 55

as well as by corpus analysis:

(27) **Productivity of + *an* + other suffixes according to data from the 112k corpus**

R2 Ranking	Tokens	*hapax*	R1	R2
+ *anut*	51	14	.2745	.4375
+ *ani*	27	17	[.6296	.5312]
+ *aniyut*	1	1		

Total *hapax*: 32

+ *ani* and + *aniyut* cannot be considered, the former because none of their *hapax* realizations are new. Two of the + *anut hapax* forms are new. Thus by both criteria, + *anut* is more productive than + *aniyut*.

The explanation lies in the semantic distinctiveness principle. Unless a semantic distinction is involved, speakers minimize use of suffixes. If it appears that an + *aniyut* form would be semantically and functionally identical to an + *anut* one, the more economical (and thus less redundant) + *anut* variant should be selected. Why, then, is the less redundant variant not selected in the following (see Schwazwald, to appear):

(28) **Less redundant nominalization not selected**

Base	Gloss	+ *i*	Gloss	+ *ut*	+ *iyut*	Gloss
dat	religion	*dati*	religious	**datut*	*datiyut*	religiousity
hemšex	continuation	*hemšexi*	continuous	**hemšexut*	*hemšexiyut*	continuity
megama	aim	*megamati*	tendentious	**megamatut*	*megamatiyut*	tendentiousness

The answer is that in cases like these, the base itself is an abstract noun. Adding the abstract nominalization suffix + *ut* directly to a morpheme that is already an abstract noun would constitute redundancy.

The nominalization of the adjective, on the other hand, is functionally and semantically appropriate. So generally speaking, the choice between +ut and +iyut is pragmatic/functional.

Even though the preference for +anut over +aniyut is attributed to avoidance of redundancy and minimization of suffixation, it still constitutes strong argument for the claim that productivity depends on the nature of the base: bases ending in +an clearly prefer +ut suffixation over +iyut.

6.2.1.4   *The relationship between* +i *and* +ut

We should now look at the relationship between the two most productive suffixes, +i and +ut, regardless of whichever suffix precedes them. The commonest combination is the sequence /+i+ut/, realized as +iyut, with 617 occurrences in the Even-Shoshan (1970) dictionary, which also contains 64 ending with +uti. So the presence of the adjectival ending +i is a very likely trigger for productive nominalizations with +ut, but the reverse is also possible. +iyut realizations also outnumber +uti ones in our 112k corpus, 83 occurrences of +iyut vs. 23 of +uti. Extraction of neologisms through dictionary comparison provides the following ordering:

(30) **Productivity of +*iyut* vs. *uti* according to dictionary comparison**

R2 Ranking	ES	ES '83	BABY	PHAS	New	R1	R2
+*iyut*	617	25	25	1	51	.0827	.9273
+*uti*	64	3	1	–	4	.0625	.0727
			Total new:		55		

The same ordering is suggested by corpus analysis:

(31) **Productivity of +*iyut* vs. *uti* according to data from the 112k corpus**

R2 Ranking	Tokens	*hapax*	R1	R2
+*iyut*	83	34	.4096	.8947
+*uti*	23	4	[.1739	.1053]
	Total *hapax*:	38		

Only +*iyut*, which includes a brand new *'iniyut* 'being in', is considered; there are no new forms among the +*uti hapax legomena*.

In part, the predominance of +*iyut* forms may be accounted for by the observation that many +*iyut* cases do not necessarily require a free-standing base ending with +i to be generated. This is the case not only in words related to roots with a historical *y* as third radical, as in

(32)
Base	Gloss	+i Form	+iyut Form	Gloss
mumxe	specialist	*mumxi	mumxiyut	specialization
pore	productive; fertile	*pori	poriyut	productivity; fertility
naki	clean	*nekiyi	nekiyut	cleanliness

but in other +*iyut* forms as well:

(33)
Base	Gloss	+i Form	+iyut Form	Gloss
nóax	comfortable	*noxi(yi)	noxiyut	comfort
gibor	hero, heroic	*gibori	giboriyut	heroism
galmud	lonely	*galmudi	galmudiyut	loneliness
guc	a very short person	*guci	guciyut	having short stature
xamor	ass, donkey	??xamori	xamoriyut	asinine behavior
hefreš	difference	*hefreši	hefrešiyut	differential status
klum	nothing; something	*klumi	klumiyut	nothingness
le'altar	immediately	*le'altari	le'altariyut	immediacy
levad	alone, by oneself	*levadi	levadiyut	being alone
matara	aim, target	*matrati	matratiyut	sense of purpose
nixóax	good smell	*nixoxi	nixoxiyut	state of freshness, good smell
kétaˤ	section, fragment	*kitˤi	kitˤiyut	state of fragmentation
komem	raise upright	*komemi	komemiyut	independence, dignity
zulat	(the) other	*zulati	zulatiyut	otherness

+*uti*, on the other hand, is almost always derived from a free-standing +*ut* base. There are only 2–3 exceptions of little significance:[14]

(34)
Base	Gloss	+uti Form	Gloss
mlaxa	work; art	mlaxuti	artificial
nagad	resistor (elec.)	nagduti	of resistor (elec.); resistive
nekeva	female	nakvuti	feminine

For +*iyut* words without a real +*i* base, +*iyut* counts as an atomic single suffix, functioning as an alternative realization of +*ut*. At least potentially, it can be appended to any stem that may take +*ut* but does not. +*ut*+*i*, as a two-suffix sequence, is limited to +*ut* cases to start with, and among them only to those that can be turned into

---

[14] These few forms are of little significance because the last two (*nagduti, nakvuti*) are quite literary, and the relationship between the form and its base in the third (*mlaxa* > *mlaxuti*) is opaque.

attributive adjectives. Thus, our measurements showing that $+i$ is generally more productive than $+ut$ are not contradicted by the predominance of $+iyut$ over $+uti$. The comparison is, actually, not between $+iyut$ and $+uti$, but rather between $+iyut$ cum $+ut$ and the sequence $+ut+i$.

The distribution ratios of cases in which $+iyut$ and $+uti$ co-occur is emphasized even further in forms where one of them is repeated more than once: $+utiyut$ and $+iyuti$. Since $+iyut$ is more common than $+uti$, one would expect $+utiyut$ to be that much more common than $+iyuti$, which is indeed the case. Of the 617 ES $+iyut$ cases, there are 15 realizations of $+utiyut$ (2 of them in the '83 supplement), and only one $+iyuti$ of the 64 $+uti$ ones ('išyuti 'of personality' < 'išyut 'personality' < 'iši 'personal' < 'iš 'person, man'). The 112k corpus, however, did not contain any such occurrences, and the dictionary cases usually involve stems in which the stem's first $+ut$ is already well-fused with the base, and apparently not as transparent as a suffix any more:

(35) **Some $+utiyut$ occurrences in the Even-Shoshan (1970) dictionary**

Base	Gloss	Bs.+ut	Gloss	Base+uti	Gloss	Base +utiyut	Gloss
yéled	child	yaldut	childhood	yalduti	childish	yaldutiyut	childishness
séfer	book	sifrut	literature	sifruti	literary	sifrutiyut	literariness
'oman	artist	'omanut	art	'omanuti	artistic	'omanutiyut	artistry
'av	father	'avhut	being a father	'avhuti	paternal	'avhutiyut	paternalism
'exad	one	'axdut	unity	'axduti	unitary	'axdutiyut	singleness
gala	go on exile	galut	exile/diaspora	galuti	exilic, diasporic	galutiyut	diaspora nature (derog.)
xaver	friend	xaverut	friendship	xavruti	friendly	xavrutiyut	sociability
kama	how many	kamut	quantity	kamuti	quantitative	kamutiyut	quantitative method
ze	this	zehut	identity	zehuti	identical	zehutiyut	being identical
ma	what	mahut	nature, essence	mahuti	essential	mahutiyut	being essential
'ecem	essence	'acmut	essentiality (lit.)	'acmuti	essential	'acmutitut	essentiality (less lit.)
maca	find	meci'ut	reality	meci'uti	realistic	meci'utiyut	being realistic
mlaxa	work, craft			mlaxuti	artificial	mlaxutiyut	artificiality
		tarbut	culture	tarbuti	cultured, cultural	tarbutiyut	cultured nature
yehudi	Jew	yahadut	Judaism	yahaduti	Judaic	yahadutiyut	being Jewish

Such derivations were made possible by the clear semantic changes in the transformation from one base to the next augmented one.

Had there been no such distinctions, suffix concatenation would have been minimized. But further suffixation would be very unlikely, again because of the semantic/functional distinctiveness constraint: *yaldu-tiyuti*, for example, would have been completely identical to *yalduti* 'childish'.

Coming back to the other suffixes discussed above, we may conclude that since +*an* is more productive than +*on*, +*ani* is more productive than +*oni* (+*i* is constant in both). Similarly, +*anut* is more productive than either +*onut* or +*a'ut*.

6.2.1.5 *Interaction of derivational suffixes in nouns/adjectives: conclusion*

The interaction of derivational suffixes in the noun/adjective system has been shown to contribute the following to the understanding of word formation:

(a) The use of derivational patterns is constrained by a requirement for semantic/functional distinctiveness from already-existing forms.
(b) Minimal semantic/functional distinctiveness is a difference of register, but with time, forms differing only in register also develop different connotations, and ultimately transparent semantic differences.
(c) In the absence of distinctiveness, speakers tend to select the simplest derivational device, with the least affixation.
(d) The productivity of an affix depends on the nature and composition of the base for derivation, and particularly on the type of affixes that had already been appended to it.
(e) When a suffix sequence has become 'atomic', its productivity is affected to some degree by how productive the final affix would have been on its own.

CHAPTER SEVEN

PARTIAL *MIŠKAL* MERGER AND BACK-FORMATION

We have already discussed in some detail two cases in which one *miškal* partially merges with another: *maCCeC* > *meCaCeC*, and *miCCaCa* > *maCCeCa*. In the case of the former, it was argued that the merger reflects the speaker's intuition that human agents and instruments are aspects of essentially the same 'performer' category. The direction of the shift was in favor of *meCaCeC*, which is more transparent, owing to the direct relationship to the base verb and to its greater prominence in sheer numbers and scope of application. The shift from *miCCaCa* to *maCCeCa*, rather than the other way around, was again attributed to the greater transparency of *maCCeC(a)* when compared with *miCCaC(a)*, and to the phonetic preference for *a* as the unmarked Hebrew vowel. But these are not the only patterns undergoing such partial mergers. There are others shifts of this kind, such as *CiCCon* > *CiCaCon*. In some others, the additional factor of back-formation comes into play. There is also one partial merger within a *binyan*. No productivity tests were designed to evaluate the extent of these phenomena, with the exception of limited tests like the Maimon (1996) one reported below. Dictionary comparison is of no value here, since even the slang dictionaries tend not to record these 'substandard' shifts, and the same applies to the 112k journalistic/literary corpus. Nevertheless, this is a significant aspect of recent productivity that requires reporting, and some interesting insights on word formation can be drawn from the underlying reasons for shifts between derivation patterns.

7.1 *Preferring* CiCaCon *to* CiCCon

As shown above, formation of abstract nouns with +*ut* and the various verb-related nominalization patterns (mostly *CiCuC*) are the most productive devices for deriving abstract nominals. But there are other nominal patterns of limited productivity, that may materialize in focused-local derivation, when the innovator is faced with a greater variety of specific realization possibilities. This wider array of choices is demonstrated, for instance, in occasional innovations by children (see Berman & Sagi 1981, Ravid 1978):

(1) | **Pattern** | **Form** | **Gloss** |
| --- | --- | --- |
| CóCeC | kórev | proximity |
| | sórax | stench |
| | xólek | smoothness |
| [at high- | 'ócev | sorrow |
| school age] | tó'am | taste |
| CaCéCet | zahémet | sickness caused by infection |
| | kašélet | repeated failure |
| CiCaCon | sigaron | state of being closed |

CiCaCon, as in *zikaron* 'memory', *bitaxon* 'security, confidence', *nikayon* 'cleanliness', is of particular interest, owing to its relationship to another pattern which in part also designates abstract nouns, *CiCCon*, as in *šilton* 'regime, government', *dimyon* 'imagination, similarity', *piryon* 'fruitfulness, productivity'.[1] A number of frequent *CiCCon* forms maintain their *CiCCon* pattern only in normative Hebrew. In the colloquial register, they always shift into *CiCaCon*, as in (data from Bolozky 1990a):

(2) ***CiCCon > CiCaCon***
     pitron 'solution' > *pitaron* (cf. *zikaron* 'memory' ~ *zixronot*)
     rišyon 'license' > *rišayon*   *yitron* 'advantage' > *yitaron*
     sirxon 'stench' > *siraxon*

Forms like *pitron* 'solution', whose plural is *pitronot* at any register, are realized as *pitaron* in analogy with *zikaron* 'memory' etc. (i.e. following *zikaron* ~ *zixronot* 'memories' rather than *šilton* 'rule, regime' ~ *šiltonot* 'authorities'). In each case, the *CiCCon* form belongs in the formal/literary register, where the colloquial *CiCaCon* variant is unacceptable.[2] A number of opacity and saliency factors combine to account for this partial merger. The direction of the shift is to some extent towards the more common pattern: 129 realizations of *CiCaCon*

---

[1] For a discussion of *CiCaCon* and *CiCCon* in BH and in MishH, see Gross (1994).

[2] In *xesron* 'shortcoming' > *xisaron*, both variants are acceptable, but the latter is preferred in the colloquial register. In two other colloquial shifts, *dimyon* 'imagination, resemblance' > *dimayon*, *šivyon* 'equality' > *šivayon*, the status of colloquial *dimayon* and *šivayon* is somewhat shaky. For some speakers, they are unacceptable, others mistakenly believe that they are the literary alternants of the *CiCCon* forms (i.e. a hyper-correction). Some even assume that *dimyon* and *dimayon* coexist, to distinguish between 'imagination' and 'resemblance', although such speakers are often inconsistent about which is supposed to be which.

were found in Even-Shoshan (1970), vs. 95 in *CiCCon*. But a 58%
majority is not sufficient to account for the shift. Even when considering only current common realizations, *CiCaCon* still does not have a
sufficient majority, only 34 of 62 (about 55%). The claim made here
is that the preference for *CiCaCon* is due more to its transparency
than to its frequency. *CiCCon* is more opaque than *CiCaCon* for a number of reasons. In some cases, it is confused with *CiCC* stems plus
the diminutive suffix + *on*, as in:

(3) **CiCC stems with diminutive** + *on*
    séfer 'book' ~ *sifron* 'booklet'   *dégel* 'flag' ~ *diglon* 'small flag'
    pésel 'statue' ~ *pislon* 'statuette'   *tipeš* 'foolish, a fool' ~ *tipšon* 'simpleton'

This could be an important factor not only for adults, but also in
child speech, where + *on*-diminutives are fairly common (Berman &
Sagi 1981). Additional opacity is caused by the *i* of *CiCCon* changing
to *e* after a formerly-pharyngeal consonant, as in *'elbon* 'insult', *xešbon*
'account, arithmetic'. *i* becomes *e* in *CiCaCon* as well, as in *te'avon*
'appetite', *gera'on* 'deficit', but since *CiCaCon* has three vowels vs. two
in *CiCCon*, the remaining two syllables make it easier to identify the
pattern, and thus a higher degree of transparency is maintained. The
strongest argument for the relatively-greater transparency and saliency
of *CiCaCon* compared with *CiCCon* is that there are 39 frequent
CiCCon/CiCaCon realizations constituting abstractions with negative
connotation or diseases, 25 of which (65%) are in *CiCaCon*, e.g.

(4) **CiCaCon nouns with negative connotation, or referring to
diseases**
    kišalon 'failure'   *dika'on* 'depression'   *šikaron* 'drunkenness'
    šiga'on 'madness'   *rikavon* 'decay'   *xivaron* 'being pale'
    'ivaron 'blindness'   *šigaron* 'arthritis'   *šimamon* 'boredom'

These illustrate a prominent, transparent morpho-semantic subgroup.
There are abstract nouns in *CiCCon* as well (*šilton* 'regime', *signon*
'style', *elbon* 'insult', *dimyon* 'similarity; imagination', *šivyon* 'equality',
etc.), some of which carry negative connotation, but they are not as
salient semantically. Thus, the preference for *CiCaCon* is to some
extent because of its frequency, but primarily because of its relative
transparency and salience, which makes it more readily available to
the non-expert innovator. It should be noted that the *CiCCon* >
CiCaCon shifts do not have to involve negative connotation, since it
is the salience *per se* that determines the direction of the shift. Dictionary
comparison would have been useful in establishing the relative productivity of *CiCaCon* and *CiCCon* as a factor determining the direction

of the shift, but the Ben-Amotz/Ben-Yehuda and the Prolog dictionaries contain no new realization of either pattern, and those listed
in ES '83 are items from Mishnaic and (mostly) Medieval Hebrew
that had been overlooked. There is only one Modern Hebrew realization in each pattern, and both are literary-rare. The 112k corpus
contains 141 tokens and 4 *hapax* forms in *CiCaCon*, and 101 tokens
and 17 *hapax* forms in *CiCCon*; 36 tokens (including 3 *hapax* forms)
included in *CiCCon* would have been realized in *CiCaCon* had the
corpus texts been oral. However, none of the *hapax* forms in either
pattern is new, which means that corpus data would not be useful
in this case either.

7.2   Back formation in the noun system

An important local strategy in the noun system is back-formation,
which is generally intended to reconstruct the singular free form from
the plural or from the construct state. This is a linear strategy that
does not involve use of affixes. Its purpose is to simplify the paradigm
by leveling. Since the paradigm often undergoes leveling with an unmarked, common or prominent alternant, Ravid (1990) characterizes derivation by back-formation as structure-preserving and thus
transparent derivation. Bolozky (1990a) deals with a number of back-
formation cases, coming to similar conclusions. Below are a few illustrations from Bolozky (1990a).

7.2.1   CaCaC > CCaC

The familiar replacement of normative *šalav* by *šlav* in colloquial
usage is not an isolated case:

(5) *CaCaC > CCaC*

CaCaC	**Gloss**	**Construct**	**Plural**	**Frequent Combinations**
šalav[3]	stage	*šlav*	*šlabim*	*šlav ʾálef* 'phase I (erron.)'
saxar	wages	*sxar*		*sxar limud* 'tuition'
badal	piece	*bdal*	*bdalim*	*bdal sigárya* 'cigarette butt'

---

[3] Even-Shoshan (1970) lists free-standing *šlav* alongside with *šalav*, in smaller print.
This apparently reflects the fact that in both BH and MishH, only the plural form
is attested, which means that *šlabim* could have also been the plural of *šlav* with
patax. Still, free-standing *šlav* is widely regarded as a non-normative form.

(cont.)

CaCaC	Gloss	Construct	Plural	Frequent Combinations
galal	dung		*glalim*	
valad	offspring		*vladot*	
marak	soup	*merak*	*merakim/*	*marak perot* 'comopte (err.)'
			marakim	(erroneous)

šalav 'stage' > *šlav* as a non-standard free form constitutes either back-formation from the plural alternant *šlabim* (or the colloquial variant *šlavim*), or analogy with the construct state form *šlav*. Structures including the construct state form *šlav* are very frequent (e.g. *šlav hatixnun* 'the planning stage'), and there also exist other combinations which mistakenly are conceived of as involving the construct state, like *šlav 'alef* 'phase I' replacing the normative *šalav 'alef*. A similar case: *saxar* 'wages' > *sxar* as a free form. *sxar* reflects analogy with the construct state *sxar* and other variants, e.g. *sxar limud* 'tuition', *sxirut* 'rental'. This is particularly common among older speakers who remain under the influence of Yiddish pronunciation of the same word for both bound and free forms. Most native speakers recognize that the use of *sxar* in isolation is unacceptable, but they would not characterize as substandard the other shifts in free forms noted above. They would accept non-normative *bdal* for *badal* 'piece, end', probably because this literary word hardly ever occurs in isolation. One only hears *bdal 'ózen* 'ear lobe', *bdal sigárya* 'cigarette butt'. *galal* 'dung' > *glal* would be taken for granted because the word is hardly ever realized in the singular. Only the plural *glalim* can be heard. The shift *valad* 'infant, offspring' > *vlad* would probably also be considered acceptable, because today it is used primarily in the plural, *vladot*, for a litter. There is also an example in which the shift is towards the stand-alone singular form: *merak perot* 'compote (literally "fruit soup")' > *marak perot*. Instead of being reduced to *merak*, the construct state form reverts back to the base *marak*. It is possible that because of the high sonority of *m* before a less sonorant consonant, one prefers not to reduce *a* to *e*, as in the colloquial *manat xerum* for normative *menat xerum* 'emergency ration'. Another possible reason is the low frequency of use of the plural of 'soup', *merakim*, which could have reinforced the construct state *merak* had it been more common. So we can conclude that what is common to all *CaCaC* > *CCaC* shifts (or the reverse, in at least one case) is paradigmatic leveling with the more frequent alternant. Attributing this phenomenon to analogy with *kfar* 'village' ~ *kfarim* 'villages', etc., would be hard to justify, since the *CaCaC ~ CCaC+im* paradigm is just as frequent as the *CCaC ~ CCaC+im* one (127 vs. 122 in Avineri 1976, respectively). Nor can we establish the relative productivity of *CaCaC* and *CCaC* as an explanation for the direction of the shift. The colloquial dictionaries list no new realizations in either pattern, and all new forms in ES '83 (5 in *CaCaC*, 4 in *CCaC*) are literary-rare. There are a few hundred tokens of both patterns in the corpus, but none of the *hapax* forms in either is new.

7.2.2   *Reduction in* +an/+ay *paradigms*

Another common back-formation process that levels the singular free stem with the rest of the paradigm is the reduction of a pretonic *a* to *e* in nouns with the suffix *+an* or *+ay*, or its deletion if no three-consonant cluster will be formed in the process:

(6) *+an/+ay* **paradigms with and without reduction**

Former Form	Gloss	Base	Construct	Plural	New Form
kalkalan	economist	kalkala 'economy'	kalkelan	kalkelanim	kalkelan
mada'an	scientist	mada' 'science'	mad'an	mad'anim	mad'an
mišpatan	jurist	mišpat 'law'	mišpetan	mišpetanim	mišpetan
totaxan	gunner	totax 'cannon'	totxan	totxanim	totxan
'urvatan	stable-attendant	'urva 'stable'	'urvetan	'urvetanim	'urvetan
handasay	engineer-assistant	handasa 'engineering'	handesay	handesa'im	handesay[4]
maxsanay	storeroom-	maxsan 'storeroom'	maxsenay	maxsena'im	maxsenay

The earlier approach was to maintain the base intact when the *+an* or *+ay* suffix was added to the base, but have the final vowel of the base reduced elsewhere, in the construct state (of both singular and plural, i.e. *kalkelaney* 'the economists of' as well *kalkelan* 'the economist of'), in the plural, and in other alternants (e.g. *kalkelanit* 'female economist'). Since pretonic reduction/deletion is a very natural phonetic process, and since it would also align the *+an* or *+ay* form with all other alternants of the paradigm, it was quite expected for paradigmatic leveling by back-formation to eventually occur. Blau (1990) points out that by now the Hebrew Language Academy recognizes these natural, expected back-formations as legitimate variants of the normative forms. In the everyday lexicon, the reduced

---

[4] As noted earlier, the *+ay ~ +a'i* distinction between nouns and adjectives, respectively, is not recognized in the colloquial register. Both tend to be realized with *+a'i*.

forms resulting from back-formation are more common, except for *maxsana'i* (*'urvatan* and *'urvetan* are equally literary).

7.2.3 CaCiC ~ CCiC

Another partial pattern merger, *CaCiC > CCiC*, may also be regarded as back-formation with the plural and the construct state:

(7) **CaCiC > CCiC**

Form	Gloss	Construct	Plural	Constr. Pl.	Colloq. Var.
šatil	plant	*štil*	*štilim*	*štiley*	*štil*
gadil	fringe	*gdil*	*gdilim*	*gdiley*	*gdil*
sa'if	clause	*se'if*	*se'ifim*	*se'ifey*	*se'if*
yadid	friend	*yedid*	*yedidim*	*yedidey*	*yedid*
kafis	beam	*kfis*	*kfisim*	*kfisey*	*kfis*
kalid	key	*klid*	*klidim*	*klidey*	*klid*

Although in these cases back-formation is modeled after the plural and the construct state, the motivation for it is apparently not analogy with these forms, but rather the existence noted above of many *CaCiC* forms that constitute passive, *+able*-type adjectives:

(8) **+*able*-type *CaCiC* adjectives**

    šavir 'fragile (= breakable)'   *xadir* 'penetrable'   *'avir* 'passable'
    ragiš 'sensitive (= "feelable")'   *savil* 'passive'   *pa'il* 'active'

The motivation for the shift is the need to make a clear distinction between these adjectives and nouns appearing to be in the same *miškal* that have nothing to do with them. There are some *CaCiC* nouns denoting agricultural terms:

(9) *bacir* 'vintage'   *katif* 'fruit picking (season)'
    'asif 'harvest'   *gadiš* 'heap/stack of wheat'

and others referring to a characteristic or occupation, as in:

(10) *nacig* 'representative' *nadiv* 'a generous person' *yariv* 'opponent'

However, while most *CaCiC* adjectives share the predictable passive adjectival meaning, the majority of *CCiC* nouns cannot be tied together semantically. They are distinguished by the absence of a feminine counterpart (unlike *nacig* etc. above):

(11) *snif* 'branch'   *švil* 'path'   *šliš* 'third'
    kviš 'road'   *kfir* 'lion'   *crif* 'shack'
    pnim 'inside'   *šviv* 'splinter'   *vrid* 'vein'
    nexir 'nostril'   *mexir* 'price'   *ktiv* 'spelling'

Apparently, speakers systematically identify *CaCiC* with +*able*-type adjectives, as well as with few but well-defined nouns, and *CCiC* with nouns devoid of a common semantic trait that have no feminine counterpart. Therefore they shift a good number of normative *CaCiC* nouns to the *CCiC* pattern, in which they fit better. This way there will also be less surface contradictions to the semantic characterization of *CaCiC* as a pattern for +*able*-type adjectives. This is a case of 'specialization' intended to facilitate further creation of adjectives of a very specific type. Thus, *šatil* may be interpreted today as 'plantable' instead of 'plant', and Ravid reports (personal communication) *'óto ganiv* 'a theft-prone car' and *tinok našik* 'a "kissable" baby' in productivity tests. The Hebrew Language Academy recognized this when it decided that in innovations, *CaCiC* will be assigned to adjectives and to nouns denoting a characteristic or occupation, as well as to agricultural terminology and a few other exceptions. Phonologically-similar nouns with no feminine counterparts will be realized in *CCiC*. This legitimized *štil, se'if* and *klid* above. *cmig* 'tire' was opted for, in spite of the fact that *camig* had already taken root, to avoid homonymity with the common adjective *camig* 'viscous'. And although *parit* had been used for a while for 'item', the decision was in favor of *prit*, to avoid similar confusion with a potential adjective *parit* 'that can broken into smaller parts' (< *parat* 'break into smaller parts'). But it was agreed that *karix* 'sandwich' and *lahit* 'hit, popularly sought item', already so well absorbed in daily usage, should be left alone. In any case, on the whole this is a case of semantic specialization, assigning *CaCiC* to passive +*able*-type adjectives and *CCiC* to phonologically-similar nouns, in a manner that clearly distinguishes between the two types. That *CCiC* is more productive than the noun pattern *CaCiC* can also be shown from dictionary comparison:[5]

(12) **Productivity of *CCiC* and nominal *CaCiC* according to dictionary comparison**

R2 Ranking	ES	ES '83	BABY	PHAS	New	R1	R2
CCiC	83	7	2	1	10	.1205	.7692
CaCiC (N)	240	3	–	–	3	.0125	.2308

Total new: 13

---

[5] The new BABY *CCiC* forms are *špix* 'ejaculated sperm' (< *šafax* 'spill, pour') and *šxif* 'emaciated person' (< *šaxif* 'very thin piece (mainly of wood); the PHAS form is *šlif* 'a quick draw' (< *šalaf* 'draw').

In the absence of new realizations of either *CCiC* or nominal *CaCiC* in our corpus, dictionary comparison provides the only useful method of measuring their relative productivity.

Note that while the *CaCiC* > *CCiC* shift is local, the actual identification of *CaCiC* with +*able*-type adjectives is by now a component (albeit minor) of the semantic global procedure of adjective formation, as shown in the adjective-selection section above (Chapter 4).

7.3   *Partial merger within a* binyan

When considering the *hitpaʿel binyan*, for instance, it is clear that the prefix *hit*+ has a central role in its marking and in its identification. Generally, it is assumed that *hifʿil* is similarly identified by the prefix *hi*+, since it is taken for granted that the past stem determines the identity of a particular *binyan*. There is, however, a significant difference between the two *binyanim* in one respect. While in *hitpaʿel* the prefix nucleus and coda are fixed, this is not the case in *hifʿil*. *hifʿil* is characterized by an indeterminable prefix, followed by the stem *(C)CiC*, since the stem vowel *i* identifies *hifʿil* more reliably that the prefix vowel does. Only the small group of 'double' root forms (like *hegen* 'protect', *hesev* 'turn') are not covered by this definition. Even when only past tense forms are considered, the prefix *hi*+ is not always sufficient to identify the *binyan*. First, there are the 'hollow' forms such as *hekim* 'raised' and *hevin* 'understood', where the prefix vowel is *e*, and forms with root-initial *n* and *yc* follow them in the colloquial (*hipil* 'dropped' > *hepil*, *hicía* 'offered' > *hecía*, etc.) The opposite shift (i.e. *e* > *i*, as in *hevánti* 'I understood' > *ivánti*) also occurs, but less frequently. The phenomenon is not new. It was already noted in Gesenius (1910: 219) for Biblical Hebrew, by Segal (1927: 85) for Mishnaic Hebrew, and by Schwarzwald (1981a: 91–92), Barkai (1978) and others for Modern Hebrew, that there has always existed a degree of analogical leveling between the different sub-classes of hollow/defective verbs, apparently because of the considerable surface similarity between them. A recent test conducted by Maimon (1996) on 15 subjects, in which the research purpose was well disguised, to assure naturalness of production, confirms that the stronger tendency is for *hiCiC* to merge with *heCiC* rather than vice versa. Below are the numbers of shifted vowels (out of a total of 15. In cases of more than a single occurrence in the Maimon data, the highest number was picked):

(13) *i* > *e* in 'hollow' *hif'il* forms

hikif 'surround' (< *n.k.r̥*) > *hekif* – 10
hicil 'save' (< *n.c.l*) > *hecil* – 10
higiš 'present, serve' (< *n.g.š*) > *hegiš* – 10
hizía 'perspire' (< *y.z.ʿ*) > *hezía* – 9
hisi 'marry (tr.)' (< *n.s.ʾ*) > *hesi* – 9
hidiax 'depose' (< *n.d.x*) > *hediax* – 9
hizik 'damage' (< *n.z.k*) > *hezik* – 8
hisig 'obtain' (< *n.s.g*) > *hesig* – 7
hišiv 'blow' (< *n.š.b*) > *hešiv* – 7
hikir 'recognize' (< *n.k.r*) > *hekir* – 6
hisik 'conclude' (< *n.s.k*) > *hesik* – 5
higía 'arrive' (< *n.g.ʿ*) > *hegía* – 3

hipil 'drop (tr.)' (< *n.p.l*) > *hepil* – 10
hibit 'look' (< *n.b.t̥*) > *hebit* – 10
hicit 'set fire' (< *y.c.t̥*) > *hecit* – 10
hiciv 'place, stand (tr.)' (< *y.c.b*) > *heciv* – 9
hikiš 'knock; deduct' (< *n.k.š*) > *hekiš* – 9
hibía 'express' (< *n.b.ʿ*) > *hebía* – 8
hiníax 'place' (< *n.w.x*) > *heníax* – 8
hisíax 'distract' (< *n.s.x*) > *hesíax* – 7
hicig 'present' (< *y.c.g*) > *hecig* – 7
hisía 'drive, transport' (< *n.s.ʿ*) > *hesía* – 5
hicía 'offer' (< *y.c.ʿ*) > *hecía* – 5

(14) *e* > *i* in 'hollow' *hif'il* forms

hekic 'wake up' (< *k.w.c*) > *hikic* – 5
hekim 'raise, set up' (< *k.w.m*) > *hikim* – 5
hetil 'throw' (< *t.w.l*) > *hitil* – 4
hemit 'kill' (< *m.w.t̥*) > *himit* – 3
heníax 'let go' (< *n.w.x*) > *hiníax* – 2
hevis 'defeat' (< *b.w.s*) > *hivis* – 2
hería 'cheer' (< *r.w.ʿ*) > *hiría* – 2
hevi 'bring' (< *b.w.ʾ*) > *hivi* – 1
hesit 'incite' (< *s.w.t̥*) > *hisit* – 1
hecif 'flood' (< *c.w.p̥*) > *hicif* – 1

hešiv 'reply' (< *š.w.b*) > *hišiv* – 5
hediax 'wash (dishes)' (< *d.w.x*) > *hidiax* – 4
heki 'vomit' (< *k.y.ʾ*) > *hiki* – 3
hevin 'understand' (< *b.y.n*) > *hivin* – 2
hegiv 'react' (< *g.w.b*) > *higiv* – 2
hesir 'remove' (< *s.w.r*) > *hisir* – 2
hemir 'exchange' (< *m.w.r*) > *himir* – 2
hefic 'scatter' (< *p.w.c*) > *hific* – 1
hexin 'prepare' (< *k.w.n*) > *hixin* – 1

According to Maimon, the mergers do not appear to be directly dependent on sociolinguistic factors, although there was certain inverse correlation between degree of education and normative choice of pattern, which may have been accidental, but may also indicate that the shift has gained acceptance. At the same time, the older the person, the higher the percentage of normative choice, which suggests that the shift is relatively new. The important question is whether the shift is morphophonological or phonetic. It might be that the predominant *i* > *e* shift is indeed a merger of the more restricted *hiCiC* pattern, which designates *n*-initial and *yc*-initial roots in *hif'il*, with the more common, and thus more prominent, *heCiC* pattern, which characterizes the large class of roots with a medial glide in *hif'il*. It is also possible that the shift is psychologically motivated, by the wish to dissimilate, particularly when the two *i*'s are so close to each other. Another possibility is that speakers realize that shifts like *e* > *i*, as in *hevánti* 'I understood' > *ivánti*, are tantamount to reassigning such forms to *pi'el* (following *dibárti* 'I spoke', etc.), which could explain why *i* > *e* is more common than *e* > *i*.

In addition to the opacity-causing shift from the prefixal *i* to *e*, one also observes today a strong substandard tendency to replace that *i* with *e* even in regular *hifʿil* forms (*higzámta* 'you exaggerated' > *hegzámta*, *hixnásti* 'I let in' > *hexnásti*, *hišmína* 'she grew fat' > *hešmína*, *hirgízu* 'they annoyed' > *hergízu*), following the normative *hifʿil* lowering of *i* to *e* before *x* from *het* (*hexlit* 'decided', *hexzik* 'held', etc.). The phenomenon is not limited to the uneducated. In December 1996, I recorded Benjamin Netanyahu making the following shifts in a broadcast statement:

(15) +*i* > *e* in regular *hifʿil* forms

hiclánu 'we succeeded' > *heclánu*	*hidgášnu* 'we emphasized' > *hedgášnu*
hivtáxnu 'we promised' > *hevtáxnu*	*hirgášti* 'I felt' > *hergášti*

This current colloquial shift also weakens the status of the prefix and its role as marker or identifier of the *hifʿil* pattern.

The first process, the *hipil* 'dropped' > *hepil* type, is analogical, and its purpose is to make all *hVCiC* forms uniform through leveling. The fact that the shift also applies to the present tense (e.g. *mapil* 'drop'> *mepil*) suggests that the motivation is not phonetic, since generally such *a* is not susceptible to phonetic reduction. *tavo* '(you will) come' is never realized as **tevo*, whereas *tišmor* '(you will) guard', for instance, may be reduced and realized as *tšmor* or *čmor*. On the other hand, the process responsible for *higzámta* 'you exaggerated' > *hegzámta* etc. appears to be essentially phonetic, a process of reduction and centralization of *i* into the minimal Hebrew vowel, *e*. Present tense *magzim* 'exaggerate', for instance, is never realized as **megzim*, since such *a* is not affected by a phonetic process. The *i* of the *hitpaʿel* prefix is not subject to a similar process. Since it is maintained in all forms of all tense paradigms, it is more stable. It might further be argued that its secondary stress throughout the *binyan* (*hitlabášti* 'I got dressed', *mìtlabéš* 'get dressed', *tìtlabšú* 'you ms. pl. will get dressed') helps to protect it from reduction. It is interesting to note that when speakers allow this prefix to get reduced today, they actually continue an early historical reduction process, through which the *a* of the *hifʿil* prefix *ha*+ was reduced to *i*.

7.4   *Partial* miškal *merger and back-formation: conclusion*

As noted above, there are no sufficient data that would enable us to evaluate the productivity of such partial mergers in current Israeli

Hebrew. But they do constitute an important aspect of productivity in the colloquial register, and should consequently be considered as a component of Israeli Hebrew word formation. Their contribution to the understanding of word formation lies mostly in the insight they allow into the reasons for shifts between derivation patterns. The main motivation for back-formation is the generalization and simplification achieved by reduction of alternation in the system, making it easier to master and reuse in new word-formation. Leveling is conditioned by a degree of morphophonological similarity, and normally favors the more common variant. It may be semantically based. In the case of *CiCCon* > *CiCaCon*, the shift is conditioned by the semantic saliency of *CiCaCon*. *CaCiC* > *CCiC* leveling is also accompanied by semantic specialization. Since *CaCiC* has become typically associated with +*able*-type adjectives, *CaCiC* nouns are assigned to morphologically-similar *CCiC* that has by necessity become specialized for nouns. In the cases of +*ay*/+*a'i* and *hiCCiC* > *heCCiC*, the motivation is phonetic naturalness.

CHAPTER EIGHT

CONCLUSION

Two major lines of conclusion, methodological and psychological, emerge from this study, based on the character of Modern Hebrew word formation, but in principle extendable across languages.

Methodologically, a combination of procedures (productivity tests, dictionary comparison, and corpus analysis) is best in order to assess lexical productivity. Dictionary comparison is relatively easy to apply, and seems to require no special improvements. Even the need to distinguish between genuine innovations and addenda due to earlier omission can easily be achieved with existing tools. The other criteria, however, need improvement and elaboration. Data elicitation procedures require more sophisticated design. For example, the fill-in-the-gap method, in writing and orally (Bolozky 1978), should be developed so as to promote natural, spontaneous responses in coinage tests. Normally, one would like to distract the subject's attention from the object of the inquiry, since it is under conditions of the least attention that natural responses arise. It is particularly important to do so in tests of this kind, since formation of non-existing words is involved, which would unavoidably constitute the focus of attention. The proposed base nouns should be more varied, to allow for the widest range of pronounceable clusters, and target meanings should be added, to cover as many potential correspondences between pattern and meaning. One should also consider whether indeed it is a good idea to use the same speakers for both types of tests. Keeping the subjects constant assures control over the individual speaker's idiosyncratic tendencies, supposedly keeping them constant, but exposure to the coinage test clearly creates biases that may affect the subsequent judgment tasks results. Corpus analysis requires larger and more varied corpora than are currently available, especially for patterns of restricted domain, which are not very likely to occur in a small corpus. The corpora used in this research were very limited, for technical reasons. None are available as yet for Modern Hebrew, and to build up a corpus is no small feat. Optical scanning is not a good option for Hebrew, since Hebrew orthography, like that of other Semitic languages, allows multiple interpretation of almost every orthographically-represented word. Ideally, every word should be tagged for maximal grammatical information, but in the absence of qualified staff to do so, the next best thing is to phonetically transcribe texts, and only in case of residual ambiguity following a search, go back and check the actual context. Another solution is to construct a sophisticated algorithm that will analyze and identify words in scanned texts with reasonable accuracy, based on contextual clues. For the present study, a very limited corpus of transcribed texts was used, partly journalistic and partly literary. In the future, one would also need to include transcribed spoken texts. A substantial body of spoken data will also enable us to incorporate the partial pattern merger and back formation phenomena characteristic of the colloquial register.

Scores obtained through each of the three investigation procedures generally reinforces findings arrived at by the other methods. Since the productivity concept is not easy to define, and some of the measures (particularly productivity tests, but to an extent the other measures as well) are difficult to control, comparing findings arrived at through different procedures is the safest evaluation measure. The higher the correlation between findings of different measurements conducted independently of each other, the higher the degree of validity.

From a psycholinguistic point of view, it was shown that selection of word formation patterns is not arbitrary. When one looks at the total Hebrew lexicon, one's first impression is that irregularity reigns, and that any attempt to make sense out of its masses of words is doomed to fail. But the total lexicon plays only a limited role in current morphological productivity, in that it determines overall prominence of a pattern in terms of sheer numbers. The new lexicon, which reflects recent tendencies in word formation, carries much greater weight. Observation of the new lexicon reveals that when a neologism is created, its formation is essentially semantically based. In fact, word formation is constrained by a requirement that each neologism be semantically or functionally distinct from any other item already in the lexicon, if not in content, then at least in register. Total semantic redundancy is not an option. The derivation process is also constrained by overriding conditions such as phonetic restrictions on pronunceability or preemption, but those are not the primary considerations determining pattern selection. They operate within the semantically-based choice, and cause the selection to shift to the closest available pattern only when a constraint is violated.

The semantic factors determining pattern choice are varied. Speakers tend to look for the most prominent and the most-readily-available pattern they observe in the recent everyday lexicon. A derivation pattern may be used widely enough to function as the default pattern for some category, but even then is still associated with some broad semantic (or at least syntactic) feature. Generally, the broader the semantic category, the more likely is the default pattern to be selected: *puʿal* for passive verbs, *hitpaʿel* for all other non-agentive verbs, *piʿel* for agentive ones; +*i* for attributive adjectives, *meCuCaC* for verb-related ones; *CiCuC* for verb-related abstract nominalizations, +*ut* for other nominalizations; +*on* for diminutives, +*an* for agentives/instrumentals, +*iya* for locatives. There are other patterns, ranked below the default ones on the productivity scale, but nevertheless significantly productive: +*ay*/+*aʾi* for agents and agent attributes, *CaCiC* for +*able*-type adjectives, etc. Beyond these primary choices, a number of general semantic factors may also play a role, resulting in additional adjustments and shifts. Such modifications usually do not upset the basic semantic classification, at least not at the highest level. Maintaining a degree of transparency for the base within the neologism is one such factor. It is often manifest in preservation of the original consonant clustering of the base. The prominence of a pattern in the new lexicon is determined not only by size, but also by semantic saliency and coherence, as well as by pattern transparency. Often, pattern transparency is enhanced by transparent suffixation. If it is evident that additional suffixation would be semantically redundant, the most economical representation (i.e. minimal suffixation) is chosen. Minor shifts between partially-similar patterns may also be caused by semantic considerations, such as preference for the semantically more salient (or more transparent) pattern, or for the pattern which speakers regard as semantically unmarked. Frequency of commonly used alternants may play a role as well.

Productivity may vary depending on the type of base undergoing derivation, as well as on previously-appended suffixes. As for the actual mechanism of derivation, it was demonstrated that although linear derivation is on the increase in Modern Hebrew, discontinuous derivation is still the mainstay of its word formation mechanism. The typically-Semitic process of discontinuous derivation, based on the fusion of extracted consonants (or original consonant clusters) from an existing lexeme and a 'canonical' *miškal*, is as strong as ever. The two derivational strategies operate quite productively alongside each other, sometimes within essentially the same morphological pattern.

The psycholinguistic conclusions confirm findings from research on morphological productivity conducted in other languages. Two of the three methods proposed for evaluating degree of productivity, productivity tests and corpus analysis, have been tried successfully in other languages. The third, dictionary comparison, has been avoided owing to some inherent inadequacies, but our research has shown that if the comparison is done correctly, it can be quite reliable, and eventually very useful. The central thesis of this book is that comparing findings from multiple methodologies would constitute a reliable evaluation measure of morphological productivity in any language. It is also proposed that the relative productivity of a particular derivation pattern in capturing some semantic category can be measured by two ratios: (a) the ratio of the number of innovations in it to the total number of its realizations within that category in the lexicon (or a corpus representing it), reflecting pattern 'internal' rate of regeneration regardless of absolute pattern size for that category, and (b) the ratio of the number of its innovations to the total number of neologisms in the semantic category concerned, reflecting relative pattern productivity within that category in the new lexicon (or the new component of a corpus representing it.) It is primarily the second ratio that determines current productivity, but the measurement is more reliable when the two ratios are consistent for each pair of patterns compared. When the two ratios are not consistent, and ratio weighting shows an advantage for the first ratio of the second pattern over the second ratio of the first, it may indicate that the second pattern would be ranked higher for productivity within a more specific semantic domain.

Finally, a consoling thought: since this book is not likely to be widely read, and since the average Israeli, though speaking English reasonably well, still hates to read in English, the damage this book might cause minimal. Just imagine how awful it would be for a native speaker to be told: this is how you coin new words. It would be like informing the fabled centipede on the mechanism it uses to move forward!

APPENDICES

I. Discontinuous word formation patterns in the English verb system

a. *drive-drove-driven, write-wrote-written, ride-rode-ridden, rise-rose-risen, arise-arose-arisen, strive-strove-striven, smite-smote-smitten, bestride-bestrode-bestridden*

b. *speak-spoke-spoken, freeze-froze-frozen, steal-stole-stolen, weave-wove-woven*

c. *grow-grew-grown, blow-blew-blown, know-knew-known, throw-threw-thrown (fly-flew-flown)*

d. *bear-bore-borne, tear-tore-torn, swear-swore-sworn, tread-trod-trodden, wear-wore-worn*

e. *take-took-taken, shake-shook-shaken, forsake-forsook-forsaken*

f. *show-showed-shown, mow-mowed-mown*

g. *sing-sang-sung, sink-sank-sunk, swim-swam-swum, drink-drank-drunk, ring-rang-rung, shrink-shrank-shrunk, spring-sprang-sprung, stink-stank-stunk (begin-began-begun, run-ran-run)*

h. *spin-spun-spun, dig-dug-dug, stick-stuck-stuck, sting-stung-stung, swing-swung-swung, wring-wrung-wrung (hang-hung-hung)*

i. *bite-bit-bit(ten), hide-hid-hid(den), chide-chid-chid(den), light-lit-lit, slide-slid-slid*

j. *bend-bent-bent, send-sent-sent, lend-lent-lent, rend-rent-rent, spend-spent-spent (dwell-dwelt-dwelt)*

k. *feel-felt-felt, kneel-knelt-knelt, deal-dealt-dealt, dream-dreamt-dreamt, keep-kept-kept, lean-leant-leant, leave-left-left, mean-meant-meant, sleep-slept-slept, sweep-swept-swept, weep-wept-wept*

l. *bid-bade-bidden, give-gave-given (eat-ate-eaten)*

m. *bleed-bled-bled, breed-bred-bred, feed-fed-fed, lead-led-led, meet-met-met, read-read-read, speed-sped-sped (hold-held-held)*

n. *bind-bound-bound, find-found-found, grind-ground-ground, wind-wound-wound*

o. *hit-hit-hit, split-split-split, slit-slit-slit*

p. *let-let-let, set-set-set, shed-shed-shed*

q. *cut-cut-cut, shut-shut-shut*

r. *hurt-hurt-hurt, burst-burst-burst*

s. *sell-sold-sold, tell-told-told (shine-shone-shone)*

t. *lose-lost-lost, shoot-shot-shot*

u. *sit-sat-sat, spit-spat-spat*

v. *pay-paid-paid, lay-laid-laid (say-said-said)*

w. *teach-taught-taught, seek-sought-sought, beseech-besought-besought*

x. *bring-brought-brought, think-thought-thought (buy-bought-bought, fight-fought-fought, catch-caught-caught)*

II. Distribution of structure-preserving and non-structure-preserving alternants in the 1978 verb productivity tests (N subjects = 50, N bases = 11) (Included are only forms whose base contains consonant clusters. CP = Cluster-Preserving; NCP = Non-Cluster-Preserving; CCP = Consonant Cluster Preservation; Co. = Coinage tests; Ju. = Judgment tests)

Base	Target Meaning	Binyan	Realization	CCP.	% Co.	% Ju.
marks 'Marx'	become a Marxist	*hitpaᶜel*	*hitmarkses*	CP	76	82
			hitmarkes	NCP	24	18
marks 'Marx'	make one a Marxist	*piᶜel*	*mirkses*	CP	62	80
			mirkes	NCP	28	18
		hifᶜil	*himriks*	NCP	8	2
šmalc 'schmaltz'	become schmaltzy	*hitpaᶜel*	*hitšmalcec*	CP	66	72
			hištamlec	NCP	22	20
			hištmalcec	NCP	8	8
šmalc 'schmaltz'	make it schmaltzy	*piᶜel*	*šmilcec*	CP	28	32
			šimlec	NCP	6	8
			šimelc	NCP	2	–
		hifᶜil	*hišmilc*	CP	64	60
talk 'talcum powder'	spray with talcum	*piᶜel*	*tilkek*	CP	46	62
			tilek	NCP	26	20
		hifᶜil	*hitlik*	NCP	28	18
patent 'patent'	register as patent	*piᶜel*	*pitent*	CP	56	68
			pitnet	NCP	44	32
zbeng 'blow'	give a blow	*piᶜel*	*zbingeg*	CP	20	28
			zibeng	NCP	12	–
		hifᶜil	*hizbing*	CP	66	72
'asfalt 'asphalt'	cover with asphalt	*piᶜel*	*'isfelt*	CP	88	98
			'isflet	NCP	8	2
		hifᶜil	*hisfilt*	CP	4	–
sport 'sports'	engage in sports	*piᶜel*	*sportet*	CP	56	50
			spirtet	CP	10	4
			sipret	NCP	2	2
		hitpaᶜel	*hitsportet*	CP	22	36
			hitspartet	CP	4	4
			histportet	NCP	2	4
			histapret	NCP	4	–
snob 'snob'	become snobbish	*hitpaᶜel*	*histaneb*	NCP	44	36
			hitsnobeb	CP	22	38
			hitsnabeb	CP	16	6
			histnobeb	NCP	6	14
			histnabeb	NCP	4	4
snob 'snob'	make one snobbish	*hifᶜil*	*hisnib*	CP	60	64
		piᶜel	*snobeb*	CP	12	22
			sineb	NCP	10	12
			'isneb	CP	12	–
			sinbeb	NCP	6	2

III. Details of 1995/96 tests on productivity of verb formation
(N subjects = 50, N bases = 23. CCP = Consonant Cluster Preservation;
CP = Cluster-Preserving; NCP = Non-Cluster-Preserving; Co. = Coinage
tests; Ju. = Judgment tests. Marking for structure preservation is limited to
forms whose bases contain consonant clusters. Variants within a *binyan* are
grouped together)

i. Focus on patient/theme suggested
Non-agentive target meaning (mostly inchoative), N subjects = 50,
N bases = 9

Base	Target Meaning	Binyan	Realization	CCP.	% Co.	% Ju.
šerif 'sheriff'	become a sheriff	*hitpaˤel*	*hištaref*		56	78
			hištarpef		2	–
			hitʾašref		–	2
		hufˤal	*hušraf*		22	10
		puˤal	*šoraf*		6	4
		nifˤal	*nišraf*		4	4
		hifˤil	*hišrif*		4	–
		piˤel	*šeref*		4	–
snob 'snob'	become snobbish	*hitpaˤel*	*histaneb*	NCP	54	54
			hitsaneb	NCP	–	10
			histnobeb	NCP	–	6
			histnabeb	NCP	2	4
			hitʾasneb	CP	–	6
			hisnobeb	CP	4	–
			histanbev	NCP	2	–
			histanbet	NCP	2	–
			histnaʾeb	NCP	–	2
			hitsnabeb	CP	2	–
			hisnabeb	CP	2	–
			hisnabneb	CP	2	–
		hifˤil	*hisnib*	CP	12	14
		nifˤal	*nisnab*	CP	4	–
		piˤel	*sineb*	NCP	–	2
			snobeb	CP	–	2
		paˤal	*sanab*	NCP	2	–
marks 'Marx'	become a Marxist	*hitpaˤel*	*hitmarkses*	CP	28	62
			hitmarksest	CP	28	14
			hitmarkes	NCP	8	12
			hitmarkest	NCP	2	6
		puˤal	*murksast*	CP	8	–
			murksas	CP	4	–
		piˤel	*mirkses*	CP	–	2
			mirkes	NCP	–	2
		hifˤil	*himriks*	NCP	–	2
šmalc 'schmaltz'	become schmaltzy	*hitpaˤel*	*hištalmec*	NCP	22	28
			hištmalcec	NCP	4	38
			hištamlec	NCP	34	6
			hitšmalcec	CP	–	24
			hišmalcen	CP	4	–

(cont.)

Base	Target Meaning	Binyan	Realization	CCP.	% Co.	% Ju.
			hitmalšec	NCP	2	–
		pi⁽el	*šmilcen*	CP	4	–
			šimlec	NCP	2	–
		nif⁽al	*nišmalc*	CP	4	4
		pu⁽al	*šumlac*	NCP	2	–
žlob 'crude/big/ strong man'	become big/ crude . . .	*hitpa⁽el*	*hižďaleb*	NCP	34	58
			hižďalbev	NCP	2	24
			hitžalbet	NCP	6	–
			hižďalben	NCP	2	–
			hižďalbet	NCP	2	–
			hižďablev	NCP	2	–
			hižtalbev	NCP	2	–
			hižtaleb	NCP	2	–
			hižďalbeg	NCP	2	–
			hitžalbek	NCP	2	–
			hižtlabet	NCP	2	–
			hižtažleb	CP	2	–
			hižlabet	CP	2	–
			hižtažleb	CP	2	–
			hižlobeb	CP	2	–
		hif⁽il	*hižlib*	CP	10	10
		nif⁽al	*nižlab*	CP	4	2
magad 'battalion commander'	become battalion commander	*hitpa⁽el*	*hitmaged*		80	84
		pu⁽al	*mugad*		12	8
		nif⁽al	*nimgad*		4	6
		huf⁽al	*humgad*		2	–
		hif⁽il	*himgid*		2	–
magav 'border police'	become border police member	*hitpa⁽el*	*hitmagev*		80	74
		pu⁽al	*mugav*		8	12
		huf⁽al	*humgav*		2	12
		hif⁽il	*himgiv*		2	2
		nif⁽al	*nimgav*		2	–
zálman 'sloppy dresser'	become sloppy	*hitpa⁽el*	*hizdalmen*	CP	60	90
			hitzalmen	CP	14	–
			hiztalmen	CP	4	–
			hizalmen	CP	4	–
		pu⁽al	*zulman*	CP	6	2
		(*huf⁽al* not possible phonetically)				
		nif⁽al	*nizlam*	NCP	–	4
		(full *nif⁽al* not possible phonetically)				
yóram 'goody-goody; obedient; a nerd'	become nerdy	*hitpa⁽el*	*hityarem*		56	86
			hityarmem		2	–
			hityatrem		2	–
			hityorem		2	–
		pu⁽al	*yuram*		2	6
		pi⁽el	*yirem*		2	2
		pa⁽al	*yaram*		–	4

Agentivity suggested, but agent not distinct from patient (reflexive, reciprocal) N subjects = 50, N bases = 3

Base	Target Meaning	Binyan	Realization	CCP.	% Co.	% Ju.
šérif 'sheriff'	make/proclaim oneself sheriff	*hitpaʿel*	*hištaref*		50	42
			hitʾašref		–	14
			hištarpef		2	2
		hifʿil	*hišrif*		16	22
		hufʿal	*hušraf*		10	4
		puʿal	*šoraf*		8	4
		piʿel	*šeref*		4	10
		nifʿal	*nišraf*		2	–
búnker 'bunker'	hide self in bunker	*hitpaʿel*	*hitbanker*	CP	92	96
		piʿel	*binker*	CP	4	2
		puʿal	*bunkar*	CP	2	–
		(*hufʿal/nifʿal* not possible phonetically)				
pitka 'note'	send each other notes	*hitpaʿel*	*hitpatkeʾu*	CP	46	44
			hitpatku	CP	14	30
			hitpatkeku	CP	2	–
		piʿel	*pitkeʾu*	CP	36	20
		hiftiku		NCP	–	2

Passive, N subjects = 50, N bases = 7

Base	Target Meaning	Binyan	Realization	CCP.	% Co.	% Ju.
bagac 'high court'	be presented to high court	*puʿal*	*bugac*		48	48
			bugcac		2	8
		hufʿal	*huvgac*		24	24
		nifʿal	*nivgac*		8	10
		hitpaʿel	*hitbagec*		6	8
šérif 'sheriff'	be made sheriff	*hufʿal*	*hušraf*		32	48
		hitpaʿel	*hištaref*		22	18
		puʿal	*šuraf*		14	–
			šoraf		2	–
			šuryaf		2	–
		nifʿal	*nišraf*		16	22
magad 'battalion commander'	be made battalion commander	*puʿal*	*mugad*		36	46
			mugdan		2	–
		hufʿal	*humgad*		30	34
			hungad		2	–
		hitpaʿel	*hitmaged*		14	14
		nifʿal	*nimgad*		–	6
panel 'panel'	be covered with panels	*puʿal*	*punal*		70	90
			punlal		–	6
			punlan		2	–
			puntal		2	–
		hufʿal	*hufnal*		10	–
		hitpaʿel	*hitpanel*		2	2
		hitpuʿal	*hitpunal*		2	–
kéres 'hook'	be fitted with a hook	*hufʿal*	*huqras*		46	38
		puʿal	*quras*		32	–
			qoras		6	38

(cont.)

Base	Target Meaning	Binyan	Realization	CCP.	% Co.	% Ju.
			qursas		–	8
		hitpaᶜel	*hitqares*		6	2
			hitqarses		–	2
		nifᶜal	*niqras*		2	6
		hifᶜil	*hiqris*		–	2
		hitpuᶜal	*hitquras*		2	–
matax 'foreign currency'	be invested in/ turned into foreign currency	*puᶜal*	*mutax*		62	48
			muštax		6	–
			mutxax		2	–
		hufᶜal	*humtax*		6	46
		paᶜal	*matúax*		–	2
talk 'talcum powder'	be sprayed with talcum powder	*puᶜal*	*tulak*	NCP	68	64
			tulkak	CP	6	14
			ʾutlak	NCP	2	–
		hufᶜal	*hutlak*	NCP	8	8
		hitpaᶜel	*hittalek*	NCP	6	2
		paᶜal	*taluk*	NCP	–	6
		nifᶜal	*nitlak*	NCP	2	–

ii. Agentive

Causative suggested (N subjects = 50, N bases = 9)

Base	Target Meaning	Binyan	Realization	CCP.	% Co.	% Ju.
šerif 'sheriff'	make one sheriff	*piᶜel*	*šeref*		22	56
			širef		30	–
			ʾišref		–	4
		hifᶜil	*hišrif*		44	40
		paᶜal	*šaraf*		4	–
snob 'snob'	make one snobbish	*hifᶜil*	*hisnib*	CP	50	54
		piᶜel	*sineb*	NCP	30	22
			sinbev	NCP	–	16
			snobeb	CP	2	2
			sinbeb	NCP	2	–
			sinben	NCP	2	–
			siben	NCP	2	–
			snibeb	CP	2	–
			snobez	CP	2	–
			snibez	CP	2	–
			ʾisneb	CP	–	2
			tisneb	CP	–	2
			sisneb	CP	2	–
marks 'Marx'	make one a Marxist	*piᶜel*	*mirkses*	CP	40	68
			mirkes	NCP	18	18
			mirksest	CP	14	10
			mirksist	CP	14	–
			markses	CP	2	–
			mirkest	NCP	2	–
		hifᶜil	*himriks*	NCP	–	4

(cont.)

Base	Target Meaning	Binyan	Realization	CCP.	% Co.	% Ju.
			himreksist	NCP	2	–
			himraksest	NCP	2	–
			hirksis	CP	2	–
šmalc 'schmaltz'	make it schmaltzy	*piʕel*	*šmilcec*	CP	10	44
			šmilcet	CP	8	–
			šmilcen	CP	2	–
			šmilces	CP	2	–
			šimlec	NCP	46	38
			šmilec	NCP	8	–
			šmilmec	NCP	2	–
			šimelcen	NCP	2	–
		hifʕil	*hišmilc*	CP	18	18
ʔáfro 'afro hair style'	make (hair) afro-style	*piʕel*	*ʔifrer*	CP	28	40
			ʔifer	NCP	16	28
			ʔifret	CP	24	12
			ʔifren	CP	4	6
			ʔifref	CP	4	–
			ʔifrep	CP	2	–
		hifʕil	*heʔefir*	NCP	4	10
		paʕal	*ʔafar*	NCP	4	4
blond(i(ni)) 'blond'	make blond	*piʕel*	*blinden*	CP	30	30
			bilden	NCP	34	22
			blinded	CP	2	10
			blined	NCP	–	12
			bilned	NCP	6	4
			blinder	CP	4	–
			ʔiblend	CP	2	2
			blended	CP	2	–
		hifʕil	*hiblind*	CP	2	10
			hivlind	CP	2	8
			hiblond	CP	4	–
			hiblid	NCP	2	–
		paʕal	*blanad*	NCP	2	–
magad 'battalion commander'	make one battalion commander	*piʕel*	*miged*		72	72
		hifʕil	*himgid*		24	24
žlob 'crude/big/ /strong man'	make one big/crude	*piʕel*	*žileb*	NCP	42	38
			žilben	NCP	2	8
			žilbev	NCP	8	–
			žilbet	NCP	6	–
			žilbeb	NCP	4	–
			žilvev	NCP	4	–
			žlobev	CP	4	–
			živlev	NCP	2	–
			žibel	NCP	2	–
			ʔižleb	CP	–	2
			tižleb	CP	–	2
		hifʕil	*hižlib*	CP	24	48
		paʕal	*žalab*	NCP	–	2

(cont.)

Base	Target Meaning	Binyan	Realization	CCP.	% Co.	% Ju.
naxs 'bad luck'	cause to be unlucky	*pi'el*	*nixes*	NCP	70	52
			nixses	CP	14	12
			'inxes	NCP	–	8
			minxes	NCP	–	8
			nixsen	CP	4	2
			nixnes	NCP	2	–
			nixser	CP	2	–
		hif'il	*hinxis*	NCP	8	16

iii. General agentive suggested (if patient involved, it is distinct from agent) (N subjects = 50; N bases = 14)

Base	Target Meaning	Binyan	Realization	CCP.	% Co.	% Ju.
šérif 'sheriff'	serve as sheriff	*pi'el*	*šeref*		8	88
			širef		78	–
			širpef		6	–
		hif'il	*hišrif*		4	6
		pa'al	*šaraf*		4	–
		nif'al	*nišraf*		–	4
		hitpa'el	*hištaref*		–	2
sport 'sports'	engage in sports	*pi'el*	*spirtet*	CP	24	28
			sportet	CP	18	24
			sipret	NCP	2	10
			sirpet	NCP	2	–
			sirptet	NCP	2	–
			spirfet	NCP	2	–
			stirpet	NCP	2	–
		hitpa'el	*hitsportet*	CP	4	16
			histapret	NCP	4	10
			hisportet	CP	8	2
			histarpet	NCP	6	–
			hispartet	CP	4	2
			hitsapret	NCP	–	4
			hitspartet	CP	2	–
			hisparet	NCP	2	–
kéres 'hook'	fit with a hook	*pi'el*	*keres*		50	48
			kirses		2	4
			'ikres		–	4
		hif'il	*hiqris*		40	40
		pa'al	*qaras*		6	4
		nif'al	*niqras*		2	–
talk 'talcum powder'	spray with talcum	*pi'el*	*tilek*	NCP	72	74
			tilkek	CP	12	16
			tilket	CP	2	–
		hif'il	*hitlik*	NCP	6	6
		pa'al	*talak*	NCP	–	4
zbeng 'blow'	give a blow	*pi'el*	*zibeng*	NCP	28	24
			zibneg	NCP	10	16
			zbingeg	CP	4	12
			zinbeg	NCP	10	4
			zimbeng	NCP	10	2

(cont.)

Base	Target Meaning	Binyan	Realization	CCP.	% Co.	% Ju.
			zinbeng	NCP	4	–
			zimbeg	NCP	2	–
			zbineg	NCP	2	–
			tizbeng	CP	–	2
		hifʿil	hizbing	CP	22	38
patent 'patent'	register as patent	*piʿel*	pitent	CP	56	50
			pitnet	NCP	20	22
			pintent	CP	12	14
			ʾiptent	CP	–	4
			pintet	NCP	4	–
			pinten	NCP	2	–
		hifʿil	hiptint	CP	–	8
panel 'panel'	cover with panels	*piʿel*	pinel		88	88
			pinlel		–	6
		paʿal	panal		6	–
		hifʿil	hifnil		–	4
ʾasfalt 'asphalt'	cover with asphalt	*piʿel*	ʾisfelt	CP	84	74
			ʾisflet	NCP	12	24
			ʾispelt	CP	4	–
bagac 'high court'	present to high court/subject to high court ruling	*piʿel*	bigec		68	58
			bigcec		8	8
			bigmec		2	–
		hifʿil	hivgic		12	26
		paʿal	bagac		2	4
		hitpaʿel	hitbagec		2	–
matax 'foreign currency'	invest in/turn into foreign currency	*piʿel*	mitax		12	50
			mitéax		50	–
			mitxen		2	4
			ʾimtax		–	4
			mimtéax		2	–
			mitxax		–	2
		hifʿil	himtiax		28	32
		paʿal	matax		2	6
buldózer 'bulldozer'	bulldoze	*piʿel*	bildzer	CP	44	68
			bildezer	CP	24	28
			bildez	CP	10	–
			bildrez	CP	2	–
			buldzer	CP	2	–
			blidzer	NCP	2	–
			*(hifʿil not possible phonetically)*			
krep 'crepe-like material'	install this material on shoes	*piʿel*	qirep	NCP	46	–
			qerep	NCP	6	40
			qirpef	NCP	6	18
			qirpet	NCP	4	–
			qirfef	NCP	2	–
			qirpep	NCP	2	–
			qirpen	NCP	2	–
			qirpfef	NCP	2	–

(cont.)

Base	Target Meaning	Binyan	Realization	CCP.	% Co.	% Ju.
			qirelp	NCP	2	–
			šilqrep	CP	2	–
		hifʿil	hiqrip	CP	22	36
		paʿal	qarap	NCP	–	4
pincéta 'tweezers'	tweeze	piʿel	pincet	CP	98	98
			pinctet	CP	2	–
			(hifʿil not possible phonetically)			
magad 'battalion commander'	serve as battalion commander	piʿel	miged		58	74
		paʿal	magad		18	8
		puʿal	mugad		6	6
		hitpaʿel	hitmaged		2	2
		hifʿil	himgid		–	6
		nifʿal	nimgad		–	2

IV. Illustrating recent verbs in the Ben-Amotz/Ben-Yehuda (1972, 1982) dictionaries, that are not listed in Even-Shoshan (1963) (the sources/bases proposed in brackets are 'best guesses'; the etymological information provided by the dictionaries concerned, if any, is not always reliable)

I. FOCUS ON THE THEME

i. *Non-agentive (mostly inchoative)*

Form	Gloss	Source	Gloss
hitpaʿel:			
hitgaleč	skid, slip (involuntary)	glič/galaš	slip, skid (N, Yid.)/slide (V)
hitxašmek	become aroused	hitxašek + šmok	desire + penis
hitfašel	fail (int.)	fášla	failure, flop; disappointment (Ar.)
hištafen	get scared	šafan	rabbit
hitbaʾes	become miserable	bá(ʾ)asa	misery, distress (Ar. ba'sāʾ)
hitmastel	become drunk	mastul	intoxicated, drugged (Ar. maṣṭul)
hitxafef	disappear; become drunk	xafif	light (Ar. xafif)
nifʿal:			
nikvač	get squeezed, crumpled	kveč	soft, mushy matter (Ger.)
nidfak	be beaten, lose	dafak	knock, screw
paʿal:			
xarap	sleep soundly	xrop	(deep) sleep (Yid.)

ii. *Agentive, where agent is not distinct from patient (reflexive, reciprocal, etc.)*

hitpaʿel:			
histalbet	indulge oneself in pleasure	stam + batala	mere + doing nothing
hitbareg	squeeze (self) in	bóreg	screw
hictalcel	phone each other	cilcel	ring
hitgaleč	skid, glide (voluntary)	glič/galaš	slip, skid (N, Yid.)/slide (V)
hitxafef	make oneself scarce	xafif	light (Ar. xafif)

iii. *Passive*

Form	Gloss	Source	Gloss
hitpuʿal:			
hitnudav	be made to volunteer	*hitnadev + nudav*	volunteer + be contributed
hitputar	be made to resign	*hitpater + putar*	resign + be fired
hufʿal:			
hoʿozav	be caused to leave, to resign	*ʿazav*	leave

II. INCHOATIVES/GENERAL AGENTIVES

hitpaʿel:			
hitbardek	be messed up; shirk work	*bardak*	chaos (< brothel (Trk.))
hitparxéax	become/behave like a hoodlum	*pirxax*	hoodlum
hitxarfen	become/be idle; go crazy; get messed up	*mexurfan*	messed up, failed (< Ar. *xárifa* 'be feeble-minded')?
hitkamcen	become/behave like a miser	*kamcan*	miser; miserly

III. AGENTIVES
i. *Causatives*

hifʿil:			
higlič	cause one to slip	*glič/galaš*	skid, slip (Yid.)/slide (V)
hilxic	cause one to be tense	*laxac*	press, pressure (V)
hiršit	get soccer ball into net	*réšet*	net
higniv	cause wonder	*magniv*	wonderful (< *ganav* 'steal')
hitrif	cause wonder	*metoraf*	crazy
piʿel:			
mistel	cause to be drunk	*mastul*	intoxicated, drugged (Ar. *masṭul*)
pindrek	overspoil (child, etc.)	*mefunak + drek*	spoilt + disgusting thing/person (Ger.)
xirteš	mess up, ruin	*xára +*	excrement (Ar.) +
smirtet	make/treat like rag	*smartut*	rag
čikmek	crumple (tr.)	*mečukmak*	crumpled, ugly, unpleasant (?)
kifer	disappoint, depress	*káfar*	depression, devastation (Ar.)
tizez	make run, torment	*tzuza/tzazit*	move/frantic activity
šixpec	reconstruct, repair	*šipec + šixzer*	renovate + reconstruct

ii. *General agentives (if patient is involved, it is distinct from agent)*

piʿel:			
birber	speak nonsense	*diber + ononm.*	speak + onomatopoeia
bimbem	make noise, hum melody	onomatopoeic	
xirtet	speak nonsense	*xáraṭa* (Ar.)	boast, lie
tirlel	nag continuously	*taralála*	crazy (Fr.?)
ʿintez	move buttocks	(Ar.?)	
filéax	steal	(Ar.?)	
fisfes	miss	(Ar.?)	

(cont.)

Form	Gloss	Source	Gloss
firgen	compliment others	*fargínen*	not begrudge (Yid.)
fišten	urinate	*šéten* +	
girbec	scratch balls; loaf	*gered* + *beycim*	scratch + balls
diveš	spend honeymoon	*(yérax) dvaš*	honey(moon)
di'wen	act so as to impress	*da'awin/ dawawin*	acts designed to impress (< Ar. *dawāwin* 'official jargon')
siben	cheat, outsmart	*sabon*	naïve person (< soap)
tixmen	conspire, deceive	? *xámana* (Ar.)	assess, appraise
hif'il:			
hiknis	fine	*knas*	fine (N)
hisnif	snuff in cocain	*snaf*	snuff (Eng.)
hiflic	fart	*floc*	fart (N) (Yid.)
hišpric	squirt	*špric*	squirt (N) (Ger.)
hikric	obtain from unknown source	?	
hitpa'el:			
hitfaléax	sneak in	*filéax*	steal (< Ar. ?) (see above)
hit'avez	pretend; make fun of one	? *háza'a*	make fun of someone (Ar.)
hit'agner	ignore	*'ignor*	ignore (Eng.)
hizdangef	walk around on Dizengof St.	*dizengof*	street named after Tel Aviv mayor
hitparper	shirk duty; be unfaithful to one's spouse	*parpar*	butterfly
hitfanen	do something pleasurable	*fanan*	wonderful; in very goof mood (Ar. *fannān*)
pa'al:			
gamaz	evaluate very negatively	*gámzu*	name of vitriolic Israeli critic

GENERAL AGENTIVES/CAUSATIVES:
pi'el:

fišel	mess up (tr. & int.)	*fášla*	failure, flop; disappointment (Ar.)

V. Some recent verbs in the Prolog Hebrew and Army Slang Lexicon (1993) that are not listed in Ben-Amotz/Ben-Yehuda (1972, 1982)

I. FOCUS ON THE THEME
i. *Non-agentive (mostly inchoative)*

Form	Gloss	Source	Gloss
hitpa'el:			
hitbarber	get lost	? *hitbalbel*	get confused, mixed up
hitxarbeš	get messed up	*xára* + *xerbon* +	excrement (Ar.) + mess up +
hitfalek	slip; come out involuntarily	? *hitxalek* +	slip +, or *tafallaqa* 'split (int.)' (Ar.)
hit'apec	be(come) drowsy	?	

ii. *Agentive, where agent is not distinct from patient (reflexive, reciprocal, etc.)*

Form	Gloss	Source	Gloss
hitpaʿel:			
histaxbek	treat as a close friend	*sáxbak*	(your) friend (Ar.)
hitkaséax	fight with and confront someone verbally	*kásax*	sweeping, cleaning out (Ar. *kásaḥ*)
hitxarden	rest and warm oneself in the sun	*xardon*	agama, lizard
hitfakes	focus oneself	*fókus*	focus
hitʿalek	stick (oneself) to someone	*ʿaluka*	leech
hitkarcec	stick (oneself) to someone	*karciya*	tick

II. AGENTIVES

i. *Causatives*

hifʿil:			
hišviz	depress, exhaust (tr.)	*šavur+zayin*	broken+penis
hišpit	impose harsh discipline	*šafat*	judge
piʿel:			
xirbeš	mess up, destroy	*xára+xarav+*	excrement (Ar.)+be destroyed+
smirkek	mess up with mucus	*smark*	mucus (Yid.)
fidéax	embarrass	*fāḍiḥa*	misfortune, calamity (Ar.)
šifcer	improve, strengthen	*šiper+bicer*	improve+fortify
kider	make one something unnecessarily difficult	*klita dérex (ha)raglayim*	absorption (= comprehension) through feet (acronym)

ii. *General agentives (if patient is involved, it is distinct from agent)*

piʿel:			
xifef	do something unprofessionally	*xafif*	light, superficial (Ar. *xafif*)
dija	work as DJ	*dijey*	disc jockey (Eng.)
milcer	work as a waiter	*melcar*	waiter
niwéaḥ	wail, complain	*nuwāḥ* (Ar.)	wailing
niylen	cover with nylon	*náylon*	nylon (Eng.)
nifes	smoke pot	*náfas*	puff; smoking pot (Ar.)
nišneš	snack between meals	*naš*	nosh (Yid.)
filek	beat, slap	*flik*	beat, slap (N) (Yid.)
pilfen	call by cellular phone	*pélefon*	cellular phone ("wonder phone")
piknek	have a picnic	*piknik*	picnic (Eng.)
fikses	send by fax	*faks*	facsimile (Eng.)
čiper	do/give something good	*čupar*	something good, pleasurable
hitpaʿel:			
hištanker	inform (on someone)	*štínker*	informer; stinker (Yid.)
hitkačkeč	talk incessantly	*káčke*	duck
hitbaxyen	complain a lot	*baxa*	cry

(cont.)

Form	Gloss	Source	Gloss
hitxaréaʿ	behave wildly; devour	?	
***paʿal**:*			
balas	devour	*balaʿ + laʿas*	swallow + chew
šaf	observe	*šāfa*	look (Ar.)

VI. Illustrating new verbs in the 1983 supplement to Even-Shoshan (1970)

A. LITERARY

I. FOCUS ON THE THEME

i. *Non-agentive (mostly inchoative)*

Form	Gloss	Source	Gloss
***hitpaʿel**:*			
hitʾavyen	become poor	*ʾevyon*	a poor man
hitʾagel	form as a drop	*ʾégel*	drop
hitʾangel	become English	*ʾangli*	English
hištaklel	become balanced	*šakul*	balanced
hittayen	become silt	*tin*	silt
hitbaser	become sick of something	*basar*	spurn, flout

ii. *Passive*

Form	Gloss	Source	Gloss
***nifʿal**:*			
nitmar	be permuted	*hitmir*	permute
***puʿal**:*			
ʾuzrar	be divided into zones	*ʾizrer*	zone (V) (< *ʾezor* 'region')
dukak	be made thin	*dikek*	make thin (< *dak/dakik* 'thin/ very thin')
sufrat	be made literary	*sifret*	make literary (< *sifrut* 'literature')
šucraf	be recombined	*šicref*	recombine (< *š + ceref* 're + combine')
suxsax	be made zigzag	*sixsex*	mix up; make zigzag
zuvad	be wrapped in bundle	*zived*	package, wrap
***hufʿal**:*			
humkal	be containerized	*himkil*	containerize (< *mexula* 'container')
hudran	be given as gift	*hidrin*	give as gift (< *doron* 'gift')
hoʿokav	be traced	*heʿekiv*	trace (< *ʿakav* 'follow')
huxlar	be chlorinated	*hixlir*	chlorinate (< *klor* 'chlorine')

II. AGENTIVE

i. *Causative*

Form	Gloss	Source	Gloss
***piʿel**:*			
ʾingel	anglicize	*ʾangli*	English
ʾivyen	make poor	*ʾevyon*	a poor man
mitev	optimize	*metav*	the best
ziter	reduce importance	*zutar*	minor
***hifʿil**:*			
heʾegid	form a concern	*taʾagid/ʾigud*	concern/union
hitri	make fresh, freshen	*tari*	fresh

(cont.)

Form	Gloss	Source	Gloss
hixlir	chlorinate	*klor*	chlorine
hiftit	crumble, crush	*ptit*	particle
hezeg	glaze	*zgugit*	glass
himkil	containerize	*mexula*	container

ii. *General agentives (if patient is involved, it is distinct from agent)*
pi'el:

kiryen	work as broadcaster/ reader	*karyan*	broadcaster/reader
bihen	do something with thumb	*bóhen*	thumb
diglel	wave flag	*dégel*	flag
xingeg	have a wild party	*xinga*	wild party
hitpa'el:			
hista'asea'	drive back and forth	*nasa'*	drive, travel

iii. *General agentive/causative*
hif'il:

hifhik	yawn a long yawn; cause to yawn	*pihek*	yawn
pa'al:			
tamar	permute	*tmura*	replacement

B. EVERYDAY

I. FOCUS ON THE THEME

i. *Non-agentive (mostly inchoative)*
hitpa'el:

hictavréax	become moody	*macav rúax*	mood

ii. *Passive*
nif'al:

nigmaz	be criticized severely	*gamaz*	criticize severely (< *gámzu*, see above)
pu'al:			
muxšav	be computerized	*mixšev*	computerize (< *maxšev* 'computer')
musgar	be put in frame	*misger*	frame (< *misgéret* 'frame')
subsad	be subsidized	*sibsed*	subsidize (< *subsídya* 'subsidy')
tupal	be taken care of	*tipel*	take care (of)

II. AGENTIVE

i. *Causative*
pi'el:

mixšev	computerize	*maxšev*	computer
nirmel	normalize	*normáli*	normal
niyed	make mobile	*nayad*	mobile
yisef	increase value	*nosaf*	additional (< *y.s.p* 'add')

ii. *General agentives (if patient is involved, it is distinct from agent)*

Form	Gloss	Source	Gloss
pi‘el:			
bilfef	lie	*bilef*	lie (*blof* 'bluff', Eng.)
birber	talk nonsense	*diber* + ononm.	speak+onomatopoeia
kiter	complain	*kúter*	cat (Yid.)
ri’ayen	interview	*re’ayon*	interview (N)
hitpa‘el:			
hištaxcen	behave arrogantly	*šaxcan*	arrogant; arrogant person

iii. *General agentive/causative*

pa‘al:			
gamaz	criticize severely	*gámzu*	name of vitriolic Israeli critic

VII. Relatively-recent *hapax legomena* verbs in a 132k-word corpus

FOCUS ON THEME

PASSIVE

Form	Gloss	Source	Gloss
pu‘al:			
ru’ayan	be interviewed	*ri’ayen*	interview (< *re’ayon* 'interview (N)')
musad	be established	*mised*	establish (< *mosad* 'establishment')
tuskal	be frustrated	*tiskel*	frustrate (< *sikel* 'preempt/ frustrate')
yusam	be applied	*yisem*	apply (< *sam* 'put, place')
duvax	be reported/briefed	*divax*	report (V) (< *dúax* 'report (N)')
muman	be financed	*mimen*	finance (V) (< *mamon* 'money, capital')
guvan	be made varied	*given*	make varied (< *gáven* 'color, hue')
huf‘al:			
hox(o)na	be parked	*hex(e)na*	park (tr.) (< *xana* 'park (int.)')
huš‘a	be removed (from office)	*hiš‘a*	remove (from office)
humxaš	be made concrete	*himxiš*	concretize (< *muxaši* 'concrete')
huvna	be built in	*bana*	build (?*hivna* not attested)

GENERAL THEME-CENTERED

hitpa‘el:			
hištofef	bend down (int., lit.)	*šafuf*	bent down
hitxaza	be seen; impersonate	*xaza*	see, foresee
hitra’ayen	be interviewed	*re’ayon*	interview (< *ra’a* 'see')
hištakem	rehabilitate oneself	*šikem*	rehabilitate
hit’ayen	become nothing	*’áyin*	nothing

AGENTIVE

CAUSATIVE/GENERAL AGENTIVE

hif‘il:			
hinšim	administer respiration, make breathe	*našam*	breathe
hifgiš	cause to meet	*pagaš*	meet
hištil	transplant	*šatal*	plant

(cont.)

Form	Gloss	Source	Gloss
hexcin	externalize	*xiconi*	external
pi'el:			
qidem	advance (tr.)	*qadam*	precede
'idken	update	*'ad kan*	up-to-here (now)
tigber	reinforce	*gavar*	be strong
širyen	armor (V); guarantee (position etc.)	*širyon*	armor (N)

CAUSATIVE/INCHOATIVE
hif'il:

hircin	make/become serious	*recini*	serious

GENERAL AGENTIVE
pi'el:

pitrel	patrol (V)	*patrol*	patrol (N)
'iyeš	man (V)	*'iš*	man
'iter	locate	*'atar*	location
tirped	torpedo (V)	*torpédo*	torpedo (N)
rixel	gossip (V)	*rexilut*	gossip (N)
biyem	direct (play etc.); fabricate	*bama*	stage
cikcek	make cricket-like noise (lit.)	*carcar*+ck	cricket + onomatopoeic
dimyen	imagine	*dimyon*	imagination
dirben	prod	*dorban*	(horse) prod
'irsel	swing (hammock, etc.)	*'arsal*	hammock
'imbet	give a bath	*'ambat(ya)*	bath(tub)
hif'il:			
hivriš	brush (V)	*mivréšet*	brush (N)
hiflic	pass wind, fart (sl.)	*floc*	fart (N) (Yid.)

VIII. Details of 1995/96 tests on productivity of adjective formation (N subjects = 50, N bases = 15. Co. = Coinage tests; Ju. = Judgment tests)

i. Tests where the suggested (adjectival) meaning involved a verb

(N bases = 5. Variants within a pattern are grouped together)

Base	Target Meaning	Pattern	Realization	% Co.	% Ju.
'anténa 'antenna'	equipped (f.) with antenna	*meCuCaC*	*me'unténet*	98	98
		mitCaCeC	*mit'anténet*	–	2
		?	*'antenáydit*	2	–
xóken 'enema'	one given enema	*meCuCaC*	*mexukan*	78	80
		[clause: that was given . . .]	*šexukan*	16	–
		CaCuC	*xakun*	–	12
		muCCaC	*muxkan*	–	6
		[clause]	*šehitxaken*	6	–
		+*(an)i*	*xokani*	2	–

(cont.)

Base	Target Meaning	Pattern	Realization	% Co.	% Ju.
		CiCuC+i	*xikuni*	–	2
		niCCaC	*nexkan*	2	–
		[Noun]	*xóken*	2	–
kével 'cable'	connected to cable	*meCuCaC*	*mexuval*	48	22
			mekuval	6	24
			mexubal	10	16
			mekubal	12	–
			mexuvlal	6	6
			mekuvlal	2	–
			mexuvlan	6	8
			mekuvlan	2	–
		[clause]	*šekuval*	2	–
		muCCaC	*muxbal*	4	10
			muxval	–	4
		CaCuC	*kavul*	6	6
		niCCaC	*nixval*	–	2
bagac 'high court'	presented (f.) to high court	*meCuCaC*	*mevugécet*	70	80
			mebugécet	4	–
			megubécet	2	–
		+i	*bagácit*	12	6
		muCCaC	*muvgécet*	–	8
		+nik+i	*bagácnikit*	4	4
		+íst+i	*bagacístit*	4	–
		CaCuC	*bguca*	–	2
		niCCaC	*nivgécet*	2	–
gril 'grill'	done on a grill	*meCuCaC*	*megoral*	6	44
			megural	26	–
			megorlal	–	4
		muCCaC	*mugral*	34	–
		CaCuC	*garul*	18	18
		+i	*grili*	6	8
		CaCiC	*garil*	4	4
		maCCiC	*magril*	2	–

ii. Tests where the suggested (adjectival) meaning did not involve a verb (N bases = 10)

Base	Target Meaning	Pattern	Realization	% Co.	% Ju.
mexdal 'criminal negligence'	criminally negligent (f.)	*+i*	*mexdalit*	82	64
		meCuCaC	*mexudal*	8	12
			memuxdélet	6	4
		+a'i	*mexdala'it*	4	8
		+on+i	*xidlonit*	–	4
		muCCaC	*muxdélet*	–	4
		CaCiC	*xadila*	–	4
kabaret 'cabaret'	of cabaret	*+i*	*kabaréti*	78	56
			kabarti	2	24
			kavarti	2	–
		meCuCaC	*mekuvrat*	12	8

(cont.)

Base	Target Meaning	Pattern	Realization	% Co.	% Ju.
			mekubrat	2	–
		+*a'i*	*kabareta'i*	–	10
		+*on*+*i*	*kabartoni*	2	–
		[*muCCaC* not possible phonetically here]			
motel 'motel'	of motel (f.)	+*i*	*motélit*	74	86
			motlit	6	–
		meCuCaC	*memutélet*	2	10
		muCCaC	*mumtélet*	–	2
			mutélet	8	–
		+*et*	*motélet*	2	–
		+*íst*+*i*	*motelístit*	2	–
šabak 'security police'	of security police (f.)	+*i*	*šabákit*	60	66
			šabakatit	2	–
		a'i	*šabaka'it*	–	18
		+*nik*+*i*	*šabáknikit*	16	–
		meCuCaC	*mešubéket*	–	6
		muCCaC	*mušbéket*	–	6
		meCaCeC	*mešabéket*	6	–
		+*an*+*ér*+*i*	*šabakanérit*	2	–
		+*on*+*i*	*šabakónit*	–	2
mis'ada 'restaurant'	of restaurant (f.)	+*i*	*mis'adatit*	34	40
			mis'adit	16	20
		+*an*+*i*	*mis'adanit*	34	34
		meCuCaC	*mesu'édet*	2	–
			meso'édet	–	2
			memus'édet	4	–
		+*on*+*i*	*mis'adonit*	4	2
		+*a'i*	*mis'ada'it*	2	–
		muCCaC	*mus'édet*	–	2
sálmon 'salmon'	of salmon	+*i*	*salmoni*	48	62
			salomomi	4	–
			salamoni	2	–
		meCuCaC	*mesulman*	14	28
		+*a'i*	*salmona'i*	2	8
		[Noun]	*sal(o)mon*	26	–
		[*muCCaC* not possible phonetically here]			
xárake 'wild driving'	wild (f.) (driving)	+*i*	*xárakit*	38	28
			xarakírit	8	2
			xarakatit	2	–
			xarikit	2	2
		+*a'i*	*xaraka'it*	16	28
			xarake'it	2	–
		meCuCaC	*mexoréket*	8	16
			mexuréket	4	–
			mexurkéket	4	4
		+*íst*+*i*	*xarakístit*	6	6
		muCCaC	*muxréket*	–	10
		CaCiC	*xarika*	2	4
		CaCuC	*xaruka*	4	–

(cont.)

Base	Target Meaning	Pattern	Realization	% Co.	% Ju.
		$+a\text{'}i+ist+i$	*xaraka'ístit*	2	–
		meCaCeC	*mexaréket*	2	–
brezent 'tarp'	of tarp	$+i$	*brezénti*	56	48
			brazénti	2	–
			barzénti	2	–
			barazénti	2	–
			brazánti	2	–
			brezanténi	2	–
		meCuCaC	*mevurzant*	6	22
			mevruzant	12	6
			mevurzan	2	8
			mevorzan	2	–
			mebruzant	2	–
		$+a\text{'}i$	*brezenta'i*	4	10
		[*muCCaC* not possible phonetically here]			
búldog	bulldog-like	$+i$	*búldogi*	56	58
'bulldog'			*buldegi*	2	–
		meCuCaC	*mevuldag*	26	22
		$+a\text{'}i$	*buldoga'i*	4	20
		$an+i$	*buldogani*	2	–
		$ist+i$	*buldogísti*	2	–
		$+ist$	*buldogist*	2	–
		$+on$	*buldogon*	2	2
		[Noun]	*búldog*	8	–
		[*muCCaC* not possible phonetically here]			
xaplap 'fast/	fast/careless (f.)	$+i$	*xaplápit*	34	50
carelessly'			*xafláfit*	18	–
			xaflápit	6	–
			xafaláfit	2	–
		meCuCaC	*mexuplépet*	20	32
			mexufléfet	16	2
			mexupléfet	–	4
		$+a\text{'}i$	*xaplapa'it*	–	8
		meCaCeC	*mexaplépet*	2	–
		mitCaCeC	*mitxafléfet*	2	–
		(*muCCaC*, as *moxoplépet*, is possible, but would be opaque, and thus not preferred)			

IX. New adjectives in the 1983 supplement to Even-Shoshan (1970)

Form	Gloss	Source	Gloss
me'uyar	illustrated	*'uyar*	be illustrated (< *'or* 'light')
megul'an	pitted	*gul'an*	be pitted (*gal'in* 'pit')
medupras	depressed	*dipres*	depress (< *diprésya* 'depression')
memuxšav	computerized	*muxšav*	be computerized (< *maxšev* 'computer')
memulkad	booby trapped	*mulkad*	be booby trapped (< *malkódet* 'trap')
menutav	routed, channeled	*nutav*	be channeled (< *nativ* 'route')
mesubsad	subsidized	*subsad*	be subsidized (< *subsídya* 'subsidy')

(cont.)

Form	Gloss	Source	Gloss
mefusfas	missed (Adj.)	*fusfas*	be missed
merumzar	with traffic lights	*rumzar*	be installed traffic lights (intersection, etc.) (< *ramzor* 'traffic light')
meto'ad	documented	*to'ad*	be documented (< *te'uda* 'document')
mešuklal	weighted	*šuklal*	be weighted (< *šakal* 'weigh')
metudlak	fueled	*tudlak*	be fueled (< *délek* 'fuel')

muCCaC (all occurrences):

muzag	glazed	*huzag*	be glazed (< *zgugit* 'glass')
mulad	inborn, innate	*hulad*	be caused to be born (< *yalad* 'give birth')
muxlar	chlorinated	*huxlar*	be chlorinated (< *klor* 'chlorine')
mo'ošar	enriched	*ho'ošar*	be enriched (< *'ašir* 'rich')
murvax	winning, gaining	*hurvax*	be won/gained (< *révax* 'gain')

CaCuC (all occurrences):

bazúa'	uneven, with bumps and holes	*b.z.'*	be uneven/full of bumps and holes
gazúa'	left with stump only (tree)	*gaza'*	cut down tree to stump (< *géza'* 'tree stump')
dafuy	imperfect, flawed	*dófi*	fault, flaw
xašuy	secretive, clandestine	*xaša'i*	secret
tanun	covered with silt/clay	*tin*	clay
ta'um	that has been tasted	*ta'am*	taste (V) (or < *tá'am* 'taste (N)')
yaduy	thrown (esp. in sport)	*yada/yida*	throw
pacuy	open	*paca*	open
camum	deformed (ear)		
šaguy	erroneous	*šaga*	err (or *šgi'a* 'error')

niCCaC (all occurrences):

noraš	inherited, inborn	*yaraš*	inherit
nexmac	unpleasant, disgusting	*xamac*	be sour (or < *xamuc* 'sour')
niflac	scary; distorted, disfigured; disgusting	*miflécet*	monster (or *palacut* 'fear')
nirhav	majestic	*marhiv*	majestic

+*i* Adjectives

btixuti	of safety	*b(e)tixut*	safety
gavšuši	with humps	*gavšus(it)*	hump
xad hori	with a single parent	*'exad + hore*	one + parent
xalifi	alternative	*maxlif/xiluf*	replacement/alternation
xozi	contractual	*xoze*	contract
matirani	permissive	*matiran*	permissive person
merabi	maximal	*merav*	most, the majority
mimsadi	of the establishment	*mimsad*	establishment
modi'ini	of intelligence, of information	*modi'in*	intelligence, information
nici	hawkish	*nec*	hawk
serugi	alternating	*leserugin*	in alternation
sifrati	digital	*sifra*	digit
svivati	environmental	*sviva*	environment
tikšorti	of the media	*tikšóret*	(the) media

(cont.)

Form	Gloss	Source	Gloss
CaCiC:			
ʾaxif	enforceable	ʾaxaf	enforce
hafix	reversible	hafax	turn over, reverse
hamir	convertible	hemir	convert
mašiš	that can be felt	mišeš	feel (by hand)
nasir	that can be sawn	niser	saw
parid	separable	hifrid	separate
kalit	that can be absorbed	kalat	absorb
šafit	fit for trial	šafat	judge, try
saxim	summable	sikem/sxum	summarize/sum
CaCeC (all occurrences):			
cadek	legitimate	cadak	be right
namek	rotting	namak	rot

X. New adjectives in Ben-Amotz/Ben-Yehuda '72/'82 not found in Even-Shoshan (1970) (or its '83 supplement)

meCuCaC:

Form	Gloss	Source	Gloss
mevurdak	disorganized	bardak	brothel (Trk.)
mejunjan	red headed	jinji	red headed (person)
mezuyan	fucked up (Adj.)	ziyen	have intercourse (< záyin 'penis')
mezupat	very bad, lousy	zift	lousy (Ar.)
mezurgag	very bad, lousy	zéreg	penis
mexurban	very bad, lousy	xirben/xerbon	shit, mess up (V)/mess up (N)
mexuryan	very bad, lousy	xaryan	shitty person (< xára 'excrement (Ar.)')
mexurkak	very bad, lousy	xára + káka	excrement (Ar.) + excrement (Yid.)
mefuclax	very bad, lousy	?muclax	?successful (ironical)
mexurfan	failed; crazy; angry	xarfãn (Ar.)/ mexurban	feeble-minded/lousy
metumbal	silly, stupid	témbel	dumb (< dumbbell (Eng.), or Trk.)
metumbax	silly, stupid		variant of metumbal
meturlal	crazy, mixed up	taralála	crazy, mixed up (Fr.)
meyukak	formal and humorless	yéke	German Jew (< ?jacket)
memustal	drunk, drugged	mastul	intoxicated, drunk (Ar.)
mesmurtat	ragged, very old	smartut	rag
mesmurkak	disgusting	smark	mucus (Yid.)
mefuzmak	humiliated	pizmek	defeat, humiliate (< ?)
muCCaC (all occurrences):			
muskal	educated (derog.)	maskil	educated
muštan	humiliated; of little value	šéten/hištin	urine/urinate
mušprac	sprayed liquid upon; miserable; drugged	špric	squirt (Ger.)
muglač	slid	glič	slide, slip (Yid.)
CaCuC (all occurrences):			
faclu(a)x	useless; ugly (belongs to this pattern?)		(cf. mefuclax above)
niCCaC (all occurrences):			
nexcac	ugly	?xacac	gravel

(cont.)

Form	Gloss	Source	Gloss
+ i Adjectives			
ʾaxul manyúki	excellent	ʾaxul manyuk	clever, "bastard" (Ar.)
ʾayumi	disgusting, terrible	ʾayom~ʾayum-	terrible
cahali	of the Israeli army	cáhal	I.D.F (Israel Defense Army) (acronym of *cva hagana le-yisraʾel*)
davkaʾi	stubborn	dávka	in spite of, on the contrary
xelmaʾi	stupid	xelm	fool-town (for a town in Poland)
mikvaʾi	from Mikve Israel	mikve yisraʾel	name of agricultural school in Israel
partáči	done sloppily	partač	sloppy work/deed (Yid.)
saxaríni	overly sweet	saxarin	saccharine
zvaʿati	terrible, horrifying	zvaʿa	horror
CaCiC (all occurrences):			
gamil	junior in vocational school	gímel	third letter of alphabet
xatix	hunk	xatixa	attractive girl
xafif	light	Ar.	
tawil	very tall	Ar.	

XI. New adjectives in the 1993 Prolog slang dictionary

meCuCaC (all occurrences):

Form	Gloss	Source	Gloss
medugam	perfectly done/made	dugma/dégem	example/model
mexučkan	acned	xečkúnim	acne
mexurman	sexually aroused	xarman	one who is always sexually desirous (? < Ar. ḥirmān 'deprivation')
meʾupas	concentrated; reasoned	ʾipes	zero in (< ʾéfes 'zero')
memunaʿ	mobile (with car)	manóaʿ	motor, engine
mevoʾas	depressed	bá(ʾ)asa	misery, distress (Ar.)
muCCaC (all occurrences):			
mutraf	exceptional, exciting	hitrif	drive crazy
CaCuC (all occurrences):			
šavuz	devastated, feeling desperate/disgusted	šavur + záyin	broken + penis
kaluk	coward; flier of light plane	?kálkar	lightweight foam material
kalul	very easy	kal/kalil	light, easy/very light, very easy
+ i Adjectives (all occurrences):			
ʿáji	of oriental descent (derogatory)	?Ar. ʿājı 'ivory' or ʿāwaja 'be crooked'	
xalavi	inaggressive, indecisive	xalav	milk
[savírski	reasonable	savir + ski	reasonable + Polish suffix]
CaCiC (all occurrences):			
[yaziz	partner (sex and friendship w/o marriage)	yadid + záyin	friend + penis]

XII. Details of 1995/96 tests on productivity of abstract nominalization formation (N subjects = 50, N bases = 21. Co. = Coinage tests; Ju. = Judgment tests)

i. Tests where a verb base was implied
(N bases = 16. Variants within a pattern are grouped together)

a. Meaning focuses on patient/theme-inchoative, reciprocal, reflexive (N bases = 5)

Base	Target Meaning	Pattern	Realization	% Co.	% Ju.
magad	becoming battalion	*hitCaCCut*	*hitmagdut*	70	80
'battalion	commander'	*CiCuC*	*migud*	8	6
commander'		*haCCaCa*	*hamgada*	6	4
		hiCaCCut	*himagdut*	4	8
		+ *ut*	*magadut*	6	2
		niCaCCut	*nimgadut*	2	–
yóram 'nerd'	becoming nerdy	*hitCaCCut*	*hityarmut*	76	90
		CiCuC	*yerum*	18	10
		+ *ut*	*yóramut*	4	–
		meCuCaCut	*meyoramut*	2	–
šérif 'sheriff'	becoming sheriff	*hitCaCCut*	*hištarfut*	56	76
			hit'ašrefut	–	4
		hiCaCCut	*hišarfut*	10	6
		haCCaCa	*hašrafa*	10	4
		CiCuC	*šeruf*	8	6
		+ *ut*	*šérifut*	8	4
		meCuCaCut	*mešorafut*	4	–
		niCCaCut	*nišrafut*	2	–
		muCCaCut	*mušrafut*	2	–
pitka 'note'	sending each other	*hitCaCCut*	*hitpatke'ut*	52	50
	notes		*hitpatkut*	24	40
		CiCuC	*pituk*	10	8
		+ *ut*	*pitka'ut*	8	2
			hitpatkekut	4	–
			hitpatkenut	2	–
zálman	dressing self	+ *ut*	*zalmaniyut*	28	40
'sloppily	sloppily		*zálmanut*	12	14
dressed man'					
		hitCaCCut	*hizdalmenut*	28	36
			hitzalmenut	6	–
		CiCuC	*zilmun*	10	8
		+ *iyáda*	*zalmaniyáda*	2	–

b. Target meaning focuses on patient/theme-passive (N bases = 3)

Base	Target Meaning	Pattern	Realization	% Co.	% Ju.
panel 'panel'	being covered with	*meCuCaCut*	*mefunalut*	46	66
	panels		*mepunalut*	16	26
			mepunlalut	2	–
		muCCaCut	*mufnalut*	18	4
			mupnalut	4	–
		CiCuC	*pinul*	12	2
			pinlul	2	2

(cont.)

Base	Target Meaning	Pattern	Realization	% Co.	% Ju.
kéres 'hook'	being fitted with	*muCCaCut*	*mukrasut*	34	40
	a hook	*meCuCaCut*	*mekurasut*	20	–
			mekorasut	16	36
			mekursasut	4	4
		hitCaCCut	*hitkarsut*	12	6
			hitkarsesut	–	4
		CiCuC	*kerus*	8	8
		niCCaCut	*nikrasut*	4	2
		haCCaCa	*hakrasa*	2	–
matax 'foreign	being turned into	*meCuCaCut*	*memutaxut*	60	46
currency'	foreign currency	*muCCaCut*	*mumtaxut*	24	48
		CiCuC	*mitúax*	8	4
			mimtúax	4	2
		haCCaCa	*hamtaxa*	4	–

c. Target meaning involves causation (N bases = 2)

Base	Target Meaning	Pattern	Realization	% Co.	% Ju.
snob 'snob'	making one	*haCCaCa*	*hasnaba*	48	54
	snobbish	*CiCuC*	*sinub*	40	36
			sinbuv	–	8
			tisnub	–	2
šérif 'sheriff'	making one sheriff	*CiCuC*	*šeruf*	42	58
			širuf	14	–
			'išruf	–	2
		haCCaCa	*hašrafa*	44	40

d. Target meaning involves general agentivity (non-causal)
(N bases = 6)

Base	Target Meaning	Pattern	Realization	% Co.	% Ju.
panel 'panel'	covering with	*CiCuC*	*pinul*	94	94
	panels	*haCCaCa*	*hafnala*	6	6
bagac 'high	presenting to	*CiCuC*	*biguc*	56	48
court'	'high court'	*haCCaCa*	*havgaca*	38	42
		CCiCa	*bgica*	4	8
		hitCaCCut	*hitbagcut*	2	2
čárter 'charter'	organizing charter	*CiCuC*[1]	*čirtur*	60	44
	flights	*+ut*	*čarteriyut*	6	4
			čartera'ut	2	18
			čárterut	2	14
			čartarut	–	8
			čarteranut	2	–
		+iya	*čarteriya*	10	6
		haCCaCa	*hačtara*	–	2
		+izm	*čarterizm*	2	–
'anténa	setting up an	*CiCuC*	*'intun*	52	78
'antenna'	antenna	corresp. inf.	*le'anten*	6	–
		'aCCaCa	*'antana*	34	8

---

[1] *CiCuC* may, of course, be realized as *CiCCuC, CCiCCuC, CCiCuCC*, etc.

(cont.)

Base	Target Meaning	Pattern	Realization	% Co.	% Ju.
		hitCaCCut	*hit'antenut*	–	12
		haCCaCa	*hantana*	2	–
šnórkel 'snorkel'	diving with snorkel	*CiCuC*	*šnirkul*	38	52
			šnikrul	6	–
			šnirklur	2	–
		corresp. inf.	*lešnorkel*	8	–
			lešnarkel	2	–
		+*ut*	*šnorkelut*	4	14
			šnorkeliyut	4	12
			šnork(e)la'ut	2	8
		hitCaCCut	*hištnarqelut*	2	6
			hitšnorkelut	2	–
			hitšnarkelut	–	2
			hišnorkelut	2	–
		corresp. inf.	*lehitšnorkel*	2	–
			lehišnarkel	2	–
		+*iya*	*šnork(e)liya*	12	–
		+*izm*	*šnorkelizm*	2	–
brezent 'tarp'	manufacturing tarp	*CiCuC*	*birzunt*	16	26
			brizunt	6	26
			birznut	4	–
			birzun	2	–
		+*ut*	*brezenta'ut*	8	18
			brezéntiyut	12	–
			brezéntut	–	14
			brezentanut		8
		hitCaCCut	*hitbarzentut*	2	2
		+*iya*	*brezentiya*	10	2
		+*ácya*	*brezentácya*	2	–
		+*érya*	*brezentérya*	2	–
		+*a*	*brezenta*	4	–

ii. Tests where no verb base was implied (N bases = 5. Variants within a pattern are grouped together)

Base	Target Meaning	Pattern	Realization	% Co.	% Ju.
šérif 'sheriff'	a sheriff's occupation	+*ut*	*šérifiyut*	58	74
			šérifut	14	10
			šerifanut	8	8
		+*izm*	*šerifizm*	6	4
		+*ológya*	*šerifológya*	4	4
		CiCuC	*šeruf*	6	–
kosem 'magician'	the magician's occupation	+*ut*	*kosmut*	60	68
			kosmiyut	2	4
			kosmanut	–	4
		CiCuC	*kisum*	16	18
		haCCaCa	*haksama*	4	–
		CéCeC	*késem*	2	2
		miCCaC	*miksam*	–	2
'axam 'V.I.P.'	V.I.P. status	+*ut*	*'axamiyut*	40	66
			'ax(a)manut	2	6

(cont.)

Base	Target Meaning	Pattern	Realization	% Co.	% Ju.
			'ax(a)maniyut	–	8
			'axamut	2	2
		CiCuC	*'ixum*	10	14
		CCiCa	*'axima*	2	4
		hitCCaCut	*hit'axamut*	2	–
		+ *izm*	*'axamizm*	2	–
		CóCeC	*'óxem*	2	–
máčo 'macho'	the macho quality	+ *izm*	*mačo'izm*	56	58
		+ *ut*	*mačo'iyut*	12	12
			mačo'ístiyut	10	20
			mačo'ut	2	4
			mačĩyut	2	–
		hitCaCCut	*hitmač'ut*	–	2
		+ *iya*	*mačiya*	2	–
		no deriv.	*máčo*	6	–
masaž 'massage'	massage art	*CiCuC*	*misuž*	32	36
		corres. inf.	*lemasež*	2	–
		+ *ut*	*masažiyut*	8	16
			masažut	4	14
			masaža'iyut	–	12
			masažístiyut	10	–
			masažanut	–	6
		+ *izm*	*masažizm*	4	4
			masizm	2	–
		CCiCa	*mesiža*	2	4
		+ *ácya*	*masižácya*	4	–
		+ *ológya*	*masažológya*	4	–
		CéCeC	*mésež*	–	2

XIII. New abstract nominalizations in the 1983 supplement to Even-Shoshan (1970)

Form	Gloss	Source	Gloss
CCiCa (all literary):			
'arisa	being betrothed	*'aras / 'arus*	betroth/betrothed
driga	grading, gradation	*déreg / dereg*	grade, echelon/grade (V)
xamisa	robbing	*xamas*	rob, robbery
hani'a	motivating	*henía'*	move (tr.), motivate
levina	brick making	*levena*	brick
nesita	downward movement	*nasat*	move downward
psida	resorption	*p.s.d / hifsid*	lose
sxixa	cover, covering	*saxax*	cover (V)
zli'a	swallowing without chewing	*zala'*	swallow without chewing
CiCuC:			
'imut	confrontation	*'imet*	confront; juxtapose
'ifrur	incineration	*'ifrer*	incinerate (< *'éfer* 'ash')
'išrur	ratification	*'išer*	ratify (< *'išer* 'confirm')
cintur	catheterization	*cinter*	catheterize (< *cinor / cantera* (Aram.) 'tube')
gerut	junking	*geret*	junk (V) (< *gruta* 'junk item')

(cont.)

Form	Gloss	Source	Gloss
xivrut	socialization	*xivret*	socialize (< *xevra* 'society')
meruv	maximization	*merev*	maximize (< *merav* 'the most')
migun	shielding	*migen*	shield (V) (< *magen* 'shield (N)')
nirnul	normalization	*nirmel*	normalize (< *normáli* 'normal')
sibsud	subsidizing	*sibsed*	subsidize (< *subsídya* 'subsidy')
šiklul	considering weight	*šiklel*	consider relative weight (< *sakal* 'weigh')
tixšuv	calculating, calculation	*tixšev*	calculate (*xišev* 'calculate, consider')

haCCaCa:

Form	Gloss	Source	Gloss
haʿacava	causing sorrow	*heʿeciv*	cause sorrow (< *ʿacuv* 'sad, sorry')
hadmaya	simulation	*hidma*	simulate, make similar (> *dama* 'be similar')
hafʿata	diminutivizing	*hifʿit*	diminutivize (< *paʿot* 'very small')
hagmada	major reduction	*higmid*	reduce significantly (< *gamad* 'dwarf')
haslama	escalation	*hislim*	escalate (< *sulam* 'ladder')
hasnaʾa	causing to hate	*hisni*	cause to hate (< *sana* 'hate')
hasmala	codification; forming terminology	*sémel*	sign, symbol
hakcana	making/becoming extreme	*hikcin*	make/become extreme (< *kiconi* 'extreme')

heCCeC:

Form	Gloss	Source	Gloss
hegev	reaction; reactance	*hegiv*	react
hegeš	feeding raw material to machine	*higiš*	present (V)
hetʿen	loading, load	*hitʿin*	load (V) (< *taʿan* 'load (V)')
hevreg	screw-type connection	*hivrig*	screw (V) (< *bóreg* 'screw (N)')

hitCaCCut:

Form	Gloss	Source	Gloss
hitʾašpezut	being hospitalized	*hitʾašpez*	be hospitalized (< *ʾišpez* 'hospitalize')
hitkarnefut	losing one's own identity in the crowd	*hitkarnef*	lose one's identity in crowd (< *karnaf* 'rhinoceros' (< a play by Eugene Eunesco)
hizdaʾavut	becoming/behaving like wolf	*hizdaʾev*	become/behave like wolf (< *zeʾev* 'wolf')
histalʿut	becoming rock	*sélaʿ*	rock

hiCaCCut:

Form	Gloss	Source	Gloss
hitaʾamut	being parallel; accommodation	*hitʾim/taʾam*	fit, match

CoCCut:

Form	Gloss	Source	Gloss
ʾorxut	being guest	*ʾoréax*	guest
ʾoyvut	being enemy	*ʾoyev*	enemy
xonxut	tutoring, instructing apprentice	*xonex*	tutor

niCCaCut:

Form	Gloss	Source	Gloss
nišʾarut	survival	*nišʾar*	stay, remain
nivxarut	being chosen	*nivxar*	be chosen

(cont.)

Form	Gloss	Source	Gloss
meCaCCut:			
mexabrut	authorship	mexaber	author
meCuCaCut:			
meʿunyanut	being interested	meʿunyan	interested
megušamut	being clumsy, awkward	megušam	clumsy, awkward
mexuyavut	commitment	mexuyav	committed
merubaʿut	being square, by-the-book	merubaʿ	square
muCCaCut:			
mufnamut	being introvert	mufnan	introvert
mušlamut	being perfect	mušlam	perfect
Other +ut:			
sridut	survivability	sarad	survive
ʿatidanut	futurology	ʿatidan	futurologist
ʾašafut	magic; great expertise	ʾašaf	magician; great expert
bareranut	selectiveness	bareran	selective
xayatiyut	animal quality	xayati	animalistic (< xaya 'animal')
xuligániyut	hooliganism	xuligáni	of hooligan (< xuligan 'hooligan')
matiranut	permissiveness	matiran	permissive (matir 'allow, pres. part'.)
mudaʿut	awareness	mudaʿ	aware
niciyut	hawkishness	nici	hawkish (< nec 'hawk')
kraviyut	being combatant	kravi	combatant (< krav 'combat, fight')
sekuláriyut	being secular	sekulári	secular
yeciratiyut	creativity	yecirati	creative (< yecira 'creation')
+izm:			
ʾelitízm	elitism	ʾelíta/ʿilit	elite
bosízm	bossing behavior	bos	boss
leninízm	Leninism	lénin	Lenin
stalinízm	Stalinism	stálin	Stalin
mačoízm	machoism	máčo	macho
paternalízm	paternalism	paternalísti	paternalistic

XIV. New abstract nominalizations in Ben-Amotz/Ben-Yehuda '72/'82

Form	Gloss	Source	Gloss
CCiCa:			
špíxa	spilled/ejected fluid (esp. sperm)	šafax	spill (may possibly belong to this pattern)
CiCuC:			
bilgun	creating chaos	bilgen	create chaos (< balagan 'chaos (Rus.)')
birduk	creating chaos	birdek	create chaos (< bardak 'brothel (Trk.)')
diskus	discussing	diskes	discuss (> diskúsya 'discussion (Pol./Rus.)')
fisfus	missing	fisfes	miss
xirbun	shitting; ruin(ing)	xirben	shit (V)/mess up

(cont.)

Form	Gloss	Source	Gloss
nijus	nagging	*nijes / nijez*	nag (V) (< Ar. *nájis* 'filthy')
kimcun	frugality	*kimcen*	be frugal (< *kamcan* 'miser(ly)')
tixmun	intrigue, intriguing	*tixmen*	do intrigue (< *taxman* 'intriguer')
kivčuč	giving a very hard squeeze	*kivčeč*	give a hard squeeze (< *kveč* 'mush (Yid.)')

hitCaCCut:

Form	Gloss	Source	Gloss
hitbalgenut	becoming chaotic	*hitbalgen*	become chaotic (< *balagan* 'chaos (Rus.)')
hitbardekut	becoming chaotic	*hitbardek*	become chaotic (< *bardak* 'brothel (Trk.)')
hitfalxut	sneaking in	*hitfaléax*	sneak in
hitfašlut	failing	*hitfašel*	fail (int.) (< *fášla* 'failure, flop (Ar.)')
hitpaperut	shirking work; sleeping with many	*hitparper*	shirk work; sleep with many (< *parpar* 'butterfly')

Other +ut:

Form	Gloss	Source	Gloss
cúcikiyut	being very small	*cúcik(i)*	very young (Yid.)
fáyteriyut	being a fighter	*fáyter*	fighter (Eng.)
mabsútiyut	being happy	*mabsut*	happy (Ar.)
mankalut	CEO position	*mankal*	CEO (*menahel klali*)
póciyut	arrogance	*poc(i)*	arrogant person, arrogant
šlúmperiyut	sloppiness	*šlúmper(i)*	sloppy person, sloppy (Yid.)
spéciyut	expertise	*spec*	expert
tafranut	being poor	*tafran*	poor person, poor (Ar. *ṭafrān*)
kvéčiyut	being whiny	*kveč(i)*	mush(y) (Yid.)

+izm:

Form	Gloss	Source	Gloss
bicuʿízm	no-nonsense, hands-on approach	*bicúaʿ*	performance, getting something done
bitxonízm	emphasis on security	*bitaxon*	security

XV. New abstract nominalizations in the 1993 Prolog Dictionary

Form	Gloss	Source	Gloss

CCiCa:

glíča sliding (may possibly belong to this pattern) *glič* slid, slip (Yid.)

CiCuC:

Form	Gloss	Source	Gloss
beʾus	disgust, despair	*mevoʾas*	in despair (< *básā'* 'misery (Ar.)')
fištun	urinating	*fišten*	urinate (< *hištin* 'urinate')
nišnuš	snacking between meals	*nišneš*	snack between meals (< *noš* 'snack (Yid.)')
girbuc	loafing	*girbec*	loaf (< *gered + beycim* 'scratch + balls')
tizuz	making run back and forth, uselessly	*tizez*	make run back and forth uselessly (< *zaz / tzuza / tzazit* 'move / a move / frenzy')

meCuCaCut:

Form	Gloss	Source	Gloss
menumasut	being polite	*menumas*	polite

Other +ut:

Form	Gloss	Source	Gloss
xelmaʾut	stupidity	*xelmaʾi*	stupid (< *xelm* 'town notorious for fools')
xorániyut	neglect, untidiness	*xoráni*	sloppy (< *xoran* 'region in the Golan')

XVI. Details of 1995/96 tests on productivity of agent formation
(N subjects = 50, N bases = 8. Co. = Coinage tests; Ju. = Judgment tests)

Base	Target Meaning	Pattern	Realization	% Co.	% Ju.
básta 'vendor	stall vendor	+ *a'i*	*basta'i*	38	38
stall'			*bastona'i*	2	–
		+ *ay*	*bastay*	2	28
			bastonay	2	–
		+ *er*	*bastyoner*	12	14
			bastoner	10	10
		+ *an*	*bastan*	8	8
		+ *i*	*basati*	4	–
			bastani	6	–
			basti	2	–
			bastoni	2	–
			bustani	2	–
		+ *ist*	*bastist*	4	–
			basatist	–	2
			basta'ist	2	–
		+ *nik*	*bástnik*	2	–
'anténa	one who assembles	+ *ay*	*'antenay*	6	46
'antenna'	antennas				
		+ *a'i*	*'antena'i*	26	–
			'antenetika'i	2	–
		+ *an*	*'antenan*	18	16
			'antan	4	12
			'antenotan	2	–
		meCaCeC	*me'anten*	16	14
		+ *ist*	*'antenist*	10	4
		+ *olog*	*'antenolog*	–	2
		+ *čik*	*'antánčik*	–	2
'omlet	one making	+ *an*	*'omletan*	36	62
'omelette'	omelette		*'amletan*	–	6
		meCaCeC	*me'amlet*	22	16
		+ *ist*	*'omletist*	18	12
		+ *er*	*'omleter*	8	–
			'omletar	2	–
		+ *a'i*	*'omleta'i*	4	2
		+ *átor*	*'omelátor*	2	–
		+ *ay*	*'omletay*	–	2
		+ *i*	*'omleti*	2	–
		+ *nik*	*'omlétnik*	2	–
		CaCaC	*'amlat*	2	–
čárter 'charter'	charter flights	+ *ist*	*čárterist*	36	30
	specialist	+ *an*	*čarteran*	20	38
		meCaCeC	*mečarter*	18	14
		+ *ay*	*čarteray*	–	14
			čartay	2	–
		mitCaCeC	*mitčarter*	2	–
			mičarter	2	–
			mičater	2	–
		CaCaC	*čartar*	4	–

(cont.)

Base	Target Meaning	Pattern	Realization	% Co.	% Ju.
			čartrar	2	–
		+*a'i*	*čartera'i*	2	–
		+*on*	*čarteron*	2	–
		+*nik*	*čárternik*	2	–
gril 'grill'	one who grills	+*an*	*grilan*	18	28
			garlan	6	–
			grileran	–	2
		+*er*	*gríler*	28	20
		meCaCeC	*megarel*	16	–
			megarlel	4	–
		+*ay*	*grilay*	–	16
		+*a'i*	*grila'i*	6	–
		maCCiC	*magril*	8	4
		+*ist*	*grilist*	4	4
		+*čik*	*grílčik*	2	–
		+*men*	*grílmen*	2	–
		+*nik*	*garlážnik*	2	–
		CoCeC	*gorel*	2	–
nagmaš 'APC'	APC-borne troop	+*an*	*nagmešan*	12	38
			nagmašan	2	–
		meCuCaC	*menugmaš*	34	–[2]
		+*nik*	*nagmášnik*	6	24
		+*ay*	*nagmešay*	4	24
		+*a'i*	*nagmeša'i*	8	10
		+*ist*	*nagmašist*	10	–
		meCaCeC	*menagmeš*	4	–
		+*er*	*nagmašyoner*	4	–
		+*ar*	*nagmašar*	2	–
		+*čik*	*nagmáščik*	2	–
		+*i*	*nagmaši*	2	–
šrimps 'shrimp(s)'	shrimp fisherman	+*an*	*šrimpsan*	18	26
			šrampsan	2	–
		+*ay*	*šrimpsay*	–	34
			šrimpay	–	4
		+*ist*	*šrimpist*	22	8
		+*er*	*šrímper*	4	4
			šrímpser	8	10
			šrimpyoner	4	–
		+*a'i*	*šrimpsa'i*	24	–
		+*on*	*šrimpson*	4	–
		meCaCeC	*mešrampes*	–	4
			mešaremp	2	–
		+*ar*	*šrimpar*	4	–
		+*olog*	*šrimpolog*	–	2
		+*men*	*šrimpsmen*	2	–

---

[2] *menugmaš* was not offered as an option, since the target meaning was an agent, not the related adjective.

(cont.)

Base	Target Meaning	Pattern	Realization	% Co.	% Ju.
		+*i*	*šrímpi*	2	–
tóšbaʿ 'Jewish oral law'	oral law specialist	+*an*	*tošbaʿan*	12	40
			tošbeʿan	8	18
			tušbeʿan	2	–
			tašbeʿan	–	2
		+*(aʾ)i*	*tošbaʿi*	34	–
			tušbaʿi	8	–
			metuššbaʿi	2	–
		+*ay*	*tošbaʿay*	6	26
			tošbeʿay	–	4
		+*ist*	*tošbaʿist*	6	6
		meCuCaC	*metušbaʿ*	10	–
		+*ar*	*tošbaʿar*	2	–
		+*nik*	*tošbanik*	2	–
		meCaCeC	*metašbéaʾ*	2	–
		mitCaCeC	*mitbašbéaʾ*	2	–

XVII. New agents and agent attributes in the 1983 supplement to Even-Shoshan (1970)

Form	Gloss	Source	Gloss
+*an*: agents or agent-attributes:			
tilan	soldier launching missiles	*til*	missile
mazlegan	forklift operator	*mazleg*	fork
ʿatidan	futurologist	*ʿatid*	future
misʿadan	restaurant proprietor	*misʿada*	restaurant
tamlilan	writer of lyrics	*tamlil*	lyrics, words to music
tafran	very poor	*ṭafrān*	pauper (Ar.)
mafsidan	loser	*mafsid*	lose (pr. part.)
mesuxan	hurdle runner	*mesuxa*	hurdle
xaryan	shitter (derog. attribute)	*xára*	excrement (Ar.)
malšan	informer	*malšin*	inform (pr. part.); informer
dagran	one studying a lot	*dagar*	hatch (tr.), sit on eggs
kaldan(it)	keyboard operator	*klid*	key (in keyboard, piano)
kanyan	purchaser	*kana*	buy
macxikan	comedian	*macxik*	funny, causing laughter
maclixan	always successful	*maclíax*	succeeding, successful
marvixan	winner	*marvíax*	win, gain, earn (pr. part.)
mecican	peeping Tom	*mecic*	peep (pr. part.)
taxkiran	one who researches for specific tasks	*taxkir*	special research
xarman	with constant sexual drive	?Ar. *ḥirmān*	deprivation
+*an*: animal/plant-related attributes:			
ʾoznan	(some) weed; pheasant; bat	*ʾózen*	ear
xanitan	a type of fish	*xanit*	lance, javelin
dabaštan	a 'hump-fish'	*dabéšet*	hump
kisan	an Australian animal	*kis*	pocket
xidkan	a shark-like fish	*xédek*	snout
gitaran	guitar-shaped fish	*gitára*	guitar

(cont.)

Form	Gloss	Source	Gloss
+ay/+a'i:[3]			
bitxonay	security conscious person	*bitaxon*	security, safety
gimlay	retiree living on pension	*gimla*	pension
kicbay	one living on annuity	*kicba*	annuity
davkay	stubborn person	*dávka*	in spite of, on the contrary
xalturay	moonlighter	*xaltúra*	moonlighting job (Rus.)
milgay	fellowship recipient	*milga*	fellowship, stipend
handasay	technician	*handasa*	engineering
palestinay	a Palestinian	*palestína*	Palestine
klinay	clinician	*klínika*	clinic
+ist:[4]			
bicu'ist	a no-nonsense hands-on doer	*bicúa'*	performance, execution of task
šminist	12th grader	*šminit*	eighth; 12th grade
+er:			
blófer	liar	*blof*	lie (< Eng. *bluff*)
konter-revolucyoner	a counter-revolutionary	Rus.	
+čik:			
'aparátčik	operator; a 'doer' (der.); party activist	Rus.	
meCaCeC:			
Agents:			
me'ahévet	lover (f)	*'ihev* (lit.)	make love (< *'ahav* 'love')
me'aper	makeup person	*'iper*	makeup (V)
mehamer	gambler	*himer*	gamble
merape	healer (non-physician)	*ripe*	heal
Agent attribute:			
mesagseg	thriving	*sigseg*	thrive
me'axzev	disappointing	*'ixzev*	disappoint
mehamem	shocking	*himem* (lit.)	shock (V) (< *hamam* 'shock (V)')
merašreš	rustling	*rišreš*	rustle
mera'anen	refreshing	*ri'anen*	refresh (< *ra'anan* 'fresh')
metaskel	frustrating	*tiskel*	frustrate
maCCiC (agent attributes):			
maftil	incriminating	*hiftil*	incriminate (< *plili* 'criminal')
maršim	impressive	*hiršim*	impress (< *róšem* 'impression')
maxris	growing a belly	*hixris*	grow a belly (< *kares/kéres* 'belly')
ma'aliv	insulting	*he'eliv*	insult
mitCaCeC:			
mitnaxel	settler	*hitnaxel*	settle

---

[3] Most +*ay*/+*a'i* innovations in the 1983 supplement to Even-Shoshan (1970) reflect the normative distinction between +*ay* as an agent noun marker and +*a'i* as its adjectival counterpart.

[4] Forms with +*ist* are often borrowed with the suffix already an integral part of the word, as, for instance, in ES '83 *'elitist* 'elitist', *fundamentalist* 'fundamentalist', *perfekcyonist* 'perfectionist;' but there are natively-formed creations as well, as in the two forms above. In other cases, the base may still be borrowed, but the alternant with +*ist* is formed after the base was borrowed.

(cont.)

Form	Gloss	Source	Gloss
CoCeC:			
Agents:			
ʾ*ocer*	curator	ʾ*acar*	safe keep, collect (< ʾ*ocar* 'treasure')
ʾ*ohed*	fan	ʾ*ahad*	like, sympathize
ʾ*oreg*	small, nest-weaving bird	ʾ*arag*	weave
xonex	tutor	*xanax*	tutor, train one as apprentice
ʿ*osek*	business owner	ʿ*asak*	deal, be in business
mošex	one who draws money from bank	*mašax*	draw
Agent Attribute:			
goʿeš	stormy, agitated	*gaʿaš*	be stormy
yoked	burning hot	*yakad*	be very hot
ʿ*okef*	bypassing	ʿ*akaf*	bypass
CaCaC:			
bataš	one beating/treading wool	*bataš*	beat, tread
capan	one who encodes	*cófen*	code
gexan	genet	*gaxan*	stoop, bend over
xamaš	one responsible for ammunition	*ximeš*	supply arms, ammunition
karsam	one who serrates, mills	*kirsem*	grind, gnaw
kalkal	one responsible for food supply and distribution; steward	*kilkel*	maintain, support, provide for
lapaf	person doing coiling	*lipef*	wind round
malat	concrete worker	*mélet*	concrete (N)
sayaʿ	collaborator	*siyaʿ*	help, assist, support

XVIII. New agents and agent attributes in Ben-Amotz/Ben-Yehuda 1972/1982 not in Even-Shoshan (1970) or its 1983 supplement

Form	Gloss	Source	Gloss
+*an*:			
kaslan	a lazy person	Ar.	
fakšešan	one who always fails	*fikšeš*	miss the target, mess up
fatyan	liar, cheat	?*fityān* (Ar.)	youth (pl.)
taxman	intriguer, manipulator	?*xámana* (Ar.)	assess, appraise
taʿaban	tired, slow	*taʿbān* (Ar.)	tired, weary, exhausted
smolan(i)	leftist	*smol*	left
zablan/ *zbalyan*	one who talks too much	*zibel*	talk too much (< *zével* 'garbage')
taktekan(it)	typist	*tiktek*	type; click, tick
malyan	very rich	*malān*	a lot (Ar.)
xarfan	one who is doomed to fail	*xarfān* (Ar.)	feeble-minded/lousy
kayfan	one who knows how to enjoy life	*kiyef*	have fun (< *keyf* 'fun (Ar.)')
fašlan	one who messes up, fails	*fášla*	failure, mishap (Ar.)
šafceran	one who talks a lot of nonsense	*šifcer*	talk a lot of nonsense

(cont.)

Form	Gloss	Source	Gloss
macigan	one who gestures in speech; one who pretends	*macig*	show; show off, pretend
mamci'an	resourceful person	*mamci*	inventor

+ *ay/+ a'i*:

Form	Gloss	Source	Gloss
dugra'i	straightforward, very frank	*dúgri*	straight, frankly (< Ar. *dúɣri*)
xelma'i	stupid, irrational	*xél(e)m*	town of legendary fools (in Poland)
xara'i	shitty	*xára*	excrement (Ar.)
yaxna'i	inferior, of lowly appearance or behavior	*yáxne*	inferior person (Yid.)
frazay	one who talks loftily	*fráza*	(lofty) phrase, expression
fatay	liar	*?fityān* (Ar.)	youth (pl.)
mikva'i	from Mikve Israel (N/Adj.)	*mikve yisra'el*	name of agricultural school
k(i)yoska'i	kiosk owner	*kiyosk*	kiosk (esp. for cold drinks, candy)
fasa'i/fasay	(one who is) doomed to fail (N/Adj.)	Ar.?	

+ *ist*:

Form	Gloss	Source	Gloss
bitxonist	one who is always security-conscious	*bitaxon*	security, safety
tixonist/ gimnazist	high school student	*tixon/ gimnásya*	highschool
grarist	one who tows	*grar*	tow truck
xalturist	moonlighter	*xaltúra*	moonlighting job
šekemist	P.X. worker	*šékem*	Israel's P.X.
sipuxist	annexationist	*sipúax*	annexation
balaganist	messy, disorganized person	*balagn*	mess, confusion (Rus.)
bardakist	messy, disorganized person	*bardak*	brothel (Trk.)
nafasist	hashish smoker		
'awantajïst	one who pretends; adventurer	*'awánta*	pretense; adventure (Ar.)
pokerist	addicted poker player	*póker*	poker (game)

+ *er*:

Form	Gloss	Source	Gloss
'ugdoner	division group commander	*'ugda*	division group
mafyoner	mafia member	*máfya*	mafia
širyoner	soldier in armor corps	*širyon*	armor
bizyoner	one responsible for disgrace/failure	*bizayon*	disgrace
fašloner	one responsible for disgrace/failure	*fášla*	failure, mishap (Ar.)
da(')awíner	braggart	*da'awin*	acts designed to impress (< Ar. *dawāwīn* 'official jargon')
miškafófer	one wearing eyeglasses	*miškafáyim*	eyeglasses

+ *čik*:

Form	Gloss	Source	Gloss
tikúnčik	handyman	*tikun*	repair
balátčik	tile layer	*baláta*	tile (Ar. *balāṭa*)

(cont.)

Form	Gloss	Source	Gloss
xarsínčik	ceramic tile layer	*xarsína*	ceramic
politúrčik	lacquer worker	*politúra*	lacquer
balagánčik	messy person	*balagan*	mess, confusion (Rus.)
da(')awínčik	braggart	*da'awin*	acts designed to impress (< Ar. *dawāwīn* 'official jargon')
napolyónčik[5]	with superiority complex	*napolyon*	Napoleon
pišalónčik	inexperienced novice; useless person'	Yid.	

meCaCeC:

metamtem	wonderful	*timtem*	make stupid, stupefy (senses)
megameret	reaching orgasm (f.)	*gimer*	finish, conclude

maCCiC:

magniv	wonderful	*higniv*	cause wonder (< *ganav* 'steal')
matrif	wonderful	*hitrif*	drive mad
malxic	causing stress	*hilxic*	cause stress (< *laxac* 'press, squeeze')

mitCaCeC:

mithapex	gay	*hithapex*	turn over
mitromem	gay	*hitromem*	rise up

CoCeC:

mokem	radar operator	*makam*	radar

CaCaC:

bašal	cook (N)	*bišel*	cook (V)

XIX. New agents and agent attributes in the 1993 Prolog dictionary

+an

Form	Gloss	Source	Gloss
balyan	one who knows how to have a good time	*bila*	have a good time
'egzozan	gay	*egzoz*	tailpipe
taf'alan	motivator/manipulator of others	*tif'el*	make operate
mecikan	one who always bothers	*mecik*	bother, torment (pr. part.)
falcan	one who farts a lot	*šalfan*	one who reacts without thinking
barzelan	officer (army slang)	*barzel*	iron (here in insignia)
'acban	quick-tempered person	*'acbani*	nervous (back formation derivation)
maški'an	one who invests great effort in whatever s/he does'	*maškia'*	invest (pr. part.)
sarfan	one who spends a lot of time on his studies	*saraf*	burn (here, time, effort)

+ay/+a'i:

šeynkina'i	Israeli yuppie (N/Adj.)	*šéynkin*	name of a trendy Tel Aviv street

---

[5] *napolyónčik* and *pišalónčik* are diminutives as well.

(cont.)

Form	Gloss	Source	Gloss
+ *ist*:			
čuparist	one enjoying special benefits	*čupar*	special benefit or pleasure
šušu'ist	intelligence worker	*šúšu*	hush hush (onomatopeic?)
+ *er*:			
distansyoner	one who keeps his distance	*distans*	distance
fantazyoner	one who fantasizes	*fantázya*	fantacy
protekcyoner	one who achieves through connections	*protékcya*	connections
***meCaCeC*:**			
meraxef	with no firm hold on reality	*rixef*	hover
meva'es	causing despair	*be'es*	cause despair (< *básā' 'misery* (Ar.)')
***maCCiC*:**			
madlik	wonderful, exciting	*hidlik*	light up (tr.)

XX. Details of 1995/96 tests on productivity of instrument formation (N subjects = 50, N bases = 8. Co. = Coinage tests; Ju. = Judgment tests)

Base	Target Meaning	Pattern	Realization	% Co.	% Ju.
pláster 'band aid'	instrument for applying band aid	*meCaCeC*	*meflaster*	40	40
			meplaster	10	16
		+ *an*	*plasteran*	18	22
		+ *on*	*plasteron*	10	14
			plasteriyon	4	–
		+ *iya*	*plasteriya*	8	–[6]
		+ *er*	*plástener*	–	4
		+ *ar*	*plastar*	2	–
		+ *ist*	*plasterist*	2	–
		+ *omat*	*plasteromat*	2	–
		+ *ik*	*plasterik*	2	–
		+ *i*	*plasteri*	2	–
kúskus 'couscous'	couscous-making instrument	+ *iya*	*kuskusiya*	50	4[7]
			kuskusiniya	2	–
		+ *an*	*kuskusan*	10	20
			kaskesan	–	2
		+ *er*	*kúskuser*	6	18
		maCCeCa	*maksesa*	2	22
		+ *on*	*kuskuson*	8	10
		maCCeC	*makses*	4	8
		meCaCeC	*mekaskes*	8	2

---

[6] By omission, + *iya* was not offered as an option for this item in the judgment test.

[7] By omission, + *iya* was not offered as an option for this item in the judgment test. They were added by hand by two subjects who opted for them.

(cont.)

Base	Target Meaning	Pattern	Realization	% Co.	% Ju.
		+ *omat*	*kuskusomat*	–	8
			mekases	–	2
		+ *ar*	*kuskusar*	–	2
		+ *it*	*kuskusit*	2	–
		CiCuC	*kiskus*	2	–
		+ *um*	*kuskusum*	2	–
		+ *prosésor*	*kuskusprosésor*	2	–
srox 'shoelace'	shoelace tying instrument	*maCCeC*	*masrex*	30	18
		+ *an*	*sorxan*	–	18
			sroxan	6	–
			sarxan	2	8
		+ *iya*	*sroxiya*	8	14
			masrexiya	6	–
			misraxiya	2	–
		miCCaCa	*misraxa*	–	18
		maCCeCa	*masrexa*	2	10
			masréxet	2	–
		+ *it*	*masroxit*	8	–
			sroxit	2	–
		+ *on*	*sroxon*	8	–
			ʿasroxon	2	–
		+ *er*	*sróxer*	–	8
		+ *iyáda*	*sroxiyáda*	6	–
		miCCaC	*misrax*	2	–
		+ *omat*	*sroxomat*	2	–
xúmus 'hummus'	hummus processing instrument	+ *iya*	*xumusiya*	16	24
			xumsiya	2	–
			maxmesiya	2	–
		maCCeCa	*maxmesa*	10	18
		maCCeC	*maxmes*	8	10
		+ *omat*	*xumusomat*	–	16
		+ *prosésor*	*xumusprosésor*	–	14
		meCaCeC	*mexames*	10	2
		+ *er*	*xúmuser*	2	10
		+ *it*	*xumusit*	8	–
		+ *an*	*xumusan*	6	–
			xamsan	2	–
		+ *on*	*xumuson*	6	–
		+ *nik*	*xúmusnik*	2	–
		miCCaCa	*mixmasa*	–	2
		+ *ína*	*xumusína*	2	–
		+ *a*	*xúmusa*	2	–
		maCCuC	*maxmus*	2	–
kótej 'cottage cheese'	instrument for producing cottage cheese	+ *iya*	*kotejiya*	22	32
		maCCeC	*maktej*	28	22
		maCCeCa	*makteja*	2	18
		meCaCeC	*mekatej*	8	6
			mekatéjet	2	–
		+ *er*	*kótejer*	6	8

(cont.)

Base	Target Meaning	Pattern	Realization	% Co.	% Ju.
		+ *on*	*kotejon*	6	–
		+ *omat*	*kotejomat*	–	6
		+ *an*	*kotejan*	2	–
		CoCeC	*kotéjet*	2	–
		CaCaC	*kataj*	2	–
		+ *a*	*koteja*	2	–
		+ *it*	*kotejït*	2	–
		+ *ik*	*kotejik*	2	–
		+ *iyáda*	*kotejiyáda*	2	–

XXI. New instrumentals in the 1983 supplement to Even-Shoshan (1970)

Form	Gloss	Source	Gloss
maCCeC:			
macnem	toaster	*canum*	thin, shrunken
madpes(et)	printer	*hidpis*	print
manpek	dispenser	*nipek, hinpik*	dispense, issue
maxzer	reflector	*hex(e)zir*	return (tr.), reflect
mavzek	flash light	*hivzik*	flash
maxlev	stapler	*hixliv*	tack, staple
makšer	two-way radio	*kišer*	connect
matmer	transducer	*tmura*	exchange, transformation
maCCeCa:			
magzera	paper cutter	*gazar*	cut
magrela	lottery machine	*higril*	draw lots (< *goral* 'lot')
maxdeda	pencil sharpener	*xided*	sharpen
malgeza	fork lift	*mazleg*	fork
manšema	respirator	*našam*	breathe
masbena	soap holder	*sabon*	soap
makrena	projector	*hikrin*	project
maklefa	peeling instrument	*kilef, kalaf*	peel (V)
makre'a	reading device	*kara*	read
meCaCeC:			
mecayéfet	machine used in weaving	*cif*	carded wool
mefaléset	grader; snow plough	*piles*	level, smooth flat
mexacec	rock crusher (to create gravel)	*xacac*	gravel
+ an:			
xaygan	dialer	*xiyeg*	dial (V) (< *xug* 'circle')
hedan	resonator	*hed*	echo
xišan	sensor	*xiša*	sensing (< *xaš* 'sense (V)')
mašvan	(the) equator	*mašve*	equate, compare (pr. part.)
+ on:			
'ašpaton	garbage receptacle	*'ašpa*	garbage
'idron	camera obscura	*'idrona*	closed place (Aram.)
halixon	walker	*halixa*	walking (< *halax* 'walk')
+ er (all borrowed with suffix):			
blénder	blender	Eng.	

(cont.)

Form	Gloss	Source	Gloss
bóyler	boiler	Eng.	
fŕízer	freezer	Eng.	
míkser	mixer	Eng.	
štéker	electrical plug	Ger.	
stóper	stopper watch	Eng.	
tréyler	trailer	Eng.	
pláyer	pliers	Eng.	

+*iya*:

mixtaviya	briefcase (loc./ instrumental)	*mixtav*	letter

***CoCeC*:**

kocev (lev)	(heart) pacer	*kacav*	allocate; provide rhythm
gorer(et)	towing vehicle	*garar*	tow (V)

CaCaC (historically with a geminated middle consonant):

'afnan	modulator	*'ifnen*	fashion; modulate (< *'ófen* 'mode')
'asaf	drain	*'asaf*	collect
'avrar	ventilation opening/ pipe	*'ivrer*	ventilate (< *'avir* 'air')
lapaf	wrapping/coiling material	*lafaf, lipef*	wrap, coil
nagad	resistor	*nagad*	be against, opposite
kabal	condenser	*kibel*	receive
katav	polarizer	*kótev*	pole

XXII. Details of 1995/96 tests on productivity of locative formation

(N subjects = 50, N bases = 8. Co. = Coinage tests; Ju. = Judgment tests)

Base	Target Meaning	Pattern	Realization	% Co.	% Ju.
kariš 'shark'	place where sharks are held	+*iya*	*krišíya*	16	60
			karišíya	18	–
			karšíya	8	–
		+*(i)yum*	*krišáryum*	–	22
			'akríšiyum	2	–
			krišváryum	2	–
			karišányum	2	–
		+*iyáda*	*krišiyáda*	2	8
		+*it*	*krišit*	–	6
			karišit	2	–
			krišonit	2	–
		'akva+	*'akvariš*	8	2
		miCCaC	*mixraš*	8	–
		maCCeCa	*makreša*[8]	8	–
		miCCaCa	*mixraša*	2	–
		miCCéCet	*mikréšet*	2	–
		+*on*	*krišiyon*	–	2
'asla 'toilet bowl'	toilet bowl factory	+*iya*	*'asliya*	36	38
			'aslaniya	2	–

---

[8] Rather than normative *maxreša*—in part to avoid merging with *maxreša* 'plough'?

(cont.)

Base	Target Meaning	Pattern	Realization	% Co.	% Ju.
			ʾasleriya	2	–
			ʾaslotiya	2	–
		maCCeCa	maʾasela	14	22
		miCCaCa	maʾasala	–	18
			mislaʾa	2	–
		+iyáda	ʾasliyáda	6	14
		+an	ʾaslan	8	–
		maCCeC	maʾasel	–	6
			maʾasélet	2	–
		+a	ʾaslata	6	–
		miCCaC	maʾasal	–	2
		+átor	ʾaslotomátor	2	–
xitul 'diaper'	diaper factory	+iya	xituliya	36	38
			xatuliya	2	–
			mexutaliya	2	–
		miCCaCa	mixtala	18	28
		maCCeCa	maxtela	10	24
		+iyáda	xituliyáda	6	8
		miCCaC	mixtal	2	–
		+on	xitulon	2	–
		beyt+	beyt xitul	2	–
			beyt xatólet	2	–
ʾomlet	place where they	+iya	ʾomletiya	68	90
'omelette'	make omelettes		ʾumletiya	6	2
			ʾomleteriya	2	–
		+a	ʾomleta	6	4
			ʾamlata	2	–
		+on	ʿomleton	4	–
			ʾamleton	2	–
			ʿumleton	2	–
		+it	ʿomletit	2	–
		+iyáda	ʾomletiyáda	2	–
		miCCaCa	mimlata	–	2
		meCuCCaC(a)	meʾumlata	–	2
masaž	massage place	+iya	masažiya	60	76
'massage'			masažeriya	4	16
			masažistiya	2	–
			masežiya	2	–
			misžiya	2	–
		+it	masažístit	2	–
			masažéstit	2	–
		+a	masaža	4	–
		miCCaC	mimsaž	2	2
		miCCaCa	mimsaža	2	2
			missaža	2	–
		maCCeCa	mamseža	2	–
			masžeʾa	2	–
			masžeda	2	–
		+on	masažon	–	2
		+or	masažor	2	–

(cont.)

Base	Target Meaning	Pattern	Realization	% Co.	% Ju.
		+ *an*	*misžan*	2	–
nagmaš 'APC'	APC repair shop	+ *iya*	*nagmašiya*	86	96
		miCCaC	*mingaš*	–	2
			nigmaš[9]	6	–
		maCCeCa	*nagmeša*	2	–
		+ *iyáda*	*nagmašiáda*	2	–
		+ *er*	*nagmášner*	2	–
kristal 'crystal'	crystal glass shop	+ *iya*	*kristaliya*	64	88
			kristeliya	8	–
			kristaler(i)ya	4	–
		maCCeCa	*krastela*[10]	–	6
		+ *it*	*kristalit*	4	–
		+ *a*	*kristala*	2	–
		+ *ácya*	*kristalácya*	2	–
		+ *iyáda*	*kristaliyáda*	2	–
		+ *órya*	*kristalórya*	2	–
		+ *ut*	*kristalut*	2	–
		+ *on*	*kristalyon*	2	–
		CiCuC	*kristul*	2	–
šnícel	schnitzel place	+ *iya*	*šnic(e)liya*	80	88
'schnitzel'			*šniceleriya*	2	–
			šnacliya	2	–
			mašnecliya	–	2
		+ *iyáda*	*šniceliyáda*	6	6
			šniceláda	–	2
		+ *er*	*šníceler*	2	–
		+ *a*	*šnicela*	2	–
		miCCaCa	*mišnacla*	–	2

XXIII. New location nouns in the 1983 supplement to Even-Shoshan (1970)

Form	Gloss	Source	Gloss
miCCaC:			
micmat	junction	*cómet*	juncture, node, crossroads
mircaf	platform (bus gate, etc.)	*racif*	platform, quay (< *ricef* 'pave')
mirtak	(place of) anchorage	*ritek*	tie, join together, confine
mivrac	spillway	*berec*	fill to overflowing
miftak	electrical 'gate'	*patak*	open a channel
macag	display	*hicig*	display (V)
miCCaCa:			
misrafa	garbage burning place	*saraf*	burn
mifxama	coal production place	*pexam*	coal
migzara	cloth cutting shop	*gazar*	cut
mikbara	cemetery	*kavar*	bury

---

[9] *nigmaš* and *nagmeša* belong to *miCCaC* and *maCCeCa*, respectively, in spite of the fact that a basic *n* replaces the prefixal *m* to facilitate pronunciation.

[10] *krastela* belongs to *maCCeCa*, in spite of the fact that a basic *k* replaces the prefixal *m* to facilitate pronunciation.

(cont.)

Form	Gloss	Source	Gloss
mivrasa	tannery	*birsek*	tan (hides) (< *burski* 'tannery', *bursi* 'tanner')
mivtaša	wool production shop	*bataš*	beat (clothes, wool)
misla'a	planting area with rocks	*séla'*	rock

+*iya*:

Form	Gloss	Source	Gloss
'arigiya	cloth production shop	*'arig*	cloth
kalbiya	dog shelter	*kélev*	dog
ma'adaniya	delicatessen shop	*ma'adan*	delicacy
migadniya	sweets and cake shop	*migdan*	sweetmeat, confection
misxakiya	child play area	*misxak*	game, play (< *sixek* 'play (V)')
steykiya	steak house	*steyk*	steak
šmartapiya	babysitter pool[11]	*šmartaf*	babysitter (< *šamar* 'guard' + *taf* 'infant')

+*iyáda*:

Form	Gloss	Source	Gloss
tremp(i)yáda	arranged hitchhiking location	*tremp*	a ride

XXIV. Abstract nouns in *miCCaC*

Form	Gloss	Source	Gloss
mivdak	checkup, test	*badak*	check, examine, test
místar	regime	*šoter*	policeman
ma'avak	struggle	*ne'evak*	struggle (V)
mifgaš	meeting, assembly	*pagaš*	meet
ma'asar	arrest	*'asar*	arrest; forbid
ma'ase	deed	*'asa*	do
ma'akav	follow up, trailing	*'akav*	follow, trail
mahalax	step, procedure	*halax*	walk
minhal	management	*nihel*	manage
mirdaf	chase	*radaf*	chase (V)
misxar	trade, commerce	*saxar*	trade (V)
mirkam	texture	*rakam*	weave, embroider
mišpat	justice; trial	*šafat*	judge (V)
mivca'	operation	*bica'*	perform
ma'amac	effort	*hit'amec*	make effort
ma'acar	detention	*'acar*	detain
midraš	study; interpretation	*daraš*	demand; inquire; interpret
mif'am	tempo, beat	*pa'am*	beat (V)
mixmah	yearning	*kamah*	yearn
mikpal	folding, bending	*kipel, kéfel*	fold (V), a fold
minšax	bite	*našax*	bite (V)
mit'am	symmetry, correlation	*ta'am*	fit, match
mizxal	crawling, slow progress	*zaxal*	crawl
mišgal	sexual intercourse	*šagal*	have sexual intercourse
mirmaz	hint	*ramaz, rémez*	hint (V), a hint
miglad	congealing	*higlid*	congeal

---

[11] In Ben-Amotz/Ben-Yehuda '82, *šmartafiya* 'babysitting area'.

XXV. Details of 1995/96 tests of productivity group/collection/ system formation (N subjects = 50, N bases = 4. Co. = Coinage tests; Ju. = Judgment tests)

Base	Target Meaning	Pattern	Realization	% Co.	% Ju.
xérek 'insect'	insect collection	+ iya	xarakiya	36	46
			xirkiya	6	–
			maxrekiya	4	–
		+ iyáda	xarakiyáda	22	28
		miCCaCa	mixraka	–	18
		+ on	xarakon	10	4
		+ an	xarkan	–	4
		+ ist	xarkanist	4	–
xatul 'cat'	group of cats	+ iyáda	xatuliyáda	42	36
		+ iya	xatuliya	32	36
			xataltuliya	4	4
		miCCaCa	mextala	–	14
		maCCeC	maxtel	–	4
		maCCeCa	maxtela	–	4
		+ on	xatulimon	4	–
matbéaʿ 'coin'	coin collection	+ iya	matbeʿiya	42	22
			matbeʿoniya	4	–
		+ on	matbeʿon	22	22
		maCCeCa	matbeʿa	4	28
		miCCaCa	mitbaʿa	–	14
		+ iyáda	matbeʿiyáda	–	14
			matbeʿotiyáda	4	–
váʿad 'committee'	a set/system of committees	+ iya	vaʿadiya	10	22
			ʿov(e)diya	10	–
			veʿidiya	4	–
		miCCaCa	mivʿada	–	14
		+ iyáda	vaʿadiyáda	–	10
		+ on	vaʿadon	–	10
			veʿidónet	4	4
		miCCaC	mivʿad	–	10
		maCCeCa	mavʿeda	4	18
		maCCeC	mavʿed	4	–
		+ it	vaʿadonit	4	4
		hitCaCCut	hitvaʿadut	–	4
		+ ut	vaʿadatiyatiyut	4	–

XXVI. Details of 1995/96 tests on productivity of diminutive formation (N subjects = 50, N bases = 6. Co. = Coinage tests; Ju. = Judgment tests. The bases for the last two were already the result of a diminutive formation process)

Base	Target Meaning	Pattern	Realization	% Co.	% Ju.
ʾomlet 'omelette'	small omelette	+ on	ʾomleton	72	84
		+ čik	ʾomlé(t)čik	2	8
			ʾomletónčik	–	2
		+ ik	ʾomletik	6	4
		+ an	ʾomletan	6	–
		+ it	ʾomletit	4	–

(cont.)

Base	Target Meaning	Pattern	Realization	% Co.	% Ju.
		+ *ist*	*ʾomletist*	4	–
		+ *íto*	*ʾomelíto*	–	2
		+ *iya*	*ʾomletiya*	2	–
		+ *a*	*ʾomleta*	2	–
		+ *ina*	*ʾomletína*	2	–
mexdal	minor act of	+ *on*	*mexdalon*	96	82
'criminal	negligence	+ *čik*	*mexdálčik*	2	8
negligence'			*mexdalónčik*	2	6
pasaž	small commercial	+ *on*	*pasažon*	66	88
'commercial	corridor area		*pasažiyon*	2	–
corridor area'			*pasažnon*	2	–
		+ *čik*	*pasážčik*	4	6
		+ *iya*	*pasažiya*	6	–
		+ *ik*	*pasažik*	4	2
		+ *tik*	*pasažtik*	2	–
		+ *it*	*pasažit*	–	2
		Redup.	*psažsaž*	–	2
		CoCeC	*posež*	2	–
gamad 'dwarf'	tiny dwarf	+ *on*	*gamadon*	78	78
			gmadmadon	–	8
			gamadonon	2	–
			gamadanon	2	–
		+ *íko*	*gamadíko*	–	6
		+ *čik*	*gmadmádčik*	–	2
		+ *an*	*gamadan*	2	–
			gamdan	2	–
		CaCiC	*gamid*	2	–
gagon 'small	very small roof/	+ *on*	*gagonon*	40	52
roof; awning'	awning		*gagnon*	2	–
		+ *čik*	*gagónčik*	18	18
		+ *it*	*gagonit*	10	24
		+ *íko*	*gagoníko*	–	6
		+ *iya*	*gagoniya*	2	–
		Redup.	*gagig*	2	–
		maCCeC	*magnen*	2	–
xataltula	tiny kitten (f.)	+ *on(et)*	*xatalulónet*	40	62
'kitten (f.)'			*xataltulon*	2	–
		+ *it*	*xataltulit*	8	28
			xatalulonit	–	10
			xatulit	6	–
		+ *et*	*xataltélet*	2	–
			xataltúlet	2	–

XXVII. New diminutives in the 1983 supplement to Even-Shoshan (1970)

Form	Gloss	Source	Gloss
+ ***on(+et)***			
ʾabuvon	small oboe	*ʾabuv*	oboe
ʾarnavon	small rabbit	*ʾarnav*	rabbit

(cont.)

Form	Gloss	Source	Gloss
ʾavatixon	small watermelon	ʾavatíax	watermellon
ʾekdaxon	small pistol	ʾekdax	pistol, handgun
ʾizmelon	small awl	ʾizmel	awl
magvon	small towel	magévet	towel
makleʿon	small machine gun	makléaʿ	machine gun
maklon	small stick	makel	stick
masrekon	small pocket comb	masrek	comb
maxševon	calculator; portable computer	maxšev	computer; calculator
takilton	diskette	taklit	disk, record
kitʿon	small paragraph	kétaʿ	paragraph, section
bdixónet	little joke	bdixa	joke
bxinónet	small exam	bxina	exam
xavilónet	small package	xavila	package
medinónet	small state	medina	state
misʿadónet	little restaurant	misʿada	restaurant
pcacónet	small bomb	pcaca	bomb

+ it:

koxavit	asterisk (small star)	koxav	star
markolit	minimarket	markol	supermarket
šapudit	toothpick-size skewer	šapud	skewer
sinarit/ sinorit	little apron	sinar/ sinor	apron

Reduplication

ʾanašnaš	little man (derogatory)	ʾenoš	man
ʾavanban	small stone	ʾéven	stone
bcalcal	small onion/bulb	bacal	onion; bulb
dragrag	step ladder	déreg	step, stage
gvarbar	adolescent pretending to	géver	man
(coll. *gvarvar*)	be a man		
smarmar	little nail	masmer	nail
beharhar	sort-of light	bahir	light (Adj.)
xadašdaš	newish	xadaš	new
sgalgal	sort-of violet	sagol	violet

REFERENCES

Aḥi'asaf, O. et al. (eds.). 1993. *Leqsiqon ha-sleng ha-ʿiwri ve-ha-cvaʾi (Hebrew and Army Slang Lexicon)*. Tel aviv: Prolog.

Alkalay, R. 1965. *Milon ʿiwri-ʾangli šalem (A Complete Hebrew-English Dictionary)*. Tel Aviv: Massada.

Almagor, D. 1993. "*Picuxiya-ya-ya.*" *Lešonenu La-ʿam* 45: 55–64.

———. 1994. "*Miloniyáda.*" *Lešonenu La-ʿam* 46: 47–58.

Ariel, S. 1972. "The functions of the conjugations in colloquial Israeli Hebrew." *Bulletin of the School of the Oriental and African Studies* 35. 514–530.

Aronoff, M. 1976. *Word Formation in Generative Grammar*. Cambridge: MIT Press.

———. 1983. "Potential words, actual words, productivity and frequency". *Proceeedings of the Thirteenth International Congress of Linguists*. pp. 163–171.

———. 1992. "Stems in Latin verbal morphology". In M. Aronoff (ed.), *Morphology Now*, Albany: SUNY Press. pp. 5–32.

———. 1994. *Morphology by Itself: Stems and Inflectional classes*. Cambridge: MIT Press.

Avineri, Y. 1976. *Heyxal ha-mišqalim (The Temple of the Mišqalim)*. Tel Aviv: Yizre'el.

Baayen, R. H. and A. Renouf. 1996. "Chronicling the *Times*: productive lexical innovations in an English newspaper". *Language* 72:1. 69–96.

Barkai, M. 1978. "Phonological opacity vs. semantic transparency: two cases from Israeli Hebrew". *Lingua* 44. 363–378.

———. 1980. "Aphasic evidence for lexical and phonological representations". *Afroasiatic Linguistics* 7. 163–187.

Barkali, S. 1964. *Luaḥ ha-šemot ha-šalem (The Complete Table of Verbs)*. Jerusalem: Reuben Mass.

Bat-El, O. 1986. "Extraction in Modern Hebrew morphology". UCLA Master's thesis.

———. 1989. "Phonology and word structure in Modern Hebrew". UCLA Doctoral dissertation.

———. 1994. "Stem modification and cluster transfer in Modern Hebrew". *Natural Language and Linguistic Theory* 12. 571–596.

———. 1996. "Phonologically-based word formation: Modern Hebrew blends." In U. Kleinhenz (ed.), *Interfaces in Phonology (Studia Grammatica 41)*. 231–250. Berlin: Akademie Verlag.

Bauer, L. 1983. *English Word-Formation*. Cambridge: Cambridge University Press.

Bauer, H. and P. Leander. 1922. *Historische Grammatik der hebräischen Sprache des alten Testaments I*. Halle: Max Niemeyer.

Ben-Amotz, D. and N. Ben-Yehuda. 1972. *Milon ʿolami le-ʿivrit meduberet (A World-Class Dictionary of Colloquial Hebrew)*. Jerusalem: Levin-Epstein.

———. 1982. *Milon ʾaxul-manyuki le-ʿivrit meduberet (A "Bastard" Dictionary of Colloquial Hebrew)*, Vol. II. Tel Aviv: Zmora, Bitan.

Ben-Asher, M. 1973. *ʿIyunim betaḥbir haʿivrit haḥadaša (Studies in Modern Hebrew Syntax)*. Haifa University/Hakibuc Hame'uxad. pp. 34–53.

Bentin, S. and L. B. Feldman. 1990. "The contribution of phonological and semantic relatedness to repetition priming at short and long lags: evidence from Hebrew". *The Quarterly Journal of Experimental Psychology* 42a (4). 693–711.

Berman, R. A. 1978. *Modern Hebrew Structure*. Tel Aviv: University Publishing Projects.

———. 1980. "Child language as evidence for grammatical description: preschoolers' construal of transitivity in the verb system of Hebrew". *Linguistics* 18. 677–701.

——. 1982. "Verb-pattern alternation: the interface of morphology, syntax and semantics in Hebrew child language". *Journal of Child Language* 9. 169–191.

——. 1987. "Productivity in the lexicon: new-word formation in Modern Hebrew". *Folia Linguistica* 21:2–4. 425–461.

——. 1989. "The role of blends in Modern Hebrew word formation." In P. Wexler, A. Bork & S. Somekh (eds.), *Studia Linguistica et Orientalia: Haim Blanc Memorial Volume*. Pp. 45–61. Wiesbaden: Harrassowitz.

——. 1989. "Children's knowledge of verb-structure: data from Hebrew". Paper presented at Boston University Conference on Language Development, October 13–15.

——. 1990. "New-root derivation in Hebrew". Talk presented at the Israel Theoretical Linguistics Society Workshop on Hebrew Grammar, Jerusalem, February 4.

——. to appear. "From known to new: how children coin nouns compared with verbs in Hebrew". In *Methods for Studying Language Production* (Festschrift honoring Jean Berko Gleason, eds. L. Menn and N. Bernstein-Ratner. Erlbaum.

Berman, R. A. and D. Ravid. 1986. "*ʿAl dargat ha-milun šel cerufey smixut* (The degree of lexicalization of structures with the construct state)". *Hebrew Computational Linguistics* 24. 5–22.

Berman, R. A. and I. Sagi. 1981. "*ʿAl darxey tecurat ha-milim ve-ḥidušan be-gil caʿir* (Word formation and neologisms at young age)". *Hebrew Computational Linguistics* 18. pp. 31–62.

Blau, Y. 1990. "*ʿAl ha-mivne ha-murkav šel ha-ʿivrit ha-ḥadaša leʿumat ha-ʿivrit še-ba-miqra* (On the complex structure of Modern Hebrew compared with the Hebrew in the Bible)". *Lešonénu* 54. 103–114.

Bolinger, D. L. 1948. "On defining the morpheme". *Word* 4. 18–23.

——. 1975. *Aspects of Language*. New York: Harcourt Brace Jovanovich.

Bolozky, S. 1978. "Word formation strategies in the Hebrew verb system: denominative verbs". *Afroasiatic Linguistics* 5:3. 111–136.

——. 1982. "Strategies of Modern Hebrew verb formation". *Hebrew Annual Review* 6. 69–79.

——. 1985. "Morpho-semantic regularity in lexical innovation: an illustration from Modern Hebrew noun formation". Middle East Studies Association of North America, New Orleans, Nov. 22–26.

——. 1986a. "Semantic productivity and word frequency in Modern Hebrew verb formation". *Hebrew Studies* 27:1. 38–46.

——. 1986b. "On discontinuous canonical patterns in the Modern Hebrew noun". Paper read at the Annual Meeting of the Linguistics Society of America, New York, Dec. 27–30.

——. 1986c. "Awareness of linguistic phenomena in the native language and its implications for learning Hebrew". *Bulletin of Hebrew Higher education* 1:2. 14–17.

——. 1990a. "On occasional morphological shifts in the noun system of colloquial Modern Hebrew". *Proceedings of the Tenth World Congress of Jewish Studies, Jerusalem, August 16–24, 1989, Division D:I*. 47–54.

——. 1990b. "*ʿAl simun ha-tnuʿot a ve-e ve-ʿal simun heʿder tnua ba-ktiv šel ha-ʿivrit ha-ḥadaša* (On marking the vowels a and e and on marking the absence of a vowel in Modern Hebrew orthography)". *Lashon Ve-ʿIvrit* 5. pp. 34–37.

——. 1993. "Evidence for productivity in Modern Hebrew word-formation". Paper read at the annual meeting of the Association for Jewish Studies, December 12–14, Boston.

——. 1994a. "On the formation of diminutives in Modern Hebrew morphology". *Hebrew Studies* 35. 47–63.

——. 1994b. "On the 'negative' character of Israeli Hebrew slang". Paper read at the annual meeting of the Association for Jewish Studies, December 18–20, Boston.

——. 1995a. "*Hasegoliyyim—gzira qavit 'o mesoreget?* (The segolates—linear or discontinuous derivation?)" O. R. Schwarzwald and Y. Schlesinger (eds.), *Hadassah Kantor Jubilee Book*. Ramat Gan: Bar-Ilan University. pp. 17–26.

——. 1995b. "Direct instruction of grammatical structure to students of Hebrew as a foreign language". *Bulletin of Higher Hebrew Education* 7–8. 30–38.

Bolozky, S. and G. N. Saad. 1983. "On active and non-active causativizable verbs in Arabic and Hebrew". *Zeitschrift für arabische Linguistik* 10. 71–79.

Bolozky, S. and M. Jiyad. 1989. "Partial mergers of morphological patterns in Modern Hebrew and in some dialects of Arabic". North American Conference of Afroasiatic Linguistics, New York, March 15–16.

——. 1990. "More on agentives, instrumentals and locatives in Modern Hebrew and in southern Iraqi Arabic". North American Conference of Afroasiatic Linguistics, Atlanta, March 28–31.

Bolozky, S. and O. R. Schwarzwald. 1990. "On vowel assimilation and deletion in casual Modern Hebrew". *Hebrew Annual Review* 12. 23–48.

——. 1992. "On the derivation of Hebrew forms with the + *ut* suffix". *Hebrew Studies* 33. 51–69.

Bréal, M. 1897. *Essai de Sémantique*. Paris: Hachette.

Bybee, J. 1985. *Morphology: A Study of the Relation between Meaning and Form*. Amsterdam: John Benjamin's.

Chomsky, N. and M. Halle. 1968. *The Sound Pattern of English*. New York: Harper and Row.

Clark, E. V. 1993. *The Lexicon in Acquisition*. Cambridge: Cambridge University Press.

Clark, E. V. and R. A. Berman. 1984. "Structure and use in the acquisition of word formation". *Language* 60:3. 542–590.

Clark, E. V. and H. H. Clark, 1979. "When nouns surface as verbs". *Language* 55:4. 767–811.

Cutler, A. 1980. "Productivity in word formation". In J. Kreiman and A. E. Ojeda (eds.), *Papers from the Sixteenth Regional Meeting*. Chicago: Chicago Linguistic Society. 45–51.

Ephratt, M. 1993. "Morphological preferences of Hebrew word formation: findings from external 'evidence". *Natural Morphology: Perspectives for the nineties*. Tonelli, I. and W. U. Dressler (eds.). Padova: Unipress. 53–73.

——. 1997. "The psychological status of the root in Modern Hebrew." *Folia Linguistica* 31. 77–103.

Even-Shoshan, A. 1963, 1970 (1980), 1983. *Ha-milon he-ḥadaš (The New Dictionary)*. Jerusalem: Kiryat Sefer.

Feldman, L. B. & S. Bentin. 1994. "Morphological analysis of disrupted morphemes: evidence from Hebrew." *The Quarterly Journal of Experimental Psychology* 47A(2). 407–435.

Gerber, N. 1992. "*Mišqal qaṭṭal umišqal qaṭlan* (The *qaṭṭal mišqal* and the *qaṭlan mišqal*). Ben-Gurion University ms.

Gesenius, W. F. H. 1910. *Hebrew Grammar*. (ed. E. Kautzsch, trans. A. E. Cowley). Oxford: Clarendon Press.

Goldenberg, G. 1981. "*Ruaḥ ha-safa u-mdiniyut lešonit le-'or hitpatḥuyot be-safot šemiyot ḥadašot* (The spirit of the language and language policy in the light of developments in new Semitic languages)". *Zixronot ha-'aqademya la-lašon ha-'ivrit* 21. 36–39.

Goshen-Gottstein, M. 1964. "Semitic morphological structures—the basic morphological structure of Biblical Hebrew". In H. B. Rosén (ed.), *Studies in Egyptology and Linguistics in Honor of H. J. Polotsky*, Jerusalem: Israel Exploration Society. 104–116.

Greenberg, J. H. 1950. "The patterning of root morphemes in Semitic". *Word* 6: 162–181.

Gross, B.-Z. 1994. *ha-mišqalim /pʕlwn/ ve-/pʕln/ ba-miqra u-vilšon ḥaxamim*. (The /pʕlwn/

and /p'ln/mišqalim in the Bible and in Mishnaic Hebrew). Jerusalem: *meqorot u-meḥqarim I, sirda ḥadaša.*

Hetzron, R. 1967. "Agaw numerals and incongruence in Semitic". *Journal of Semitic Studies* 12: 169–197.

Jespersen, O. 1924. *The Philosophy of Grammar,* London: George Allen and Unwin. p. 239.

Junger, J. 1987. *Predicate Formation in the Verbal System of Modern Hebrew.* Dordrecht: Foris.

Kutscher, E. Y. 1969. "Two 'passive' constructions in Aramaic in the light of Persian". *Proceedings of the International Conference on Semitic Studies,* Jerusalem. 132–151.

——. 1982. *A History of the Hebrew Language.* Jerusalem-Leiden: Magnes Brill.

Lieber, R. 1992. *Deconstructing Morphology.* Chicago: University of Chicago Press.

Lyons, J. 1977. *Semantics.* Cambridge: Cambridge University Press.

Maimon, Y. 1996. "*Netunim 'adkaniyim 'al ha-vare'ácya hevin~hivin* (Updated data on the *hevin~hivin* variation)". Ben-Gurion University ms.

Malone, J. L. 1971. "Wave theory, rule ordering, and Hebrew-Aramaic segolation". *Journal of the American Oriental Society* 91:1. 44–66.

McCarthy, J. J. 1979. Formal problems in semitic phonology and morphology. Doctoral dissertation, MIT, Cambridge, MA.

——. 1981. "A prosodic theory of nonconcatanative morphology". *Linguistic Inquiry* 12: 373–418.

McCarthy, J. J. and A. Prince. 1986. "Prosodic morphology". University of Massachusetts, Amherst and Brandeis University ms.

——. 1990. "Foot and word in prosodic morphology: The Arabic broken plural". *Natural Language and Linguistic Theory* 8: 209–283.

Mirkin, R. 1968a. "*Le-hašlamat he-ḥaser ba-milonim* (Filling in gaps in dictionaries)" *Lešonenu la'am* 19:3. 72–76.

——. 1968b. *Mišqal mefo'al* (The *mefo'al* pattern). *Lešonenu* 32. 140–152.

Mor, G. 1994. *Cura u-mašma'ut: 'iyun bi-lšon ha-proza šel david fogel (Word-Formation and Meaning: A Linguistic Study of David Vogel's Prose).* Beer-Sheva: Ben-Gurion University of the Negev Press.

——. 1995. "*Ha-benoni ke-gar'inan šel gzirot ḥadašot be'ivrit 'axšavit* (The present participle as the nucleus of new derivations in current Hebrew)." *'am va-Séfer* 9. 13–29.

——. 1996. "*Ma meta'er šem ha-to'ar gzur šem 'ecem +i* (What do adjectives derived from noun plus *i* describe)". Paper read at the meeting of the Israeli Branch of the European Linguistic Society, Tel Aviv.

——. 1996. "A new tendency in contemporary Hebrew: infinitive is preferred to gerund". Paper read at the 29th meeting of the European Linguistic Society (Societas Linguistica Europaea), September 4–8, Klagenfurt.

——. to appear, a. *Beyn ha-'ivrit ha-mithadéšet la-'ivrit ha-ḥadaša: 'iyun morfo-semánti ba-maqbilot ben lešono šel d. fógel šel šnot ha-'esrim li-lšon yaménu* ([Differences] between the reborn Hebrew and modern Hebrew: studies of morpho-semantic parallels between the language of D. Vogel in the twenties and current Hebrew.) In *Biqóret u-Faršanut.*

Muchnik, M. 1997. "*Darxey tecurat-am šel šmot ha-tó'ar bi-lšon ha-sleng* (Strategies of adjective formation in slang)." Paper read at the Third Conference on Hebrew as a Living Language, Oranim College, December.

Neradim, E. 1995. "*Ha-hebet ha-morfológi šel ha-basis bi-gzirat te'arim be-'emca'ut sufiks +i ba-'ivrit ha-xadaša* (The morphological aspect of the base in deriving adjectives by means of the suffix +i in Modern Hebrew)". Bar-Ilan University master's thesis.

Nir, R. 1978. "New trends of word fomation in Hebrew". *Proceedings of the Twelfth International Congress of Linguists,* W. U. Dressler and W. Meid (eds.). Inngbruck. 447–450.

——. 1984. *Lašon, medyum u-meser (Language, Medium, and Message).* Jerusalem: Posner.

———. 1990. "Ha-śafa ha-'iwrit liqrat ha-me'a ha-'eśrim ve-'aḥat (The Hebrew language towards the twentieth century)". Lašon ve-'iwrit 1.

———. 1993. Darxey ha-yecira ha-milonit be-'iwrit bat yameynu (Lexical Formation Strategies in Modern Hebrew). Tel Aviv: The Open University.

Ornan, U. 1971. "Binyanim u-vsisim, netiyot u-gzirot (Binyanim and bases, inflections and derivations." Ha-'universita 16:2. 15–22.

———. 1983. "Tecurat ha-mila ha-'iwrit keycad (How do we build a Hebrew word?)," in M. Bar-Asher et. al. (eds.), Hebrew Language Studies Presented to Zeev Ben-Hayyim. 13–42. Jerusalem: Magnes Press.

Plada, N. 1958/9. "šexiḥut ha-hagayim be-'iwrit (phoneme frequency in Hebrew)" (with an introduction by Chaim Rabin)". Lešonenu 23. 235–242.

Ravid, D. 1978. "Word-formation processes in Modern Hebrew nouns and adjectives". Tel Aviv University M.A. thesis.

———. 1990. "Internal structure constraints and new-word formation devices in Modern Hebrew". Folia Linguistica 24:3–4. 289–347.

Ravid, D. and Shlesinger, Y. 1987. "'Al miyunam ve-'al darxey gziratam šel šmot to'ar ba'aley sofit i ba-'iwrit ha-ḥadaša (Regarding the classification and derivation of adjectives with the suffix i in Modern Hebrew)". Hebrew Computational Linguiustics 25. 59–70.

Rosén, H. B. 1956. Mefo'al ba-'iwrit ha-yisre'elit (Mefo'al in Israeli Hebrew). Lešonenu 20. 139–148.

———. 1977. Contemporary Hebrew. The Hague: Mouton.

———. 1992. "Zutot me-hitgabšuta šel ha-'iwrit ha-yisre'elit (Bagatelles from the formation process of Israeli Hebrew". Divrey ha-mifgaš ha-šnati ha-šmini šel ha-ḥug ha-yisre'eli šel ha-ḥevra ha-'eyropit le-valšanut (Proceedings of the Eighth Annual Meeting of the Israeli Circle of the European Linguistic Society) 5. 33–39.

Saussure, F. de. 1916/1968. Cours de Linguistique Générale. Paris: Payot.

Schlesinger, I. M. 1989. "Instrumentals as agents: on the nature of semantic relations". Journal of Linguistics 25. 189–210.

Schultnik, H. 1961. "Produktiviteit als morfologisch fenomeen". Forum der Letteren 2: 110–125.

Schwarzwald, O. 1974. "šorašim, bsisim, u-miwne ha-morfemot (Roots, bases, and the structure of morphemes)". Lešonenu 38: 131–136.

Schwarzwald, O. R. 1981a. Diqduq u-meci'ut ba-pó'al ha'iwri (Grammar and Reality in the Hebrew Verb). Ramat Gan: Bar Ilan Press.

———. 1981b. "Frequency factors as determinants in the binyanim meanings". Hebrew Studies 22. 131–137.

———. 1982. "šxiḥut usdirut ba-lašon: 'iyunim ve-hašlaxot (Frequency and regularity in language: observations and implications)". 'iyunim ba-ḥinux 35. 163–174.

———. 1996. "Syllable structure, alternation, and verb complexity: Modern Hebrew verb patterns reexamined". In S. Izre'el and S. Raz. Israel Oriental Studies XVI: Studies in Modern Semitic Languages. Leiden: E. J. Brill.

———. 1997. "Theoretical and practical issues in Modern Hebrew word foreignness". Paper read at the 25th meeting of the North American Conference on Afroasiatic Linguistics, Miami, March 21–23.

———. to appear. "Praqim be-morfolgya 'iwrit (Topics in Hebrew Morphology)". Tel Aviv: The Open University.

Schwarzwald, O. R. and E. Neradim. 1994/95. "š.p.'.l 'iwri (Hebrew s.p.'.l)." Lešonenu 58: 145–152.

Segal, M. Z. 1925. "Ha-ze'eyrut be-'iwrit (diminution in Hebrew)". Mada'ey Ha-Yahadut I (Yedi'ot Ha-Maxon Le-Mada'ey Ha-Yahadut III). pp. 139–152.

Segal, M. H. 1927. A Grammar of Mishnaic Hebrew. Oxford: Clarendon Press.

Siegel, D. 1979. Topics in English Morphology. New York: Garland.

Sivan, R. 1976. *'Al 'ovney lešon yameynu (Developments in the Hebrew Language of Today)*. Jerusalem: E. Rubinstein.

Sivan, R. and E. A. Levenston. 1967/77. *The Megiddo Modern Dictionary, Hebrew-English*. Tel Aviv: Megiddo.

Spencer, A. 1991. *Morphological Theory*. Oxford: Basil Blackwell.

Steriade, D. 1988. "Reduplication and syllable in Sanscrit and elsewhere". *Phonology* 5 v. 1 73–155.

Tobin, Y. 1995. *Invariance, Markedness and Distinctive Feature Analysis*. Beer Sheva: Ben-Gurion University of the Negev Press.

Treivish, B. and R. Matiash. 1996. *"Produktiviyut ha-binyanim: kal, pi'el ve-hif'il bi-lšon ha-'itonut 'al pi bdika statistit* (The productivity of the binyanim: *CaCaC, CiCeC* and *hiCCiC* in journalistic Hebrew according to a statical sample)". Ben-Gurion University ms.

Tsafrir, Y. 1995. *"šxixut pe'alim be-tekst sifruti* (Verb frequency in a literary text)". Ben-Gurion University ms.

Van Marle, J. 1985. *On the Paradigmatic Dimension of Morphological Creativity*. Dordrecht: Foris.

Walden, Z. 1982. "The roots of roots". Harvard University doctoral dissertation.

Werner, F. 1983. *Die Wortbildung der hebräischen Adjektiva*. Wiesbaden: Harrassowitz.

Wexler, P. 1990. *The Schizoid Nature of Modern Hebrew: A Slavic Language in Search of a Semitic Past*, Volume 4 in *Mediterranean Language and Culture Monograph Series*, A. Borg, S. Somekh and P. Wexler (eds.), Wiesbaden: Otto Harrassowitz.

INDEX

STUDIES IN SEMITIC
LANGUAGES AND LINGUISTICS

3. Corré, A.D. *The Daughter of My People*. Arabic and Hebrew Paraphrases of Jeremiah 8.13-9.23. 1971. ISBN 90 04 02552 9
5. Grand'Henry, J. *Les parlers arabes de la région du Mzāb (Sahara algérien)*. 1976. ISBN 90 04 04533 3
6. Bravmann, M.M. *Studies in Semitic Philology*. 1977. ISBN 90 04 04743 3
8. Fenech, E. *Contemporary Journalistic Maltese*. An Analytical and Comparative Study. 1978. ISBN 90 04 05756 0
9. Hospers, J.H. (ed.). *General Linguistics and the Teaching of Dead Hamito-Semitic Languages*. Proceedings of the Symposium held in Groningen, 7th-8th November 1975, on the occasion of the 50th Anniversary of the Institute of Semitic Studies and Near Eastern Archaeology of the State University at Groningen. 1978. ISBN 90 04 05806 0
12. Hoftijzer, J. *A Search for Method*. A Study in the Syntactic Use of the H-locale in Classical Hebrew. With the collaboration of H.R. van der Laan and N.P. de Koo. 1981. ISBN 90 04 06257 2
13. Murtonen, A. *Hebrew in its West Semitic Setting*. A Comparative Survey of Non-Masoretic Hebrew Dialects and Traditions. Part I. *A Comparative Lexicon*.
   Section A. *Proper Names*. 1986. ISBN 90 04 07245 4
   Section Ba. *Root System: Hebrew Material*. 1988. ISBN 90 04 08064 3
   Section Bb. *Root System: Comparative Material and Discussion*. Sections C, D and E: *Numerals under 100, Pronouns, Particles*. 1989.
   ISBN 90 04 08899 7
14. Retsö, J. *Diathesis in the Semitic Languages*. A Comparative Morphological Study. 1989. ISBN 90 04 08818 0
15. Rouchdy, A. *Nubians and the Nubian Language in Contemporary Egypt*. A Case of Cultural and Linguistic Contact. 1991. ISBN 90 04 09197 1
16. Murtonen, A. *Hebrew in its West Semitic Setting*. A Comparative Survey of Non-Masoretic Hebrew Dialects and Traditions. Part 2. *Phonetics and Phonology*. Part 3. *Morphosyntactics*. 1990. ISBN 90 04 09309 5
17. Jongeling K., H.L. Murre-van den Berg & L. van Rompay (eds.). *Studies in Hebrew and Aramaic Syntax*. Presented to Professor J. Hoftijzer on the Occasion of his Sixty-Fifth Birthday. 1991. ISBN 90 04 09520 9
18. Cadora, F.J. *Bedouin, Village, and Urban Arabic*. An Ecolinguistic Study. 1992. ISBN 90 04 09627 2
19. Versteegh, C.H.M. *Arabic Grammar and Qurʾānic Exegesis in Early Islam*. 1993. ISBN 90 04 09845 3
20. Humbert, G. *Les voies de la transmission du Kitāb de Sībawayhi*. 1995. ISBN 90 04 09918 2
21. Mifsud, M. *Loan Verbs in Maltese*. A Descriptive and Comparative Study. 1995. ISBN 90 04 10091 1
22. Joosten, J. *The Syriac Language of the Peshitta and Old Syriac Versions of Matthew*. Syntactic Structure, Inner-Syriac Developments and Translation Technique. 1996. ISBN 90 04 10036 9
23. Bernards, M. *Changing Traditions*. Al-Mubarrad's Refutation of Sībawayh

and the Subsequent Reception of the *Kitāb*. 1997. ISBN 90 04 10595 6
24. Belnap, R.K. and N. Haeri. *Structuralist Studies in Arabic Linguistics*. Charles A. Ferguson's Papers, 1954-1994. 1997. ISBN 90 04 10511 5
25. Talmon R. *Arabic Grammar in its Formative Age. Kitāb al-ʿAyn* and its Attribution to Ḥalīl b. Aḥmad. 1997. ISBN 90 04 10812 2
26. Testen, D.D. *Parallels in Semitic Linguistics*. The Development of Arabic la- and Related Semitic Particles. 1998. ISBN 90 04 10973 0
27. Bolozky, S. *Measuring Productivity in Word Formation*. The Case of Israeli Hebrew. 1999. ISBN 90 04 11252 9
28. Ermers, R. *Arabic Grammars of Turkic. The Arabic Linguistic Model Applied to Foreign Languages & Translation of ʾAbū Hayyān al-ʾAndalusī's* Kitāb al-ʾIdrāk li-Lisān al-ʾAtrāk. 1999. ISBN 90 04 113061
29. Rabin, Ch. *The Development of the Syntax of Post-Biblical Hebrew*. 1999. ISBN 90 04 11433 5